Praise for *New Ideas from Dead Economists*

"If you only read one economics book this year, read this one."
—Lawrence H. Summers, former U.S. Treasury secretary, professor
of political economy, Harvard University

"Readable . . . enjoyable . . . valuable to the lay reader who wishes
to speak intelligently about economics and world markets."
—*National Review*

"A first-class book."
—*Christian Science Monitor*

"Witty . . . accessible . . . a history of economic thought that
won't scare even the worst econophobes." —*Phoenix Republic*

"A sorely needed and well-written guide to the still-living ideas
that fashion our prosperity."
—Alfred L. Malabre Jr., author of *Understanding the New Economy*

"Lights up economics with a wickedly sparkling wit."
—Associated Press

"An excellent review of contemporary macroeconomic theories and issues. . . . It does not get any better than this."
—*Choice*

"Effective and entertaining . . . highly recommended."
—*Library Journal*

"Successfully puts a wide range of economic theories and philosophies into an understandable, everyday perspective."
—*Booklist*

NEW IDEAS
FROM DEAD
ECONOMISTS

NEW IDEAS
FROM DEAD
ECONOMISTS

THE INTRODUCTION TO
MODERN ECONOMIC THOUGHT

COMPLETELY REVISED
AND UPDATED, 4TH EDITION

Todd G. Buchholz

With a Foreword by Martin Feldstein

PLUME

℗

PLUME
An imprint of Penguin Random House LLC
penguinrandomhouse.com

🐧

Library of Congress Cataloging-in-Publication Data
Names: Buchholz, Todd G., author.
Title: New ideas from dead economists: the introduction to modern economic thought, 4th edition / Todd G. Buchholz.
Description: Completely revised and updated. | New York: Plume, Penguin Random House LLC, 2021. | Revised edition of the author's New ideas from dead economists, c2007.
Identifiers: LCCN 2020041051 (print) | LCCN 2020041052 (ebook) | ISBN 9780593183540 (paperback) | ISBN 9780593183557 (ebook)
Subjects: LCSH: Economists—Biography. | Economics—History. Classification: LCC HB76.B83 2021 (print) | LCC HB76 (ebook) | DDC 330.092/2—dc23
LC record available at https://lccn.loc.gov/2020041051
LC ebook record available at https://lccn.loc.gov/2020041052

First Plume hardcover edition: December 1989
First Plume trade paperback edition: December 1990
First Plume trade paperback edition ISBN: 9780452265332

Printed in the United States of America
2nd Printing

Contents

Preface to the Revised Edition

Vincent van Gogh painted twenty-eight portraits of himself in just two years! I have avoided such introspection and have managed to keep both ears attached to my head. I had not read *New Ideas from Dead Economists* since early 1989, when I delivered a manuscript to the offices of E. P. Dutton for its hardcover debut. I suppose some authors reread their works often, reminiscing about a skillful turn of phrase or prescient thought. Rather than reread my work, I continually watched the world economy over the subsequent years to see how the book's ideas and the great economists' ideas held up. This newly revised edition benefits from a careful study of economic trends and crises from my perch as a White House economist, Wall Street adviser, investment fund manager—and father. I was none of those when I drafted the first edition.

The world has changed in staggering ways. Mostly for the good. New medicines, new technologies, more jobs, less inflation, and less crime have blessed the United States. In 1989, we had no Internet, no anti-baldness drugs, few automobile airbags, and no hope that the jobless rate could plunge below 5 percent or that U.S. stock prices would more than triple during the 1990s and then jump by another 75 percent in the early 2000s (with some cliff-hanging moments along the way). The pandemic in 2020 did not bring massive bank failures and soup kitchens like the Great Depression of the 1930s did, but instead a Great Cessation as people were forced to stay in their homes and away from shops and friends.

In the years since the first edition, we have also witnessed a phenomenon I call the "scissors economy." Technology has permitted Americans to cut out the middleman from many purchases. Who needs a stockbroker or an insurance agent when the Internet allows people to comparison shop? You can buy a sockeye salmon direct from Alaska within seconds or an airplane ticket to Timbuktu. Consumers have more control than ever before and can customize purchases with an ease that only a prince or a potentate could have afforded in past epochs. Even bespoke dog food can be ordered online, tailored for a hound's age, weight, fur type, and preference for poultry, bison, or vegan protein.

In a tech-driven economy, consumers spend more of their income on digital products like video games and streaming entertainment. Digital products often have "zero marginal cost," meaning the seller does not pay much to make an extra copy. In past eras, vinyl records, cassette tapes, and CDs were made up of advanced plastics, pressed and assembled by machines, and then shipped to stores. Every time a music studio churned out another record, it spent money on raw materials, processing, and shipping. Today, when artists invite you to download a tune, your extra download costs them virtually nothing. Of course, plenty of resources may go into the initial creation of an item. I co-founded an educational software company that makes math games for children based on the Math Arrow matrix. Designing the game, writing software code, and hiring cartoonists to draw Kyle the Kangaroo cost a great deal. But when a parent or child downloads the game to play, it costs the company very little. This model is vastly different from what Adam Smith, our first great economist, encountered in 1776. He observed a pin factory, not bytes zooming through a digital stream.

Across the United States, old monopolistic utilities have broken down as cable, satellites, fiber-optic, and wireless technologies compete for your television, smartphone, and streaming business. Every time your eye catches the glint of a rooftop solar panel on a home, a centralized power company sheds a tear. A striking advertisement once appeared in the Washington, D.C., area, touting a new telecommunications company. Posters displayed a statue of Lenin with a rope around his neck and the headline "No Empire Lasts Forever—Especially One That Keeps You Waiting 5 Hours for a Repairman."

The scissors economy has not snipped out every middle person, of course. In a modern economy, most of us cannot avoid toiling in the middle. Very few of us spend the morning picking strawberries by hand or hammering steel on an anvil. But the scissors economy has placed a new burden on middle people: they must prove their value. Traditional retailers may lament the "Amazonization" of sales, but Amazon has carved itself a prosperous place directly in the middle of transactions, as have PayPal, Venmo, and others. Amazon's success comes from stunning innovations: same-day delivery, rapid refunds, easily read customer ratings, and algorithms that may display sensible recommendations. Sears, a once mighty competitor that built the world's tallest skyscraper in 1973 and was the nation's largest retailer throughout the 1980s, trumpeted the slogan "Where America Shops." By 2018, Sears had not innovated much and found itself booted from its tall building and instead in bankruptcy court. Will Amazon hold on to its lead, or will nimbler new competitors emerge to humble it?

Sweeping changes in European and Asian political economy command our attention. Europe has been stitching itself together and then breaking itself apart again. The Berlin Wall came tumbling down in 1989, freeing hundreds of millions of Eastern Europeans from Soviet drudgery and pushing them into competitive markets, where many have thrived and others have struggled. Within a few years of the Berlin Wall's crumbling, Czech and Bulgarian versions of *New Ideas from Dead Economists* appeared, as newly freed minds searched to understand a market economy. In 2000, Western European nations gave up sovereign currencies like the German deutsche mark, Italian lira, and French franc in order to embrace the euro currency. In 2020, the United Kingdom, which clung to the pound sterling, waved good-bye to the European Union, frustrated by its political and legal demands. In Asia, the Japanese economy transformed itself from a threatening giant in the late 1980s into a humbled midget in the 1990s. The key Tokyo stock market, which climbed to 39,000 in 1989, collapsed and stood at just 19,000 in 2020. What happened to all those stories of superior Japanese management techniques? Meanwhile, China emerged as a powerhouse in world trade, its factories churning out more goods than any other country's. This from a nation whose GDP barely showed up on a chart in the 1970s.

The Berlin Wall

As the Soviet Union and the United States waged the Cold War, each had intercontinental ballistic missiles poised and aimed at the other, ready to destroy humanity. Most geopolitical strategists believed that a standoff—that is, a "stable Cold War"—was a good outcome that could, hopefully, be extended well into the twenty-first century. Not even Ronald Reagan, surely the most optimistic Cold Warrior, thought that the Soviet empire would crumble as swiftly and peacefully as it did after 1989. Many of his advisers and almost all his opponents urged caution. When Reagan implored then Soviet leader Mikhail Gorbachev to "tear down this wall," State Department "experts" objected to the forceful yet fanciful dare. Why rile the Soviet bear and ask for an impossible task? It turned out that the bear was not so strong and the task not so farfetched. Only a few years later, East Berliners and West Berliners took picks and hammers to the wall in all-night celebrations while their radios blared the youthful, uplifting tunes of American rock and roll. Similar rejoicing took place in Warsaw, Prague, and Budapest.

Under German chancellor Helmut Kohl's bold leadership, West Germany adopted East Germany, funneling generous financial gifts and resources to its poorer brethren. A fascinating study showed that East Germany would have been even further behind in 1989 had its communist government not engaged in spying and stealing secrets from West German technology companies![1] Today, residents of eastern Germany still earn less money than their countryman cousins, but they have surely adapted to Western capitalist ways. The Polish, Czech, and Hungarian economies have also strived to transform themselves. Despite economic turbulence, democratic elections have largely reinforced a pro-market approach and buried Soviet ideology. Even when former communist officials win parliamentary seats, they generally support market reforms. During a recent visit to Gdańsk—home of the Solidarity movement that brought down communism in Poland—I was impressed by the entrepreneurial energy of young Poles who had opened up shops throughout the medieval Baltic port city. Prague and Budapest and Tallinn, Estonia, also bustle in living color, rather than in the drab grays of the communist era.

In Russia, the path has been bumpy. In 1998, Russia looked economically defunct, as the ruble lost most of its value and panicked sellers hammered the Russian stock market into rubble. Foreign investors who held Russian bonds could use them for wallpaper. Why did Russia's capitalist experiment fail? A not-so-funny thing happened on the way to the free market: the country took a dangerous detour into "crony" capitalism, in which former communist bosses exploited their connections, twisting former state monopolies into private monopolies that they continued to control. Managers of mines made fortunes by smuggling precious metals out of the country by rail, by truck, and even tucked in the pockets of trench coats. The iron hand of the Soviet police lost its grip, and the new democratic Russia had only a flimsy legal system to deal with crime and settle business disputes. Moscow, with its fancy clubs populated by newly rich racketeers, more closely resembled Chicago under Al Capone than a developed country. Billionaire barons set up their own private security forces. Moreover, President Boris Yeltsin's government could not figure out how to force these barons to pay taxes. Thus, the Russian government ran up a huge budget deficit, forcing it to borrow money from foreigners by selling them bonds. After a frenzied bubble of stock market gains in 1996 and 1997, the country looked corrupt, bankrupt, and ready to erupt. So Russians and foreigners snuck their money out of the country, erasing the modest wealth built up by a new middle class.

Is there a lesson here, or just a depressing tale? Russia's 1998 debacle teaches us that a market economy must rest on a dependable legal system. A free market does not mean utter chaos; it requires ground rules. Without courts to enforce contracts, police to punish mafiosi, and agencies to collect taxes, Russia detoured into crony capitalism, a voyage of the doomed. In the West, they say that justice is blind. Russia's problem was that she was blind to justice. Of course, Russia has failed before. The entire twentieth century was an economic failure. Visiting regal old cities like Saint Petersburg and Odessa (in Ukraine) and witnessing breathtaking nineteenth-century architecture and stunning opera houses teaches one that the problem with communism was *not* that it couldn't keep up with capitalism; the problem was that it couldn't even keep up with the standards of the czars in 1917. Let's hope for a new Russian revolution in this still-young twenty-first century, a revolution that finds a place for both economic liberty and the rule of law. Over the past twenty years, President Vladimir Putin has presided over periods of strong growth, but he has yet to shatter the iron shackle on Russia's economy: its reliance on selling heavy metals and slick sludge to others. Rich in oil, natural gas, and gold, Russia booms when world commodity prices soar but stumbles when they crash. The rebirth of the

U.S. energy industry, which now pumps out more oil than any other country, threatens Russia's future profits. Until it further diversifies, Russia cannot boast of a nimble economy but can only brag that it is the world's best-stocked pantry.

Japan: Land of the Setting Sun?

When I wrote the first edition of *New Ideas from Dead Economists*, scholars and journalists were crowning Japan as the king of the world economy. Books with titles such as *Yen! Japan's New Financial Empire and Its Threat to America* and *Trading Places: How We Are Giving Our Future to Japan* painted a picture in which Japan would take over the world, and Americans would be reduced to flipping hamburgers to make ends meet. Japanese speculators collected Van Goghs, Monets, and golf course memberships as if they were souvenir tokens. They bought up downtown Los Angeles and the best properties in Hawaii. Their banks dominated the financial industry, and analysts calculated that the land beneath the Imperial Palace in Tokyo was worth more than all the land in California. A prominent Japanese politician wrote a bestselling book condemning U.S. hegemony, called *The Japan That Can Say No.* How the mighty have fallen! Japanese investors turned out to have a reverse Midas touch, turning precious assets into worthless trinkets. Along with a devastating slide in the Tokyo stock market, the price of Impressionist paintings sank along with that of Hawaiian real estate. Their investments in movie studios left them with staggering losses, as slick Hollywood producers ripped them off. Back in Japan, arrogance turned to humility and fear, as property prices and incomes dropped. In 1998, interest rates fell to zero, meaning that you could borrow money from the government for free. The only thing that rose was the jobless rate.

What happened? The quick answer is that in 1989 the Japanese central bank jacked up interest rates to deliberately pop a bubble in the stock market. But that does not explain a nearly ten-year plunge. Two culprits come to mind. First, the Japanese government encouraged its premier corporations to dominate the manufacturing sector, while the United States was shifting toward service industries like finance and health care. Though Japanese banks dominated the world in *size,* they lagged way behind in profitability and sophistication. Most of the new financial products, from stock index funds to complex derivatives, were made in the United States or the U.K. Why didn't Japanese companies develop these ideas? They faced little competitive pressure at home. The Ministry of Finance protected the insurance companies from the savings banks and the savings banks from the corporate banks. Whereas in the United States these industries faced ferocious competition from each other, the Japanese government created fiefdoms that were safe behind bureaucratic walls. The ministry basically forced households to pour their money into pitifully low-yielding bank accounts, giving firms a captive audience. Adam Smith would have seen it coming. By keeping their home turf sedate, they imperiled their ability to fight in the real world.

Japan looked feeble in information technologies, too. When a Japanese friend of mine first encountered the Internet and noticed that almost all the websites were in English, he shook his head and said, "We're toast." Although Japanese businesses successfully won market share in manufactured goods like electronics, they found their prices undercut by South Korean and Malaysian factories. Soon they gave up the fight and closed down Japanese factories and opened up cheaper ones in China. The concept of "lifetime employment" died, deflating the confidence of working men and women. Japanese commentators called the phenomenon the "doughnut" economy, as the economy turned hollow.

These structural flaws came along with incompetent fiscal and monetary policy. Essentially, the Bank of Japan waited too long before cutting interest rates, and the Ministry of Finance actually pushed up tax rates in the middle of a recession. John

Maynard Keynes (see chapter 9) taught the world that during the Great Depression, you shouldn't punish consumers when the economy is rushing down the drain. The message apparently did not make it into Japanese until recently, though *New Ideas from Dead Economists* has been available there since 1991! Under Prime Minister Shinzō Abe's "Abenomics," Japan finally made some forward progress. Abe urged the central bank to disregard inflation fears and to instead flood the economy with yen to encourage consumers. Abe's biggest problem is more structural. The population is aging as fast as sushi left out in the sun: by 2050, senior citizens will make up 40 percent of the population; and by 2100, Japan's population will be one-third smaller than in 2000. Abe has tried to get around the demographic stumbling block by encouraging more women to enter the workforce. He declared that "Abenomics is Womenomics," and now a higher proportion of women hold jobs in Japan than in the United States or Europe. But of course those female employees are aging and will eventually retire. To avoid becoming the land of the setting sun, Japan may have to become the land of the rising robots.

China Awakens and Roars

China's emergence since 1990 looks awesome and a little frightening, as it galloped along at a pace of 10 percent GDP growth each year between 1990 and 2012. When I traveled to Shanghai in 1993, the city's beautiful old art deco buildings along the Bund dominated the skyline. The Peace Hotel, which my father had visited as a seventeen-year-old sailor at the end of World War II, still captured the imagination. By 2005, an entire new city with dozens of futuristic skyscrapers had emerged across the river in Pudong, casting literal and metaphoric shadows over the colonial past. Between 1990 and 2005, about half a billion people had been lifted from poverty.[2]

This is likely the greatest victory in the war on poverty in the history of the world.

If you read the financial press, you will hear that nearly every hiccup in the world economy may be blamed on China. High oil prices? China must be hoarding. Low interest rates? China must be snapping up too many U.S. Treasury notes. Fewer manufacturing jobs? China must be stealing them. A lethal pandemic? Someone must be noshing on an undercooked bat in a Wuhan "wet market." True, China is a mammoth force in the global economy today, especially considering that the country was an economic invalid just thirty years ago. In chapter 6, on Karl Marx, we will see how Deng Xiaoping dismissed Maoism and sent his people scurrying not for copies of Mao's Little Red Book of communist quotations, but for copies of Harvard's crimson MBA manual. Despite China's current triumphs in world trade, the next ten years will pose extreme challenges. Like Japan, China will hit a demographic wall when it has to support more senior citizens with fewer young workers. Its quick-rising middle class will spend more abroad on tourism, health care, and luxury goods. When countries move from poverty to middle-class status, they desire three things: cars, protein (meat and grains), and health care. This provides enormous opportunities for foreigners to sell goods there, if the Chinese government permits more imports. The switch to cars has already taken off, and you can see Beijing choked with automobiles that spew fumes and trample over traditional bicycles. China's future will be rocky, fascinating, and, hopefully, a force for global prosperity.

Attitude Over Latitude

Most people, including many professional economists, think about a country's economy like a potential home buyer thinks about a model home. It's awfully hot in Costa Rica! How lucky that Venezuela has oil! Too bad Australia is so far away from the action! The cliché "location, location, location" might work well for buying a three-bedroom colonial in Peoria, but it's hardly worth a hill of beans when analyzing a country. Take Mexico, please. Mexico has enjoyed a great location, right on the U.S. border. It hasn't moved. Yet America's wealth and technology have not rubbed off much. Now look at prosperous Australia—a twelve-hour flight even after you change planes at LAX! And settled by criminals who sailed on leaky boats!

Economic textbooks spend a lot of time focusing on "factor endowments," telling us that a country blessed with lots of minerals and natural resources has a big advantage. Really? Hong Kong is a pile of rocks. The Netherlands was a sinking Venice, but without the charming bridges or the spumoni, and yet in the seventeenth century it leapfrogged its better-endowed neighbors. And then there's Israel today. It may be settled by God's chosen people, but He chose not to give them a drop of oil, while gushers spout across Arabia. Read Mark Twain's description of the arid and empty land. Israel's terrain doesn't naturally grow enough green for a sprig of parsley on your dinner plate, and yet there she blooms. In the race for economic development, would you rather bet on a country with a million tons of endowed zinc or one with a couple of extra IQ points and a free flow of ideas?

A big endowment of riches may even be a curse. The earth under many parts of Africa bulges with metals. And yet some of the most promising economies are retarded, as oligarchs like Robert Mugabe in Zimbabwe hung on to power for four decades, preventing capital from diffusing through society. Think back to the schoolbook atlases that displayed the natural resources of each country. As a kid, I always thought it unfair that the evil Soviet Union seemed to have all the great stuff, even bauxite, which sounded like a mysterious, earthly version of kryptonite, a bad thing in an enemy's arsenal. But the Soviet system had a reverse Midas touch, too. It turned precious metals and rich soil into famine and poverty. Way back in 1500, when Yuan dynasty vases were being baked, the Chinese had all the technology they needed to beat England to the Industrial Revolution. But the mandarins of the time stomped on trade and financial flows. Because leftists refused to believe that "attitude beats latitude," they felt sorry for and made excuses for the Soviet Union's seventy years of bad weather. As Ronald Reagan put it, there are just four things wrong with communist farming: "spring, summer, winter and fall."

What counts most, then? *Attitude, not latitude.* And the best indication of a country's attitude may be the wisdom it gleans from the great economists.

The history of economic thought teaches us that success often goes to the hungry, the humble, and the limber. And that is what you will learn in the pages ahead.

The 1990s and early 2000s gave us plenty of opportunities to test the wisdom and assess the musings of the great economists. And now as we head toward the middle of this century, we will face fresh and sometimes baffling challenges—and the ideas of the dead economists will be there to help.

San Diego, California
January 2020

Foreword

All of us are affected by government economic policies and by private economic decisions. No one can be an informed voter or even an understanding reader of the daily newspaper without a knowledge of economics. And who can plan for the future in which we and our children will live and work without a sense of the forces that shape our economic life?

The economic policy issues that we debate today—trade policy, inflation, the proper role of government, the eradication of poverty, and the means of raising the rate of economic growth—have been discussed by economists for more than two centuries. Many of today's economic policies—both the good ones and the bad—are the result of the ideas of those past economists. And many of today's debates about economic policy can be understood only by those who have at least some familiarity with the ideas of earlier economists.

The giants of economic science during the past two hundred years have been men concerned with the critical policy issues of their time. They studied the working of the economy in order to advocate better economic policies. But despite their concern with policy, they were not polemicists or politicians but men who sought to persuade their contemporaries in government and in the broader public by analysis and evidence that would meet the standards of professional debate.

Like any scientific discipline, economics advances by discovering the limitations of earlier ideas. Although economics does not have the opportunities for experimentation that characterize the natural sciences, economists can use systematic observation and the analysis of experience to reject old theories and develop new ones.

The changes in technology and in the political and institutional environment impede the process of drawing firm conclusions about the likely effects of alternative economic policies. It can take decades before issues are settled, and new generations of economists and policy officials may have to learn that the conclusions of the past continue to be valid in the changing environment of today.

Adam Smith, the eighteenth-century founder of modern economics, rejected the conventional wisdom of his day by arguing that government interference in the economy is generally harmful and that the public's interest is best served by competition among private buyers and sellers. In recent years, governments around the world have recognized the virtues of a market economy based on private enterprise rather than on government planning and public ownership. The reduction of tax rates in the United States, the privatization of nationalized industries in England and France, the resurrection of family farms in China, and the Soviet economic restructuring that has been labeled "perestroika" are the direct descendants of the early ideas of Adam Smith.

The theories of John Maynard Keynes, developed in England during the Depression of the 1930s, have helped governments avoid a return to mass unemployment. But the Keynesian arguments against saving and in favor of increased consumer spending are being gradually abandoned as inappropriate for the very different conditions of today's economy. Now we understand that increased saving can in general be the basis for increased investment in new plants and equipment and therefore for faster economic growth and a higher standard of living.

When Federal Reserve officials make decisions about monetary policy and interest rates, they are relying on ideas and evidence that can be traced back to nineteenth-century economists like John Stuart Mill as well as on the latest data being developed in Washington. When Treasury officials debate appropriate tax rules for businesses and individuals, they may make use of analytic arguments that date back more than a century to David Ricardo and Alfred Marshall. Similarly, the analysis of trade policy, energy and environmental regulation, and antitrust legislation are based on ideas that have developed through the centuries. A familiarity with these economic ideas is important for anyone who wants to understand how new policies are likely to affect the economy and why certain policies are chosen.

In this book, Todd Buchholz provides a lively and intelligible introduction to the key ideas of economics through the study of the great economists who have shaped the discipline. Instead of the formal models and complex diagrams that are the focus of standard economics textbooks, Buchholz provides clear, nontechnical explanations and timely examples.

I first met Todd Buchholz when he was teaching a section of the introductory economics course at Harvard. Buchholz was an excellent teacher who was selected from among the thirty other teachers in the course to receive the annual prize for outstanding teaching of introductory economics. His skills in the classroom are well displayed in this very readable book.

—Martin Feldstein
Cambridge, Massachusetts
June 1989

NEW IDEAS
FROM DEAD
ECONOMISTS

CHAPTER I

Introduction: The Plight of the Economist

It's not easy being an economist. Corporate executives attack them for not calculating costs and benefits with enough precision. Altruists accuse them of being too fussy about costs and benefits. To politicians, economists are party poopers who won't let them promise prosperity without sacrifice. Some of the wittiest writers, including George Bernard Shaw and Thomas Carlyle, have taken time out to insult them. Indeed, it's been open season on economists ever since Carlyle called economics the "dismal science."

Economists feel wrongly accused, however, for they are usually not the cause of bad news but simply the messengers. And the message is simple: human beings must make difficult choices. We are no longer in Eden. The world does not flow with milk and honey. We have to choose among cleaner air and faster cars, bigger houses and bigger parks, more work and more play. Economists do not tell us that any of these is bad. They tell us only that we cannot necessarily have them all—all at once. Economics is the study of choice. It does not tell us what to choose. It only helps us understand the consequences of our choices.

The great economists, of course, were not content to be merely messengers. Though they have been ridiculed with irreverent epithets—Smith the bumbler, Mill the egghead, Keynes the bon vivant, and so on—they cannot be disparaged for their motives. It is ironic that economists themselves receive so much virulent criticism in our day, for, as Keynes noted, most of the eminent practitioners started as do-gooders, searching for ways to improve the world. Alfred Marshall in particular saw economics as a profession that should blend shrewd science with a devotion to people. Whereas the medieval world saw three grand professions—medicine aimed at physical health, law aimed at political health, and theology aimed at spiritual health—Marshall hoped to make economics the fourth noble vocation, aimed at better material health not just for the rich but for all. Marshall tried valiantly to mediate between two powerful, regrettable strands: a trend toward arid mathematical economics without practical application and a trend toward sheer emotional radicalism without careful theoretical reflection. The curriculum he fought to establish at the University of Cambridge drew together the most scientific minds with the most passionate. Keynes was the most stellar result.

The strongest link between economics and the real world has always been politics. Indeed, until this century economics was called "political economy." Almost all the stellar economists served at some level of government. Two of them, David Ricardo and John Stuart Mill, won election to the British Parliament. Among the greatest economists, we consistently see not just a spark of scientific interest but a surge of passion. Among the numerous symbols of calculus and statistics, we see bold exclamation points.

Throughout the history of economic thought, we see confrontations and sometimes cooperation between government and economists. Modern economics received its initial push when Adam Smith denounced the incestuous marriage between the monarchies and the merchants of Europe. One of the few things Adam Smith, Karl Marx, and Thorstein Veblen had in common was their realization that businessmen love to use politics in order to help themselves. In a famous statement, Smith warned that businessmen seldom meet without plotting against the consumer. You can be sure that even today, the orator at the local chamber of commerce meeting who exalts the free market would jump at the chance of securing a monopoly, an exclusive government contract, or a regulation that guarantees his profits. Thankfully politicians have not always been obliging. After World War II, Great Britain's socialist leaders promised prosperity and near paradise through unionism and nationalization, but instead the British economy only got worse and worse. One of Winston Churchill's biographers tells the story of Churchill meeting the leader of the Labour Party in the men's room outside the House of Commons. The Labour leader entered first and took up a standing position. Churchill entered a moment later on the same mission and, seeing his opponent, stood all the way at the other end of the row. "Feeling standoffish today, are we, Winston?" the Labour leader asked. "That's right," barked Churchill. "Why, every time you see something big, you want to nationalize it!"[1]

Most of our presidents have shown little grasp of economic principles. John F. Kennedy once admitted that the only way he could remember that the Federal Reserve Board controlled monetary policy, not fiscal policy, was that Chairman William McChesney Martin's name began with the letter "M." Apparently, Kennedy couldn't have appointed a Volcker, Greenspan, or Powell to the post.

Election campaigns are the most trying time for economists. Whenever a politician promises his or her constituents more margarine *and* more munitions, economists must warn of the calamitous consequences. Any progress that economists make in raising economic literacy can be wiped out in a second by the pie-in-the-sky ravings of a candidate. An election-year speech is the political equivalent of prime-time television. When a presidential candidate appears on television, he cannot allow himself to appear any more sophisticated than Joey Tribbiani of *Friends*. For some politicians, this is not a great challenge.

It is not hard to see why politicians misunderstand their economic advisers. Economists speak a different language to one another than they do to the public. They speak the language of models. In their attempt to explain a complex world, they must first simplify out those few factors at any given time that are most important, for every economic phenomenon may be affected by thousands of events. For example, the level of a consumer's spending in the United States may depend on some of the following: weather, musical tastes, weight, income, inflation, political campaigns, and the performance of U.S. Olympic team. To isolate and rank which are most important, economists must design models that exempt some of the infinite number of possible causes. The best economists are those who design the most durable, robust models.

Of course, all scientists must construct models. For years physics rested on a Newtonian model of gravity. Astronomers still use a Copernican paradigm. Thomas Kuhn's classic and controversial *The Structure of Scientific Revolutions* traces the development of these models.[2] So why is economics more difficult than these "hard" sciences? An example may help here. Imagine a surgeon operating on a kidney. After inspecting an X-ray report, the surgeon knows that the patient's right kidney lies one inch below the colon. Imagine, however, that as the surgeon makes an incision, the kidney changes position. In just this way, as an economist isolates causes and estimates their influence, the degree of influence changes. As human relationships and social institutions change, so does the subject of our scientific inquiry. Economics may not be a "hard" science. But that does not mean it is an easy science. Because it is so fluid, it is hard to hold in place and to study.[3] No wonder Lord Keynes insisted that the master economist fulfill a set of attributes more extraordinary than those needed for knighthood or even sainthood:

> He must be mathematician, historian, statesman, philosopher. . . . He must understand symbols and speak in words. He must contemplate the particular in terms of the general, and touch abstract and concrete in the same flight of thought. He must study the present in the light of the past

for the purposes of the future. No part of man's nature or his institutions must lie entirely outside his regard. He must be purposeful and disinterested in a simultaneous mood; as aloof and incorruptible as an artist, yet sometimes as near the earth as a politician.[4]

The Genesis of Economics

Where shall we start in studying the history of economic thought? We could start with the Bible, which contains many statements on land, labor, capital, and debt forgiveness. But the Bible presents more commandments than careful analyses.[5] Although Adam Smith got his name and his moral posture from the Bible, it provided little inspiration for his economic theorizing.

We could also explore Aristotle's articulate remarks praising private property and denouncing the accumulation of wealth for wealth's sake. But Aristotle knew just enough about economics to know that time was a scarce resource. Therefore, he devoted more of his time to philosophy and to educating Alexander the Great than he did to economic theory. It shows. Aristotle remains one of the giants of philosophy, but at the risk of insulting ardent fans of college courses on Western civilization, we must admit that Aristotle left few marks in the annals of economic discipline.

In the Middle Ages theologians debated economic issues. The Catholic Schoolmen struggled over questions of justice and morality in the marketplace. In particular, they devised the doctrine of the "just price" and refined the Church's view of usury. Whereas the Old Testament specifically forbade lending at interest to members of the same community, medieval theologians tried to separate the different components of interest—such as risk, opportunity cost, inflation, and inconvenience—in order to perforate the solid prohibition and permit loopholes. The theologians faced excruciating choices. If they continued to deliver orthodox biblical inter-pretations that challenged commercial activities, the School-men would lose their relevance, because many people were willing to take their chances with divine retribution. On the other hand, if the theologians simply condoned commercialism in all its forms, they would lose credibility as Church leaders. They devised most of their economic theories while straddling the secular and the sacred. This is neither a comfortable posi-tion nor one terribly conducive to studying economics. They spoke on economics because it was a duty to their flock. But the duty was to guide the flock to heaven, not to a higher stan-dard of living. When Protestants split the flock, the task grew even less manageable.[6]

We cannot sprint so swiftly past the mercantilists. Generally speaking, they were a group of writers and courtly advisers to European monarchs during the sixteenth through the eigh-teenth centuries. They did not share a common "good book," and they certainly had different interests. As royal families of England, France, Spain, Portugal, and Holland consolidated their boundaries and battled for colonies across the seas, law-yers and merchants began advising kings and queens on how to manage their economies.

In retrospect, we can list several tenets often found in their recommendations: First, a nation should keep its house in or-der by awarding monopolies, patents, subsidies, and privileges to loyal subjects of the crown. Second, a nation should pursue colonies for the purpose of extracting precious metals and raw materials, which were good measures of national wealth, for they could pay for wars of conquest. Third, a nation should restrict its foreign trade so that it exported more finished goods than it imported. A consistently positive balance of trade would bring in gold (wealth) from debtor nations.

Thus under mercantilism, we see nations expanding their borders. At the same time, however, we see a tightened control over the internal economy, as guilds, monopolies, and tariffs distribute economic power to political favorites. In some nations the control extended further than in others. Finance Minister Jean-Baptiste Colbert thoroughly regulated the manufacture of many goods during the reign of Louis XIV and bestowed great authority to the guilds. In a stunning display of imperial power, he once announced that fabric from Dijon would contain 1,408 threads!

The mercantilists provided the perfect target for Adam Smith, with whom it seems reasonable to start our study of modern economic thought. He excoriated their theories on several levels. First, they measured wealth on the basis of coin and precious metals, while Smith believed that real wealth should be gauged by the standard of living of households. Bags of gold do not necessarily translate into bags of food. Second, he said that wealth must be measured from the viewpoint of a nation's consumers. Tactics that placed money in the hands of prime ministers or sycophantic merchants did not necessarily help the citizens of a nation. Third, Smith knew that individual motivation, invention, and innovation inspire an economy to greater prosperity. By bestowing gifts of monopoly and protection, mercantilist policies paralyzed the body politic. Thus began modern economics.

Should We Ignore the Economist?

Since the days of Adam Smith, we have produced few master economists. Mainstream economic theory does not explain everything. In particular, economists today have a difficult time looking back to explain the drop in productivity growth from the early 1970s through the early 1990s, or looking forward to design the optimal way to pay back government debts in the mid-2000s. Yet economists agree on enough to say that countries and individuals take foolish risks in ignoring the basic tenets of economic theory. The nation that raises trade barriers in an atavistic yearning for stable mercantile times hurts its own consumers. The nation that keeps farm prices high hurts its own consumers and finds itself with a surplus of grain rotting in silos. On these two points few economists would disagree. Yet too few politicians in the world will listen.

Even if governments do not always take the advice of economists, we can look to economists to tell us where our standard of living has been and where it may be going. Ever since the Industrial Revolution sparked England, Americans have always looked forward to getting bigger and better. We see the present as the minimum. Yet history provides no precedent for continual progress. Every year that the industrialized nations avoid a new dark age, we set a record for humankind. Listen to the words of Georges Duby as he describes Europe in the eleventh century. It is frightening to think that these horrible decades came after and not before the relative affluence of ancient Greece, Rome, Babylon, and Egypt:

> . . . the Western world in the year 1000. A wild world, ringed round by hunger. Its meager population is in fact too large. The people struggle almost bare-handed, slaves to intractable nature and to a soil that is unproductive because it is poorly worked. No peasant, when he sows one grain of wheat, expects to harvest more than three—if it is not too bad a year; that means bread to eat until Easter time. Then he will have to manage on herbs, roots, the makeshift food that can be gleaned from forest and riverbank and, on an empty belly, he will do the heavy summer tasks and wither with fatigue while he awaits the harvest. . . . Sometimes, when too heavy rains have soaked into the ground and hampered the autumn ploughing, when storms have pummeled and spoiled the crops, the customary food shortage becomes a famine, a great death-dealing wave of starvation. The chroniclers of the times all described such famines, not without a certain satisfaction. "People pursued one another in order to eat each other up, and many cut the throats of their fellow men so as to feed on human flesh, just like wolves."[7]

Will the developed world ever know such horrors? Will it ever slip back into the frightening state of some of its Third World neighbors? Not even the master economist of Keynes's most fantastic dreams would know. We do know that the goal of the great economists was to teach us to avoid such a dark abyss.

It is striking that so many of the lessons of the great economists still speak to us. Each of their wisest theories has a practical point or an analogy today. This book seeks their wisdom by looking at mainstream economics and asking, Who first had these insights and built these durable models? We can learn from the masters. Some of the contemporary examples in this book are meant to be humorous. David Ricardo did not have access to the cast of *Gilligan's Island* to explain the Law of Comparative Advantage. But my using the castaways to do so, I hope, does no disrespect and provides some help in understanding the difficult paradigm. Economics need not be dull. Why not have the last laugh on Carlyle by using the dead economists themselves to reverse their bad reputations and to teach the lessons they left us? Better the ghosts of economists past roll over in their graves in laughter than toss and turn, disappointed that we forgot their work and fearful that we will drive ourselves back to the eleventh century.

CHAPTER II

The Second Coming of Adam Smith

When Ronald Reagan won the 1980 presidential election, conservative supporters in Washington rejoiced. At cocktail parties and meetings they congratulated one another and looked forward to prosperity under "Reaganomics." They also noticed that they were wearing the same neckties, which featured the profile of Adam Smith.

Why were politicians and activists who prided themselves on patriotism parading the profile of an eighteenth-century Scotsman? Why not Theodore Roosevelt, Thomas Jefferson, or even Barry Goldwater? Could Adam Smith really be more relevant to contemporary economic crises than the thousands of economists and political leaders who had followed?

Adam Smith believed that his ideas would be relevant forever. This was a common trait of intellectuals in the eighteenth century, a truly revolutionary age. Political ferment began to bubble in France and America. By the time Smith wrote his greatest work, *The Wealth of Nations*, dealers were trading within the British Isles and across the seven seas, population was expanding, merchants were organizing small factories, and banking systems were spreading throughout Britain and the Continent. But the most powerful and profound revolution of the Enlightenment was sparked by thinkers probing for new explanations of the world around them. No wonder Smith once proclaimed in his lectures, "Man is an anxious animal."[1]

From the Middle Ages until roughly the time of Columbus,

theologians had dominated European intellectual thought. Church elders interpreted natural phenomena in accordance with religious doctrine. But in the century leading to Smith's birth, more and more people began following the bold paths of Francis Bacon and Nicolaus Copernicus in searching for rational explanations for natural events. Eventually, scientists emerged independent of ruling churches, applying the "scientific method" for laws of nature regardless of controversial conclusions.

Galileo Galilei attacked the religious cliché that God gave man only two books, the Bible and nature. Claiming that the language of the book of nature was mathematics, Galileo proved by mathematics and experiment, without the help of holy scriptures, his law of falling bodies. Galileo knew that he was treading on treacherous ground and tried to avoid condemnation. Fearful when, in 1632, his telescope experiments confirmed Copernicus's heresy that the earth revolved around the sun, he dedicated his findings to the pope. He was right about the earth. And he was right to fear the Church's wrath, for a tribunal consequently condemned him "for vehement suspicion of heresy."

Toward the end of his *Discourse on Method* (1637), René Descartes foreshadowed the explosion of thought in the eighteenth century by arguing that through practical science men can be the "masters and possessors of nature."

The shining figure in the Enlightenment, though, was Isaac Newton. He pursued Galileo's scientific quests, searching beyond religious texts for answers, which he revealed in his theory of gravity, laws of physical motion, and discovery of calculus. Newton seemed to portray God as a key player only at the beginning of time, as responsible for the world today as a pawnshop owner is after a pawned watch leaves the shop. The German philosopher Gottfried Wilhelm von Leibniz thought that Newton compounded the blasphemy by depicting God as a clumsy watchmaker.

Adam Smith was born into this movement. Like Galileo and

Newton, Smith sought out cause-and-effect relationships. Before he touched economics, Smith tried to master astronomy and gave lectures on Copernicus. But soon he shifted his lens from planets to the orbits of people. He had one wish: to make sense of the seemingly chaotic clanging he heard in the streets, at the docks, and in the emerging factories.

Born in 1723, Smith grew up with his mother, Margaret, in Kirkcaldy, a small port located across the Firth of Forth from Edinburgh. His father, a comptroller of customs, had died months before his birth. Some men born without fathers reinvent themselves and make up their own world, like Tom Sawyer and Saul Bellow's Augie March. Others search for a father figure somewhere else—for example, in the heavens. Smith managed to do both. We will later see that Smith's concept of the "invisible hand" provides a natural order for all the confusion he saw about him.

Smith was a sickly lad who never married and spent a good part of his adult life living with his mother. Margaret was hearty, though, and lived to age ninety. When she died, he was distraught, writing, "I certainly loved and respected [her] more than I ever shall either love or respect any other person. I cannot help feeling . . . a very heavy stroke upon me."[2]

Although it was not apparent from the Adam Smith neckties worn in Washington, Smith was an odd-looking Scotsman. He had a large nose, bulging eyes, a protruding lower lip, a nervous twitch, and a speech impediment. Smith once acknowledged his unusual features, saying, "I am a beau in nothing but my books." A good student, Smith entered the University of Glasgow at age fourteen and later rode on horseback to Oxford to accept a scholarship at Balliol College. Like most other college students of his day, Smith intended to study theology and enter the clergy. Like many college students of any day, Smith complained about his teachers and wrote that "it will be his own fault if anyone should endanger his health at Oxford by excessive study."[3] He especially denounced the lecturers: "In the University of Oxford, the greater part of the public professors have, for these many years, given up altogether even the pretence of teaching."[4] More important, Smith lashed out at academic censorship and complained to friends that college officials had confiscated his copy of David Hume's heralded *Treatise of Human Nature*. Although he was permitted to read all the ancient Greek and Latin classics, Smith was forbidden from reading one of the most potent works of his own time.

Despite academic restrictions, Smith was so influenced by Hume's skepticism (*A Theory of Human Nature* is subtitled *An Attempt to Introduce the Experimental Method of Reasoning into Moral Subjects*) that he refused to continue preparing for the clergy. Instead, he returned to Kirkcaldy, where he later delivered popular public lectures on rhetoric and law.

In 1748, Smith returned to the University of Glasgow to teach logic. The next year he filled the chair in moral philosophy vacated by his former teacher Francis Hutcheson. A "campus radical," Hutcheson had stirred administrators by refusing to lecture in Latin. The Presbytery then prosecuted him for spreading the following "false and dangerous" doctrines:

1. The standard of moral good is promotion of happiness to others.
2. It is possible to know good and evil without knowing God.

As we will see, Smith had absorbed many of Hutcheson's dangerous declarations. Hutcheson stood nobly for academic freedom in the face of ruling dogma. Unlike Galileo, Hutcheson did not try to avoid censure by dedicating his teachings to the pope, which, in any event, would not have done much good in Protestant Scotland.

It is interesting to note that Smith's ideas are usually associated today with conservative politics, yet because his intellectual roots were rather radical, some contemporary conservatives feel a bit uneasy about Smith. Anti-globalists and über-nationalists who denounce international trade blame Smith for the troubles they see. Libertarians, however, seek to place his capitalist theories on the same altar as God, Mom, apple pie, and democracy.

Far from following the sleepy style of the Oxford dons he had assailed, Smith the professor quickly gained a reputation for lucid lectures and concern for his students. Though he lectured, tutored, and held informal discussions, Smith also found time to serve as the college treasurer and later the dean of faculty.

Smith never taught a course in economics. In fact, Smith never took a course in economics. Nobody did. Until the nineteenth century, academics considered economics a branch of philosophy. Not until 1903 did Cambridge University establish an economics program separate from the "moral sciences." Nonetheless, Smith squeezed his preliminary thoughts on economics into lectures on jurisprudence. The following notes, taken by a student, point to the genesis of his key analysis of labor later elaborated in *The Wealth of Nations*:

"Division of labor is the great cause of the increase of public opulence, which is always proportioned to the industry of the people, and not to the quantity of gold and silver, as is foolishly imagined."[5]

So far we have discussed Smith's education and his appearance but have avoided his personality quirks. It's a touchy subject. Sigmund Freud observed that people have a tendency to puff up the status of their forefathers. He called this the "family romance." Budding economists might be disappointed to discover that their forefather was not as intelligent as Newton, not as witty as Voltaire, and not as scandalous as Byron. In fact, despite the "family romance" tendency, economic historians admit that Smith was a bit of a bumbler. Although in his lectures Smith shared precise observations—pointing out that John Milton wore shoelaces rather than buckles—in his own life Smith noticed not much at all.

Professional economists are now weary of the many stories of Smith acting absentmindedly. Nonetheless, these tales can still amuse the beginning scholar.

One day while the Right Honourable Charles Townshend was in Glasgow, Smith took him on a tour of a tanning factory. While rhapsodizing on the merits of free trade, Smith walked right into a huge, nauseous pool of goop. After workers dragged him out of the goop, stripped him, and threw a blanket over him, Smith complained that he could never keep his life in order.

On another day, Smith climbed out of bed and began to walk. And walk. And walk. Fifteen miles later, the sound of church bells stirred him from sleep. The most famous economist of his time was found running back to his house, nightgown flapping in the breeze.

Smith the Philosopher

Even before Smith wrote *The Wealth of Nations*, he gained fame in 1759 with his book on ethical behavior, *The Theory of Moral Sentiments*. As sales burgeoned, he became known as "Smith the philosopher." *A Theory of Moral Sentiments* followed in the Enlightenment tradition. Just as scientists searched for the origin of the solar system, Smith searched for the origin of moral approval and disapproval.

How can a man who is interested chiefly in himself make moral judgments that satisfy other people? After all, each person stands at the center of his own system, just as the sun stands at the center of the planets. Does the sun care what the smaller planets think? Smith struggled with this paradox, asking himself why, if people are selfish, each town does not resemble the vicious state of nature that the political theorist Thomas Hobbes portrayed in *Leviathan*. Hobbes argued that man's life is "solitary, poor, nasty, brutish, and short" until governments emerge.

Finally, Smith concocted a clever answer. When people confront moral choices, he said, they imagine an "impartial spectator" who carefully considers and advises them. Instead of simply following their self-interest, they take the imaginary observer's advice. In this way, people decide on the basis of sympathy, not selfishness.

Many critics vilify modern economists for assuming only selfish motives, for caring only about costs and benefits, and for ignoring man's more noble side. The economist is, they declare, a moral dwarf. The attack may apply to some—but not to Adam Smith. Not just aware of sympathy and sentiment, he devoted the entire book to these emotions. Furthermore, *A Theory of Moral Sentiments* pointed to many concepts developed by Freudian psychoanalysis more than a century later. Freud's concept of the "superego," the conscience that restrains humans from certain acts and makes them feel guilty when they do not listen, is not so far removed from the adviser that Smith described.

Smith's reputation soared as his book spread throughout Britain and the Continent. Wealthy students, whose parents heard of the Scotsman's achievements, left their schools in France, Switzerland, and Moscow to enroll at the University of Glasgow. Ben Franklin, who had invented swim fins and the Franklin stove, and had already flown his kite in a thunderstorm, came to visit. One imagines Smith in the twenty-first century, appearing on podcasts and television talk shows plugging his book. Given his chronic absentmindedness, he might have been an entertaining guest, especially appearing on late-night television in his nightgown. Smith certainly was not content to stay locked in an ivory tower. At Glasgow he mixed town and gown, meeting with bankers, merchants, and politicians. At the Political Economy Club, he tried to figure out how businessmen really operated. As we will see, he learned not to trust the motives of merchants.

To France and Physiocrats

Soon, even cosmopolitan Glasgow began to bore Smith, and he resigned his professorship in 1764 to become the tutor of the son of the late Duke of Buccleuch. The boy's mother, the Countess of Dalkeith, had just married Smith's admirer Charles Townshend, who later emerged as chancellor of the exchequer and found his way into history books when his taxes inspired some colonists across the Atlantic to make a teapot of Boston Harbor. Smith's tutoring job involved touring Europe, helping the boy develop a proper polish, attending lavish balls, and accepting £300 per year plus expenses and a £300 per year pension (roughly twice his former income). Smith was not fond of what today we would call a "gap year." The man who would never know a son or a father surmised that "by sending his son abroad, a father delivers himself, at least for some time, from so disagreeable an object as a son unemployed, neglected, and going to ruin before his eyes."[6] With the tutoring proposal in hand, Smith consulted his impartial adviser, who sympathetically approved. He took the job. Forced by the offer to leave Glasgow in the middle of the term, Smith attempted to refund the fees he had collected from his devoted students by grabbing the coats of young students, shoving cash into their pockets, and then shoving them away from him. The students refused and dumped the contents of their pockets back into Smith's.

The first and the most boring stop on the tour was Toulouse, France. Smith's displeasure recalls the old vaudeville line about spending a week in Brooklyn one night. Smith would have been happier with one week in Brooklyn, for at least they speak a form of English there, whereas Smith could hardly speak French. Instead of a week, they stayed for a year and a half. Samuel Johnson once said that nothing concentrates a man's mind so wonderfully than knowing he is to be hanged in a fortnight. Toulouse was not quite a scaffold, but it did inspire Smith to concentrate and write about economics. In a rather humble letter to Hume, he reported, "I have begun to write a book in order to pass away the time."[7]

After the south of France, the entourage moved on to Geneva, where Smith met Voltaire, and finally to Paris. Paris was bubbling with artistic and intellectual creativity. Smith enjoyed the theater, met exciting personalities, and discovered a vibrant school of economics known as physiocracy. Founded by François Quesnay, a court physician for Louis XV with friends in high places and a high opinion of himself, the physiocrats presented some rather simple ideas in inscrutable language and a mysterious chart called the *Tableau économique*. Quesnay gathered together obsequious disciples who called him master, father, "the Confucius of Europe," and "the modern Socrates."[8] The physiocrats vigorously advanced the Enlightenment quest for the laws of nature, but they did not believe that man could completely control nature—only that people could thrive if they understood its laws. In fact, *physiocracy* means "rule of nature."

The *Tableau économique* brilliantly illustrates physiocratic thought. Just as medical doctors such as Claude Bernard began dissecting the human body and charting the path of blood, Quesnay charted the circulation of income in the economy. Instead of hands, feet, arms, and legs, Quesnay saw the body politic as three naturally interdependent classes: farmers, artisans, and proprietors (landlords and other sovereigns). Unfortunately, he so riddled the chart with zigzags that only he seemed to understand it. Quesnay admitted that even his chief disciple, Mirabeau the elder, was too "bogged down in the zigzag."[9] Nonetheless, in sycophantic style, Mirabeau praised the table as an invention as extraordinary as writing.

Physiocrats energetically argued two points: first, that wealth arose from production, not from acquisition of gold and silver, as mercantilists thought; and second, that only agricultural enterprise produced wealth, whereas merchants, manufacturers, and other workers did not. On an economics exam they would score 50 percent correct. They rightly claimed that a nation that produces goods is wealthier than a nation that simply stockpiles precious metals, but they lose points by arguing that manufacturing, commerce, and service industries are "sterile," unproductive, and mere shifters of wealth. Without zigging and zagging through the model, let us note that the physiocrats advocated policies to make agriculture, the only productive sector, even more productive. For instance, they urged the government to release the economy from trade restrictions, which kept farm rents artificially low and discouraged investment in land. Further, they proposed taxes on landlords, not to punish them, but because only they could afford to pay, for only they owned a "productive" sector of the economy. In sum, the physiocrats enthusiastically embraced the concept of private property and private gain but saw concomitant responsibilities for owners. After all, their analysis insisted, it's only "natural."

Adam Smith listened attentively to the Frenchmen. Their analysis confirmed some of his ideas, but he did not accept their pronouncements on productive and sterile sectors. Nor did Hume, who asked a friend to "thunder them, and crush them, and pound them, and reduce them to dust and ashes."[10]

Perhaps Smith's impartial conscience restrained him from wishing pulverization. Physiocracy is, Smith admitted, "with all its imperfections," perhaps "the nearest approximation to the truth that has yet been published upon the subject of political economy." But, he added with some condescension, it is "a system, which never has done, and probably never will do any harm in any part of the world."[11] Thus, he gently patted the powdered wigs of the physiocrats, who gave the world an innocuous doctrine.

In 1766, sorrow struck when the duke's ill younger brother died in Paris. Smith's tour ended, and he returned to Kirkcaldy via London. For the next ten years Smith worked on his book, traveled to the Literary Club in London to discuss ideas and hoist glasses with Edward Gibbon and Edmund Burke, and exchanged nasty vulgarities with Samuel Johnson and James Boswell. Johnson called Smith a "dull dog," and Boswell deemed him an "infidel with a bag wig." Despite their vitriol, Smith received rave reviews from conversationalists whenever he visited Paris.

The Wealth of Nations

Finally, in March 1776, *The Wealth of Nations*, that book Smith wrote to pass away the time, was published. Smith's hero Hume praised it loudly but warned that popularity would come only slowly. For the first time Smith rejoiced in a Humean mistake. An instant success, the first edition sold out in six months. Robert Burns, whose poems give us "Auld Lang Syne" and "Mice an' Men," declared that he "could not have given any mere man credit for half the intelligence Mr Smith discovers in his book."

But is it a good book? It is not only a good book; it is a great one. With the hubris that goaded the gods into striking down Greek tragic heroes, Smith stared confidently at the world and delivered nine hundred pages of analysis, prophecy, fact, and fable—most of it clear, charming, and aimed at helping the reader to understand. *The Wealth of Nations* introduces readers to the world of philosophy, politics, and business, with the sharp, skeptical, yet ultimately optimistic Smith as a guide. Just when the Industrial Revolution explodes, Smith confidently points to every player, from farmer to friar to merchant to shipper, masterfully making sense of the social upheaval. Furthermore, Smith approaches economic policy without a biased brief for a particular party or class. No one could accuse him of sycophancy or insincerity. Though he finally endorses the rise of the bourgeoisie, he warns society not to naively succumb to bourgeois blandishments. In a way, the 1776 publication of *The Wealth of Nations* brought forth a declaration of independence for economists.

The full title reveals the key to Smith's masterpiece: *An Inquiry into the Nature and Causes of the Wealth of Nations.* Notice that Smith focuses on a particular goal: to uncover causal laws that explain how to achieve wealth. The title alone places him in the Enlightenment tradition. The text confirms the suspicion by explaining the laws that guide "economic actors" and then drawing the implications of these behavioral laws for society. "Economic actors" may sound somewhat technical, but Smith simply means people, for everyone at some point in the day is an economic actor. And just as there could be no *Hamlet* without the Prince, Smith could construct no economics without understanding people. In this he follows the leads of Machiavelli and Hobbes, each of whom saw men as they were, not as they should be. Hobbes spoke of life as "but a motion of limb. . . . For what is the *heart* but a *spring* and the *nerves* but so many *strings*; and the *joints* but so many *wheels* giving motion to the whole body?" (original emphasis). Man is scrutable and peccable.[12]

The important natural drives or "propensities" Smith discovers in human nature form the basis of his analysis and the foundation of classical economics. All humans want to live better than they do. Smith finds a "desire of bettering our condition, a desire which, though generally calm and dispassionate, comes with us from the womb, and never leaves us till we go to the grave."

Between the womb and the grave "there is scarce perhaps a single instant in which any man is so perfectly and completely satisfied with his situation, as to be without any wish of alteration or improvement of any kind."[13] Then, Smith points to "a certain propensity in human nature . . . to truck, barter, and exchange one thing for another. . . . It is common to all men."[14]

To increase the wealth of nations, Smith argues that society should exploit these natural drives. Government should not repress self-interested people, for self-interest is a rich natural resource. People would be fools and nations would be impoverished if they depended on charity and altruism. Smith states that man almost constantly needs help from others, but it is hoping in vain "to expect it from their benevolence only. He will be more likely to prevail if he can shew them that it is for their own advantage." In the most cited passage in the history of economic thought, Smith proclaims: "It is not from the benevolence of the butcher, the brewer, or the baker, that we expect our dinner, but from their regard to their own interest."[15] Even those who enjoy slaughtering cattle, brewing beer, or baking cakes would not want to do it all day if they were not compensated. Smith never suggests that they are motivated only by self-interest; he simply states that self-interest motivates more powerfully and consistently than kindness, altruism, or martyrdom. Put succinctly: Society cannot rest its future on the noblest motives but must use the strongest motives in the best possible way.

But if everyone charges ahead in his own direction, why does society not resemble anarchy, something like a complex highway intersection with broken traffic lights? Shouldn't we hear a frightening crash when self-interests clash? If roads cannot be safe without a traffic authority designating who shall move, can a community survive without a central planning authority to decide who produces and what is produced?

Yes. Not only will it survive, but the community will thrive far more than any community with central planning. More surprising, it will surpass both in output and social harmony any economic system based on altruism. Smith had studied astronomy and embraced the idea of a natural harmony in the planets, even if each planet moved in its own orbit. People, he thought, could move in different paths yet harmonize and help each other—but not intentionally. In his classic statement, Smith announces that if all seek to promote their self-interest, the whole society prospers: "He . . . neither intends to promote the publick interest, nor knows how much he is promoting it. . . . . He intends only his own gain, and he is in this, as in many other cases, led by an invisible hand to promote an end which was no part of his intention."[16] That "invisible hand" becomes the transparent symbol of Adam Smith's economics.

Yet Smith did not rest his argument on any apparition. The invisible hand merely symbolizes the true orchestrator of social harmony, the free market. Friedrich von Hayek, one of the twentieth century's most vigorous proponents of the free market, said that if the market system had not arisen naturally, it would have been proclaimed the greatest invention in human history. For market competition leads a self-interested person to wake up in the morning, look outside at the earth, and produce from its raw materials, not what he wants, but what others want. Not in the quantities he prefers, but in the quantities his neighbors prefer. Not at the price he dreams of charging, but at a price reflecting how much his neighbors value what he has done.

The Free Market at Work

Let us start with our self-interested neighbor John as an example. In contrast to Adam Smith, John wakes up in his own bed, rather than in the town square. While reading the newspaper, John admires the lovely wood sculpture of a vulture that hangs above his dining room table, as if ready to swoop down on table scraps. John really enjoyed carving the vulture. An idea strikes him: Why not sculpt more vultures and sell them? After all, the specially treated wood imported from Tasmania would only cost $50 per vulture, and he can sculpt one per week. He decides to sell the vultures for $200 each, since big profits could make him rich and bring him the things he dreams of, like big cars and riotous vacations in Acapulco. Most important, though, he loves sculpting.

He begins working and rents a shop, inviting neighbors and local art critics to a gala opening. They laugh. He cries. They think the vulture sculptures are hideous. He cries louder. No one buys. Finally, his mother offers $49 for one. He gives in—and goes out of business. The invisible hand gives a "thumbs-up" approval. Why?

Instead of producing something his neighbors wanted, John produced what he wanted. Instead of charging a price they were willing to pay, John charged an exorbitant amount. But in John's case, no one would pay him as much as it actually cost him to produce the vultures. Didn't John have to charge more than his costs? No. The answer is not to charge more, but not to produce at all! Why should the invisible hand approve of John going out of business? To make the sculptures, John used up scarce resources. The earth gives us only so much to work with. If John used the valuable Tasmanian wood, no one else could. The invisible hand forces people to give up if they do not produce something more valuable than what they started with. John took $50 worth of wood, carved it up, and gave the world vultures worth less. Societies cannot afford to squander resources by subtracting from their value. People who take wood and produce Stradivarius violins or crutches for the disabled increase the value of those resources and enrich society. They deserve applause from the invisible hand. John deserved a punch.

Back to the drawing board for John. He pours a cup of tea, curses the vulture above his dining room table, and slams his fist down. Tea jumps out of the cup onto the table. Now he curses himself for spilling tea on the new table he made just a month ago. Inspiration strikes again. Why not, he asks, build tables and sell them? A bit wiser now, he finds a lumber mill that will supply wood to him at a cost of about $100 per table. Carving, planing, and fitting will take about two weeks per table. His time, he figures, is worth $200 per week, based on his previous job as a carpenter. Taking into account tools, rent, and other incidentals, he calculates the total cost per table at roughly $575. John window-shops for similar dining room tables and discovers he could sell the tables for $585. Not only will he be able to pay himself $200 per week, but he will also earn a profit.

The invisible hand finally gives John a thumbs-up. He's taken scarce resources and brought forth something more valuable than what he started with—not according to his own tastes but according to society's.

So far we have seen the invisible hand encourage and discourage production. But Adam Smith also shows us how the market regulates prices. Remember that Smith's characters are self-interested. Why does John not raise his table prices above $585 to increase profits? He cannot. If John boosts his prices, profits will plunge, because people will simply by-pass his shop and buy from competitors who charge less. Of course, all the furniture makers could get together and agree to raise prices. But even if they were able to agree, other self-interested people would see the high profits in the furniture business and open shops. Such entrepreneurs could earn enormous profits by underselling and stealing business away from the cartel.

Prices and profits signal to entrepreneurs what to produce and what price to charge. High prices and high profits sound alarms in the ears of entrepreneurs, screaming at them to start producing a certain good. Low profits or losses grab the businessman by the shirt collar and shake him mercilessly until he stops producing.

Prices and profits are not simply abstractions, though. What does it really mean if profits are high? It means that people need or want a product. When homeowners and automobile drivers decided they preferred streaming audio devices to compact disc players, demand rose for the streaming-device technology and producers were able to charge more. In turn, compact disc manufacturers responded to the signals by producing fewer players; workers shifted from one type of factory to another; and the price returned to normal. Between 2000 and 2018, the number of CD sales plummeted by 90 percent, while the cost of listening to a song also decreased.[17] Consumers bought fewer CDs in 2018 than they did in 1987, when *Dirty Dancing* hit the charts. Likewise, in 2004 Blockbuster video had more than nine thousand stores worldwide. Today there is one remaining outpost that attracts tourists nostalgic for the 1990s to Bend, Oregon. Despite the churn in the video industry, the cost of watching a movie at home is cheaper. Over the past decade, prices for personal computers and flat-screen TVs have dropped, not only because costs have dropped, but also because so many high-technology manufacturers have entered the competition for profits. In the long run, no industry should earn more than a normal profit. The free market automatically induces self-interested Johns to satisfy strangers. No central planner need call, no taskmaster need coerce.

Division of Labor

Adam Smith delivered on his promise to show how the invisible hand regulates output, price, and profit. But the cheery Scotsman also promised to teach us what increases the wealth of nations. If he failed to answer that question, he'd score no higher than the physiocrats. Happily, he won again with a neat three-word answer: division of labor. Smith argued his case logically and empirically. The empirics come to life as he describes a pin factory, again in one of the most famous passages in economic thought. Mark Twain said that classics are books everyone owns but no one ever bothers to read. Even more sad, classics often become rather boring clichés, and we can miss the force and drama they packed when they originally appeared. Imagine the initial power of the following passage, for it appeared before factories were common and when groups of only three or four people produced most of the world's goods:

A workman not educated to . . . the trade of the pin-maker . . . could scarce, perhaps, with his utmost industry, make one pin in a day, and certainly could not make twenty. But in the way which this business is now carried on, not only the whole work is a peculiar trade, but it is divided into a number of branches, of which the greater part are likewise peculiar trades. One man draws out the wire, another straights it, a third cuts it, a fourth points it, a fifth grinds at the top for receiving the head; to make the head requires two or three distinct operations; to put it on, is a peculiar business, to whiten the pins is another; it is even a trade by itself to put them into the paper; and the important business of making a pin is, in this manner, divided into about eighteen distinct operations, which, in some manufactories, are all performed by distinct hands . . . I have seen a small manufactory of this kind where ten men only were employed, and where . . . each person . . . [averaged] four thousand eight hundred pins a day. But if they had all wrought separately and indepen-dently, and without any of them having been educated to this peculiar business, they certainly could not each of them make twenty, perhaps not one pin in a day.[18]

Just by specializing and dividing the tasks, one day's output can explode by 400,000 percent! How can Smith possibly ex-plain this? Are we about to be introduced to the invisible foot or another impartial ghost who actually works for us while we sleep? To be fair to Smith, he never promised a 400,000 per-cent leap in every situation. But he did proclaim three ways in which division of labor lifts output: First, each worker devel-ops more skill and dexterity in her particular task. Second, workers waste less time changing from one task to another. This makes sense, especially if changing tasks forces one to change uniforms, tools, or location. And third, specialized workers will more likely invent machinery to help with the par-ticular task they focus on daily. Smith believed that workers, rather than engineers, often propel invention:

A great part of the machines made use of in those manufactures in which labour is most subdivided, were originally the inventions of common workmen, who, being each
of them employed in some simple operation, naturally
turned their thoughts towards finding out easier and readier
methods of performing it. Whoever has been much accus-
tomed to visit such manufactures, must frequently have
been shewn very pretty machines, which were the inventions
of such workmen.[19]

Notice that while Smith begins by praising division of labor
for its heightened productivity, he ends up crediting division
of labor for technological advancement.

From the mid-1970s until the late 1980s, when the Japanese
stock market bubble burst, business consultants, economists,
and business writers studied Japanese factories in quest of the
secret behind their successes that toppled the "Big Three" automakers in Detroit and bankrupted U.S. tech firms like Pola-
roid and Compaq. In some ways, Japanese workplaces appear
less divided and less Smithian, employing work circles rather
than assembly lines. Yet Japanese businesses claim that their
workers invent and innovate much more than their American
counterparts do. The glorification of Japanese methods has
inspired some emulation and a few fables, such as the tale of
the Japanese, French, and American corporate executives,
each sentenced to death. The executioner offers a final request. The Frenchman says, "I'd like a bottle of cabernet sau-
vignon and a feast featuring escargot, pheasant, and crème
brûlée." The Japanese executive responds, "I'd like to give a
lecture on the merits of Japanese corporate management." Finally, the American gives his last request: "Would you please
kill me before the lecture on Japanese management?"

To spark efficiency, jobs should be divided by task, Smith
submitted. But he warned that division of labor leads to a
divergence in wage rates for different tasks. Smith's complex
hypotheses for wage rates preclude a neat and concise discus-

sion. But he did give economic theorists cogent grounds for explaining why one group gets paid more than another:

1. A job may entail disagreeable conditions, and thus few accept employment unless wages compensate them ("compensating differentials"). A window washer at the top of the Empire State Building receives more than a busboy who wipes down a Formica lunch counter. Of course, the window washer also gets a better view.

2. Some jobs require special training. Courtroom stenographers earn more than bailiffs.

3. An irregular or insecure job may pay more. Construction workers receive more per hour than other similarly trained laborers because weather conditions prevent them from working as many hours.

4. When high degrees of trust are required, wages rise. Because lay persons cannot assess the value of a diamond, many people feel more comfortable buying from a pricey but trustworthy store like Tiffany's than from a discounter.

5. When the probability of success is low, the payoff for success will be high. Lawyers in civil suits often accept cases on a contingency—that is, they get paid only if they win. But if they do win, they can earn even more than stenographers. Smith did not believe that all economic actors displayed perfect rationality. He suspected that people in risky professions overestimate their chances of success and therefore end up with lower incomes than they expect.

Division of Labor Among Towns and Countries

Smith never promised that division of labor alone brings wealth to a nation. Free trade among manufacturers, suppliers, towns, and cities is also necessary. What good are ten thousand pins if they cannot be traded because of restrictions or high transportation costs? The manufacturer might as well make twenty or perhaps none. Furthermore, division of labor can take place among towns, not just among workers in a factory. Particular towns can specialize, just as particular individuals can. Boise may produce wheat while Boston produces Bose headphones. The point is, the wealth of a nation grows if markets expand—that is, if more and more areas are hooked up to trade routes.

Consider the United States in 1750. Trade routes along the Eastern seaboard delivered goods relatively smoothly from Baltimore to Boston, yet settlements west of Pennsylvania had to fend for themselves. A self-sufficient settlement is analogous to a pin worker who must cut, bend, attach, and deliver by himself. In the United States, as transportation routes over rivers and land developed and distribution costs shrunk, more and more towns could be brought into a common market, boosting the wealth of the individual communities and of the nation as a whole. In fact, as the maritime industry built safer ships and developed better navigational skills, it drove down shipping costs over the Atlantic, which invigorated the colonies and Britain throughout the eighteenth century. Even the defeat of pirates contributed to the wealth of nations.

Emersonian self-reliance may be part of the American psyche, but the American pocketbook fattened in spite of it.

While pleading for free trade, Smith insisted that England would gain from trade if it could buy a good from another country for less than the cost of producing that good in England. The English might not like the French, but if a bottle of French white wine costs one pound and an English counterpart costs two pounds, England is foolish to produce wine. France has an "absolute advantage" in wine. Of course, if French wine costs twice as much as English wine, England is foolish to buy French wine. Smith's point is well taken, for why should England waste scarce resources that could be used to produce wool at a lower cost than France rather than grapes at a higher cost? According to Smith, nations should import only those products in which another country has an absolute advantage. (Keep Smith's argument in mind, for David Ricardo shows true brilliance when he reforms it and persuades almost all economists thereafter that trade can enrich a nation, even when no other country produces more cheaply.)

Using his overcoat as an example, Adam Smith cited all the varied and geographically divided laborers who together made it possible for him to stay warm: shepherds, wool sorters, wool combers, dyers, spinners, weavers, merchants, and sailors (presumably elements of his coat were imported). Most striking, none of these laborers had to know each other, know Smith, or know why Smith wanted a coat. All they needed to know was that the wage for shepherding or dyeing was high enough to make their labor worthwhile; that is, someone was willing to pay them for contributing to the final product. Hayek would take Smith's argument further in an important article, pointing to the dispersion of information as one of the biggest obstacles for society. No central planner could possibly gather all the information needed to decide whether society should produce a coat for Adam Smith; and even if he had all the information, it could change. But the market-price system tells individuals all they need to know. Hayek uses the example of tin in the following passage:

> Assume that somewhere in the world a new opportunity for the use of . . . tin, has arisen, or that one of the sources of supply of tin has been eliminated. It does not matter for our purposes—and it is very significant that it does not matter—which of these two causes has made tin more scarce. All that the users of tin need to know is that some of the tin they used to consume is now more profitably employed elsewhere, and that in consequence they must economize tin. There is no need for the great majority of them even to know where the more urgent need has arisen. . . . If only some of them know directly of the new demand, and switch resources

over to it, and if the people who are aware of the new gap thus created in turn fill it from still other sources, the effect will rapidly spread throughout the whole economic system and influence not only all the uses of tin, but also those of its substitutes and the substitutes of these substitutes, the supply of all the things made of tin, and their substitutes, and so on, and all this without the great majority of those instrumental in bringing about these substitutions knowing anything at all about the original cause of these changes.

A striking quotation from the philosopher Alfred North Whitehead emblazons that point: "It is a profoundly erroneous truism, repeated by all copy-books and by eminent people when they are making speeches, that we should cultivate the habit of thinking what we are doing. The precise opposite is the case. Civilization advances by extending the number of important operations which we can perform without thinking about them."[20] Through symbols and signals that we do not understand, we take advantage of the knowledge of others.

Hayek also applies his "ignorance" argument to attack the utopian hope of an economy based on complete altruism. An individual is the world's foremost expert on what she wants. Nobody else knows better; nobody else can better judge the effects of alternative choices on her achieving what she wants. Therefore, people should look after their own interests. If all sought to do "the public good," they would have to know as much about everyone else as themselves. Jill, a saintly woman, may love Jack, whom she has never met; but how does she know what he wants and how much he values what he wants? Suppose Jill and Jack are both altruists. Jill is selling her house. Since she loves Jack, she wants to sell the house to him for only $100,000. Since Jack loves Jill, he would not dare pay so little. He offers $200,000. She refuses and offers to accept $110,000. Insulted that she refuses his gift, Jack insists on $210,000. We do not know where this will end, which is precisely Hayek's point. No market signals emerge, and society loses the ability to allocate scarce resources, because nobody admits how much they value the house. As Adam Smith put it: "By pursuing his own interest he frequently promotes that of the society more effectively than when he really intends to promote it. I have never known much good done by those affected to trade for the public good."[21]

Hayek's logic was influenced by his teacher Ludwig von Mises, who argued against socialism in 1920 on the grounds that no government could perform all the calculations needed to organize an efficient economy. Von Mises was the leader of the Austrian school of economics, which took a laissez-faire view and was very skeptical of mathematical models. Because von Mises believed that economic truths were self-evident and opposed models based on real data, his views fell out of favor until fairly recently. Today, neo-Austrians try to expand on his work and that of his Viennese teachers, Carl Menger and Eugen von Böhm-Bawerk.

Milton Friedman follows in the Smith-Hayek tradition. If you pick up a copy of his book *Free to Choose*, you will see a picture of Friedman holding up a pencil as a symbol of the wonders of free trade. No single person, Friedman insisted, knows how to make a pencil.[22] To make a pencil, you must learn how to chop down a big tree in Oregon. But first you would need steel for the saw. So you would book a flight to an iron mine in Brazil and strap on a miner's helmet. Then make your way to Pittsburgh to figure out how to turn iron ore into steel. Do not forget the pencil's metal tip, graphite center, and rubber eraser. They require trips to Sri Lanka and Indonesia. After all that traveling and learning all the chemistry, engineering, and foreign languages necessary for the transactions, do you think you could you churn out a single pencil for the thirteen cents that Dixon Ticonderoga charges, whose pencils also come in a handy cardboard box with attractive graphic printing and attract faithful fans? (George Lucas wielded a Dixon Ticonderoga before he gave Luke Skywalker a lightsaber, and Willy Wonka writer Roald Dahl would sharpen half a dozen each morning before his first morning scribble.)[23] Remarkably, not the iron miner, the tree chopper, the rubber farmer, nor the graphic artist ever has to gather together in a conference room to conjure up the miracle of the pencil. No central planning bureaucrat needs to direct the operation. The price system and the invisible hand of the market coordinate all this. And in your lifetime, have you ever heard of a shortage of pencils? Or price gouging by pencil makers? Pencils are surely a trivial matter (unless you show up without one on the morning of your SAT test). But far more sophisticated examples, from an aspirin (one penny for each pill) to an airline jet engine ($11 million), come to us through the same mechanism. Over time, markets drive producers to deliver better products and better prices.

A Theme for the Common Man

Although Smith constantly praised free trade and the causes of merchants, he was not a hired gun of the bourgeoisie. *The Wealth of Nations* bristles with criticism of merchants. Nor is it a brief for the rich. Smith vigorously praised free trade and division of labor because he was convinced that they helped the common man even more than they helped the prince:

Without the assistance and cooperation of many thousands, the very meanest person in a civilized country could not be provided. . . . Compared, indeed, with the more extravagant luxury of the great, his accommodation must no doubt appear extremely simple and easy; and yet it may be true, perhaps, that the accommodation of a European prince does not always so much exceed that of an industrious and frugal peasant, as the accommodation of the latter exceeds that of many an African king, the absolute master of the lives and liberties of ten thousand naked savages.[24]

As do his followers, Smith fondly suggests that under a market system, even the poor and the politically impotent can prosper. In contrast, under a centrally guided system, political power determines economic position: only the friends of the king and lords can grow rich. Again, Milton Friedman expanded on Smith's point in his *Capitalism and Freedom*, arguing that the market system reduces effective racial or ethnic discrimination because consumers buy from whoever offers the best price, not from whoever offers the proper prayer or complexion; and on the other hand, he points out that under a socialist system, a member of a minority group must gain the political favor of a planner in order to advance.[25]

Friedman's beliefs remain controversial, and critics have offered many counterexamples, suggesting, for instance, that corporate executives promote minority workers only if they score highly on such "soft" variables as "leadership ability" and "personality." Furthermore, critics insist that economic power can translate into political power through campaign contributions, leaving the economically poor without a political voice. Friedman accepts the latter point but hurls it back at his critics by arguing for a smaller government that is barred from interfering in most economic events. The debates rage, and the literature expands.

Although Smith was confident that he had exposed the secrets to greater wealth, he was not driven to establish an infallible catechism. He readily admitted some faults in dividing labor, and again, he proved himself sensitive to more than costs and benefits. Recall that his first love was moral philosophy. A firm believer in the influence of physical conditions on the human mind, Smith feared that an assembly line could rob workers of their intelligence and spirit: "The man whose whole life is spent in performing a few simple operations, of which the effects too are perhaps, always the same . . . has no occasion to exert his understanding, or to exercise his invention in finding out expedients to removing difficulties. . . . He, naturally, therefore loses the habit of such exertion, and generally becomes as stupid and ignorant as it is possible for a human creature to become." In one of his paternalistic moments, Smith recommended public education as a remedy for public dullness, because educated workers are more likely to invent and to exercise their minds while performing physical tasks. Said Smith: "For a very small expense the publick can facilitate, can encourage, and can even impose upon almost the whole body of the people, the necessity of acquiring those most essential parts of education."[26]

At this point, let's summarize *The Wealth of Nations*. Adam Smith saw labor as the chief engine of economic growth, accelerating when (1) the labor supply increased, (2) labor subdivided, or (3) labor quality rose through new machines. As long as new ideas for profitable investment and invention continued to spring from imaginations and free exchange was permitted, economic growth would go forward. And most important, the general public could enjoy a higher standard of living. The Nobel Prize–winning economist Paul Samuelson, whose disagreements with Milton Friedman fill volumes, reexamined Adam Smith's growth theories using modern mathematical techniques, finding that if "inventions keep recurring . . . profit rates and real wage rates average out above their subsistence levels." Samuelson announced "the happy finding that Adam Smith comes through with flying colors from a modern postmortem."[27]

Policies and Practice

Adam Smith was no ivory-tower theorist. He wanted the world to follow his precepts, and he eagerly met with politicians and power brokers. He was thrilled when Prime Minister William Pitt took his advice or when opposition leader Charles James Fox quoted him and called the "truth" of his work "indisputable." He would have forgiven Fox for quoting famous passages without having read any of his books. In *The Wealth of Nations*, Smith speaks with prescience and sympathy toward the American colonies. He was disappointed that English leaders could not see that the colonies would win their fight for independence and become "one of the greatest and most formidable [empires] that ever was in the world."[28]

President Harry Truman once begged for a one-armed economist. Why? He was "damn tired" of economists who said that "on the one hand, we could . . . but on the other hand maybe." Adam Smith had two hands, but he confidently pointed his finger at the best policies for the polity to follow. He warned legislators that special interests would press hard against those measures that increase the wealth of nations. His warning should still resound in parliaments and congresses throughout the world. Smith's free-market approach to economics did not condemn him to the naive optimism of Voltaire's Dr. Pangloss, who lives "in the best of all possible worlds" despite all the evidence surrounding him. On the other hand, he was not, as speechwriter William Safire so alliteratively put it (through the lips of Spiro Agnew), a "nattering nabob of negativism." Instead he recognized obstacles and showed how to avoid them. Let us look at two policy concerns.

Domestic Trade Restrictions. Recall the competitive market system described earlier, in which entry into an industry forces prices and profits down to the cost of production plus a normal return on investment. Smith saw that sometimes merchants clearly took home exorbitant profits. Why didn't his model work? Smith described two different scenarios that explain excess profits.

In the first case, entrepreneurs cannot enter the outrageously profitable industry simply because of natural phenomena. For example, only the land near Jerez, Spain, can grow the proper grapes for sherry. Enterprising Englishmen cannot grow grapevines for sherry around Buckingham Palace, even if the royal family volunteers to crush the grapes with their own royal feet.

Thus, landowners in Jerez may enjoy high profits. Of course, entrepreneurs could try to persuade people to drink port instead, which would erase the exorbitant profits.

What if the royal family could manage to grow grapes for sherry in their English garden at Buckingham Palace? Should they be able to call the brew "sherry"? The European Union insists on protecting many agricultural items from geographical copycats. For example, champagne can be produced only in Champagne, France. No doubt, Italian winemakers can figure out how to age grapes for a champagne product, but they would be arrested if they slapped the word "champagne" on the label. Instead they call their fruitier, bubbly wine Prosecco, from grapes grown north of Venice. But do not feel sorry for the Italians. Only they can legally produce Parma ham, while only the French can call a blue cheese Roquefort. A consortium of Parmigiano-Reggiano cheese makers in Italy specifies exactly how many hours cows may be milked and what portion of milk may be devoted to cheese-making.[29] And as you would guess, only the Swiss can make authentic Swiss cheese, despite the availability of hole-punch machines all over the continent.

By limiting competition, these "geographical indicators" and trademarks keep profits higher for traditional producers and prices higher for consumers.[30] A salesman for Kraft's cheap, canned, parmesan-cheese sprinkle would not receive a warm welcome at a pizzeria in Parma. Champagne producers in France know that Prosecco and California sparkling wines can be made more cheaply and can perform rather well in blind taste tests against their bottles. The European bureaucratic insistence on agricultural protection could be called a "reign of terroir"—"terroir" meaning the "character of the terrain." It is caught up in a heartfelt, nostalgic notion that produce is tied to the land and to the cultural traditions of a place. Kalamata olives taste like Kalamata olives because the soil, the rains, and the sweat of the Greek worker make it so. One does not have to look hard to spy the word "culture" in "agriculture."

Europe is not the only place that imposes geographical indicators. Try brewing Kentucky bourbon in New Jersey and you may be chased down by a Paducah sheriff and his shotgun. In general, though, the United States has a more lenient view of geographical trademarks and has tried to negotiate through the World Trade Organization for weaker standards. It is a tough negotiation. When modern European politicians try to water down the rules and regulations, they face a backlash of terror. In 2019, French farmers suspected that French president Emmanuel Macron was loosening restrictions that keep out South American beef. They launched battalions of tractors rumbling through Bordeaux to protest. Macron was lucky. In the 1990s, the French agriculture minister was chased through the streets of Paris by farmers wielding pitchforks. Please note that this pitchfork chase took place in the 1990s, not the 1790s.

Nostalgia plays a role in this passion. In Proust's *Remembrance of Things Past* (1913), the narrator Marcel drowns in a flood of feelings as he dunks his baked madeleine in his tea. He tries to recall the memories of youth: "After the people are dead, after the things are broken and scattered, taste and smell alone . . . remain poised a long time, like souls, remembering, waiting, hoping amid the ruins of all the rest." In a modern economy, as commerce and science allow us to enjoy more food, live longer, and climb to a higher standard of living, we also may feel as if we are losing something. Marcel remembers a fresh-baked madeleine. Today I am more likely to eat a madeleine delivered by truck to a Starbucks or sold in a wrapper by Nabisco. Perhaps we miss the taste of an earlier day—or the artisans who conjured up those tastes. Despite the higher standard of living, we might occasionally feel the nostalgic twinge. I call this feeling "melancholia madeleine"; for amid the hustle of modern times and the beeping of devices, we all sometimes feel like Marcel.

But is it better to call off modernity and to swear off international trade? The last time Europe tried "buying local," it was called the Middle Ages. But even in medieval times, residents invited traveling merchants to set up shops in town squares. Modern consumers have the luxury of year-round, 24-7 access to goods grown, gathered, stitched, or forged from every continent but Antarctica, unless you are Mr. Popper looking for a penguin. In the 1940s, a Cole Porter lyric recalled an ex-lover who was not worth the ransom on "asparagus out of season." Isn't asparagus now available year-round, along with kiwi, sushi, and farm-raised branzino?

The second case Smith pointed to is more pernicious. Abnormal profits may persist when small groups of merchants join in pacts to keep prices high. "People of the same trade seldom meet together, even for merriment and diversion, but the conversation ends in a conspiracy against the public, or in some diversion to raise prices," he wrote.[31] According to Smith, devilish pacts among merchants are usually not strong enough by themselves. Therefore, the traders entice government to do the work of the devils. Conspiracies will usually not prevent market entry unless the government supports the cartel. Smith fired salvos at many contradictory restrictions that limited trade and the division of labor for the benefit of identifiable groups. Apprenticeship laws and guilds especially choked competition. Smith described one fatuous result: a coach maker could not legally make wheels for his coaches, but a wheel maker could make coaches to place on top of the four wheels he made! If wheel makers could prohibit competition through law, they could charge high prices. Besides the Statute of Apprenticeship, Smith also disparaged the English Poor Laws. To get relief, citizens had to fulfill residency requirements, which meant that they could not fluidly move from industry to industry or town to town as demand changed for different types of laborers. Smith viciously lashed out at monopolies granted by the government, which, by "keeping the market constantly understocked, by never fully supplying the effectual demand, sell their commodities much above the natural price, and raise their . . . wages or profits."[32]

And how has Smith's fear of conspiracy been addressed on this side of the Atlantic? The United States has been more concerned with monopolies and oligopolies (a small group of firms that together dominate an industry) than with apprenticeship rules, which were never as common in America as they were in Europe and Asia. Every high schooler learns about robber barons, those nineteenth-century industrialists like Vanderbilt, Carnegie, and Rockefeller who stomped on competitors and ruled over trains, steel, and oil. In 1898, William McKinley launched the trust-busting era to bring down the titans of the time, a program later enforced by Theodore Roosevelt. But here is what many schoolbooks leave out: during the robber-baron era (often defined as 1865 to 1900), consumer prices in the United States were flat to falling, while per capita GDP steadily rose. It is hard to understand why those barons would have used their sweeping power to increase output and cut prices. Economic theory teaches us that monopolists do the opposite. The answer: their market power was not permanent and they were constantly fighting off invaders, which required them to keep prices down. Nonetheless, American economists and politicians feared that large corporations could protect themselves from competition and thereby rake in high profits. Thus, over the years, the government dragged into court thousands of corporations, which kicked and screamed through their lawyers, and sued them for price-fixing and restraining competition under the Sherman Antitrust Act and the Clayton Act. Further, the Justice Department frequently tried to block corporate mergers. Trust-busting continued throughout the twentieth century. The Nixon administration launched a thirteen-year breakup fight against IBM (alleging that Big Blue was monopolizing the computer business) before slinking away in 1982. IBM doesn't even make personal computers anymore. In 2005, the Federal Trade Commission battled a merger between Blockbuster and the Hollywood Entertainment video company, apparently worried that these hapless firms were locking up the VHS and DVD markets. (Was the FTC protecting consumers against those pesky VHS players that kept blinking "12:00"?) Throughout the 1970s, some economists and law professors, frequently the former students of University of Chicago dons Milton Friedman, George Stigler, and Richard Posner, contended that while price-fixing was evil, "bigness" through mergers may not be, for bigness does not necessarily prevent entry and may, in fact, foster efficiency.

Amazon and Walmart are the two biggest retail companies in the world. Walmart was started by Sam Walton, a crafty, penny-pinching guy from Arkansas who named his first store Walmart because he didn't want to spend money to buy the extra letters to spell out Sam Walton's 5-10.[33] Jeff Bezos launched Amazon by selling books in his garage and warned early investors that there was a 70 percent chance he would go bankrupt. Instead, Bezos became the richest man in the world. From modest beginnings, these two retailers have grown into far-flung enterprises that have rewritten the rules of retail and driven storied competitors like Toys "R" Us, Barneys, and Kmart into bankruptcy court. Nonetheless, their principal impact on consumers has been to drive prices lower.

Many contemporary scholars maintain that old-fashioned trustbusters look at the market too narrowly. Modern competition includes foreign corporations, not just domestic ones. As evidence, they can point to the failures of General Motors in the 1980s versus the victory of Hyundai, a Korean car manufacturer that within months of landing on America's shores drove right through Detroit and left skid marks on GM's balance sheets. In the television market, Sony crushed Zenith and RCA, before Samsung and Sharp stole market share from Sony. Motorola dominated early cellphones in the 1990s but seldom shows up now except in a game of trivia.

In the 1990s, the hottest antitrust case was launched by the Justice Department against Microsoft. The government's antitrust regulators argued that Microsoft's monopoly on computer operating systems permitted it to block competitors

from getting their products in front of consumers. Many journalists analogize Microsoft founder Bill Gates to John D. Rockefeller, suggesting that by monopolizing the computer system,
Gates can act as Standard Oil did by cornering the market in
oil. Microsoft opponents cheered when one of the leading
Chicago School thinkers, former judge and Yale professor
Robert Bork, issued a brief attacking the monopolist. After
dramatic video footage of Bill Gates, then the world's wealthi-
est man, fidgeting on the witness stand, Microsoft settled the
case with the Department of Justice. Yet, to the regret of Microsoft's opponents, the settlement did not force the company
to rip out the guts of its software code, or prevent it from tying
new programs to its Windows program. In fact, the settlement
did little more than obligate Microsoft to "share" its interfaces
with others. Quite often, while lawyers argue in court, new
leaps in technology make courtroom solutions both obsolete
and wasteful. At the very moment Gates was held hostage in
Seattle, Steve Jobs was in Cupertino unveiling the iMac and
plotting to rip open markets with the iPhone and iPod.

In a remarkable commencement address at Stanford, Steve
Jobs recalled dropping out of college on his way to challeng-
ing IBM: "I didn't have a dorm room, so I slept on the floor in
friends' rooms. I returned Coke bottles for the five-cent deposits to buy food with, and I would walk the seven miles
across town every Sunday night to get one good meal a week at
the Hare Krishna temple. I loved it. And much of what I stumbled into by following my curiosity and intuition turned out to
be priceless later on."[34] For more than thirty years, the Justice
Department was attacking IBM. But it took a dropout like
Steve Jobs, not starchy antitrust lawyers, to create more in-
tense competition.

The world economy is as ferociously competitive as ever.
Many barriers to entry in the modern economy are falling, not
rising. Invaders are poised nearly everywhere, threatening to
steal market share. Procter & Gamble owned a 70 percent
share of the men's razor market until some daring dude

launched the Dollar Shave Club with an outrageous YouTube ad called "Our Blades Are [Expletive] Great," which went viral in 2012 and attracted millions of subscribers. Amazon is scaring firms in various sectors, not with higher prices but with lower prices and quicker delivery—even delivery by drone.

The gig economy, too, is delivering bargains. Airbnb has effectively added 25 percent to the number of available rooms in U.S. cities. Uber is worth more than Hertz and Avis. In the heyday of antitrust enforcement in the 1960s and 1970s, start-up firms needed to raise tens of millions of dollars to build factories and hire employees. Nowadays, firms with compelling intellectual property and strong leadership can take on market leaders with just a website, a few swivel chairs, and a single-serve coffeemaker.

Even areas that seemed entirely off-limits to the private sector attract competition. The hit movie *Hidden Figures* tells the inspiring story of black women who helped NASA do the math to get John Glenn into orbit. But even the risky, previously untouchable space sector has grown supercompetitive, with Bezos's Blue Origin, Richard Branson's Virgin Galactic, Elon Musk's SpaceX, Boeing, and Arianespace vying for business.

Antitrust enforcement should focus on cases where mergers would damage consumers through persistently higher prices. For example, local hospital mergers tend to raise prices, and limping patients are not usually in a physical or psychological position to shop around.

Despite the low inflation environment of the past decade, the Trump administration has been more aggressive than its predecessors on trust-busting. The Trump Justice Department, for example, tried unsuccessfully to block a merger between AT&T and Time Warner, arguing that a merger could drive up the cost of consumers watching movies and television programs at home. The Federal Trade Commission sued Qualcomm for imposing allegedly onerous contract terms on Apple. This new concern about corporate powerhouses has received support in past years from some academic economists who have pointed to a rising concentration of market share in various industries. They have warned that rising prices are on the way.[35]

Nonetheless, it is extremely difficult to forecast the impact of corporate deals when technology moves so quickly. AT&T and Time Warner might someday display awesome powers, but the combined firm must grapple with the fact that 30 percent of millennials have "cut the cord" with their cable provider. Netflix, Disney, Hulu, YouTube, Amazon, and half a dozen others offer streaming services. Meanwhile, Snapchat, a nimble new content company, attracts 160 million viewers who watch more than 10 billion videos daily. Who is the underdog?

The greatest irony is already apparent, though. For a good part of the twentieth century, many eminent economists such as Joan Robinson, Edward Chamberlin, and John Kenneth Galbraith pronounced that Adam Smith's simple world of perfect competition grew less relevant as the years went by and corporations swelled. Yet many modern economists insist that because of international competition Adam Smith's vision grows more radiant and relevant every day![36]

International Trade Restrictions. "What is prudence in the conduct of every private family, can scarce be folly in that of a great kingdom," Smith wrote.[37] Having proved the theory of absolute advantage, he mercilessly blasted merchants who lobbied for, and governments that surrendered to, demands for protection from foreign producers. Through tariffs or quotas, the government forces consumers to subsidize merchants, because consumers pay higher prices than necessary. Without foreign competition, domestic merchants raise their prices and profits. The forces that fight free trade look "like an overgrown standing army . . . formidable to the government, and upon many occasions intimidate the legislature." Smith lamented that officials who opposed free trade were rewarded with flattering publicity, while those who battled for the public interest received insults and infamous abuse.[38]

In a quick debate, anti–free traders usually come up with

pithier lines. Senator Bernie Sanders, an avowed socialist, calls free trade "a race to the bottom." President Donald Trump called free trade agreements a "trade war on the American worker."[39] Some years ago I debated a boisterous union leader who literally took off his shoe and began slapping the lectern with it, eliciting cheers from a crowd gathered at a massive, dingy Chicago hotel. No doubt, the shoe was made abroad, which reinforced his point. Advocates for free trade usually need at least two sentences to make their point, with or without shoes.

The data does not prove that trade makes people more jolly, but it does make a compelling case that trade pushes up living standards. Perhaps the best way to look at the benefits is to ask, how many hours does an average person have to labor in order to get enough food to live and to buy the things they desire? In 1870, children typically began work at age 13. What was the retirement age? Death. People labored in the fields or factories roughly 3,000 hours a year and somehow managed to squeeze in 1,800 hours of household chores. They spent 61 percent of their waking hours working. By 1950, children did not work until age 17.6, and adults spent only 45 percent of the day on the job. Today, we start working at age 20, look forward to a 16-year retirement, and spend only 28 percent of our waking hours on the job.[40] Child labor laws emerged in the early 1900s. Nowadays parents are more likely to worry that their children have not been exposed to even a part-time job and, therefore, lack a sturdy work ethic.

Before the Internet, American shoppers who did not want to get in their cars would flip through the Sears and J. C. Penney catalogs before placing their orders. Thankfully those old catalogs are still in libraries and allow economists to compare prices over time. In 1959, for example, an average worker would labor for about two weeks to afford a refrigerator. Today, it takes a few days' labor. A vacuum cleaner would require more than a week of labor; today it takes less than one day's labor.[41] And while the United States has a wide disparity of incomes, poor households have surely benefited, too. In 1971 only about 20 percent of American homes owned a dishwasher and about 40 percent watched television in color. By 2005 about 40 percent of *poor* families no longer had to wash dishes by hand, 78 percent had air conditioning, and nearly *all* owned at least one color television. Other countries enjoyed similar wonders. As recently as the mid-1960s, one-third of British families did not own a refrigerator, which might explain the lingering tolerance for tepid beer.[42]

Countries that shun trade tend to stagnate or sink. After the Soviet Union imploded in 1991, I took a few days off from my job at the White House to visit Leningrad, which had just changed its name back to Saint Petersburg, Russia. Wandering through the flaking hallways of the Hermitage, I realized that communism's problem was not failing to keep up with the rising standards of 1980s America but failing to keep up with the standards of 1917 Russia. Cuba's GDP per capita was near the top of Latin America's rankings before Fidel Castro's revolution in 1959. Then as Cuba's leaders confiscated private property and banned entrepreneurs from earning profits, Cuba slid to the bottom. Castro's acolytes might blame the plunge on a U.S. trade embargo, but that makes my point: countries cut off from trade (voluntarily or not) stagnate. On average, Latin American living standards have doubled since 1959. Cuba's per capita GDP has hardly budged.[43] And when you see photos of skinny peasants pushing their vintage 1956 Chevy Bel Airs through dusty roads, you see who has to do the budging. Someday we might expect a more prosperous Cuba, provided Raúl Castro's successors permit a more active entrepreneurial class.

In the 1800s, Japan's fearsome Tokugawa shogun rulers felt shock, awe, and panic when English and Portuguese traders steamed into their harbors under a cloud of coal-fired power. The leaders had cordoned off Japan for hundreds of years but suddenly realized that their country was economically and militarily retarded.

The World Bank compared pairs of countries that chose starkly divergent paths in the 1980s and 1990s. The first of the pair opted to globalize, while the other stuck to its own bubble: Vietnam versus Burma; Bangladesh versus Pakistan; and Costa Rica versus Honduras. Those countries that opened up grew at an average pace of 3.5 percent in the 1980s and 5 percent in the 1990s. The isolated economies grew by merely 0.8 percent in the 1980s and 1.4 percent in the 1990s.[44] Over time, when a country folds itself into a self-contained bubble, the economy grows stale and fetid, like a poorly aerated terrarium. Or a dank prison, which pretty much describes North Korea. After fighting in the Korean War subsided in 1953, the North was slightly wealthier than the South. In the 1950s and 1960s, the USSR, China, Poland, and even Albania sent massive aid to rebuild North Korea, on top of the Japanese-built factories north of the thirty-eighth parallel. Despite joint communist assistance, the South today is about twenty times wealthier, and South Koreans live ten years longer and stand several inches taller. The Koreans call it "the Miracle on the Han River." North Korea does excel in a few categories: for example, executions without trial and infant mortality rate (six times higher). South Korea produces world-class Samsung flat-screen televisions, super-smart LG refrigerators, smooth-riding Hyundai and Kia cars, and charismatic K-pop singers who bring raving audiences to their feet around the world. What does the North produce? Death threats against Hollywood actors who star in dopey movies (like *The Interview*). And presumably the jumpsuits once worn by Kim Jong-il.

The Free Market Is Not a Pain-Free Market

The free market is not a pain-free market. And we should admit that some people lose when a country opens its markets. It is hard to find a shoe that is made in America. In 2015 President Obama visited Nike's headquarters in Oregon to cheer a new global trade agreement that he said would help Americans. If Obama looked down at his wristwatch in order to time his speech, he probably would not have seen "Made in USA." The United States wristwatch industry is shrunken, having fallen first to the Swiss, then to the Japanese, then to the Chinese, and then to the Swiss again. Perhaps the Detroit-based Shinola company, named for a once-famous shoe polish, or Apple's iWatch will bring it back (though most components come from Asia).

If we accept Smith's basic theory, does he allow any exceptions to free trade? Yes, but not many. He pondered and rejected the "infant industry" argument, which asks for "temporary" tariffs just for the early years of development. Alexander Hamilton embraced the infant argument in the United States a few years later, and Japan would nurse an infant semiconductor industry two hundred years after that. Smith doubted that government could ever gather the political will to remove the subsidies once the industry matured. The industry would learn to scream and cry like a baby despite its adult appetite. Or, in a new version of the argument, the industry will wheeze and drool as a senile corporate citizen demanding help against competition. The U.S. steel industry has clamored for protection on both grounds, first as a dotard and lately as a born-again infant. But protection for steel can be particularly pernicious, because it drives up the prices of everything from dishwashers to dump trucks and impairs American exports of machinery.

In 2018, President Trump pulled the gates down in front of foreign steel makers, slapping tariffs of 25 percent on their sales to the United States. Auto and appliance makers quickly felt as if they were stuffed into a vise, as U.S. steel prices jumped up by about 10 percent. While Trump trumpeted that the tariffs spurred U.S. Steel to spend $1 billion upgrading a plant and led the industry to hire 12,700 more workers, think tank economists calculated that the higher cost of items such as autos, motorcycles, and washing machines was so burdensome to consumers that each new steel job cost the economy about $900,000.[45]

Smith had little sympathy for tariffs as reprisals against another country's protectionism, for a retaliatory tariff only erased more potential wealth from the world. Of course, a successful reprisal that persuades the original transgressor to roll back is tautologically good. But how does one know a priori whether or not the retaliatory tariff will incite a third tariff? President Obama slapped 35 percent tariffs on low-end Chinese automobile tires and was surprised to find that the Chinese retaliated by jacking up tariffs on American chickens by 50 to 100 percent. As a result of a rubber dispute, poultry farmers in Maryland and Arkansas lost $1 billion in sales.[46] The Great Depression of the 1930s surely deepened because nations erected high tariffs partly in retaliation for others. Smith snidely stated: "To judge whether such retaliations are likely to produce such an effect, does not, perhaps, belong so much to the science of a legislator . . . as to the skill of that insidious and crafty animal, vulgarly called a statesman or politician."[47]

Although the United States clearly protects certain industries, politicians and economists often cite Japan as a flagrant violator of free trade. Two reprisal techniques are worth mentioning. Since Japan allegedly protects through its inscrutable regulations, Harvard economist Henry Rosovsky drolly suggested that Japanese imports enter the United States by way of customs agents in Boise, Idaho. Rosovsky would beef up the staff and extend their hours to nine to five, open only on Mondays, in months whose names end in "r." In another case, John Connally, former governor of Texas, contended while campaigning for the Republican presidential nomination in 1980 that stronger measures were needed. He suggested completely blocking Japanese imports into the United States and telling them to "listen to their Sonys and sit in their Toyotas on the docks of Yokohama." Connally, who spent millions on his campaign, received about the same number of votes in the United States as he would have in Yokohama.

Only occasionally Adam Smith's free trade logic bowed to protectionist requests. For example, he allowed tariffs to counterbalance an internal tax on a domestic product. He also submitted to tariff pleas for national defense reasons by acknowledging that Britain's safety demanded a healthy ship-building industry. He knew the story of Venice's demise in the 1600s. Venice, once known as the Serenissima Repubblica di Venezia, gained great wealth as the hinge between Asia and Europe, engaged in trading spices, glass, books, and banking services (you can still admire the glass on the island of Murano). But the doges of Venice decided to outsource their military to French and Dutch mercenaries. The problem with mercenaries is obvious: if your enemy is willing to pay more, the sailors will turn their cannons on you. When the Ottomans dangled gold in front of the mercenary Venetian navy, the navy merely switched flags, Venice lost overseas possessions, and in 1615 mercenaries threatened to blow up the doge's palace and murder its senators. In *Othello*, Shakespeare admires the brave Moor because he keeps his word in Venice, despite his tragic flaws and mercenary standing. Although Smith carved out such exceptions to free trade, he maintained that protection for domestic industries stunted "the growth of opulence."

In Smith's time, national defense was about cannonballs and muskets. In today's technological world, we must ask, what is national security, anyway? When the coronavirus struck the United States in 2020, many American politicians and ordinary citizens were shocked to learn that a large proportion of U.S. antibiotics came from China, along with ventilators. If the deadly virus had hit China and the United States at the exact same time (rather than sequentially), would China have embargoed those items for its own population, leaving sickly patients in the United States to suffocate? In the face of the choking global pandemic, even free traders had to consider that such vital goods are not like children's toys.

If government should not protect its industries, regulate labor, or distribute favors to merchants, what should it do? When would Smith release the manacles on the visible hand of government? Smith clearly defined the proper role for government: first, providing for national defense; second, administering justice through a court system; third, maintaining public institutions and resources such as roads, canals, bridges, educational systems, and the dignity of the sovereign.

The Second Coming

The wearer of the Adam Smith necktie in 1980 generally believed in a limited national government, fewer social welfare programs, less government price regulation, and less federal intervention in and aid for local government affairs; the free market would provide most of what citizens require in life. When Ronald Reagan took office in 1981, his chief economic adviser reputedly joked, "Don't just stand there. Undo something!" Though a trend toward deregulation began under the Carter administration with the Airline Deregulation Act of 1978, Reagan accelerated the pace, leaving natural gas, oil, and airline prices to the direction of the invisible hand, while abandoning Carter's wage and price guidelines.

Despite Reagan's initial victories, the deregulatory effort faltered when mighty maritime, trucking, and construction interests began battling the administration. After the first Reagan term, deregulation forces found more to cheer about in Moscow than in Washington. The cable television industry, for example, found Congress regulating it, then deregulating it again, depending on how angry voters were with their cable rates. The banking industry, though, successfully fought for new freedoms to link up with securities firms, while the federal government stayed mostly on the sidelines as the private sector launched the revolutionary Internet. By throwing open so many sectors to cutthroat competition, the government forced U.S. firms to get lean and tough—characteristics that served them well in the global market. During the 1990s, European and Japanese firms were not prepared to face such awesome competitors, and so U.S. companies gained world market share.

Opponents of deregulation frequently point out that countries like Austria and Norway are much more regulated than the United States is, yet families there earn about the same amount of money and seem just as happy. Therefore, they argue, government regulations must not hinder economic growth. The "Buchholz critique" addresses this point by arguing that a relatively unregulated economy like that of the United States produces more marketable innovations than other countries. As a result, even highly regulated nations benefit from the supercompetitive U.S. market. For example, the Internet was largely developed here, but now consumers throughout the world get to log on. Students as far away as Tibet use the advanced microprocessors developed by Intel in Santa Clara, California. If U.S. firms were as tightly bound as Tibetan firms, there would probably not be an Internet or a superfast microprocessor. Therefore, to simply compare economic levels among countries ignores the spillover effects, in which ideas and technologies slosh across borders, usually emanating from the freest economies.

Andy Warhol said that in the future everyone would be famous for fifteen minutes. Adam Smith has been famous for more than two centuries. How do we remember him? In the most revolutionary age of Western civilization, when the tumult of social rebellion, intellectual upheaval, and explosive economic growth baffled lesser men, Adam Smith gave the world order. He did not invent the market, nor did he invent economics. But he taught the world about the market and economics. For nearly seventy-five years, *The Wealth of Nations* supplied most of what economists knew.

Two hundred years after *The Wealth of Nations*, Smith's ideas were resurrected and exalted. But what happened to Smith, the man who searched for a father and instead found a profession? He lived happily ever after. Truly. Ironically. Truly, because he socialized with the most famous men of his day, saw his book translated into almost every European language, earned honors throughout Britain and the Continent, and watched government officials assiduously take notes whenever he spoke. Ironically, because he spent the thirteen years before his death in 1790 working for the government as His Majesty's commissioner of customs, a post similar to his father's. Upon taking the position, Smith did the logical thing for a bachelor and looked into his closet for something appropriate to wear. He found, to his "great astonishment," that he "had scarce a stock, a cravat, a pair of ruffles, or a pocket handkerchief" that was not considered contraband, furtively smuggled in from abroad.[48] Faced with this comic situation, he took two actions: First, he burned the clothing. Second, he began a campaign to persuade the prime minister and his aides to snip the "unjust and oppressive restraints" on Irish and American imports.

Despite the cognitive dissonance of the job, Smith took pride in his post and was made an honorary captain of the city guard, marching through the streets with his cane propped over his shoulder like a soldier carrying his musket. He died on July 17, 1790, after musing to his friends that he must leave the room but would see them in "some other place." That place is found wherever and whenever men and women show up at a market—whether a corner stand, an online auction, or a gleaming superstore. By proudly marching on behalf of trade, Adam Smith helped increase the wealth of nations.

CHAPTER III

Malthus: Prophet of Doom and Population Boom

Once upon a time, back in 1908, the Chicago Cubs faced the New York Giants in a decisive game for the National League pennant. During a dramatic play in the bottom of the ninth inning, the Giants' substitute first baseman, a young, competent player, inadvertently failed to touch second base, which was duly protested and the game ordered replayed. The Cubs went on to win the ensuing one-game playoff for the pennant.

The young man's name was Fred Merkle, but from that moment on until he died, he was haunted by a new name, "Bonehead" Merkle. Despite the daring and noble efforts that followed, he never shed his epithet.

Almost everybody today seems to know of Sigmund Freud, Freudian slips, and sexual symbols. Any educated person who denies knowing about Freud must be repressing it.

Thomas Robert Malthus never played baseball and never saw a psychoanalyst. Yet his name became as famous as Freud's and his infamy as undeserved as Bonehead Merkle's. Byron, who probably needed a psychoanalyst more than Malthus did, composed poetry about him, and children sang rhymes mocking him. Decades after his death, Marx viciously attacked him. A century after his death, Keynes glorified Malthus and predicted that on the bicentenary of his death, "We shall commemorate him with undiminished regard." But undiminished compared with what?

What dastardly crime did Malthus perpetrate that led even

Romantic poets like Coleridge to lament: "Behold this mighty nation, its rulers and its wise men listening . . . to Malthus! It is mournful, mournful"?

In 1798 Malthus robbed romantic dreams from people who looked to the nineteenth century with utopian faith. He was tried in newspapers and found guilty of predicting that over-population would produce a future not of rapture but of so-cial ruptures and decay. On the eve of a new century, Malthus was the ultimate party pooper. Or at least his theory was.

Born February 13, 1766, in Surrey, England, at the Rookery, the country seat of his eccentric father, Daniel, Malthus at the age of only three weeks met his two "fairy godfathers," David Hume and Jean-Jacques Rousseau, whom Daniel Malthus wor-shipped. Robert, as the boy was called, flashed signs of high intelligence at an early age and soon received private tutoring. He grew to be tall and striking, and in 1784 entered Jesus Col-lege, Cambridge, where, while studying for the clergy, he also read mathematics and philosophy. Like Adam Smith, Malthus was impressed by Newton and read carefully his *Philosophiae Naturalis Principia Mathematica*. Despite his weighty intellec-tual interests and aspirations for holy orders, Malthus was a popular, witty Cambridge man, ready to put on a mocking comic expression or voice. Malthus wore his fair hair in curly ringlets down to his neck, while most others wore pigtails. He might have been a trendsetter, for ten years later, almost all undergraduates wore their hair in ringlets. More shocking, while most students powdered their hair white, Malthus some-times used pink. A punker before his time, perhaps. Unfortu-nately, we do not have any paintings that display Malthus's eye-catching looks, because Malthus refused to sit for a por-trait. Despite his effervescent manner, he was embarrassed by a hereditary harelip and cleft palate. Perhaps he colored his hair to distract from his face. Not until a year before his death did Malthus finally agree to have his image memorialized, but the painter skillfully massaged the oils so that Malthus looks serious, conventional, and proud. Interestingly, he holds a book in his hands, and his index finger cleaves his book precisely in half.

Before graduating in 1788, the master of Jesus College warned Malthus that a speech defect resulting from the cleft palate would hurt his chances of rising within the Church. This despite Malthus's winning prizes for Greek, Latin, and English orations at Cambridge! Malthus discarded the advice, took holy orders anyway, and briefly practiced at a church in Okewood, returning to Jesus College as a fellow in 1793. Although he never again committed himself full-time to the clergy, economists still refer to him as Parson Malthus, perhaps because the image of Puritanical pessimism fits his population theory better than that of a happy, humorous layman. Recall H. L. Mencken's definition of a Puritan: one who has a haunting fear that someone, somewhere, at some time, may be having fun. Psychologically, perhaps we feel more comfortable dismissing Malthus and his warnings if we portray him as a Puritan.

Bursting Utopian Bubbles

The tides of revolution rolled high and rough when Malthus returned to Jesus College. In 1793, revolutionaries guillotined Louis XVI, and the French Republic declared war on England. Despite the harrowing times, some writers and preachers pronounced that high tides would eventually bring the calmest, most idyllic time man had known since Eden. Rousseau had earlier written utopian prose, suggesting that man was born happy and free yet corrupted by society. Voltaire quipped that Rousseau's hypernaturalism aroused a yearning to walk on all fours while reading his work. In England, Wordsworth captured the rapture, writing, "Bliss was it in that dawn to be alive / But to be young was very heaven!"[1] But Malthus resisted the vision of utopia. In particular, he rebelled against

William Godwin, a minister, a pamphleteer, and the author in 1793 of *An Enquiry Concerning the Principles of Political Justice, and Its Influence on General Virtue and Happiness*. Godwin quite simply believed that "Man is perfectible, or in other words susceptible of perpetual improvement." (His daughter, Mary Shelley, author of *Frankenstein*, might have disagreed!) And because "truth is omnipotent," man could transform himself into a creature better suited for happiness and harmony with his neighbor: "Every man will seek, with affable ardour, the good for all."[2] Following Rousseau's claim that the history of civil society was the history of human sickness, Godwin envisaged the abolition of government, courts, crime, war, melancholy, and anguish as man achieved perfection. Though he married one of history's founding feminist philosophers, Mary Wollstonecraft, author of *A Vindication of the Rights of Women* (1792), Godwin thought that marriage itself was evil. Even death and sleep could be put to rest, in Godwin's vision: "Generation will not succeed generation. . . . Before death can be banished, we must banish sleep, death's image. Sleep is one of the most conspicuous infirmities of the human frame. It is . . . an irregular and distempered state of the faculty."[3] Similar visions of sugarplums danced in the head of Marquis de Condorcet, a French philosopher and mathematician, whose *Sketch for a Historical View of the Progress of the Human Mind* was published in 1794. Condorcet showed striking optimism for a fugitive from Robespierre soon to be caught and put to sleep permanently.

Most annoying to Malthus, Godwin and the Archdeacon William Paley argued that an increasing population was a good sign, for it meant more total happiness. Paley proclaimed that a decay of population was the greatest evil a state could suffer. As the eighteenth century ended, some scholars equipped with bits of discredited data estimated that population had grown very slowly during the past one hundred years, while others even contended that the population had plummeted. Since a strong labor force supported economic growth, Prime Minister William Pitt introduced a bill that increased poor relief payments for couples with children, a precursor of modern-day programs like Aid to Families with Dependent Children (launched in 1935 during the Great Depression) and its successor, Temporary Assistance for Needy Families.

As expected, Daniel Malthus nodded in blissful agreement with the coalition of Godwin, Paley, and the posthumous Rousseau. But while father nodded, son shook his head. They talked and walked in the woods; each tried to persuade the other of the conclusion that reason required. Finally, Robert, frustrated with his misty-eyed, quixotic foe, dashed off in a fury *An Essay on the Principle of Population as It Affects the Future Improvement of Society, with Remarks on the Speculations of M. Godwin, M. Condorcet, and Other Writers*. Father, now misty-eyed at his son's intellectual prowess, arranged for the essay's anonymous publication.

The Frightening Theory

Few essays have ever been more shocking. Imagine the earth shrinking at a furious pace. Every twenty-five years it splits in half, one half remaining in orbit, the other spinning toward the sun, igniting, and exploding. People must scramble and trample toward the half that survives, carrying with them children, grandparents, and whatever sacred possessions they can carry. Even worse, they do not know which half of the earth will survive. Malthus's prophecy is slightly different, yet only a bit less frightening. Instead of the globe cleaving and bursting, Malthus describes the population swelling and spreading at an explosive pace, while food supplies only inch along. Malthus assumed that farmers were currently planting, plowing, and harvesting from the most fertile fields. More population would force them to tame rockier, less fecund soils, yielding "diminishing returns." Though Malthus lived long after the fourteenth-century black death, which wiped out one-third of

Europe's workers, lingering memories taught him that wages *rose* after the plague. With fewer workers, landowners needed to pay the survivors more. Better-paid peasants started demanding more protein, leading to a shift from growing crops to raising cattle and sheep for meat and also for the leather and wool trade. Though Henry VIII's chancellor, Sir Thomas More, decried this trend and described "meek and tame" sheep devouring "men . . . whole fields, houses, and cities," the shift to animal husbandry opened up new opportunities for women, allowing them to delay marriage and put off their own husbands. In a perverse way, the plague appeared to raise the standard of living! A man like Malthus, who could see the bright side of the black plague, could see the black side of bright things, too.[4] Using contemporary data from the United States supplied by Benjamin Franklin, Malthus asserted that population tends to double every twenty-five years. Of course, it could double even faster. Actually, Malthus chose relatively conservative examples. Franklin reported that some villages double in only fifteen years! Though armed with no reliable data from Franklin on the food supply, Malthus concluded that output could never keep pace with population. Unchecked population grows at a geometric ratio, Malthus posited, whereas food increases at merely an arithmetic ratio.

What do these ratios mean? A geometric ratio (or exponential rate) means that a number continually multiplies itself by a constant—for example, a perpetual doubling. An arithmetic ratio simply adds a constant. Malthus provides a good example: If the present population is one billion, humans would increase by 1, 2, 4, 8, 16, 32, 64, 128, 256, while food would grow by 1, 2, 3, 4, 5, 6, 7, 8, 9. Whereas each person had one basket of food at the beginning, two hundred years later, 256 people would have to share nine baskets. Only one hundred years after that, 4,096 people would have to share thirteen baskets!

Geometric ratios can be extremely powerful, surprising, and misleading. A few examples might help. If Scott wants to borrow Dennis's television to watch the Super Bowl on February 2 and promises to pay one penny on January 1 and double that each day until the football game begins, Scott had better be very rich or Dennis had better be foolish enough to accept Monopoly game money. Scott would owe Dennis $42,949,672.96 at kickoff time! Compound interest rates at banks also illustrate geometric ratios.[5] Recall the story of the Dutch who bought Manhattan island from the Indians for about $24. If the Indians had placed the money in a compound interest account, their heirs could afford to buy back the island today, including the Empire State Building, Lincoln Center, the skating rink in Central Park, and all the "improvements" since the seventeenth century.

Compound interest can also mislead, as we can see in a more recent example. In 1981, Congress passed a bill permitting Individual Retirement Accounts, essentially allowing people to put away up to $2,000 per year in a fund that would not be taxed until retirement. Advertisements immediately appeared in newspapers proclaiming that a twenty-five-year-old could easily retire with more than $1 million just by saving $2,000 a year. Graphs showed dollar bills soaring into the stratosphere, launched by the magic of compound interest. But the very small print told the real story. The banks assumed an interest rate of 12 percent over the next forty years, but did not tell the reader that if interest rates averaged 12 percent for forty years, inflation would likely rage for forty years, wiping out most of the gain. Imagine the frugal yuppie, slumped over his desk for forty years with little contact with the outside world. In the year 2021, he finally retires. With the yellowed 1981 advertisement in trembling hand, he finds the last remaining coin-operated telephone and asks his banker to arrange for an armored car to pick up his treasure. The banker explains that nearly $10 million plus a blender await the yuppie. The yuppie weeps with joy, supporting himself on his pasta maker. He hears a click. The operator interrupts: "Please deposit four hundred thousand dollars for another minute."

In fact, the advertisements from the early 1980s were remarkably misleading; between 1981 and 2020, banks rewarded savers with an average annual return of about 4 percent, not 12 percent!

The conclusions of *An Essay on the Principle of Population* were not entirely new either to Malthus or to others, since Franklin and Sir James Steuart, a Scottish rival of Adam Smith's, each had previously published foreboding essays. Malthus himself had put forth his fears two years earlier in an essay that searched without success for a publisher: "I cannot agree with Archdeacon Paley, who says, that the quantity of happiness in any country is best measured by the number of people. . . . The actual population may be only a sign of the happiness that is past." Even if unoriginal, the Malthusian thesis, backed by pithy phrases and striking images, displayed a new virtuosity in the art of persuasion. Malthus captured the theory and with it the attention of Britain.

If the earth halved and halved again, we would see a frenzied rush. But what exactly happens when mouths exceed spoonsful? Long before geometric growth soars off the graphs, two kinds of obstacles block the advance: "positive" checks and "preventative" checks. By "positive," Malthus clearly did not mean optimistic. He meant checks that raise the death rate. What are the positive forces that can "save" us from geometric ratios? War, famine, and plagues. The black death lurks in every alley ready to rescue us. Infant mortality liberates us from overpopulation. And famine haunts us always:

Famine seems to be the last, the most dreadful resource of nature. The power of population is so superior to the power of the earth to produce subsistence for man, that premature death must in some shape or other visit the human race. The vices of mankind are active and able ministers of depopulation. They are the precursors in the great army of destruction; and they often finish the dreadful work themselves. But should they fail in this war of extermination, sickly seasons, epidemic, pestilence and plague, advance in terrific array, and sweep off their thousands and ten thousands. Should success be still incomplete; gigantic, inevitable famine stalks in the rear, and with one mighty blow, levels the population with the food of the world.[6]

Preventative checks, which lower the birthrate, seemed less severe, but also less likely. If only people would bridle their passion and delay marriage, they would be better off, Malthus suggested. After all, having children lowers a family's standard of living. But Malthus saw little hope here, for he was preaching to the converted. The middle and upper classes who would read his essay would embrace his argument. But what chance did he have of persuading the lower classes, who always appear more fruitful and multiplicative, to forbear from marriage or childbirth, especially when the Poor Law encouraged couples to have children? Malthus portrayed a recurring cycle in which population growth controlled by grim natural checks would keep wages at only a bare subsistence level. If wages rose higher, workers would have more children, leading to food shortages and an inescapable decline in the standard of living.

In a splendid understatement, Malthus admits that his scenario has a "melancholy hue." (Can one call black a hue?) Later, Malthus mourns that to "prevent the recurrence of misery, is, alas! beyond the power of men." You can imagine the book of Genesis (3:17) ringing in the preacher's ears: "Cursed is the ground for thy sake; in sorrow shalt thou eat of it all the days of thy life." Nonetheless, Malthus tries to sustain a smile and his homiletic humor. Life is "a blessing independent of a future state . . . and we have every reason to think, that there is no more evil in the world than what is absolutely necessary."[7] God, not Malthus, presents the Malthusian trap, hoping mankind will show sympathy and virtue.

The force of the anonymous pamphlet was a plague on the houses of Paley and Godwin, decimating their followers and leaving their theories to look as though intellectual famine had struck utopia. Paley turned and followed his apostates. Godwin battled back, but on Malthus's grounds, suspending his utopian mirages and arguing that moral restraint could forestall disaster. The vital victory for Malthus, however, was winning over Prime Minister Pitt. Though in 1796 Pitt had eloquently advocated for poor relief in Parliament, only four years later he adopted Malthus's thesis and withdrew his support for a new bill. Pitt now argued Malthus's position that since poor relief only encouraged the poor to have children, it brought closer the date for "positive checks" to ravage the populace. Erasing poor relief from the public ledger would actually be a "palliative," by increasing work incentives and decreasing claims on the food supply. Likewise, Malthus was not enthusiastic about public vaccinations, even though he lived to see a country doctor named Edward Jenner successfully immunize his gardener's son against deadly smallpox.

Malthus cannot be disparaged as a heartless hater of the poor, even though Charles Dickens would put Malthusian words into the mouth of Ebenezer Scrooge, who thunders that many of the poor should hurry and die to "decrease the surplus population." In fact, *An Essay* rings with sympathetic statements that the poor suffer most when positive checks rage. As Keynes later insisted, a love of truth and a discerning public spirit drove Malthus to his conclusions. But how strong Pitt's throat muscles must have been to swallow his own words from 1796: "Let us make relief a matter of right and honour. . . . This will make a large family a blessing and not a curse; and this will draw a proper line of distinction between those who are to provide for themselves by their labour, and those who, after enriching their country with a number of children, have a claim upon its assistance for their support."[8]

Even with Pitt's support, Malthus remained skeptical of the future. Handsome men, beautiful women, and wine irresistibly arouse people to venery. And as some preachers were well aware, words are often impotent when the listeners are not.

As the nation trumpeted his alarm, Malthus began to feel

uneasy about the breezy scientific method he had used. After all, he had based his shattering, universal conclusions on scattered bits of information from a former colony. In addition, he felt uncomfortable with the nearly fatalistic pessimism of his books. A revised edition of *An Essay* seemed appropriate. Malthus began exhaustive research, traveling to Sweden, Norway, Finland, Russia, and even France and Switzerland during the 1802 peace with England. He studied civil records and laws, learning that Austria and Bavaria still upheld seventeenth- and eighteenth-century edicts prohibiting paupers from marrying. In 1801, Britain published its first comprehensive census, surprising Malthus, yet strengthening his argument. According to the study, during the late 1700s, population had advanced dramatically, whereas most had previously believed that the growth was very slow. About a hundred years earlier, in 1696, the pioneer statistician Gregory King had wrongly predicted that population would not double for six hundred years.

In 1803, Malthus presented a new edition, complete with new title: *An Essay on the Principle of Population, or A View of Its Past and Present Effects on Human Happiness, with an Inquiry into Our Prospects Respecting the Future Removal or Mitigation of the Evils Which It Occasions.* Gone are Godwin and Condorcet from the marquee. Reduced are discussions of Utopian prophecy. Everything else in the book was expanded, if not in geometric ratio, at least in terms of length, depth, and weight. Malthus illustrated theoretical points with endless anecdotes and examples from Africa, Siberia, Turkey, Persia, Tibet, China, and again the United States, this time including American Indians. No one could attack him for not being empirical. In tone, the second edition sounds slightly less dire, offering hope that the working class might change their habits and show "moral restraint" before multiplying. Of course, altering attitudes takes time. The more temperate tone also affected discussion of the Poor Laws. Rather than scratching them forthwith, Malthus proposed "their *gradual* and *very gradual* abolition" so that no one presently alive or born within two years is injured (original emphasis).[9] And relief would be withdrawn only from the able-bodied. To promote food supply, Malthus also urged restrictions on food imports and exports. Restrictions would boost the price in England and would therefore spur domestic production. Though generally a free trader, Malthus proposed an exception for food. We will examine his trade arguments when we discuss David Ricardo in the next chapter.

With the new edition, reputable writers and politicians again admitted the force of Malthus's logic. Reviews from leading journals and magazines praised Malthus (whose name now appeared on the previously anonymous work) for his insight and diligence, if not for his brevity. His work was read from Turin to Tasmania, and a pirated copy showed up in the United States before the official printing arrived. Less than two years later, the *Monthly Magazine* announced the preparation of a third edition, which appeared in 1806, followed by a fourth edition the next year. No surprise, controversy erupted with each new edition. Intellectual enemies sniped even more wickedly and vulgarly at the second edition than they had at the first, since they now had a target (rather than an anonymous author) for their attacks. The poet Robert Southey wrote to a friend: "Malthus is as great a favourite with the *British Critic* as with the other voiders of menstrual pollution. I shall be very glad to lend a hand in some regular attack upon this mischievous booby. . . . We may in a few evenings effectually demolish him."[10] Hardly a sonnet. Southey's blank verse venom even exceeded Coleridge's, which merely called Malthus "monstrous." Coleridge's grudge against Malthus had festered from the time Malthus voted to expel Coleridge from Jesus College for leaving to join the army without permission. Despite the vitriol, Malthus earned points with economists and soon emerged as a leader of the profession. James Mill, David Ricardo, and later John Stuart Mill and Alfred Marshall accepted *An Essay*, though sometimes ignored its implications in their own writings.

Malthus's work inspired and irked more than economists.

Years later, he won points with an intrepid bug collector sailing to the Galápagos on the H.M.S. *Beagle*, namely, Charles Darwin. If Malthus's cataclysm takes place, who exactly makes it out alive? The fittest, of course. Darwin, who was not so fit himself and often distracted by depression, listlessness, indigestion, and awful itches, wrote that while reading Malthus "for amusement," he was "struck" by the idea that a struggle for existence would lead to "the formation of new species." Meanwhile, Darwin's rival, Alfred Russel Wallace, wrote in his autobiography that Malthus provided the "long-sought clue" to understanding evolution.[11]

Soon after Malthus's second edition appeared, he put aside moral restraint and at the age of thirty-eight married Harriet Eckersall. Since marriage violated the tenets of a Jesus College fellowship, Malthus resigned and in 1805 accepted a post at Haileybury College, the training school for the East India Company, which administered India for the British government. Named professor of general history, politics, commerce, and finance, Malthus became the first professor of political economy in England. Thus, we may consider Malthus, despite his holy orders, the first professional economist. (Incidentally, disciples of Adam Smith assailed the East India Company as a pernicious monopoly, while followers of the utilitarian Jeremy Bentham defended the company, arguing that new British entrants into the business of India would exploit the natives.

At Haileybury, Malthus proved once again that the man who depicted miserable plagues and famines loved to have fun. A friend described his mood as habitually playful, as ready to engage in all innocent pursuits and pleasures of the young as to encourage them in their studies. Within three years Malthus had three young children of his own to play with. Critics loved to jeer at the multiplication of his own offspring, and although the Malthuses had only three, somehow the 1958 and 1967 Everyman's Library editions of *An Essay* awarded him eight more—all girls!

A Good Soothsayer?

Malthus spawned thousands of disciples, many of whom burst forth in the 1960s, 1970s, and 2000s, pleading for the modern-day relevance of their master's prophesies. Before examining the recent literature, let us with hindsight assess Malthus's predictions. Malthus was 99.99 percent correct—until approximately the time he lived. In other words, from approximately 300,000 B.C., when *Homo sapiens* figured how to walk upright, until the 1700s, when people created more babies and ran low on foodstuffs, and thereby suffered more misery. But starting around the time of his birth, Malthus's predictions began to swerve off the rails. Population did not continue to expand geometrically. Food supplies did not creep along. Misery may have visited the poor, but not for Malthusian reasons. On the contrary, in Britain and on the Continent, where Malthus focused his attention, people ate better, lived longer, and exhibited more "restraint" than Malthus could ever have expected.

Malthus missed some of the most important trends in history, as well as some obvious statistical blips. On the trivial side, he forgot to ask Benjamin Franklin whether the rising population figures distinguished immigrants from natural-born Americans. In other words, by lumping Franklin's data together, Malthus in effect assumed that mothers of English descent in remote villages were giving birth to Dutch children arriving in New York by boat. Since he saw rising numbers, he declared the English mothers extremely fertile—certainly a painless childbirth system, even if a flawed statistical method. More crucial, Malthus missed the advances in medicine, an agricultural revolution, and the start of an Industrial Revolution, all of which would twist his projections like taffy into novel geometric shapes, not steady geometric trends.

While Daniel Malthus took walks in the woods with Jean-Jacques Rousseau and contemplated man's perfection, eighteenth-century farmers were perfecting powerful methods to expand output. At the beginning of the eighteenth century, European agricultural productivity was no higher than it was twenty centuries earlier. But from 1700 to 1800, output per worker doubled in England. In France, despite the effects of revolution and war, output grew by roughly 25 percent between the time of Malthus's birth and the first edition of *An Essay*. Several innovations accounted for the leap, including crop rotation, seed selection, better tools, and the use of horses instead of oxen, reducing plowing time by nearly 50 percent. By 1750, rapid progress allowed England not only to feed her citizens but also to export an additional 13 percent in cereals and flour. If a country advances in agriculture, more citizens can work in urban or nonagricultural areas. Whereas 75 percent of Englishmen worked in agriculture in 1690, by 1840 only 25 percent did.[12] In the United States today, only a tiny fraction of the population is needed to feed all of America and export millions of tons of corn, pork, wheat, and other foodstuffs abroad. In the past fifty years, the United States population has grown by 130 million, but its 331 million citizens can manage to eat only half as much soy as its farmers grow. That is a lot of edamame and soy milk to load onto ships. New forms of farming have emerged in recent years, and aquaculture—the farming of fish and shellfish—now yields more seafood than traditional wild fishing, whether done with hooks or nets. Far from limiting population growth, expanding food supplies permitted more parenthood. Further, they have expanded waist sizes, as the average adult weight has ballooned by more than twenty-five pounds.

Remarkably, though, a higher standard of living in Malthus's time did not lead to a birth spiral. When looking at population statistics, Malthus did not see that an increase in population might stem from a decrease in the death rate. From 1740 onward, mortality rates declined in Europe as a result of the improved diet made possible by the agricultural revolution and better health and medical treatment. Until the eighteenth century, doctors probably killed more than they cured; an operation on a voodoo doll by a witch doctor was likely to be as effective as surgery by a scalpel-wielding "leech" doctor. In the 1700s, life expectancy at birth was approximately thirty years, rising to forty years in 1850, fifty years in 1900, and nearly eighty years today.[13] Because of the agricultural revolution, large fluctuations in harvests diminished, and except for in Ireland in the 1840s, famines disappeared from western Europe. The last famine in Great Britain struck nearly a century before the appearance of *An Essay*.

But why did population not steadily soar? Economists point to four stages in the "demographic transition." In preindustrial societies, high death rates balance high birthrates, ensuring steady population. In the second stage, early industrial development, better health lowers death rates, so birthrates appear excessive, and population spurts upward. Since Malthus collected his data in this era, he did not and probably could not have seen what would come next. In the third stage, urbanization and education persuade many to have fewer children. Thus, the death rate continues falling, but so does the birthrate, which flattens the population curve. Finally, in a mature society, with successful birth control and often both spouses working, couples seem to desire between one and three children, and the population stabilizes.

The role of children has changed through history. In peasant societies, more children were needed to work as field hands or to crawl into mines. Our great-grandparents and great-great-grandparents may have had six, seven, or more siblings. In peasant societies, the number of children was a sign of virility. Wealthier couples had more of them. In Rodgers and Hammerstein's *The King and I* (based on the nineteenth-century King Mongkut of Siam), the monarch boasted of 106 children, and Broadway audiences oohed as they scurried to the king's feet and kowtowed to their father, who somehow seemed not weary. Today royal families may have just a few princes and princesses, though even a small number may be enough to stir trouble for the crown. Among upper- and middle-income families, rather than being a sign of virility, children may be seen more as accessories, like Chanel handbags or a new Tesla plugged into the socket.

I would posit the following rule of thumb: in modern times (following industrialization), if a nation exceeds a 2.5 percent annual average growth in GDP for two consecutive generations (twenty-five-year periods), the fertility rate will drop to just over the replacement level—that is, 2.5 children per female. If GDP continues to grow for a third consecutive generation, the fertility rate will tend to drop below 2.1, and the population will require immigration to maintain a stable size.

Karl Marx once said that whenever the train of history goes around a bend, all the intellectuals fall off. Malthus did not foresee stages three and four. When the figures fell off his plotted chart, Malthus fell off the train.

Can we blame him? After all, he had few hard facts to work with. Indeed, the Panglossian arguments he rebutted were so lofty and fanciful that his efforts appear painstakingly detailed in comparison. If we apply his own criteria, as later stated in his *Principles of Political Economy*, though, he is guilty: "The principal cause of error, and of differences which prevail at present among the scientific writers on political economy, appears to me to be a precipitate attempt to simplify and generalize . . . [and not to] sufficiently try their theories by a reference to that enlarged and comprehensive experience, which, on so complicated a subject, can alone establish their truth and utility."[14] Given his oversight of an agricultural revolution and too cursory analysis of why population figures rise, he simplified and generalized too much to escape a verdict of guilty.

The most important moral of Malthus's errors is this: never, ever, extrapolate from past data without bold-faced, underlined, capitalized disclaimers and due modesty. If Aeschylus lived in the modern world, he would write a tragedy about a noble researcher smote by the gods for immodest extrapolation. If Aeschylus wanted modern protagonists, he could look to disciples of Malthus, who, like Cassandra, cried of doom to come (the difference being that Cassandra was right).

In fact, Aeschylus may have had a clue to the demographic transitions to come. My research on ancient Greece and ancient Rome shows that those rich and storied societies began to buck the Malthusian model as they gained wealth.[15] The tale of three hundred Spartans fighting off thousands of Persian soldiers under Xerxes the Great in 480 B.C. has been told in books, films, and video games. In Sparta, soldiering began in the crib, in a survival-of-the-fittest manner. A public committee would inspect babies to determine which was hearty enough to deserve nourishment. At age seven, boys would be taken to camps to begin battle training, eating in mess halls and sleeping in barracks. As adults, adorned in red cloaks, protected by bronze shields, and swinging bronze spears, the Spartan phalanxes looked untouchable.

But where did all the mighty Spartans go? DNA tests do not identify for Spartans, and they did not leave much of a written record. We know a bit from Aristotle and a few other scribbler historians. In short, when the Spartans conquered others, for example, Laconia and Messenia, they dragged the vanquished back to Sparta to be slaves, who performed the farmwork for them. Meanwhile, with slaves at their disposal, Spartan women did not have to do housework and instead helped manage the family farms. Spartan law granted women the right to inherit property and to become educated, which was in some ways more progressive than the law in Athens. But with others to do the hard work, the Spartans chose to have fewer babies, which concentrated wealth and land into fewer heirs. Aristotle pointed out that the Spartan population began to shrink *after* its military victories: "Although the country is capable of supporting fifteen hundred cavalry and thirty thousand heavy-armed troopers, they number not even a thousand."[16] By the early fourth century, Sparta's population had shrunk by 80 percent, and when the Thebans came marching toward them in 371 B.C., there were too few Spartan warriors to pick up the bronze spears locked in the armory.

Ancient Roman legislators also noticed a drop in Rome's birthrate following conquests and bumper crops. Pliny the Elder complained that even one child was a heavy burden. The emperor Augustus became so worried that he prodded the Senate to pass laws penalizing the unmarried, the celibate, and the childless. One of the laws put a 50 percent inheritance tax on a man who did not have children (*lex Papia Poppaea*). It did little good, and so Rome had to enlist German tribesmen to man the army and navy, "barbarians" with little loyalty to the emperor.

Around this time, the geographer Strabo, who straddled Greek and Roman culture, noted that the ancient lands seemed to have more statues than people. The ratio of statues per baby is worth watching today, as the birthrate drops below the replacement rate in much of the industrialized world.

Doomsday Postponed?

Spurred by concerns about pollution, population, and rising energy prices, some groups in the 1960s and 1970s tried to map the world's future. Again, sad sooths were said: assuming current trends, resources would dwindle; industry would befoul those natural resources that did not dwindle; output would collapse; and population would streak past food supplies. Who said these sooths? Among others, in 1968 the Disney company released a ten-minute cartoon starring Donald Duck warning families that if they have more than a few children, the mothers will be "tired and cross, . . . the children will be sickly and unhappy," and the family will not have enough food to feed their ox, leaving the dad to push a plow. Moreover, they won't be able to afford "modern conveniences," at which point the film shows a clunky radio.[17] One of the most frightening studies was compiled by the Club of Rome, a group of European academics, and presented in a bestselling book, *The Limits to Growth*.[18] Using advanced computer techniques, the Club of Rome extrapolated trends and predicted disaster within one hundred years unless preventatives more severe than Malthus suggested were taken. The preventatives: immediately stop economic growth, stop population expansion, and recycle resources. So shocking were the predictions that the club reevaluated them and shortly afterward issued a much happier study. An economist described the club as "the computer that cried wolf." Nonetheless, the original report got the publicity. In 1973, Robert S. McNamara, then president of the World Bank, compared the "population explosion" to the threat of nuclear war. In 1974, Robert Heilbroner published *An Inquiry into the Human Prospect*, in which he displayed absolutely no hope for mankind in the modern world. Projecting industrial trends, he concluded that resources could not keep up with industrial demand. And even if they did, we would all burn up in a hotter atmosphere. Perhaps switching to a more monastic lifestyle would be prudent, he suggested. So far, most people have responded to the suggestion with the malapropic advice of movie mogul Samuel Goldwyn: "Include me out."

In 1980, in response to an earlier request from President Jimmy Carter, the State Department and the Council on Environmental Quality released *The Global 2000 Report to the President*. Though much more rosy and reasonable than the Club of Rome study, the report proclaimed: "If present trends continue, the world in 2000 will be more crowded, more polluted, less stable ecologically, and more vulnerable to disruption than the world we live in now. . . . Barring revolutionary advances in technology, life for most people on earth will be more precarious in 2000 than it is now . . . unless the nations of the world act decisively to alter current trends."[19] The *Washington Post* approved, writing that "the report's projections clearly erred on the side of optimism."

Still, most economists remain skeptical of these reports. Those who programmed the models installed the same kind of pessimistic and static assumptions that Malthus used. Some branded the models "PIPO": pessimism in, pessimism out. One key assumption violated a central tenet of economics—namely, prices signal to economic agents when to conserve or economize. Recall our earlier discussion of Adam Smith and Hayek's example of tin. If demand for tin grew, the price would rise, people would try to use less tin, and entrepreneurs would be spurred into looking for substitutes for tin or additional supplies of tin. Under the original Club of Rome report, if demand grew, nothing would happen except that the world would run out of tin. Yes, for some products there may be a fixed supply, no substitutes, and a rising demand unresponsive to higher prices. But these are surely exceptions. Nobel laureate Wassily Leontief studied the question for the United Nations in 1977 and reported: "Known world resources of metallic minerals and fossil fuels are generally sufficient to supply world requirements through the remaining decades of this century . . . to support world economic development at relatively high rates. But . . . these resources will most probably become more expensive."[20]

In retrospect, even Leontief was too pessimistic. Starting in the 1980s, energy prices began a slow slide that would last through the end of the century (aside from a brief jump in 1990 when Saddam Hussein's Iraqi army invaded Kuwait). By the mid-1990s, oil prices were lower in inflation-adjusted terms than they had been in the early 1960s, long before the OPEC oil embargo of 1973. By 2020, inflation-adjusted oil prices were roughly equivalent to the prices that prevailed in the 1970s. Even the price of gold, which had leapt to $400 an ounce in the 1970s, drifted down to just under $300 in 1998 before climbing again in recent years. In 1980 an optimistic economist named Julian Simon challenged a pessimistic biologist named Paul Ehrlich, who had earned his academic credentials studying butterflies but reached worldwide fame through his books *The Population Bomb* and *The End of Affluence*. During the 1970s, Ehrlich had appeared twenty times on NBC's *Tonight Show* and had forecast that hundreds of millions of people would starve to death in the decade unless the world immediately embraced "zero population growth." Simon dared Ehrlich to choose any commodities, wagering that the prices would fall over time, not rise (showing that there was no shortage). Ehrlich purchased $1,000 worth of five metals. In 1990, they would check the prices. If they had gone up, Simon would pay Ehrlich the increase. If they had fallen, Ehrlich would pay Simon the difference. Sure enough, Ehrlich had to pay up, for resource prices dropped, even though the world economy and the world's population expanded. Simon received a check for $576. Why did Simon win? First of all, the "oil scare" model did not imagine that entrepreneurs would pump vast sums of oil from the North Sea or from Mexico. Second, they, like Malthus, missed an agricultural revolution that showed farmers how to grow more with less. In the 1950s, a plant geneticist and pathologist named Norman Borlaug helped launch the Green Revolution by figuring out how to mate a sturdy-stalked dwarf wheat with a heavy-headed strain. His results yielded bumper golden harvests that have fed millions in India, Mexico, and Africa. Third, they underestimated the incentive to invent substitutes for scarce goods. Right now, aluminum, steel, and plastics companies vigorously compete to fight their way into new automobiles. In the 1967 movie *The Graduate*, a middle-aged character gives the young college grad played by Dustin Hoffman a hot investment tip, "plastic." It turned out to be a smarter idea than most of those dispensed by "professional" Chicken Littles. The Stone Age didn't end because we couldn't find any more rocks. We won't stop using fossil fuels because we've used up the last drop. We will stop because they have become relatively more expensive, either through cheaper alternatives or government regulation.

The doomsday models assume that technology cannot outpace resource demand. While technology may not be the dependable deus ex machina of Greek theater or the cavalry of Hollywood Westerns, we cannot be too disparaging, either. For example, the models condemn automobiles for pollution and portend an end to fossil fuels such as oil. According to the models, automobiles and oil, though crucial to modern society, are destructive. But what did these replace during the twentieth century? The horse for transportation and wood for energy. Near Central Park in New York, only a few dozen horse-drawn carriages operate today. Yet the smell can be pungent. Imagine the stench and disease spread a century ago in cities where horses reigned supreme for transport! Wood may be more renewable than oil, but fossil fuels have proved cheaper. The switch was promoted by prices, not by a foreboding model. The point is that long-term forecasts regarding economic resources and technology require divine gifts, not degrees in economics.

Does this mean that economists must wear silly smiles and let the invisible hand take care of pollution and starvation in less developed nations? No. We will discuss pollution more fully later, but for now, economists must admit that pollution often indicates a gap in the simple Adam Smith model. Think of pollution as a cost of doing business. But how does smoke differ from labor cost or machinery cost or rent? The corporation pays for these other costs. They are "internal" to its operation. But the corporation does not pay for the pollution. It is an "external" effect that society pays for by breathing dirty air. The result? The manufacturer produces more goods than it should, because the cost of producing seems cheaper than it really is. To get the ideal amount of production, the manufacturer should be forced to absorb the usual costs plus the cost of pollution to society. Taxes on pollution are frequently suggested by economists to achieve this.

The Malthusian trap seems more pertinent in less developed nations, where better health services reduce death rates, while birthrates continue at high levels. But despite pessimism, fertility figures in many poor countries have declined in the last twenty years as a result of educational campaigns, subsidized birth control, and the natural "demographic transition" that accompanies economic development. In Brazil, some social scientists credit the middle-class attitudes displayed on television for a stunning drop in the birthrate, which confounded forecasts of the 1970s. On the other hand, the effort to reduce birthrates is controversial in some societies. In China the government's one-child policy, which reigned from 1979 to 2015, cut the birthrate dramatically, though it also may have contributed to female adoptions abroad, infanticide, and a mismatch in the ratio between young men and young women. Now that the Chinese government has lifted the restrictions, however, the birthrate has not significantly rebounded, suggesting that Chinese couples have voluntarily adopted a puny birthrate of roughly 1.6 children per couple. In other countries, birth control policies defy tradition and religious precepts. Nonetheless, dramatic declines have been registered in Sri Lanka, Indonesia, and several Indian states. Between 1960 and 2000, fertility fell in 183 countries surveyed by the World Bank (and rose in only four: Chad, Congo, Equatorial Guinea, and East Timor). Malthus's suggestion that better education would help constrain the birthrate does seem reasonable, as literacy rates have risen dramatically. Has the birth dearth gone too far? We will discuss this in later chapters when we discuss retirement programs and government debts. For now, note that Singapore has seen the birthrate of Chinese ethnics plummet so fast that it worries about underpopulation. After twenty years of the slogan "Two is enough," Singapore officials declared: "Have three—more if you can afford it!" To boost its birthrate, Russia has promised young couples free motel visits and even the chance to win a new refrigerator.

At the same time, poor countries are boosting their agricultural output. China and India constitute more than 40 percent of the world's population and most of its poor people. Yet over the last twenty-five years, both these countries have become nearly self-sufficient in agriculture, and India is now an export powerhouse in wheat and rice. To battle terrible starvation and malnutrition, India imported eighteen thousand "miracle seeds" developed by Norman Borlaug in his Green Revolution. The seeds sprouted and grew, and within ten years India began conquering widespread starvation.[21] In 1978, China began to restructure the agricultural sector, shifting from centrally controlled production units to decentralized market forces. Finally permitted to float, prices became signals to China's economic actors, and output leaped forward.

African states have sometimes found success elusive in both slowing population and raising production. Although babies are born at a slower rate than in the 1950s, the overall population growth rate is higher because life expectancy has risen dramatically. Until recently, the ghost of Malthus seemed to frown upon countries such as Ethiopia, where drought and war act as positive checks. Nonetheless, such ravaged countries have the potential to feed their populations. Economists point to two primary problems. First, poor countries cannot afford to save and invest in new technology because incomes are low. And incomes are low because production techniques are inefficient. Thus they are caught in a vicious cycle, which foreign aid attempts to break. Second and much more important, many governments with unstable political roots placate urban consumers by keeping food prices low. But artificially low prices decrease investment by farmers and stunt further output. As a result, consumers happily see low price tags but sadly look up to see empty shelves.

Third World countries often compound the problem by propping up their currencies, which encourages imports and discourages exports. In recent years, many scholars have reexamined the basic question of whether population growth hurts Third World countries and concluded that for some countries, especially those with plenty of arable land, rapid population growth may not be destructive. A denser population may lower the costs of transporting goods to customers and stimulate domestic demand for goods. The World Bank suggests that most developing countries can absorb up to 2 percent growth without a decline in the standard of living.[22] While African countries average annual increases of 3 percent, Asian and Latin American countries average about 2 percent. Certainly, there is reason for hope. But hope rests to a large extent on whether governments will enact productive economic policies that encourage trade among adults and education among children.

Since the first edition of this book, in 1989, a number of African nations have actually tossed aside the rigid, wrong-headed policies that condemned their populations to continuous famines. Ethiopia, once the poster country for drought and agricultural desperation, has made a remarkable turn-around in past years, doubling its grain output in the 1990s and more than quadrupling its per capita GDP since 2000. While the Marxist dictator Mengistu had forced farmers into cooperatives, and then paid them low prices, his successors since 1991 have permitted farmers to charge market prices, encouraging them to produce more grain and to take better care of their fields.[23] Foreign investment has poured in, and Ethiopia has achieved one of the highest growth rates in the world. Fortunately, Ethiopia is not alone, as Ghana and Uganda have also declared war on starvation, rather than war on farmers. In recent decades, sub-Saharan African citizens have boosted their daily food consumption by one hundred calories, while life expectancy has climbed by about ten years.[24] Alas, Zimbabwe, which was led by Robert Mugabe's autocratic regime for four decades, has not joined in.

Malthus and the Immigrants

When Malthus warned that economic growth in Europe would spur overcrowding, his readers immediately came up with a nifty solution: ship the poor to the sparsely settled and sweeping plains of the New Worlds. Surely, North America and Australia offered an inexhaustible supply of soil for them to toil on. Malthus was skeptical. He figured that as soon as the Europeans boarded the crowded ships, a new generation of poor would simply rush into the towns and hamlets to take their places. Further, he surmised that settlers in North America would end up chopping down trees, poisoning the environment, and plundering native populations. He had previously condemned Spanish pioneers for wiping out many indigenous villages. Malthus was wistful about the idea of people leaving their homelands, stating that emigration "snaps the cords" of nature and that crossing the turbulent sea would be like the "separation of death from all their former connexions."[25] Eventually, over the course of new editions of his masterwork, Malthus softened his stand against emigration and eventually supported government plans to send poor Irish and Scottish peasants to America. He expressed sympathy for Celtic paupers and deemed their living conditions and government policies "degrading." But Malthus added a proviso to his evolving emigration views: the government should raze the cottages of those who leave so that the newly poor did not refill them. It was better to hand over the land to woolly sheep and meaty cattle.

While in his day Malthus warned that the whole planet would get too crowded, many present-day protesters worry that their specific native countries are overflowing—with too many immigrants. In Italy, Sweden, and Germany, new political parties suggest throwing out the newcomers. In the post–World War II era, Germany opened its doors for 7 million foreigners, many of them Turkish and Arab guest workers. But lately they are viewed less like guests and more like unwanted squatters. Even in Australia, Anglos are protesting the influx of Asians. This in a country once populated by British prisoners!

The European dynamic has become more severe in the past few years, following German chancellor Angela Merkel's 2015 decision to open the borders to one million refugees, primarily from Syria. Merkel and her economic advisers defended their decision on two grounds. First, they said that it was Germany's and Europe's moral obligation to help war refugees. Second, she and her economic advisers argued that Germany needed more workers because of its shrinking birthrate. But Germany had no organized method to deal with the influx. A government study showed that violent crime jumped by 10 percent within the first year, with 90 percent of the crime committed by young males.[26] No doubt, the veritable stampede of refugees helped fuel the Brexit movement in the U.K., as many British voters perceived that their country had surrendered the right to control its own borders and to battle its own crime rate. Separate from the Syrian crisis, Italy has struggled to contain refugee flows from North Africa. Between 2016 and 2018, three hundred thousand arrived on leaky boats primarily through Sicily, severely straining public services and prompting citizen outrage. The harried escape from African ports and the fifteen thousand deaths during the Mediterranean transit (as reported by the United Nations) appeared to be a Malthusian nightmare. But keep in mind, the refugees were not fleeing from famine but from warfare, terrorism, and dismal economic prospects.

In America—a nation of immigrants—we sometimes hear people denounce newcomers, especially during periods of slower economic growth, when the jobless rate rises. Even a lenient abolitionist like Ben Franklin called Protestant German immigrants "Palantine Boors." Few "nativists" (not to be confused with Native Americans) worry à la Malthus that immigrants will eat all their food. Instead, they claim that immigrants drive down the standard of living by taking jobs from those born in this country while undermining the "cultural integrity" of the United States. Of course, these arguments are not new. Between 1845 and 1855, more than a million Irish crossed the Atlantic, fleeing the blight of festering potatoes. They soon made up more than one-quarter of New York's population, and they were not always welcomed warmly.[27] Irish Americans bitterly tell of their great-grandfathers reading help-wanted ads that included the tag line "No Irish need apply." As a character in the 1991 film *The Commitments* announces, "The Irish are the blacks of Europe. So say it loud—I'm black and I'm proud!" Yet through the eyes of today's Mexican immigrant, Irish Americans look like they sailed over with Miles Standish on the *Mayflower*. A book called *How the Irish Became White* shows how the derided Irish claimed their place in America.[28] The careers of outstanding, patriotic sons like George M. Cohan undoubtedly helped the immigrant cause. Cohan claimed that he was born on the Fourth of July, and even inserted that claim into his song "Yankee Doodle Dandy." The grandson of slaves, Louis Armstrong later pulled the same patriotic stunt, though he was off by only one month.

But "this time it's different," nativists argue. First of all, immigrants in the past few decades have not assimilated as quickly as the millions who arrived in the great waves of European refugees at the turn of the twentieth century. Why not? Let's consider three factors: cacophony, communication, and calluses.

The earlier waves fled from a polyglot of European countries and spoke a *cacophony* of different languages. In 1910 every immigrant language except English was a minority tongue. Germans made up a plurality, at 18 percent, but no group had a big enough "market share" to dominate or create a durable enclave. From 1915 to 1965, Europeans composed about 75 percent of 11 million newcomers. In contrast, nearly half the recent immigrants come from Latin America, mostly from Mexico (only about 15 percent come from Europe). Because there is strength in numbers, many families can live and work speaking in Spanish. Spanish-speaking cable and satellite television has been sweeping Florida, Texas, and California. The Spanish-language network Univision often beats out the English-language networks Fox, NBC, CBS, and ABC in prime-time viewing among eighteen- to thirty-four-year-olds. Modern *communication* technologies help, since newcomers can easily telephone, text, email, or even fly to see their relatives back home. Long-distance telephone rates have plummeted from dollars per minute to a few cents, giving even minimum-wage workers the "luxury" of phoning home. In contrast, in 1912 the Hamburg Shipping Line carried mailbags from Germany, the only way for a fräulein to communicate with her frau back home. The "melting pot" metaphor has been locked in the cupboard, replaced by the "salad bowl," suggesting that each ethnic group should maintain its identity and resist assimilation. While peer pressure used to prod immigrant children to learn English, even Chinese youths are quick to mock each other as "bananas" (yellow on the outside; white on the inside) if they take up American habits too quickly.

Economists care much more about the third factor. Are immigrants catching up to native incomes, as the Irish, German, Italians, Poles, and Jews eventually did, or are they slipping behind and leaning too much on public assistance programs? While most economists start out very sympathetic to lenient immigration rules, the latest data troubles them. Here's the problem: the economy has grown so technologically advanced that unskilled laborers have little hope of jumping into the mainstream. In the 1880s, Isaac and Joseph Breakstone could start by selling dairy goods from a corner pushcart and eventually build a successful nationwide brand. But pushcart capitalism does not stand much of a chance today. During the earlier waves, immigrants had *calluses* on their hands. The country needed calluses in 1900, since 69 percent of the population worked on farms, in forests, in coal mines, or in factories.[29] As soon as newcomers disembarked from boats, they learned to put their calluses to work, even if they faced discrimination. My grandfather, Sam Lewis, who arrived from London, told me that when boats from Ireland docked in

Manhattan, male steerage passengers were offered a choice: "A hook or a club?"—meaning they could either haul crates as a longshoreman or wield a billy club as a policeman, since Irish bosses dominated both vocations.

In 1900, even a high school degree was rare, with fewer than 14 percent of Americans earning a diploma, and fewer than 3 percent going on to college. Today, can an immigrant who comes from a country that has not yet passed through the Industrial Revolution, much less the semiconductor, cloud, and artificial intelligence revolutions, stand a chance? Sure, numerous skilled Chinese and Indian immigrants have earned fortunes in Silicon Valley designing computer equipment, software, and new media, but these stories are certainly rare among the Mexican-born gardeners of Southern California. Whether explained by discrimination, family traditions, legal structures, or educational backgrounds, the data do reveal ethnic differences in outcomes. Recent migrants from Latin America start off earning about 30 percent less than natives, with halting progress from that point on. Guatemalans who arrived before 1980 were making 28 percent less by the 1990s. Even within Asia, however, there were differences. While the Chinese had on average fully caught up, Laotians stayed 22 percent behind.[30] Furthermore, when unskilled immigrants come ashore, they may push down wages for unskilled natives, particularly urban blacks, by 2.5 to 5 percent, according to some researchers.

Of course, the data could change (and a revolution in our school systems would help!). Even so, because the data is aggregated, it tells us little about *individual* contributions by immigrants. What if Albert Einstein had stayed in Germany and been forced to help the Third Reich? Certainly his genius offset all the German immigrant rabble that angered anglos in the 1930s. Steve Jobs's biological father fled Syria and managed a modest coffee shop in Sacramento, California. The immigrant's son reinvented how we share our music and our stories. And in any case, the Statue of Liberty was not placed in New York Harbor as an economic symbol. Despite occasional backlashes, the United States has welcomed the huddled masses, who have longed to breathe free, and have made us richer in the process.

One more reason keeps economists hopeful: when millions of baby boomers retire over the next two decades, the United States will need *more* workers to support the pensioners. It will be a new opportunity for new members of the workforce. We will see whether they take advantage of it.

Global Warming: Malthus's Revenge?

Mother Nature is fickle. The seas in which we now sail, swim, and jet-ski once boiled. Dinosaur fossils lie buried near traces of tropical ferns in Montana. In a real Jurassic Park, tropical ferns left coal deposits near the South Pole. Millions of years later, the Vikings hunted in a truly green Greenland, and Englishmen drank English wine amid flourishing vineyards in the Midlands. Later, in the time of the Renaissance, the Little Ice Age took hold. Bitter winters inspired the Flemish painter Pieter Bruegel the Elder to create his seminal work, *Hunters in the Snow*, while Dutchmen enjoyed skating on canals, a rare treat today.[31] Shortly before the Carter administration released *Global Report 2000*, which forecast environmental disaster and soaring energy prices, Congress held hearings on the climate. In particular, the 1960s and 1970s had been a chilly decade marked with blizzards, and some scientists warned of a new ice age, since temperatures had peaked in the 1940s. Computer models warned that the earth might have jumped onto a long-term track toward global *cooling*. After all, the last ice age had temperatures just 10 degrees Fahrenheit cooler than ours. Small shifts could lead glaciers to spread from the poles, covering New York in hundreds of feet of bluish ice, as it had been millions of years ago.

Almost immediately after these warnings, the weather turned warm again. By 1990 international scientists gathered under the United Nations' auspices and predicted that the earth was warming dangerously fast and could send the thermometer up perhaps by 9 degrees Fahrenheit by the year 2100. Not only would more people sweat, but global warming would incite terrible floods as well as devastating droughts that would threaten food and water supplies. What would cause this calamity? Following the work of a Swedish scientist, Svante Arrhenius, the Intergovernmental Panel on Climate Change (IPCC) theorized that fossil fuels build up carbon dioxide, creating an insulating layer that permits the sun's hot rays to penetrate but doesn't let warmth escape. Over a hundred-year period, as the number of automobiles throughout the world multiplies, so will CO_2 levels. Already, the shrinking glaciers of northern Europe are revealing bones and fossils that date prior to the last ice age. A hotter climate would lift sea levels, disintegrate glaciers and polar ice sheets, and intensify storms. Many places would turn wetter, inciting tropical diseases such as malaria and devastating world agriculture.[32] All in all, a bleak, Malthusian story of population growth destroying the ability of the world to sustain human life.

Could it be true? Perhaps. Skeptics cite a number of arguments against the doomsday scenario. For example, the earth's temperature has crawled up by about 1.8 degrees Fahrenheit in the last century, and the data is awfully fuzzy (satellite readings show a smaller rise). Some scientists believe that the sun could have brightened up enough to explain that small rise. They also argue that the formation of clouds is still too tricky a process for computers to model. In addition, some glaciers around the world have actually started spreading rather than shrinking. Finally, skeptics argue that even if the climate perks up by 4.5 degrees Fahrenheit (the IPCC's midrange forecast), many parts of the world would benefit from a longer growing season and less brutal winters. A group of optimistic economists have dubbed their analysis the "Ricardian" approach, named after the hero of our next chapter.[33] In the Ricardian analysis, farmers would take advantage of global warming by switching to warmer-weather crops; they would replace wheat fields with cotton, for example. Already, a wine-growing culture has sprung up in the English countryside, where it had died out seven hundred years ago. Of course, countries that are already terribly hot and wet would have few new choices. What's good for the farmer in Kansas may be terrible for the man who tends the rice paddies in Vietnam when the monsoons hit.

Economists do point out, however, that a wealthier world can better afford to take more action and absorb geological threats. Early-warning systems for hurricanes save thousands of lives. In September 1900 a wicked storm smacked into Galveston, Texas, killing 8,000 unsuspecting souls. It is the most lethal natural disaster in U.S. history. Why were the victims unsuspecting? Because radar, radio, and satellites had not yet been invented. Death rates from droughts and extreme weather events have plunged by about 90 percent in the past one hundred years. Between 1982 and 2002, the United States suffered eighteen major earthquakes, claiming a total of 143 lives. India, with flimsier buildings, cruder sewage systems, and less effective firefighting forces, suffered only fourteen major earthquakes, but those disasters killed 32,117.[34] A rising GDP will not tame the force of Indian earthquakes, but it will protect more people from rubble. As the world's GDP rises, defensive options against climate change become more affordable. Miami Beach has literally lifted up roads and bridges to accommodate periodic flooding. As recently as 1990, one in three humans around the world lived in extreme poverty, according to the World Bank. That number has dropped by two-thirds. It is one of the most extraordinary achievements in human history and gives human beings the wherewithal to fight and endure the impact of climate change.

Many strategies to fight global warming include taxing carbon emissions, such as those outlined by Yale economist William Nordhaus, whose climate change model earned him a

Nobel Prize in 2018. The idea of taxing pollution goes back to the English economist Arthur Cecil Pigou, who was born in the middle of the Victorian era and lived to see Queen Elizabeth II crowned in the 1950s. Pigou developed the idea of "externalities," meaning that a company's operations might have spillover effects on neighbors. Consider, if you sat next to Winston Churchill while he smoked a cigar, or lived next door to a Snoop Dogg concert venue, you might absorb some fumes. If a hot dog company smokes meat and emits vapors that make you choke, it is imposing a cost on its neighbors. Pigou pointed out that since the hot dog company does not pay the cost of this annoyance, it likely churns out more hot dogs than it would if it had to pay for its pollution. In sum, the world gets too many hot dogs and too much smoky air. Pigou argued that the market would be more efficient if a tax were levied on the factory to more closely align the total benefits and total costs of the factory's work. Following this model, Harvard economist Greg Mankiw keeps track of leading economists and thinkers who support taxes on externalities, including carbon taxes, and collectively calls them the "Pigou Club."

Global warming, by itself, does not prove Malthus right. The real test comes if humankind has to respond to a warmer, more threatening climate. Will they keep pumping CO_2 into the atmosphere until they either asphyxiate or destroy the vegetation? Or will he they find the technological tools to let the species survive? Our great-grandchildren might learn the answer.

His Last Days

Malthus would be surprised to learn that the world is in good enough shape to dispute his thesis more than 150 years after his demise.

Malthus spent the last thirty years of his life in Haileybury and London, hobnobbing with the greats and near greats. In Samuel Johnson's term, he was "clubbable" and became a member of the King of Clubs (a dining society) and the Political Economy Club. In 1824, *The Gentlemen's Magazine* of London reported that the Royal Society of Literature named both Malthus and his foe Coleridge "Royal Associates," and each received a lifetime stipend for research and, presumably, bickering with each other.[35] Malthus continued to publish books and pamphlets, most notably his *Principles of Political Economy*. More important, in friendly yet forceful tones he debated David Ricardo on trade policy and the question of economic depressions, which we will discuss later.

Even until his death of heart disease in 1834, Malthus felt obliged to deny that he was an enemy of mankind. He left behind a widow and two children, having buried a teenage daughter a decade earlier. Many lecturers and authors still portray him at best as a dour parson and at worst as a goblin well suited for Halloween. Yet his critics, he thought, donned the merry masks that marred their vision—preventing them from seeing that the light at the end of the tunnel was a train coming at them.

CHAPTER IV

David Ricardo and the Cry for Free Trade

David Ricardo never attended college. But he delved into economic theory with more competence than any academic. He never formally studied financial markets. Yet he made millions of pounds in the stock market. His powerful mind and practical knowledge so dominated intellectual foes that he could win fiery debates and then dismiss the rival argument, saying that only a university professor would be silly enough to believe it.

One university professor was "silly" enough to disagree with Ricardo. His name was Thomas Robert Malthus. But critics had so viciously slandered Malthus that he actually enjoyed Ricardo's thoughtful attacks. After those of Shelley and Coleridge, Ricardo's snipes must have seemed more like a serenade. And at least Ricardo agreed with his population principle.

The relationship between Ricardo and Malthus began in the press, when each published essays on currency and trade issues criticizing the other. Malthus finally sent a letter to Ricardo in 1811, suggesting, "As we are *mainly* on the same side of the question, we might supersede the necessity of a long controversy in print . . . by an amicable discussion in private." At almost the same time, Ricardo was composing nearly the same note. They met a few days later, and it was the beginning of a lifelong friendship. Ricardo composed reams of charming letters to his unlikely friend, punctuated by detailed policy points. Shortly after their first meeting, he wrote that he was "anxious for an opportunity of introducing Mrs. Malthus and Mrs. Ricardo," adding: "And we have a bed always at your disposal, so that I shall hope on your very first visit to London you will favor me by occupying it."[1] Before his death in 1823, Ricardo wrote to Malthus, stating, that despite numerous disputes, "I should not like you more than I do if you agreed in opinion with me." Only three people shared in Ricardo's will, and Malthus was one of them. Later Malthus announced, "I never loved anybody out of my own family so much."

Malthus never knew anybody who was so outside his "family" as Ricardo. Whereas Malthus came from a stable old English family and took holy orders in the Anglican Church, Ricardo was born the son of a Jewish immigrant in 1772, whose family had fled persecution in Portugal, worked as coral cutters in Livorno (near Pisa, Italy), washed up on the shores of the Netherlands, and then sailed across the North Sea to arrive in England.[2] His father, Abraham Ricardo, was one of the twelve "Jew brokers" permitted to practice as a stockbroker at the Royal Exchange in London. An early-nineteenth-century map shows that different national and ethnic groups were assigned to specific stations around the Exchange, like a food court at a modern shopping mall. Jews' Walk lies in the southeast corner of the Exchange, across from French Walk and sandwiched between Spanish Walk and Portugal Walk.[3] How ironic that the saga of the Ricardo family's travels ended up bringing them just feet from the Portuguese flag they had once fled. In addition to the Royal Exchange, Abraham also listed his business address as Garraway's Coffee House, a bustling café built after the fire of 1666, where traders, booksellers, and lawyers would sip a strong brew and gab about monarchs and money.

While Malthus received careful tutoring and schooling at Cambridge, Ricardo went to work with his father at fourteen as a messenger and soon began to learn intricate financial systems and strategies on the job, so to speak. And he learned well. By his mid-twenties, the man with the Midas touch had established his own business and amassed a fortune through stocks, bonds, and real estate investments worth hundreds of millions of dollars (in today's dollars). While the Ricardo family began by trading stocks and commodities, with success and heightened credibility, they began to represent the English government in selling bonds to the public. The only investment money Malthus ever earned, Ricardo made for him. A primary example of their contrasting acumen occurred during Napoleon's reign. Ricardo had bought some British government stock for himself and Malthus, but after the proclamation of a new French constitution, Malthus grew nervous, fearing that a good turn of events for the French leader would hurt the stock. In tones so timid that they show Malthus better suited for a church bingo game than the stock market, he requested that Ricardo sell the shares, unless "it is either wrong, or inconvenient to you, and whatever may occur . . . I shall always be sensible of your kindness, and not disposed to repine." Ricardo sold Malthus's shares but held on to his own a bit longer, earning almost double Malthus's premium.[4]

David Ricardo's hard work and ingenious manner made his father proud, until they didn't, at which time all hell broke loose, if not literally then theologically. David's wife, Priscilla, whom he wanted to introduce to Mrs. Malthus, was neither Jewish, like David, nor Anglican, like the Malthus clan. She was a Quaker. Neither Priscilla's nor David's parents approved of their marriage. When David refused to bow down to his parents' wishes, they recited the prayer for the deceased and mourned for a son who was now dead to them. The parents never spoke to their son again. Perhaps David so valued Malthus's friendship because his own family had fractured.

By marrying a Quaker, Ricardo had not exactly elevated himself in the eyes of high society, for Quakers were also a suspect group whose legal rights were restricted. But for David's charm and wealth, they would have been a very isolated couple. David's successes, however, allowed him to buy an estate in Gloucestershire and a house in London's posh Grosvenor Square, where he and Priscilla raised their six children, one of whom became the high sheriff of Gloucestershire.

Although wealth surrounded Ricardo, he did not read *The Wealth of Nations* until he was twenty-seven, and then only by "accident." During a boring vacation in the English resort of Bath, the future leader of classical economics came upon the founder's greatest work. Recall that Adam Smith began *The Wealth of Nations* during a dull stay in France. Since economics seems to owe more to boredom than any other discipline, perhaps students should not complain if their professors occasionally repay the favor or commemorate the founding.

In 1809, Ricardo debuted as an economics writer—with newspaper articles and pamphlets on currency and inflation—to rave reviews. At the urging of James Mill, a political economist and the father of philosopher John Stuart Mill, Ricardo entered London's intellectual society, later becoming a member of Malthus's Political Economy Club and of the King of Clubs. A splendid raconteur and host, Ricardo especially impressed the novelist Maria Edgeworth, who reported having had "a delightful conversation, both on deep and shallow subjects. Mr. Ricardo, with a very composed manner, has a continual life of mind, and starts perpetually a new game in conversation. I never argued or discussed a question with any person who argues more fairly or less for victory and more for truth."[5]

The son of an immigrant soon became the very model of a major English gentleman, wise to the Industrial Revolution and smart in the drawing room. At the bullying of James Mill, in 1817 Ricardo finally wrote a treatise, *On the Principles of Political Economy and Taxation*, providing a full commentary on Adam Smith as well as contemporary issues. Two years later, and again at Mill's urging, Ricardo won a seat in the House of Commons, where his high-pitched voice rang out for political freedoms and free trade. Though he took his oath swearing on "the true faith of a Christian," we will never know whether in deference to his estranged family he kept his fingers crossed behind his back.

A Tricky but Brilliant Theory

We also do not know how many members of Parliament actually understood Ricardo, especially his views on trade. This was not because his views were cloudy or he was inarticulate, but because Ricardo tried to argue perhaps the most complex and counterintuitive principle of economics. Once, President Gerald Ford gave a televised speech on the federal budget deficit using a calendar as a visual aid, all carefully rehearsed so that he would not make any embarrassing hand gestures. No modern president would attempt to do what Ricardo tried to do. Unfortunately, the perplexing principle is the key to modern economic understanding. An insolent natural scientist once asked a famous economist to name one economic rule that is neither obvious nor unimportant. Ricardo's Law of Comparative Advantage was the immediate response. Regrettably, few politicians then or now can follow the analysis. As a result, quotas, tariffs, and trade wars mar the world's economic history.

Before examining the principle, let's see why Ricardo bothered to explain it. As in Adam Smith's vision, businessmen love to shout about free enterprise at Rotary Club meetings, yet whisper requests for favors into the ears of politicians on Capitol Hill. During Ricardo's time, landowners whispered and waved their wealth at Parliament, securing protection from the import of grain after the Napoleonic Wars. The price of grain had soared during the wars, partly as a result of Napoleon's embargo, and landowners feared a sudden drop at the onset of peace. On the other side of the aisle sat the rising bourgeoisie, the new businessmen of the Industrial Revolution. Since the bourgeoisie employed laborers, they preferred to see lower prices for food, so they wouldn't be forced to pay higher wages. The landowners won the battle of influence, and in 1815 Parliament passed an act that prohibited imports of grain below a certain price, virtually granting farmers a monopoly. British dictionaries define "corn" as grain such as oats, rye, wheat, and barley. Thus, the acts were called Corn Laws. Across Britain today, you can find grand old nineteenth-century buildings called the Corn Exchange, where traders and farmers would haggle. In Leeds, the dramatically domed Corn Exchange resembles Rome's Pantheon, and is now a shopping mall.

Ricardo saw two futures for Britain: first, as an insular, protectionist island barricaded against foreign goods; second, as an extroverted trader, acting as the "world's workshop." The choice was critical. For if Britain chose the former, the self-reliant economy would soon become decrepit. We will first learn why Ricardo preferred the open-door policy and then examine the tricky question of Ricardo's "stationary state."

Recall Adam Smith's absolute-advantage trade model. Imagine him espousing his theory and insulting the French by saying, "We don't like them. They eat frogs. And I had a tedious time in Toulouse. But if they can make wine cheaper than we can, we should toast them and drink their wine. If they cannot make wine more cheaply, let's just snicker at them across the English Channel." A logical, intuitively correct statement.

To understand Ricardo's response, imagine the old television series *Gilligan's Island*. Hapless, hopelessly clumsy Gilligan is washed ashore along with the competent, self-assured skipper. Two tasks must be done: fishing and building shelter. Assume that the skipper can catch a fish dinner in 10 hours and build a thatched hut in 20, and that Gilligan usually hooks himself and takes 15 hours to catch fish and 45 hours to build a hut. By Adam Smith's logic, the skipper should move as far away from Gilligan as possible, building and fishing on his own, since he outperforms Gilligan in everything. But economists still shudder with reverence when Ricardo shows that the skipper should split the chores with Gilligan!

Let's first calculate how many fish dinners and huts they could build on their own, spending half their time fishing, the other half building. Assume that during a year, the skipper will work a total of 2,000 hours, and his younger first mate Gilligan is ordered to work 3,600. If the skipper spends 1,000 hours on fishing, he will garner 100 fish dinners; and 1,000 hours of hut building by him will produce 50 huts. Gilligan's 1,800 hours of fishing will bring 120 dinners; and 1,800 hours of hut building will make 40 huts. So the total number of dinners on the island is 220, eaten in the comfort of 90 huts.

What happens if they specialize? If the skipper spends all his time on huts, he will construct 100; if Gilligan concentrates on fish, he will return with 240 fish dinners. Thus, the island has increased output dramatically just by specializing, even though Gilligan is far less competent at both tasks!

Imagine Ricardo responding to Smith's hypothetical insult of the French by saying, "I dislike the French as much as Adam Smith did. But I do not snicker at them just because they cannot do anything as cheaply as we can. I would trade with them despite their inferiority."

The next key question is how do we know what to specialize in? Let us return to the island. Since it takes the skipper twice as long to erect a hut as it does to catch dinner, he gives up two dinners every time he builds a hut. But Gilligan, who takes three times longer to build a hut than to catch dinner, gives up three dinners every time he builds a hut. Since building huts is a smaller sacrifice for the skipper, he should build huts. Ricardo showed that people and countries should specialize in whatever leads them to give up the least. This is their "comparative advantage." And the sacrifice they make by not producing a good is their "opportunity cost." Thus, specialization is determined by whoever has the lower opportunity cost.[6]

The point of Ricardo's analysis: free trade makes it possible for households to consume more goods *regardless* of whether trading partners are more or less economically advanced. The point of Ricardo's Corn Laws position: if French farmers are willing to feed us for less than it would "cost" us to feed ourselves, let us eat French food and spend our time doing something else.

The Battle Against Protectionists

Let's say that Santa Claus began delivering free toys, cookies, and clothing all across the United States. Would the United States be better off? Yes, because we could spend our time making other things while our kids enjoy the gifts. Here's the unavoidable follow-up question: Would *everyone* be better off? No. Employees of Mattel and Hasbro might find Santa a particularly unfair trade competitor as they are laid off and sent to stand in line at state unemployment offices.

The problem confronting Ricardo and all free traders is that bakers, toy makers, and tailors would prefer that the government intercept and destroy Rudolph. They would claim that jobs depend on sewing and cobbling for ourselves. But they forget the benefits to consumers throughout the country, especially to the lower classes, for whom cheaper food means a substantially better life. Let's remember how hard life could be for typical families. We know the biblical saying "Man shall not live on bread alone." At the time Ricardo wrote and argued before Parliament, workers spent 75 percent of their wages on food and more than half their wages buying grain so that they could knead and bake dough for bread. They had just enough money left to smear on some bacon fat, mutton, or cheese and wash it down with a literal splash of tea, less than one-tenth of an ounce per day. The average diet amounted to about 2,300 calories, on par with that of hunter-gatherers in the Congo and New Guinea in 1800. They consumed about 40 percent fewer calories than we do today, stunting growth to an average of five feet, seven inches for adult males. Laborers and farmers exerted themselves six days a week, nearly every hour after the sun would rise. While Shakespeare had portrayed magical midsummers and paeans to pastoral life in *As You Like It*, Malthus noted that in the countryside "the sons and daughters of peasants will not be found such rosy cherubs in real life, as they are described to be in romances. . . . [They] are very apt to be stunted in their growth, and are a long while arriving at maturity."[7]

It was not difficult for Ricardo to see how blocking cheap grain imports injured workers and hampered their employers.

Beyond the damage to consumers, protectionists forget that jobs are created by selling goods and services to other countries. No wonder Ricardo became an enemy of the upper class by declaring that the "interest of the landlords is always opposed to the interest of every other class in the community." Despite the force of his intellect and argument, Ricardo could not persuade Parliament to relent. The Corn Laws persisted until 1846. Ricardo did, however, persuade subsequent generations of economists that protection is almost always bad for an economy as a whole, though good for a particular group. People sometimes insult economists for frequently disagreeing about policy prescriptions. George Bernard Shaw predicted, "If all economists were laid end to end, they wouldn't reach a conclusion." Yet several times during the twentieth century, thousands of economists signed petitions begging the U.S. government not to block imports. Every time the domestic economy appears stagnant, some politicians try to placate voters by threatening foreign economies. The United States imposed its highest tariffs of this century when it and the world needed free trade the most, during the Great Depression. When economies turn inward, they almost always turn downward. There is no such thing as an inward and upward spiral in economics.

During the 1980s, Japanese automakers began "voluntarily" restricting exports to the United States to avoid even harsher measures from Congress. Because the supply of Japanese cars was limited, their prices rose, and American manufacturers were able to charge more for their own cars. Economists estimated that American consumers lost $350 million as a result in the first year, and car prices rose by nearly $3,000 in the first three years of the restraints. Even if, at most, ten thousand jobs were "saved," the American economy could have paid each worker $35,000 a year just to sit at home. Instead, fewer consumers could afford cars, and those who bought had fewer dollars left to purchase other goods, reducing jobs in other sectors. "Domestic car makers could and probably should cut prices, but the government handed the American consumer to them on a platter, and they couldn't resist carving them up," charged Robert Crandall of the Brookings Institution.[8]

In 1989, automotive lobbyists beseeched the Treasury Department to classify imported minivans and SUVs as trucks. If the Treasury had given in to the pressure, tariffs on such vehicles would have increased tenfold. The British government especially protested the proposal on behalf of Land Rover. Its embassy in Washington, D.C., informed the White House that the queen herself drove a Range Rover, and that the queen would *never* drive a truck.

Abraham Lincoln put one protectionist argument pithily: "I don't know much about the tariff, but I do know if I buy a coat in America, I have a coat and America has the money—if I buy a coat in England, I have the coat and England has the money." He was right—he did not know much about the tariff. Like the mercantilists, Lincoln did not understand that a country is wealthy if it consumes lots of goods and services, not if it stockpiles metals or paper currency with portraits of presidents on them. If Lincoln buys the London coat he prefers, he cashes in some dollars for British pounds. So someone in London now has dollars. Londoners do not give up pounds just to wallpaper their flats with greenbacks. The Londoner will either (1) buy an American product or (2) trade in the dollars for pounds. If she buys an American product, Lincoln is happy because he preferred the London coat, and the Londoner is happy because she liked the American good. If she dumps her dollars, she will dump them on someone else who wants to buy American goods.[9]

What if we could just stuff a million rowboats full of American money in exchange for the *Queen Mary 2* filled with British goods? Then the Treasury could print billions of five-dollar bills. According to Lincoln's logic, we would get beautiful sweaters, teapots, and tweed suits, while the British would get paper! Although Lincoln did not realize it, this would be a wonderful deal! But the joke's on us. Lincoln did not understand that the British accept dollars *because* they can buy American goods and financial assets with them. Money may not make the world go around, but money certainly goes around the world. To stop it prevents goods from traveling from where they are produced most inexpensively to where they are desired most deeply.

The issue is not whether coats will be produced in the United States or not. It is whether we will use our valuable resources to produce goods with a higher or a lower opportunity cost. By allowing trade, nations coerce their citizens to shift resources away from low-productivity industries and toward high-productivity industries. If nations shift, households can enjoy more goods with less sacrifice.

Shifts do cause pain, however, to workers and owners in low-productivity industries. But protection often costs consumers so much, the government would do better to directly compensate the displaced workers and pay to retrain them. Protecting one steelworker's job cost more than $100,000, while "saving" a shoemaker's job cost $77,000 in the early 1980s.[10] From 2002 to 2006, punitive duties on Canadian lumber drove up the cost of a new American house by about $1,000.[11] Further, the logic of protection points toward economic stagnation. Most industries and inventions that have raised our standard of living have forced others out of their jobs. Xerox once produced an award-winning television advertisement depicting a monk working at a monastery, laboriously transcribing pages of ancient prayers. One day his superior praises his handwritten parchment but then asks for five hundred more copies! The harried monk first panics before strutting around the corner to a new copier machine, which does the job in seconds. When he delivers the five hundred copies to his superior, the head monk stares blissfully toward heaven and proclaims "it's a miracle." Can you imagine how a well-organized political action committee of monks might demand protection? Picture thousands of monks marching on Washington. How many monks could be displaced by electronic copiers?

Again, the free market is not a pain-free market. The invisible hand does not protect us the way a mother protects her child. If people prefer more stability, perhaps they should opt for protection. But the benefits of economic growth and progress do not usually come to those who huddle in the corner while their government protects the harbors from Greeks bearing gifts and goods.

The world does not admire economists for their sense of humor. But the highlight of social science satire came from the French economic pamphleteer Frédéric Bastiat during the 1840s, when France augmented import duties:

From the Manufacturers of Candles, Tapers, Lanterns, Candlesticks, Street Lamps, Snuffers, and Extinguishers, and from the Producers of Oil, Tallow, Resin, Alcohol, and Generally of Everything Connected with Lighting To the Honorable Members of the Chamber of Deputies.

Gentlemen:
    . . . We are suffering from the ruinous competition of a foreign rival who apparently works under conditions so far superior to our own for the production of light, that he is *flooding* the *domestic market* with it at an incredibly low price. . . . This rival . . . is none other than the sun. . . .

We ask you to be so good as to pass a law requiring the closing of all windows, dormers, skylights, inside and outside shutters, curtains, casements, bull's-eyes, deadlights and blinds; in short, all openings, holes, chinks, and fissures. . . .

If you shut off as much as possible all access to natural light and thereby create a need for artificial light, what industry in France will not ultimately be encouraged? . . .

If France consumes more tallow, there will have to be more cattle and sheep. . . .

The same holds true for shipping.[12]

More seriously for our time, Ricardo's analysis implies that protectionism by wealthy nations condemns less developed countries to stagnation. It seems contradictory to offer millions of dollars in foreign aid and loans while at the same time planting hurdles in front of the recipients. For example, the U.S. Congress, under pressure from domestic sugar producers, has thwarted the development programs of many Caribbean nations. Import quotas tightened from about 6 million tons of sugar in 1977 to just 1.2 million tons in 1998. Should we be surprised that many farmers south of the border found coca a more attractive crop and the underground American drug industry a more willing trading partner?

Sometimes it helps to imagine protectionist arguments on a small scale. Would a wealthy man be hurt by trading with a poor man? Should Elon Musk make his own shoes rather than buying them? If not, why would the United States be hurt by buying shoes from Malaysia? Would the nation be richer if all people were self-sufficient? If all neighborhoods were self-sufficient? Should individual counties erect trade boundaries? Few would answer yes, and the Constitution would prevent it. But why should a nation be enriched by turning away goods produced more cheaply abroad?

After World War II, many nations entered into the General Agreement on Tariffs and Trade, an organization designed to promote free trade and the forerunner of today's World Trade

Organization. Later, multinational trade negotiations took place, reducing world tariff barriers. Yet the threat of severe isolationist efforts always lurks. Protectionists gathered academic ammunition during the 1980s and 1990s, when some top theorists began poking a few holes in Ricardo's analysis. Nobel laureate and high-profile columnist Paul Krugman began asking good and tough questions. For example, typical Ricardian examples compare two countries with disparate talents and natural resources, and thereby explain why British looms might need Egyptian wool. But Krugman pointed out that after World War II, most of the increase in trade crossed the checkpoints of countries with similar incomes and resources. Today, the world's second busiest trading border lies between the United States and Canada, countries that look a great deal alike, except for a fondness for hockey on one side and for firearms on the other. In Europe, even though the Global Skills index shows Germany and Sweden almost precisely matched, Germany sells Porsches to Sweden, and Sweden ships Volvos to Germany (though the Volvo car company is Chinese-owned).[13] Why are both countries producing cars? This is not exactly Ricardo's tale. The developers of Strategic Trade Theory and New Geography Theory (building on the late-nineteenth- and early-twentieth-century work of Alfred Marshall at Cambridge and Bertil Ohlin and Eli Heckscher in Stockholm) explain that companies gain economies of scale by specializing, which drives down their average costs. But to keep costs low, a company will not try to cater to everyone. Volvo caters to people who prize safety above all. It advertises to soccer moms and dads, and doesn't worry about winning over fanboys who dream of throwing a stick shift into fifth gear. Porsche does. Porsches are faster, and Germany's traffic fatality rate is 40 percent higher than Sweden's. Ferraris are fast, too. Soon after Italy passed a law requiring seat belts, merchants in Naples began selling white T-shirts embossed with diagonal black stripes, fooling the traffic police, but probably not fooling *dame fortuna*.[14]

Companies often target a plurality of consumers in their home country, leaving foreign companies to rush in to handle the outliers. This spurs a wider variety of products, which is why American car buyers can choose among hundreds of models, made anywhere from Spartanburg, South Carolina, to Chennai, India. Citizens of the old Soviet Union, self-blockaded from free trade, could choose among only a handful of obsolete cars that would break down soon after arrival. Ronald Reagan joked about the Soviet car buyer who hands over his money and is told to come back in ten years. The buyer asks, "Morning or afternoon?" The dealer replies, "In ten years, who cares what time of day?" The buyer says, "Well, the plumber's coming at nine."

How does specialization drive down costs, even when two countries, companies, or individuals start off evenly matched? Consider Mike and Manny, two friendly surfers from the Jersey Shore. They both know how to make a foot-long sandwich; they just can't agree whether to call it a submarine, hero, gyro, po'boy, hoagie, or grinder. Regardless of the name, they know it requires buying a long bread roll, slicing meat and cheese, slapping on mustard, squirting oil and vinegar, adding a tomato, lettuce, etc. If Mike and Manny walk into the same supermarket, it will cost them the exact same amount to make the sandwich (assuming their time is worth the same). But what if Mike decides he really enjoys making sandwiches and wants to start grinding them out for friends, neighbors, and strangers? Instead of strolling down the supermarket aisles and paying the retail price, he starts buying in bulk at lower wholesale prices. He invests in his own slicing machine, and can now churn out submarine sandwiches at a much faster pace. Pretty soon, he might call himself Jersey Mike and operate the fastest-growing restaurant franchise in the United States, with 1,600 locations. Manny, who still shops in the supermarket, cannot compete on price. For a study on restaurants, I developed an index called "cost per gram of protein" and discovered that fast food and casual dining have driven down the cost of protein for consumers (grilled chicken, sliced turkey, hamburger, and fish sandwiches). One may have divergent opinions on the relative tastes of takeout joints, but the relative efficiency of places like Jersey Mike's is impressive.[15] What happens to Manny in our scenario, who started off with talent and resources equal to Mike's, but had less ardor for sliced meat? Perhaps Manny prefers performing oil changes on automobiles, invests in car lifts and tire changers, and becomes president of the Pep Boys: Manny, Moe, and Jack, with nearly one thousand locations.

Strategic Trade theorists point out that if bigger firms grow even more efficient, in some sectors only a few companies might satisfy world demand and still earn profits. The best example comes from the aircraft sector, where Airbus and Boeing divide up large commercial jetliner sales, with Embraer of Brazil picking up the smaller commuter jets. In one of the most frequently cited papers on international economics, Barbara Spencer and James Brander of Canada warn that in a sector with just a few players, a government might decide to bankroll a particular company so that the firm could wipe out its rivals. Moreover, a rival of this favored firm might shrink back and realize that it cannot win if it is in the boxing ring with a buffed-up company bolstered and subsidized with public treasure and negotiating muscle.

Whenever a market shrinks to a few players, it may begin to resemble a game in which players must guess how their foes will react. If Airbus jacks up prices, will Boeing follow along or swoop in with discounts? If AT&T throws in free international calls, will Verizon match the offer? In the 1940s, long before video games began to dominate entertainment, a young man named John Nash emerged from his childhood home in Appalachia with a brilliant mind and a tempestuous mental life (portrayed in the movie *A Beautiful Mind*). Nash latched on to game strategy as a key to understanding markets that are not perfectly competitive. Today, professors of economics, mathematics, political science, and philosophy all discuss the "prisoner's dilemma," named by Nash's doctoral adviser at Princeton, Albert Tucker. Here's how it works. If the police arrest two suspects and keep them together, they can both agree to deny the crime and might be let free, if there's no other evidence. But if the police throw them into separate cells, the suspects cannot collude, and one may decide to "rat out" the other, as they might say in a Martin Scorsese movie, in exchange for leniency. Separated prisoners must calculate, Is my compatriot loyal or a fink? Likewise, if Uber and Lyft can collude, they can maximize profits by coordinating their prices. But if they cannot collude because of antitrust laws, one of them might try to gain market share by undercutting prices.

Strategic Trade Theory and Prisoner Dilemma games do not prove that Ricardo's accounting is wrongheaded. They merely imagine certain circumstances in which other options could be optimal. Krugman, the most famous developer and practitioner, is cautious about governments nudging aside Ricardo and pursuing their own hunches. In 2009, the Obama administration was determined that the United States would "own" the solar panel industry and beat Chinese competitors. The Departments of Energy and Defense funneled more than half a billion dollars into a start-up called Solyndra, which quickly built a gleaming plant the size of five football fields in the California desert. It included robots that whistled Disney tunes—possibly the mining song from *Snow White and the Seven Dwarfs*. Within two years Solyndra collapsed into bankruptcy, and some leftover glass tubes showed up as an outdoor sculpture at the University of California, Berkeley, Botanical Garden, where at least they could provide visual entertainment, if not electrical power. Government bureaucrats could not understand or forecast the changing price for solar inputs such as polysilicon. In a sharp essay titled "Ricardo's Difficult Idea," Krugman blasts pop-policy pundits like former labor secretary Robert Reich who do not take the time to grapple with Ricardo and instead pretend that there is an obvious role for governments to reorient trade and pick winners. Krugman ends his essay, "Ricardo's idea is truly, madly, deeply difficult. But it is also utterly true, immensely sophisticated—and extremely relevant to the modern world."[16]

A Fork in the Future

Earlier we noted that Ricardo saw two futures for Britain: a bright future as an extroverted trader and a gloomy one as an isolationist. Through comparative advantage, Ricardo foresaw England emerging as the workshop of the world. And he cheerfully declared before Parliament that "this would be the happiest country in the world, and its progress in prosperity would be beyond the powers of imagination to conceive, if we got rid of two great evils—the national debt and the corn laws." Far from predicting doom, Ricardo directed his audience toward national progress: "Man from youth grows to manhood, then decays, and dies; but this is not the progress of nations. When arrived to a state of the greatest vigour, their further advance may indeed be arrested, but their natural tendency is to continue for ages, to sustain undiminished their wealth, and their population."[17]

Despite such raptures about trade, some authors persistently portray Ricardo as a pessimistic analyst, just as gloomy but more clever than that other goblin, Malthus. In fact, Ricardo did spend much time analyzing a depressing isolationist future. But we cannot forget that this future was used as a foil for the first path in order to frighten politicians into more laissez-faire policies.

What was the second path? Let us start with the sequence of steps before turning to an analysis. Accepting Malthus's population principles, Ricardo saw that (1) increasing population leads to a higher demand for food, (2) which leads to extending farming to less fertile lands, (3) which leads to higher costs in farming, (4) which leads to higher prices for food, (5) which leads to paying workers more, (6) which leads to lower profits for entrepreneurs, (7) which leads to higher payments to those who own the best lands.

To understand Ricardo's game plan, we must open the program and identify the players. First and most plentiful are workers. In accord with Malthusian principles, they multiply when wages rise, which in turn reduces their wages. Thus, over the course of a long game, payments will stay at a level high enough to sustain them, according to the customs and expectations of the day. Ricardo does not condemn them to bare biological subsistence, scrounging for scraps and tottering in rags:

> It is not to be understood that the natural price of labour, estimated even in food and necessaries, is absolutely fixed and constant. It varies at different times in the same country, and very materially differs in different countries. It essentially depends on the habits and customs of the people. An English labourer would consider his wages under their natural rate, and too scanty to support a family, if they enable him to purchase no other food than potatoes, and to live in no better habitation than a mud cabin.[18]

Second, we have tenant farmers. But note that they do *not* own the land they cultivate. Ricardo depicts them as capitalists who rent the land, hire workers, and earn profits. Instead of owning tools in a factory, the farmer owns plows. Ricardo agrees with Adam Smith that capitalists/farmers have a "restless desire" to follow market signals and shift resources and investments to the most profitable projects. Thus, they perform very important tasks for society, but not necessarily because they like society.

Third, and most powerful, Ricardo describes the wealthy landowners who rent the land to the farmers. The landowners live a leisurely life yet ultimately realize more wealth than the other players.

Ricardo revamped economic conventions and the definition of "rent." Recall the Corn Laws debate. Some claimed that corn cost more because landlords were charging farmers more in rent. Ricardo disagreed, arguing that the price rose because of wartime shortages, which lured entrepreneurs into the farming industry. As they entered, landlords found more capitalists knocking at their doors and bidding up the rental price of land. Thus, land rents were high because the price of corn was high, not vice versa. When blockades tumbled, so would the price of corn, and landlords would have to charge lower rents. In modern economic terms, the desire for renting land is a "derived demand," determined by the supply and demand for corn.

Ricardo next argued that landlords can charge rents only if there is a demand for their property. Some landowners' property will be more fertile than others', and rent levels will be established on the basis of this difference in fertility. If Al owns a plot of land that yields one thousand tons of grain, and Joan owns a plot nearby that yields only five hundred tons, Al will be able to charge a higher rate to a capitalist farmer.

Rents arise because all land is not created equal:

When in the progress of society, land of the second degree of fertility is taken into cultivation, rent immediately commences on that of the first quality, and the amount of that rent will depend on the difference in the quality of these two portions of land. When land of the third quality is taken into cultivation, rent immediately rises on the second, and is regulated as before by the differences in their productive powers. At the same time, the rent of the first quality will rise.[19]

If Ricardo is right, rents emerge as populations grow. When few people need food, they can raise enough by farming only the best land. As mouths multiply, farmers begin cultivating the second-best land. Because the second-quality land produces less, the owner of the better land can now charge rent. Wages and a normal profit on the secondary land will determine the price of grain. And since costs are lower on better land, a surplus exists. The landlord takes the surplus.

Why did Ricardo's vision incite frowns and fright? According to it, the path of economic growth ended at a ditch, literally and figuratively. For a while capitalists could expand industrial production and even pay workers higher wages. But soon the happy workers would breed more workers, bidding down wages. How would England feed the hungry crowds? By farming more land. But remember, the additional lands would be less productive and most costly to cultivate, since farmers began by exploiting the richest land first.

The price of grain would rise. But the capitalist would not profit, because he must pay the workers more so that they can survive. If resources are "to be divided between the farmer and the labourer, the larger the proportion to the latter, the less will remain for the former."[20] Furthermore, the landlords who own the best lands collect higher rents when farmers begin tilling inferior land. Who wins? The landlords. Who loses? The capitalists. Who stays the same? The workers, although ultimately starvation could strike when farmers exhaust the lands. Ricardo calls the somber plight the "stationary state." Literally, hunger forces society to cultivate even ditches. Figuratively, the capitalists and workers are left waving their arms and shouting for help from within a ditch.

Why does Ricardo diverge so strongly from Adam Smith's merry dream? Smith generally assumes that agriculture will not decay into low productivity and that industry will continually grow more productive. In modern terms, Smith sees constant returns to agriculture and increasing returns to industry, which allows all parties to prosper. Ricardo depicts constant returns to industry and decreasing returns to agriculture. Ricardo does hold some hope that technology will periodically rescue the economy. The tendency for profits to fall "is happily checked at repeated intervals by the improvements in machinery, connected with the production of necessaries, as well as by the discoveries in the science of agriculture which enable us to relinquish a portion of labour before required, and, therefore, to lower the price of the prime necessity of the labourer."[21] Still, we cannot confidently depend on technology always to save us.

But remember Dickens's *A Christmas Carol*. The ghost tells the tale of the gruesome future Christmas, defiled by hunger, dread, and despair. Scrooge timorously asks, Is this the way Christmas must be? With the ugly clang of chains and a haunting, raspy wheeze, the ghost leaves tomorrow to Scrooge.

Ricardo is not the goblin some depict, but more like the ghost from *A Christmas Carol*, warning England that insular, greedy policies will bring harder and greedier times, while an open, extroverted trading position can promise happier days. "I contend for free trade in corn, on the ground that while trade is free, and corn cheap, profits will not fall however great be the accumulation of capital," he wrote. Economic growth confronts no ditches. And although obstacles arise from "the scarcity, and consequent high value of food and other raw produce . . . let these be supplied from abroad in exchange for manufactured goods, and it is difficult to say where the limit is at which you would cease to accumulate wealth."[22]

Ricardo's analyses proved fertile for criticism and extension. Like Malthus, he underestimated the "restraint" of workers. They did not propagate as quickly as he feared. Milton Friedman, as noted previously, holds a pencil as his emblem of economic freedom. Sometimes the classical economists sound as if they should be holding rabbits' feet—not for luck, but to symbolize their perception of man's breeding propensity. Like Malthus, Ricardo bitterly opposed the Poor Laws because they ultimately brought hunger, insisting that "every friend to the poor must ardently wish for their abolition."

Ricardo's blasts at landlords and depiction of rents came to the United States in earthy and fervent language through Henry George's *Progress and Poverty* in 1879. George, a journalist with messianic visions, led disciples in the "single-tax move-ment." Incensed by undeserved gain, George condemned landowners who simply collect rents while others struggle to generate wealth. Proposing a massive tax on land to absorb rents, George divined with more verve than any Old Testa-ment prophet that it would abolish poverty; tame the ruthless passions of greed; dry up the springs of vice and misery; light in dark places the lamp of knowledge; give new vigor to inven-tion and a fresh impulse to discovery; substitute political strength for political weakness; and make tyranny and anar-chy impossible.[23]

There are several problems with the proposal. First, econo-mists distinguish between "economic rent," which Ricardo discussed, and the simple rent that tenants pay landlords. Ac-cording to Ricardo, economic rent is a payment beyond what is necessary to keep land or labor or capital in its present use. Since land can be used only for grain in Ricardo's analysis, nothing has to be paid to keep it as farmland. Owners have no choice but to use it for grain. Therefore any payment to land-lords is economic rent. Baseball great Willie Mays used to say that he would play for free. If he would, any payment he re-ceived would be economic rent, because it was beyond what was necessary to get him to play.

Movie stars receive economic rents also. Let's say that Sylves-ter Stallone constantly makes the choice between acting and working as a professional seamster. If he received less than $30,000 per movie for acting, he would switch to sewing hems and cuffs. Thus if a new movie, *Rocky Meets Rambo II* in 3-D, paid him $5 million, we would say that $30,000 was "transfer earnings" and $4,970,000 was economic rent. Maybe Henry George would have been brave enough to take away all the rent.

The point is that part of a payment that keeps land, labor, or capital in a particular use is not economic rent, but transfer earnings. Any payment above that is economic rent. There-fore, if a property owner would convert his land into a carnival tenting ground if he did not receive $1,000 per month from tenants, the first $1,000 he receives is not economic rent. Beware of the ambiguity of the language. What apartment tenants usually call "rent" is not economic rent unless it exceeds the necessary payment. But how would Henry George know which part of the total payment is economic rent to be taxed? Here he would need even more heavenly help than he has revealed.

The single-tax-on-land movement also faces moral hurdles to either leap or transcend. If fairness demands taxing economic rents, fairness requires taxing economic rents from land, labor, and capital. How would George distinguish between Stallone's transfer earnings and economic rents? What about salaries of senators and famous economists? Not everyone is as honest as Willie Mays.

Although George never accomplished his mission, he became famous throughout the United States and England, where devotees set up single-tax societies to spread the good word. And the good book *Progress and Poverty* spread more quickly than laborers multiply. Despite the movement's ultimate decline, George fans can proudly point to property taxes as a source of state and local finance. But they cannot point as confidently as they could sixty years ago. George overestimated the future importance of rents and rental income. Governments at every level have grown tremendously in the last century. Even if governments could take all rents without rebellion or severe recession, rents would not come close to covering expenses. In 1929, property rents accounted for about 6 percent of national income. The percentage has steadily dropped to well under 1 percent today. Whereas property taxes once provided 65 percent of state and local budgets, they now supply about 17 percent.

Over the past twenty years, as brick-and-mortar retail stores have lost business to online merchants, many pedestrians walk past empty storefronts. Vacant storefronts used to signal a recession. Now they represent technology and changing tastes (and a lack of imagination for alternative uses). It is hard for a mom-and-pop hardware store to compete with same-day home delivery from Home Depot and Lowe's. In a bizarre, neo-Georgian manner, some cities like San Francisco and Oakland attempt to battle empty storefronts by raising taxes on land-owners. Civic leaders portray the landlords as greedy asset-sitters, waiting for a big payday. Meanwhile, the neighborhood looks glum and gritty. The landlords, of course, think of them-selves as victims of structural change who would be delighted to find solvent tenants in an era when once-famous names like Forever 21, Borders, and RadioShack have folded. In San Fran-cisco between 2015 and 2018, despite a strong economy and an overall job growth of 13 percent, the number of retail jobs slumped by 8 percent.[24] Landowners also point out that city regulations often prohibit them from leasing to viable tenants—for example, restricting many storefronts from converting to restaurants. In 2019, a falafel restaurant in San Francisco used the city's convoluted rules to try to prohibit a competitor from opening up a new shop nearby.[25] Regardless of the falafel wars and the arguments about vacancy taxes, George might find it amusing to hear that his progeny, instead of levying high taxes on rents, are taxing the *absence* of rents!

If George caught a Ricardian pitch and ran amok, Ricardo's contemporary Malthus tried to bat it back. On the Corn Laws question, Malthus accepted much of Ricardo's analysis regard-ing rent and diminishing returns from farming. But he pos-ited a four-part rebuttal. First, he maintained that the Corn Laws actually induced more domestic grain output because they boosted grain prices. Second, Malthus thought grain was too important a commodity to be left to foreign producers. Third, he concluded that higher grain prices actually in-creased wages to workers, since workers are paid according to the price of grain. Malthus thus claimed that higher wages would more than compensate for higher food prices. Ricardo disagreed. In modern terms, he thought that higher "nomi-nal" wages would not be higher "real" wages; that is, they would not allow laborers to buy any more than they could before. To Ricardo, Malthus's argument sounded like the dictator who, smiling and winking at the masses, promises a doubling of salaries. The crowd cheers. They salute the five-story posters of the despot and rejoice. The next day they go to the stores and find that the employees of the stores spent the whole night marking up the prices by 100 percent.

Fourth, Malthus rather feebly defended the landlord by complimenting Ricardo, who had

> now become, by his talents and industry, a considerable landlord; and a more honourable and excellent man, a man who for the qualities of his head and heart more entirely deserves what he has earned . . . I could not point out in the whole circle of landlords.[26]

Flattery got Malthus nowhere, except perhaps an invitation to Ricardo's country retreat. For Ricardo never said that landlords intentionally suck the lifeblood from a nation. Like vampires, they are compelled by forces outside their power. Ironically, Ricardo, the lavish landlord, angered the landlords; while Malthus, the modest teacher, infuriated the humble folk.

Ricardo versus Malthus on Gluts and Method

The Ricardo-Malthus show featured more than landlord debates, however. The two economists also disagreed about economic depressions. Malthus believed in "general gluts," an ugly phrase meaning that business sometimes supplies more goods and services than people want to buy. Ricardo would have sooner believed in a Godwinian utopia than in general gluts. Ricardo embraced Say's Law, named for the Frenchman Jean-Baptiste Say, who proved logically that general gluts were fantasies. (Scientists love to discover laws and graphical curves, perhaps because custom lets the laws and curves be named for the discoverer. In economics, we also have the Lorenz curve, Okun's Law, and Harberger triangles.)

What is Say's Law? Workers and owners of land and capital are paid wages, rents, and interest that add up to the sale price of the product. Every cost in manufacturing becomes someone's income. Therefore, consumers—who are simply laborers, capitalists, and landlords after they get home from work—can afford to buy all that has been produced. Say's Law is generally known by the slogan "Supply creates its own demand."

Say never forbade "partial gluts," which occur when consumers decide to purchase less of a particular product. Eventually, the seller will erase the partial glut by lowering the price. But to Say, Smith, Hume, and Ricardo, a general glut remains impossible, because the consumers must do something with their money, and people have infinite desires for more material goods.

Malthus cried nay. First of all, he noticed that in the post–Napoleonic Wars depression of 1818, unemployment seemed very high. But how could he invade the tight circle that Say drew and Ricardo emboldened? He began by tracing the circle and agreeing that consumers *could* buy all the goods offered, but what if they did not feel like spending all their money? What if they preferred to save or hoard? Would this not leak out of Say's circle of buying and leave the merchants sitting on top of unsold merchandise?

Ricardo swiftly struck back. If consumers save, they keep their money in banks, which then lend to those who do want to spend money on consumer goods or investment goods. Either way, someone is spending. Even Adam Smith knew that: "What is annually saved is as regularly consumed as what is annually spent, and nearly in the same time too; but it is *consumed* by a different set of people."[27] Ricardo then scolded his friend "Mr. Malthus," who "never appears to remember" this simple point.

Though he convinced few economists, Malthus still sensed

a gap between savings and investment. To cure a general glut, he proposed "the employment of the poor in roads and public works, and a tendency among landlords and persons in property to build . . . and to employ workmen and menial servants" as "the means most within our power and most directly calculated to remedy the evils."[28]

But Ricardo responded that Malthus's *Principles* present "hardly a page" without "some fallacy."

Even if Ricardo won the day, a century later, John Maynard Keynes resurrected the loser. In a resplendent paean, Keynes paid tribute to the "first of the Cambridge economists" for his theory on depressions and at the same time denounced Ricardo: "If only Malthus, instead of Ricardo, had been the parent stem from which nineteenth-century economics proceeded, what a much wiser and richer place the world would be today!"[29] Keynes surely exaggerates here in both the extent of Ricardo's dominance (he "conquered England as completely as the Holy Inquisition conquered Spain") and the similarity between his own analysis and Malthus's. Though Keynes and Malthus both rejected Say's Law, Malthus made little headway relating saving to investment and urged public works to slow investment, not to stimulate sales of goods, as Keynes did. Nonetheless, if Keynes says Malthus inspired him, who are we to disagree?

The real difference between Malthus and Ricardo did not revolve around gluts, rents, or protection, but rather around method. Both lived in an age of scientific discovery. Both searched for cause-and-effect links. Both predicted what would occur because of these links. But Ricardo focused more intensely on the intricate sequence of steps along the way. Malthus seemed content to find a general principle and then apply it to the world. Recall Ricardo's careful seven-step path to the stationary state. Neither Smith nor Malthus constructed such rigorous models. Under the guidance of James Mill, Ricardo attempted long, deductive chains of reasoning. He wanted to derive propositions as certain as Euclidean geometry or Newtonian mechanics. Sometimes his assumptions or first premises were simply wrong. But given those premises, his theory was impregnable. Impregnable, yes; useful, perhaps not. Keynes and Joseph Schumpeter both accused Ricardo of choosing assumptions or examples that ensured the result he desired. Schumpeter called this the "Ricardian vice." And whom else did Schumpeter accuse of suffering from the Ricardian vice? Keynes.

Ricardo discussed his methodological differences amiably: "Our difference may in some respect, I think, be ascribed to your considering my book as more practical than I intended it to be. My object was to elucidate principles, and to do this I imagined strong cases." Ricardo also preferred long-run analysis to short-run descriptions, telling Malthus, "You have always in your mind the immediate and temporary effects of particular changes—whereas I put these . . . aside, and fix my whole attention on the permanent state of things which will result from them."[30] No wonder correspondence shows that Ricardo refused to grant Malthus's empirical observations. They either did not fit into Ricardo's strong case or appeared to be fleeting. But because Malthus never constructed sophisticated analytical models, he gained the reputation for fickleness. His contemporary Robert Torrens wrote that "in the leading questions of economical science, Mr. Malthus scarcely ever embraced a principle which he did not subsequently abandon."[31] Later, Keynes earned the same reputation, permitting his most acerbic critics to praise his eclecticism—in choosing the worst from the best.

Despite the attacks by Keynes and Schumpeter, exalted economists including Karl Marx, Léon Walras, Alfred Marshall, and Knut Wicksell have declared Ricardo's preeminence. One prominent twentieth-century student of economic method proclaimed that "if economics is essentially an engine of analysis, a method of thinking rather than a body of substantial results, Ricardo literally invented the technique of economics."[32]

One gets the impression that when Malthus died, some

came to the funeral to mourn, others to make sure he really was dead. Ricardo attracted more admirers for his intellect, for his kindness, and for his character. In his last year, his fifty-first, he battled slavery proponents and denounced their cause as a stain on the nation's character. Here was a wealthy man who could have spent his life luxuriating in the country and traveling throughout the world. Instead he used his leisure to study perplexing questions and derive abstract, abstruse, and, he thought, correct solutions. Upon teaching himself about the world, he taught others by book, by newspaper, and by parliamentary speech. His law of comparative advantage and theory of economic rent still appear in textbooks, as persuasive and important as ever.

Although Ricardo's theories are taught throughout the world, it is the European nations that may best test his legacy. In a bold effort to knit themselves together so tightly that they might avoid a replay of the two world wars that began on their soil in the twentieth century, European Union states fulfilled their 1992 pledge to dismantle all remaining trade barriers among themselves, giving Ricardo a partial victory. For a complete victory, the European Union countries must also keep their second pledge: not to erect fortresses on their shores that would prevent countries in the Americas, Africa, Asia, and post-Brexit United Kingdom from participating in their free-for-all program. So far, the results are mixed. Though U.S. financial firms have made strong inroads (often by merging with European entities), somehow European farmers continue to win special favors to the annoyance of American, Australian, and Latin American agriculture. Despite trumpeting support for struggling Caribbean and African farmers, E.U. nations dump millions of tons of subsidized sugar onto the world market, depressing prices; German potato farmers protest imports of foreign spuds; and French winegrowers fight to keep out South African chardonnays. The most divisive issue might be bananas! Former U.S. secretary of state Madeleine Albright was once interrupted during a tense meeting over battle lines in Kosovo and noted, "I never in my life thought I would spend so much time on bananas." Europe protects its former colonies in Africa from the banana growers of the Caribbean and Latin America. So far, bananas have been a strong weapon against free trade. Ricardo would be disappointed but hopeful. If there's a way to gauge the world's attitude to Ricardo's legacy, it is this: follow the bananas.

CHAPTER V

The Stormy Mind of John Stuart Mill

Almost all renowned British economists since Adam Smith have been linked through close friendships. Remember that Smith's good friend David Hume was a "godfather" to Thomas Malthus, who was an intimate friend of David Ricardo, whose comrade James Mill encouraged his economics. James begot John Stuart Mill. A slight break occurs since Mill did not befriend his successor Alfred Marshall. But Marshall learned from Mill's works (and from the economist F. Y. Edgeworth, nephew of Ricardo's friend Maria Edgeworth) and then taught Keynes, whose ideas dominated Western economics until the end of the twentieth century.

The life of John Stuart Mill presents a fascinating personal history shaped by the force of ideas. Through him, we see the philosophical conflicts underlying classical economics. Although economists sometimes debate the originality of his contributions to economic theory, all admit that Mill asks troubling questions about the ethical foundations of economics and capitalism.

One of old-time comedian Jimmy Durante's most famous lines was "Everybody wants to get into the act." Nearly every intellectual after Isaac Newton wanted to get into the scientific act and discover precise answers to their questions. Smith, Ricardo, and Malthus wanted to be the Isaac Newtons of economics by discovering laws of nature. The law of comparative advantage, Say's Law, and the law of population all arose in this period. Around the same time, Jeremy Bentham sought to be the Newton of the moral universe, a *moral* scientist. James Mill fell under the spell of the potions brewed by moral scientists as well as by economic scientists. In love with the taste of Bentham's ideas, James Mill forced his son to drink.

Born in London in 1806, John Stuart still had the taste for mother's milk when his rigorous education began. James taught him Greek at the age of three. By eight, the boy had read Plato, Xenophon, and Diogenes in Greek and begun learning Latin. His mother was not a warm figure to her nine children. With baby John Stuart's premature knowledge of the classics and her frigidity, he might have mistaken her for the Venus de Milo. Between the ages of eight and twelve, Mill exhausted well-stocked libraries, reading Aristotle and Aristophanes and mastering calculus and geometry. During his spare time he was forced to teach Latin to his brothers and sisters. Any hobbies? He read histories. Any friends? Not a one.

At fourteen, his father began strolling with John Stuart through the woods while delivering lectures on Ricardo's economics: "He expounded each day a portion of the subject, and I gave him next day a written account of it, which he made me rewrite over and over again until it was clear, precise, and tolerably complete."[1] Imagine the poor boy trying to scribble notes on Ricardo's complex theories while his father leads him down wooded paths.

Because of such rigors, which turned Mill into an intellectual thoroughbred and an emotional hobbyhorse, he remained humble, denying that he had an unusually quick mind, accurate memory, or energetic character. In "all these natural gifts I am rather below than above par; what I could do, could assuredly be done by any boy or girl of average capacity." Nor was Mill sure he knew any more than other children until his father took him for a walk through Hyde Park and assured him so. But do not feel proud, James warned: anybody could have done it—given a father like him. John Stuart was both the beneficiary and the victim of such a father, who

gave his son "an advantage of a quarter century" over his contemporaries.[2]

But this advantage robbed from his heart what it had added
to his brain. What could be more pathetic than his remark "I
was never a boy"?[3] He socialized with his father's friends, none
of whom played tag or other children's games, and appeared
as solemn as a loser on election day. James sent his son to
France for a year, where he stayed with Bentham's brother,
and briefly with Jean-Baptiste Say (the economist who taught
that "supply creates its own demand"). As spring 1822 turned
the thoughts of other boys his age to young lasses in meadows,
it excited only Mill's intellect, for it was then that he discovered Jeremy Bentham's utilitarianism in the three-volume
Treatise on Legislation.

> When I laid down the last volume . . . I had become a differ-
> ent being. The "principle of utility" understood as Bentham
> understood it, and applied in the manner in which he ap-
> plied it . . . fell exactly into place as the keystone which held
> together the detached and fragmentary component parts of
> my knowledge and beliefs. It gave unity to my conception of
> things. I now had opinions; a creed, a doctrine, a philoso-
> phy; in one among the best senses of the word, a religion;
> the inculcation and diffusion of which could be made the
> principal outward purpose of a life. And I had a grand con-
> ception laid before me of changes to be effected in the con-
> dition of mankind through that doctrine.[4]

For the next few years Mill joined his boyhood "friends"
James Mill and David Ricardo in preaching the Benthamite
gospel through the *Westminster Review.* The *Review*

> made considerable noise in the world, and gave a recog-
> nized status, in the arena of opinion and discussion, to the
> Benthamite type of Radicalism, out of all proportion to the
> number of adherents. . . . The air of strong conviction with

which they wrote, when scarcely anyone else seemed to have an equally strong faith in as definite a creed . . . made the so-called Bentham school in philosophy and politics fill a greater place in the public mind than it had held before.[5]

By the time he reached adulthood, Mill had a slight build and a bulge on his forehead over his left eye. His beady, gray eyes overlooked a prominent beak, which itself overshadowed thin lips that emitted an even thinner voice. After losing his hair, he gained the look of the sort of parsimonious chemist who would dispense morphine only one tiny pill at a time. Soon enough this odd visage would shake, shudder, and reveal the turmoil below.

Jeremy Bentham: Pleasure, Pain, and Arithmetic

What was this Benthamite gospel that attracted such a persuaded and persuasive flock? Just as nature placed the earth under the force of gravity, he said, nature "has placed mankind under the governance of two masters, pain and pleasure."[6] From these laws Bentham discovered both a descriptive and a prescriptive religion. Since all human beings like pleasure and hate pain (masochists notwithstanding, although they prefer pain only because it gives them pleasure), they choose to do that which gives them pleasure. In its prescriptive chapters, the doctrine implores human beings to choose the path of pleasure. So far this sounds like fun, like the hedonism of the ancient Greek Aristippus. But Bentham adds one ethical caveat: when choices affect others, individuals should choose the alternative that maximizes the total pleasure of all. "Greatest happiness for the greatest number" is the cry of the utilitarian movement. And responsible government should engrave this in legislators' minds.

In words that made democrats misty-eyed, Bentham argued that all people count equally when determining happiness. If the king stubs one toe, this counts half as much as his serving wench Jane stubbing two. If giving Jane a bandage helps her more than it hurts the king, she gets the bandage. No wonder aristocrats prayed for Bentham to stub his tongue before he could spread this gospel.

Still, this formulation was not mathematically precise enough for the Newton of the moral universe. Bentham devised a method of quantifying the amount of pleasure and pain, called the *felicific calculus*. As we all know, some experiences are more pleasurable or painful than others. Why? Any single experience can be measured by four factors: (1) intensity, (2) duration, (3) certainty, and (4) propinquity. People prefer long, certain vacations to the mere possibility of a weekend off. Hilarious comedians bring more pleasure than mildly amusing ones.

Bentham apparently gave himself so much pleasure devising this calculus that he prolonged it by adding three more factors: fecundity, impurity, and the effect on others. Some pleasures lead to more pleasures. If by attending a summer frolic, Mark increases the chances of making new friends, the frolic shows the fifth felicific factor, fecundity. If the frolic might bring pain, because Mark befriends the football player's wife, the frolic shows the sixth factor, impurity (the chance it has of producing opposite sensations). Finally, if many people will laugh when the football player rearranges Mark's face, we must consider their pleasure.

With these tools Bentham added complex instructions. At first glance they remind one of the assembly directions that accompany certain do-it-yourself Chinese furniture, which might as well be written in the original language, because indecipherable Mandarin is at least prettier than unintelligible English. A closer look, though, reveals that Bentham actually made sense:

Begin with any one person . . . and take an account,

1. Of the value of each distinguishable pleasure which appears to be produced by it in the first instance.
2. Of the value of each pain which appears to be produced by it in the first instance.
3. Of the value of each pleasure which appears to be produced by it after the first. This constitutes the fecundity of the first pleasure and the impurity of the first pain.
4. Of the value of each pain which appears to be produced by it after the first. This constitutes the fecundity of the first pain and the impurity of the first pleasure.
5. Sum up all the values of all the pleasures on one side, and those of all the pains on the other. The balance, if it be on the side of pleasure, will give the good tendency of the act upon the whole, with respect to the interests of that individual person; if on the side of pain, the bad tendency of it upon the whole.
6. Take an account of the number of persons whose interests appear to be concerned; and repeat the above process with respect to each. Sum up the numbers expressive of degrees of good tendency . . . do this again with respect to each individual, in regard to whom the tendency of it is bad. . . . Take the balance; which, if on the side of pleasure, will give the general good tendency of the act . . . if on the side of pain, the general evil tendency with respect to the same community.[7]

Bentham must have taken step 3, long-term pleasures, quite seriously. He bequeathed his body to the University of London, to be wheeled out for major administrative meetings. His body, post-taxidermy, still resides there. Unfortunately, some sporting, pleasure-seeking students stole his head—which just shows how difficult it is to measure fecundity and purity.

Reading Bentham satisfied John Stuart Mill's cravings for

scientific precision and gave him a new way of looking at social intercourse. He quickly joined the fight for Bentham and his Philosophical Radicals, who included some prominent Parliament members as well as writers. Ironically, these champions of pleasure were about as joyful as Kafka.

In politics, Bentham's Radicals battled bravely for democracy and free speech. From free speech comes truth, they declared. They fought the Stamp Act, which taxed periodicals, and opposed various restrictions on assembly. Mill was briefly arrested for passing out birth control literature, and later in life he would raise the banner of women's suffrage. On Ricardian grounds they attacked the Corn Laws. Jeremy Bentham denounced the barbaric English prison system, arguing that punishment should be used only instrumentally, to deter, not to wreak vengeance masquerading as justice. After all, a criminal is just a person who decides that crime pays, Bentham submitted. The real answer is to adjust the costs. Although Bentham once proposed that the motto of the government be "Be quiet," the Radicals were ready to abandon laissez-faire whenever the benefits outweighed the costs: "I have not, I never had, nor ever shall have, any horror sentimental or anarchical, of the hand of government. I leave it to Adam Smith . . . to talk of invasions of natural liberty."[8] Their god was utility, not an invisible hand, even if their god usually worked through the invisible hand.

Incidentally, their god certainly was not the one associated with churches, synagogues, and mosques. James Mill simply could not reconcile an evil world with a good maker. John Stuart Mill vividly recalled his father's atheistic rantings.

I have a hundred times heard him say, that all ages and nations have represented their gods as wicked, in a constantly increasing progression, that mankind have gone on adding trait after trait till they reached the most perfect conception of wickedness which the human mind can devise, and have called this God, and prostrated themselves before it.[9]

During the 1820s and 1830s, the Radicals won many political wars and skirmishes, far beyond anyone's expectations, including John Stuart Mill's. To support himself, Mill joined his father as a clerk at the East India Company in 1823. Like Malthus and Keynes, who would later work for the government's India Office, Mill never made it to India and never learned Hindi or Sanskrit. He did work hard without much distraction, breakfasting at ten o'clock each morning on a single boiled egg, and eating nothing else until the working day was over.[10] During the same year he joined the company, Mill founded the Utilitarian Society, where he and other young Benthamites would debate and study regularly for long periods of time with intensity and in propinquity. Their chief opponents were romantics, utopians, and socialists, who all seemed too high in the clouds of Coleridge's poetry to win earthly debates.

The Thinking Machine Conks Out

During this period Mill may have taken Benthamite precision too far and completely forgotten the ultimate goal, happiness: "The description so often given of a Benthamite, as a mere reasoning machine, though extremely inapplicable to most . . . was . . . not altogether untrue of me."[11]

He had his midlife crisis at the age of twenty. The reasoning machine broke, and springs, gaskets, and wires flew about. For years he had "what might truly be called an object in life; to be a reformer." Yet one winter day in 1826, he was "in a dull state of nerves . . . one of those moods when what is pleasure at other times, becomes insipid or indifferent." He asked himself a fateful question and received a devastating answer:

Suppose that all your objects in life were realized; that all the changes in institutions and opinions which you are looking forward to, could be completely effected at this very instant: would this be a great joy and happiness to you? And an irrepressible self-consciousness distinctly answered, "No!" At this my heart sank within me: the whole foundation on which my life was constructed fell down. All my happiness was to have been found in the continual pursuit of this end. The end had ceased to charm, and how could there ever again be any interest in the means? I seemed to have nothing left to live for.[12]

For six months he despaired, often contemplating suicide. He simply had never developed any human feelings. He saw only the veins in flowers. While romantics wore roseate glasses, his eyes stripped the world of all tints and hues, like turpentine. Years later Nietzsche would announce that "God is dead." For Mill, robbed of love by a frigid father and left with nothing but reason, man was dead. About his father, Mill wrote: "For passionate emotions of all sorts, and for everything which has been said or written in exaltation of them, he professed the greatest contempt. He regarded them as a form of madness."[13]

In an age of reason, Mill longed for passion. Mill was not so much the dupe of rationalist philosophers but the victim of their incompetent, zealous disciples. Hume, for one, insisted that reason always be the "slave of the passions." Indeed, even Bentham introduced reason only as a method of comparing passions, not replacing them.

Psychoanalysts have quite a case before them. Perhaps Mill was tortured by guilt springing from a repressed death wish directed against his tyrannical, inescapable father. But Mill was worse off than the Greek hero. At least Oedipus had a loving mother. In his three-hundred-page autobiography, Mill does not even mention his mother! An early draft suggests why:

A really warm hearted mother would in the first place have made my father a totally different being and in the second would have made the children growing up loving and being loved. But my mother with the very best intentions only knew how to pass her life in drudging for them. . . . I thus grew up in the absence of love and in the presence of fear.[14]

His mother did not leave an autobiography. Who knows whether marriage to James Mill depleted her ability to love? Suffice it to say that the Mill home was not a place to drop by for hot chicken soup and warm company.

Rebirth as Romantic

Just as Mill floundered in the intellectual tide called rationalism, he was saved by an undertow called romanticism. In his *Birth of Tragedy*, Nietzsche depicted two powerful forces clashing in the human psyche: Apollonian and Dionysian. Apollo is the spirit of reason, order, and Mozart symphonies. Dionysius is the spirit of caprice, emotion, and Puccini operas. When eighteenth-century rationalism drove Mill to despair, he turned to the poetry of Wordsworth and even Coleridge. Wordsworth's lush portraits of natural beauty finally inspired feelings of joy and the discovery of imagination. The world finally seemed sensuous. By embracing beauty, Mill could battle to drive outward the narrow borders of his mind and the imperial reign of his father.

Like Coleridge's ancient mariner, Mill embarked on an intellectual odyssey, visiting Carlyle and the French philosopher Auguste Comte, whose empirical emphasis influenced Mill. Sometimes the mariner seemed to go overboard in praising his new godfathers and rejecting the old ones. After befriending Mill, an arrogant Comte demanded financial support. Mill acquiesced and even asked friends to give money to Comte. After about a year, the charity stopped. Instead of thanking his benefactors, Comte mailed a nasty letter to Mill lecturing him on the duty to support penniless pundits. Although Mill was sometimes known as the "Saint of Rationalism," this episode in his life must be headed "The Saint as Sap."[15]

After Mill's father died in 1836, John Stuart began publishing articles that showed how far he had sailed from the Philosophical Radicals. His 1838 essay "Bentham" savaged Benthamism for impoverishing the spirit. Spiritual perfection should be a personal goal in its own right, regardless of pain and pleasure. Bentham was better when he stuck to legislative questions, rather than personal morality, Mill added condescendingly. Two years later, Mill glorified Coleridge beyond reason.[16]

His father's death was probably both liberating and troubling for Mill. Gertrude Himmelfarb reports that on James's death, John Stuart suffered a "brain fever," leaving him with a twitching eye. Placing the son on the psychoanalyst's couch again, could the twitch have resulted from attempts to repress relief at his master's passing?[17]

The odyssey was not just intellectual and aesthetic. For the first time, John Stuart Mill fell in love—balding head over tattered heels in love. Unfortunately, Harriet Taylor was married with children. But this did not stop Mill, who was still Benthamite enough to pursue pleasure. Their "affair" took the form of a nonsexual ménage à trois, with secret rendezvous at the London Zoo near the rhino exhibit. Harriet lived with her husband, but Mill visited when John Taylor was out, and Harriet spent many summer weekends with Mill. This odd arrangement lasted from 1830 until 1851, when Mill and Harriet married. John Taylor had died two years before, but Mill thought that a long engagement would sanitize a scandalous liaison. Mill attributed almost all his famous works to Harriet's wisdom. She was a goddess to him. If Mill himself resembled a squinty-eyed pharmacist, Harriet as a young woman had the large-eyed gaze of a Disney princess. A dinner companion described her body as moving with an "undulating grace," her lovely head sitting atop a "swan-like throat and complexion like a pearl." Her low, sweet voice created an "engrossing" presence.[18]

All the warmth and strength Mill had longed for in his marble mother, he found in a loving wife:

> Her mind was the same perfect instrument, piercing to the very heart and marrow of the matter; always seizing the essential idea or principle. The same exactness and rapidity of operation, pervading as it did her sensitive as well as her mental faculties, would, with her gifts of feeling and imagination, have fitted her to be a consummate artist, as her fiery and tender soul and her vigorous eloquence would certainly have made her a great orator, and her profound knowledge of human nature and discernment and sagacity in practical life, would, in the times in which such a *carrière* was open to women, have made her eminent among the rulers of mankind. Her intellectual gifts did but minister to a moral character at once the noblest and the best balanced which I have ever met with in life.[19]

Many of Mill's friends thought he was hallucinating. Historians still argue among themselves in assessing Harriet's contributions. One thing is certain: Mill felt privileged that such a beauty would choose to love him, and she ended up influencing him immeasurably.

With Harriet in hand and romance spinning in his head, we might expect Mill to have lived out his life composing odes to Grecian urns. But having traveled the world metaphorically and literally, our romantic hero returns home—more of a man than he was before. Home was Benthamism. But Mill would alter and improve it. The rest of his writings and political career reflect an enlightened utilitarianism. Mill insisted that the greatest happiness depends on more than mere pleasure. The joy of sensing a Beethoven symphony or Michelangelo masterpiece is more than just pleasure. Great works and deeds bring joy by lifting the spirit. Bentham had suggested that poker is as good as poetry, if the pleasure given is equal. Mill disagreed. Switching metaphors, Mill countered that he would rather be a discontented Socrates than a well-fed pig. Mill enhances utilitarianism by invoking Platonic virtues of honor, dignity, and self-development. For this reason, Mill became an ardent advocate of public education. To him, statecraft must be soulcraft.

In 1848, Mill published his chief work on economics, *Principles of Political Economy*. For decades it dominated the book market like the monopolies Mill discussed within its pages. Oxford relied on the *Principles* until 1919, probably because its successor was written by Marshall, a Cambridge man. Indeed, the works of all the great economists illuminate long paths. From 1776 to 1976 just five books reigned over economics in nearly unbroken succession: Smith's *Wealth of Nations*, Ricardo's *Principles*, Mill's *Principles*, Marshall's *Principles*, and Samuelson's *Economics*. What they lack in imaginative titles, they make up in endurance.

Mill's Method

Mill's struggle with rationalism and romanticism finds its way into his *Principles* when he discusses economic methods. James Mill, following Hobbes, thought of social science with the same precision with which one performs geometric proofs. From general premises, James Mill deduced specific conclusions and policies. The general premises usually centered on "laws" of human nature such as self-interest. There could be no doubt about the inferences, any more than one could deny that a triangle has three angles and three sides. From his father, Mill learned economics as syllogistic sequences, or rationalism.

During his crisis and reeducation years, Mill learned a less precise method, induction. In many cases, social scientists can only spy on their subjects and hypothesize patterns or trends, rather than proclaim incontrovertible laws. Induction has two humble goals: discover behavior patterns and make predictions based on those empirical patterns. That induction is less precise does not mean that it is necessarily inferior to deduction. Some subjects do not lend themselves to deduction. Social sciences cannot be deductive and precise, because people do not always behave rigidly and consistently. Deduction may be more appropriate for predicting the behavior of corpses. In a veiled jab at his deceased father, Mill warned that a "wise practitioner" would not "deduce the line of conduct proper to particular cases from supposed universal practical maxims, overlooking the necessity of constantly referring back to the principles of the speculative science."[20]

In accepting induction as a proper scientific tool, Mill did not discard deduction. With seemingly Solomonic wisdom, Mill sliced out a role for each. Each method could balance the other. If some economists deduced from flawed a priori principles, empiricists could throw observed counterexamples in their faces. For example, Malthus's law of population was first presented as a deductive truth. We can disprove Malthus's law by observing well-stocked supermarket shelves. On the other hand, deductive theoreticians can check the work of empiricists for logical consistency. For instance, a softheaded empiricist could argue that because the migration of storks is highly correlated with the human birthrate in New York, a good policy for controlling the human population would be to shoot down storks. Through logic a rationalist could show that the flawed observations do not make sense. (Naturally, a hardhearted empiricist would discover the independence of the events for himself once he started shooting storks and counting babies.)

Mill did not always blend the two methods. In fact, *Principles* proposes a schizoid approach to production and distribution. Fixed, universal laws control production: "There is nothing optional, or arbitrary in them." Therefore, deduction applies. But "it is not so with the Distribution of Wealth. That is a matter of human institution solely. The things once there, mankind, individually or collectively, can do with them as they like."[21]

Whereas Ricardo based both his production and his distribution analyses on carefully identified roles played by landlords, workers, and capitalists, Mill rejected such eternal divisions in the distributive process. Yes, the landlord would receive rents under the Ricardian analysis. But society may decide not to let him, Mill insists.

For two reasons Mill's bifurcated scheme seems mistaken. First, production laws may not be fixed. For example, technological advance cannot be predicted or assured. Mill does hint at this objection. Second, distribution cannot be neatly separated from production.

One does not have to be a tax-slashing fanatic to suspect that confiscatory tax rates might change an individual's activity. Boris Becker was a wealthy German tennis player. Germany taxed wealthy people heavily. How much tax did Becker pay to Bonn from his million-dollar purses? None. He moved to Monaco. He shifted his production because of distributional measures (and later stumbled into legal trouble). In 2013, actor Gérard Depardieu, a Chevalier of the French Legion of Honor, flipped his French château for a Belgian château and even picked up a Russian passport from Vladimir Putin in order to avoid a planned 75 percent income tax rate. Of course, taxes do not explain everything. Only a fool would conclude from the Becker story that Mikhail Baryshnikov left the Soviet Union because of tax rates. In 2006, the Irish rock star Bono and his U2 bandmates quietly moved their business office from Dublin to the Netherlands to avoid higher Irish taxes. Some of Bono's fans were disappointed since, at Dublin concerts, Bono had scolded the Irish prime minister for not spending more tax money on Third World poverty relief. While U2's music may be original, apparently their tax strategy is not. Mick Jagger and the Rolling Stones have been tax exiles in the Netherlands and assorted Caribbean isles for decades.

In subsequent chapters and editions of *Principles*, Mill relents on his claim of a clear methodological distinction between production and distribution.

To summarize all the important models presented in *Principles* might take more space than the original work, because Mill attempted a comprehensive review of economic doctrine, adding numerous improvements. He wrote convincingly about the management of the firm; supply and demand as an equation rather than a ratio; Say's Law; and demand as a major factor in Ricardo's Law of Comparative Advantage. As Nobel laureate George Stigler observed, Mill's advancements form a very peculiar list: they are only vaguely related to one another.[22] Rather than building a new foundation, Mill replaced many weak stones at many different levels.

Because Alfred Marshall performs similar repairs on Mill's work, we might better spend this chapter examining Mill and the economics of social policy. Except for Marx, Mill may have been the last of the "political economists," as famous for his political tracts *On Liberty* and *Utilitarianism* as for his economics. By the end of the nineteenth century, economics as a science grew so specialized that few could master both it and philosophy. By the mid-twentieth century, few could master more than a couple of topics in economics alone. We have a choice, states Nobel laureate Robert Solow, between saying more and more about less and less, or less and less about more and more.

In Mill's earlier book *On Logic*, he posited a crucial distinction between *positive* and *normative* works. Positive economics describes and predicts what actually takes place in the world. Normative economics advocates what should take place based on one's moral philosophy. Mill as reformer is a normative role. Of the five books of the *Principles*, the first three tend to be descriptive, while the latter two show Mill in his normative role, fervently devoted to enhancing the human condition through greater wealth equality, women's rights, and education.

Anyone can carry placards and shout slogans demanding equality, happiness, or the presence of an NFL team in Oakland. But results do not come from banners alone, any more

than good weather comes to Siberian towns that rename
themselves "Paradise." The majesty of Mill is that he tied his
normative goals to realistic analyses.

Taxation and Education

Mill delicately balanced the positive and normative in his
chapters on taxation. In fact, his position on income tax reflects the spirit of the landmark 1986 U.S. Tax Reform Act,
which attempted to "flatten" the progressive income tax. Like
Adam Smith, Mill called for a proportional income tax. This
takes the same percentage of income from earners regardless
of their income level. Contrast this with a progressive income
tax, which takes an increasing percentage as income rises.
Mill's analysis here actually mirrors our earlier Mick Jagger
example, for Mill fears that a progressive tax might discourage work:

> To tax the larger incomes at a higher percentage than the
> smaller, is to lay a tax on industry and economy; to impose a
> penalty on people for having worked harder and saved more
> than their neighbors.[23]

Although the proportional tax would apply to most of the
population, Mill would exempt the poor from paying taxes.

For most of the twentieth century, the United States rejected
Mill's advice and accepted a progressive income tax. By the
mid-1980s, taxpayers could fall into one of fourteen brackets,
ranging from 11 to 50 percent. If a person received a raise, she
likely moved to a higher bracket. But President Reagan and
Congress finally took Mill's advice and passed the landmark
1986 Tax Reform Act. The act collapsed those fourteen brackets into two: 15 and 28 percent. Although not a "flat" tax system, the act appeared as two plateaus, rather than as an

increasingly steep mountain. Also in line with Mill, the act exempted more poor people from paying any income taxes. Though Congress has amended the 1986 act a number of times, and has created more "plateaus," the basic logic continues: fewer loopholes and lower rates than in the 1960s and 1970s. Today Washington, D.C., is corrosively divided. But the gray-hairs of the nation's capital say that the extraordinary 1986 tax reform was one of the last examples of Republicans and Democrats coming together to rebuild highly complex and combustible laws.

Why did Congress finally honor Mill, even if partially and inadvertently? A variety of good and bad reasons explains any committee act. As someone once said, chaos in the world proves conclusively that God is a committee. Proportional-tax advocates argue that progressive taxes distort the incentive to augment income. Moreover, a progressive code encourages people to evade taxes as their income rises. They may do this legally, through tax shelters and creative accountancy, or illegally. Even if the published tax code is progressive, if people evade well enough, the results may not be. In fact, prior to the 1986 act, the actual tax returns filed with the Internal Revenue Service illustrated a relatively proportional tax. People used loopholes to thwart and transform the progressive system. The 1986 act, supported by Democrats and Republicans, eliminated many loopholes and made evasion less attractive. Some quirky loopholes did find their way into this tougher bill, however, including one that induced Eskimos to sell their business losses to corporations, which could then deduct the Eskimos' losses on their corporate tax forms.

Critics who reject these arguments against progressivity insist that proportional taxes are simply not as fair as progressive taxes. Despite this attack, it appears the ghost of Mill is still winning many battles, keeping the number of U.S. tax brackets at half the pre-1986 number, while the U.K. maintains just three basic brackets.

If Mill let the rich off easy on income tax, he tightened the screws on inheritance taxes. In his philosophical and economic works, Mill urged "equal opportunity" rather than "equality of results." If some children inherit huge sums from their parents, they possess an unfair advantage over others. And those with silver spoons may coast along on their parents' wealth rather than create more. Why is Mill cautious on income taxes but confiscatory on inheritance taxes? His penetrating insight here is that high inheritance taxes do not discourage work, as progressive income taxes do. "It is not the fortunes which are earned, but those which are unearned, that it is for the public good to place under limitation," he wrote.[24]

His analysis is not irrefutable, though. In practice, even inheritance taxes grow messy, for parents can simply transfer wealth before they die. Thus, gift taxes become necessary, along with gift inspectors. Moreover, high inheritance taxes could discourage older people from working or encourage them to spend their wealth on extravagances rather than save or invest in productive ventures. In sum, even inheritance taxes are not foolproof. In the 1980s, Sweden's inheritance tax reached 70 percent, forcing many spouses and children to sell family homes, holiday cottages, and small businesses to pay the tax collector. Even the founder of IKEA, Ingvar Kamprad, picked up his put-it-together-yourself furniture and decamped to Switzerland. Finally, a coalition government of Social Democrats, the Green Party, and the Left Party totally repealed the tax, beginning at midnight on January 1, 2005. But here's where the behavior gets interesting. Somehow Swedes were 10 percent more likely to die on January 1, 2005, than on December 31, 2004.[25] Either those elderly folks were utterly determined to drink a final midnight toast, or their devoted heirs kept them plugged into life support systems a few seconds longer to avoid the taxman.

President George W. Bush disagreed with Mill on inheritance and estate taxes, which he deemed a "death tax." In 2001, Bush convinced Congress to chop the estate tax down to zero in 2010. However, the legislation was to expire on December 31 of that year. Thus, on January 1, 2011, the top tax rate would bounce back to its old 55 percent level. If the Swedish example could be called "Keep Pappy Breathing," the U.S. counterpart could be called the "Throw Momma from the Train Act." Just in time, however, Congress, under Presidents Bush, Obama, and then Trump, saved solvent mommas by passing more permanent changes, which now exempt the first $11.6 million of an estate from taxation. Nobel laureate Joseph Stiglitz, a strong voice for progressive policies, cautions that high estate taxes present a prickly paradox: they can spur more inequality, not less. His tricky argument posits that high-taxed, wealthy families would put less of their income into savings, which would drive up the returns on capital. Since wealthier families tend to own more capital, they could grow even wealthier in the process.[26] Mill's scrutiny of the rich did not end with inheritance taxes. Despite his love affair and Benthamite breeding, Mill was Victorian enough to oppose sheer sybaritism by the rich. He eagerly proposed taxing riotous parties and luxuries flaunted for status. Long before Thorstein Veblen, Mill declared that an item "on which money is spent . . . from regard to opinion" is "a most desirable subject of taxation."[27] Sometimes Mill sounded as if he would receive as much pleasure from taxing the rich as the rich received from being rich. Given some of the affluent people Mill knew and the poor people he cared for, we cannot blame him. Mill always appreciated how social circumstances helped mold opinions.

Mill also wondered how society could give relief to the poor without dissuading them from getting jobs. No clear answer appeared. Mill distinguished the able-bodied from the disabled, elderly, and very young. Certainly, Mill reasoned, society should not worry about dissuading the disabled and should not cut their relief. Mill accepted the findings of the Royal Commission on Poor Law Reform and opposed the elimination of aid to the handicapped. Yet he felt less lenient toward the physically fit. He proposed that recipients exchange labor for welfare payments. After ignoring Mill's call for decades, in 1988 the U.S. federal government and several states adopted "workfare" programs in which healthy welfare recipients must accept employment or job training. The father of the federal legislation, Senator Daniel Patrick Moynihan, had labored for many years to redefine welfare as a transition to eventual employment. While the 1988 program had plenty of loopholes, it spurred a heated national debate on the subject. Americans had grown used to conservatives excoriating the welfare state, as President Reagan did by campaigning against "welfare queens" who drove Cadillacs to the bank to cash their government checks. A controversial 1985 book, *Losing Ground*, earned applause and denunciations for arguing that welfare payments actually tore apart black families. The "conservative" workfare argument got its biggest boost, though, in 1992, when Governor Bill Clinton of Arkansas announced that he would reform welfare "as we know it" if he were elected president. Suddenly, liberal politicians could jump on the anti-welfare bandwagon without embarrassment. After a few years of bickering with Congress, in 1996 President Clinton signed the Personal Responsibility and Work Opportunity Reconciliation Act, which put a time limit on public assistance and paid bonuses to states that successfully moved welfare recipients into jobs. While Republicans lauded the law they helped write, some White House advisers quit in protest, believing the bill too tough on recipients. Combined with a stunningly healthy job market that brought the jobless rate down to thirty-year lows (hitting 3.9 percent in April 2000), the new workfare system surpassed expectations, cutting the welfare rolls by several million while raising the employment rate of never-married mothers from 63 to 76 percent. A Federal Reserve Bank of San Francisco study concluded that "reform has made even the most vulnerable single mother economically more self-sufficient."[28] Of course, such a strong job market would have induced some people to get off the dole anyway; but there is little doubt that the new law gave them an extra push.

Wisconsin's heralded model had preceded the federal law by several years. The state counsels former claimants through a transition period, giving them "trial jobs," child care, and medical services, if necessary. New York City emulated the Wisconsin model, enjoying a dramatic drop in the welfare rolls. From 1960 until 1993, New York City welfare rolls had surged from 250,000 to 1.2 million. By 2019, they had fallen to 330,000. Welfare programs in Arizona, Florida, and eleven other states do not give any additional money to a welfare mother even if she gives birth to another child, a "family cap" concept also applied in South Korea and Singapore. Researchers at Rutgers and Princeton Universities found that this strict rule persuaded more poor women to use birth control, thereby curbing their birthrate. Reforming welfare is as much a cultural revolution as an economic one. The Massachusetts Department of Public Welfare has changed the name on its door plate to the Department of Transitional Assistance. Florida calls its program the Work and Gain Economic Self-Sufficiency Program. To critics, this smacks of George Orwell. To supporters, it puts the jobless in a proper frame of mind to fight back for their self-respect.

Mill's plan was more severe, however, for he thought that the jobs should necessarily be as arduous as those held by the least fortunate independent workers. Modern versions correctly find no reason to prevent recipients from training for more worthwhile jobs. Nonetheless, Mill shows remarkable prescience again.

Mill feared that if welfare were too easily doled out, generations of poor people would be born into families weaned of a work ethic. Even more pernicious, he thought that higher welfare payments would only promote higher birthrates. Thus, Mill rejected socialist and romantic proposals for raising relief benefits or wages. Such normative efforts ignored positive information about human tendencies. Mill needed to ground his normative policies in mature, reasoned models.

Falling back on his early memories, Mill recalled the power of education. He backed public education for paupers. But education would not consist simply of the three Rs. Mill saw nothing wrong in inculcating a taste for capitalist values. Capitalist societies have a duty to teach all their citizens how to succeed in a commercial community. What Max Weber later called the "Protestant work ethic" is not a biological trait. To assume that it is deprives poor people of their only hope for rising out of poorhouses: "It appears to me impossible but that the increase of intelligence, of education, and of love of independence among the working classes, must be attended with the corresponding growth of the good sense which manifests itself in provident habits of conduct."[29] Mill wanted to combine moral education with economic incentives, proposing, for instance, that the government provide to the poor what we now call home-improvement loans.

Volumes could be written on Mill's attitude toward laissez-faire policies versus government intervention. In brief, he stayed in the middle of the road and usually did not get run over. Rejecting a doctrinaire laissez-faire position, he embraced only a presumption of laissez-faire. That is, the burden is on the proponent of government to show that the greater happiness requires intervention: "Every departure from [laissez-faire], unless required by some great good, is a certain evil."[30] Obviously the state should tax, coin money, defend against enemies, establish courts, and so forth. But "optional" functions such as consumer protection, education, and business regulation should be approached on a case-by-case method. For example, Mill preferred private charity to state welfare, but he knew that charity might be only partly successful. The poor would happily accept any money, but the rich wouldn't give (partly because of "free rider" effects—people assume that others will bear the burden). Thus, the state should use its taxing power to maintain the poor.

Mill's approach again appears very modern. He would have approved, and indeed anticipated, many of today's governmental institutions. Nonetheless, he made sure that all proposals passed the crucial presumption test, for "impatient reformers, thinking it easier and shorter to get possession of the government than of the intellects and dispositions of the public, are under a constant temptation to stretch the province of the government beyond due bounds."[31] His reading of Alexis de Tocqueville's classic *Democracy in America* taught him the virtue of local rather than centralized plans.

In many ways Mill's positions reflected his government's at the time. England moved toward free market economics in many significant ways but set up safeguards against exploitation. William Gladstone led Parliament to finally abandon the Corn Laws in 1846 and to reduce income taxes. Even as the alarum of free trade finally shook Europe, Parliament restricted in 1802, 1819, and 1833 the hiring of children through the Factory Acts, providing landmark shields. Mill would approve of both, not out of a knee-jerk ideology but from careful reasoning.

Looking Forward

Most economists cannot resist predicting the long-term future. Like Smith, Malthus, Ricardo, Marx, and Keynes, Mill painted an impressionistic vision of the future, blending tones from Ricardo and Saint-Simonian socialism, a utopian movement that glorified industrial workers. From Ricardo, Mill sketched the possibility of a stationary state. From Saint-Simon, Mill brushed on cheerful colors. The stationary state would be happy. Whereas Ricardo constructed a theoretical model to track the results of diminishing returns, closed markets, and falling profits, Mill portrayed a nearly theological model of heaven on earth. In some distant time the scramble for money would stop, and the human race would exalt itself instead of wealth. Keynes would present a similar vision during the Great Depression.

Recall that Mill's enlightened utilitarianism had a place for Platonic ideals in its calculus. Mill yearned for a time when human beings would care more about dignity, integrity, and justice than overtime and overdrafts:

> I cannot . . . regard the stationary state of capital and wealth with the unaffected aversion so generally manifested towards it by political economists of the old school. I am inclined to believe that it would be, on the whole, a very considerable improvement on our present condition. I confess that I am not charmed with the ideal of life held out by those who think that the normal state of human beings is that of struggling to get on; that the trampling, crushing, elbowing, and treading on each other's heels, which form the existing type of social life, are the most desirable lot of human kind, or anything but the disagreeable symptoms of one of the phases of industrial progress.[32]

Like Marx, Mill thought that humans would eventually surpass the "realm of necessity" and arrive at a time when they could choose not to struggle for subsistence, but to strive to enhance their humanity. Only the "backward countries of the world" truly need more economic growth, Mill thought. The advanced countries need only a better distribution, or at least a better ethos. He decried the United States, where he thought poverty was eliminated but "the life of one sex is devoted to dollar hunting, and of the other to breeding dollar hunters."[33] One wonders whether Mill would prefer our new world, in which all are equally free to hunt.

What are we to make of Mill's portrait? It is too impressionistic to deduce or even induce any firm conclusions. As new editions of *Principles* arrived, they sounded somewhat more sympathetic to socialism. Yet Mill never sounded empathetic.

He could feel for the utopians, but never sign the petitions or march beside them. As Lord Byron said, "I stood among them, but not of them." Mill never abandoned his faith in competition and a Tocquevillian fear of centralized power: "I utterly dissent from the most conspicuous and vehement part of [socialist] teaching, their declamations against competition. . . . They forget that wherever competition is not, monopoly is."[34]

Few of us ever give up our longings for paradise. The rich can look for it on some tropical isle. Religious men and women can rely on a hereafter. Optimists can rely on tomorrow. John Stuart Mill fought for today and hoped for some idyllic day after tomorrow.

Mill fought for his principles in his *Principles* and in Parliament during the 1860s. A consistent voice for human rights, Mill championed women's suffrage, voting rights for the poor, and the North in the American Civil War. According to Lord Balfour, "Mill possessed an authority in the English Universities . . . comparable to that wielded . . . in the Middle Ages by Aristotle."[35]

His *Autobiography* depicts a far-from-conventional politician. When first asked to run for office, he "was convinced" that hardly anyone "really wished to be represented by a person of my opinions." He openly refused to campaign or spend money. He did make one promise: if elected, he would not devote any time to local interests. One famous writer declared at the time that "the Almighty himself would have no chance of being elected on such a program." Toward the end of the "campaign," Mill attended a public meeting of workers. An opponent flashed a placard that quoted Mill bluntly describing the English working class as "liars." However, they are better than the foreign working classes, the quotation continued, because they feel guilty. Almost any other politician would have been tarred and feathered at this point. Mill recalls, "I was asked whether I had written and published it. I at once answered 'I did.'" His supporters panicked, fearing for their lives. "Scarcely were these two words out of my mouth, when vehement applause resounded through the whole meeting." The workers had finally found someone they could trust.[36]

When his beloved Harriet died, Mill arranged a monument formed of Carrara marble, from the same quarry as Michelangelo's *David* and the Marble Arch that had stood in front of Buckingham Palace. After her passing, Mill began to rely more on his stepdaughter, Helen Taylor, for advice and administrative assistance. In spring 1873, while conducting botany experiments near his home in France, Mill contracted erysipelas, a deadly skin infection. His death sparked tributes and special issues of magazines from economics to philosophy to *Popular Science*. A leading Oxbridge scholar of the day noted that over the prior twenty years, Mill was "the author who has most powerfully influenced nearly all the young men of the greatest promise."[37] Just as today's students may hang in their dorm rooms posters of the dashing (and murderous) Che Guevara, the brooding Franz Kafka, or the daring Frida Kahlo, Mill was—despite his wan visage—the veritable pinup of his day. His English admirers raised funds to build a memorial statue for him along the Thames, but Mill wanted to be interred next to Harriet in a modest cemetery in a small French village near Avignon. Five people attended the burial. Though he fought in no wars and seldom raised his voice or threw down a gauntlet, he lived a life of struggle. He battled bigots, elitists, rationalists, and socialists. He challenged the ethos etched in his brain at a tender age. Edmund Burke once lamented that "the age of chivalry is gone. That of sophists, economists, and calculators has succeeded, and the glory of Europe is extinguished forever."[38] Chivalry still inspired Mill. And his most gallant duels and conquests were over the windmills of his mind.

CHAPTER VI
The Angry Oracle Called Karl Marx

When he was a child, Adam Smith was once kidnapped by some shrewd gypsies. After a few hours of holding the boy captive, the gypsies left him on a roadside, and he was returned to his family. A biographer remarked that the naive, absent-minded economist would not have made a good gypsy. One might also say that it's a good thing Karl Marx was never kidnapped by capitalists. He would not have made a good capitalist. Nor was he a good consumer. Marx was always in debt.

In powerful words and an incendiary manner, Marx foretold the collapse of capitalism. But not before he performed a penetrating inquiry into the laws of capitalism and the hidden code that rules the development of civilization.

Marx's place in the history of economic thought is difficult to locate. In many ways, mainstream economists today banish Marx to bourgeois cocktail conversation. Yet a billion people have struggled to survive under regimes that have claimed to be Marxist. Along with Freud and Darwin, Marx had a tremendous impact on the twentieth-century mind. But during his own lifetime, Marx found little fame and little following. John Stuart Mill, the most erudite man of Marx's era, never heard of him.

Marx the man enjoyed a bourgeois beginning in the German town of Trier in the Rhineland. Born in 1818, he mixed with the upper and middle classes of Trier. Marx later expressed pride that his father, Heinrich, a distinguished lawyer, also owned a vineyard. Marx's childhood friend and future wife, Jenny, lived nearby. Her father, Baron von Westphalen, became like an uncle to young Marx.

After his older brother died at the age of four, Marx inherited the role of eldest son and began terrorizing his younger and less brilliant sisters. A favorite game included "driving" his sisters like horses through the streets of Trier at full speed. In addition to equestrian events, Marx also forced his sisters to enter cake-tasting tournaments, in which they would eat cakes he would bake with dirty dough and unwashed hands. Nonetheless, the Marx sisters admired Karl for his intelligence and entertaining stories. Marx's schoolmates also loved and feared the boy, who brought smiles with pranks and shudders with sarcastic verse.

All his life Marx had a facility and proclivity for biting criticism and ad hominem abuse. He saved some of his most vicious attacks for Jews. Both Marx's parents were descended from eminent lines of rabbis; his uncle served as chief rabbi of Trier. Yet anti-Semitic laws persuaded Marx's father to convert to Christianity, even if he spoke of Jews as his "fellow believers." His son, however, rejected his Jewish ancestors with almost perverse pleasure. Scholars may debate whether he was really anti-Semitic. But undoubtedly Karl Marx uttered numerous venomous insults.[1]

Like John Stuart Mill, Marx imbibed both rationalist and romantic potions. His father provided eighteenth-century French rationalism mellowed by British empiricism, advising his son to "submit" to "the faith of Newton, Locke, and Leibnitz."[2] Meanwhile, the highly cultured Baron von Westphalen enchanted young Marx by strolling through idyllic woods and telling stories of Shakespeare, Homer, and the romantics. Ironically, it was the aristocratic baron who first introduced Marx to classless, utopian socialism. Without the influence of his father's sharp, discerning mind, Marx might have believed the fuzzy, wistful notions of the utopians. But where they would see bliss, he would see struggle.

At the University of Bonn, the biggest struggle Marx faced was against his eagerness to drink and to spend his father's money. He lost the struggle, and Heinrich lost a lot of money. Marx studied law and gained some practical legal experience when he was imprisoned for drunkenness. Since the university had its own drunk tank, imprisonment wasn't severe—visitors could play cards and continue drinking with the condemned man. The escapade proved useful. Marx's first political victory left him president of the Trier Tavern Society.

After a year of Bonn parties, Heinrich transferred his son to the University of Berlin, a more sober place, he hoped. Heinrich lost hope rather quickly: "As though we were made of gold my gentleman-son disposes of almost 700 thalers in a single year, in contravention of every agreement and every usage, whereas the richest spend no more than 500."[3] Creditors sued Karl several times, forcing him to move at least ten times during his five years at Berlin.

Heinrich complained of more than profligacy: Karl was a slob, a patron saint of unwashed, unkempt college students. His swarthy complexion earned him the nickname "the Moor," later used affectionately by his children and friends. With dark skin and long, matted hair, he appeared a shaggy excuse for a student.

Heinrich also objected to Karl's academic meanderings through philosophy and law. If Karl wandered, he certainly did it outside the classroom. During his last few years he took only a few courses and became a "bohemian student, who merely regard[ed] the university as his camping ground."[4] Nonetheless, Marx learned philosophy on his own and joined the Young Hegelians, radical critics of religion and eclectic followers of G. W. F. Hegel, the Berlin philosopher who had died only a few years before Marx's university career began. Marx would ingeniously adopt the Hegelian method and prove to the world that skipping classes sometimes pays (though not financially).

Unfortunately, Marx would never prove this to his father, who died in 1838. Marx retained strong affections for his father, whose photograph he always carried. Incidentally, Marx never showed such affection for his mother, seeing her merely as a stingy source of funds. He neither attended her funeral nor shed a tear when she died.

After his father's death, Marx thought it prudent to finish his studies. Suddenly eager to leave academia, he refused to submit his thesis on Greek philosophy to the rigorous Berlin procedures. Instead he sent it to the University of Jena, a noted diploma mill. A six-week correspondence course would have taken longer. In just a few days, Jena took out its well-worn rubber stamp and awarded a doctorate.

Young Man as a Journalist

With diploma in hand, Marx meandered into journalism, writing and then editing the *Rheinische Zeitung*, a liberal middle-class newspaper. Ironically, he bridled in its more radical writers, who tended toward communism. The repressive Prussian government eagerly censored criticism, and Marx often dealt with nearly moronic officials. One censor forbade an advertisement for a translation of Dante's *Divine Comedy*. Why? In Prussia, thou shalt not mock divine subjects through comedy.

An observer of Marx's tenure at the newspaper left a striking portrait of the young editor:

Karl Marx from Trier was a powerful man of 24 whose thick black hair sprung from his cheeks, arms, nose and ears. He was domineering, impetuous, passionate, full of boundless self-confidence, but at the same time deeply earnest and learned, a restless dialectician who with his restless Jewish penetration pushed every proposition of Young Hegelian doctrine to its final conclusion and was already, then, by his concentrated study of economics, preparing his conversion to communism. Under Marx's leadership the young newspaper soon began to speak very recklessly.[5]

The government responded to Marx's brashness by presenting a choice: either the newspaper shuts its doors or Marx walks out of them. Marx resigned.

He had lost a job, but in the meantime he had gained a wife, Jenny von Westphalen. Her relatives thought that the nobleman's daughter had married beneath her, but they had no idea how far down she would descend.

In 1843 the Marxes moved to Paris, where Marx edited a new political review, began to flirt with communism, and mingled with other young, arrogant radicals whom Heinrich Heine described as a "crowd of godless, self-appointed gods."[6] The journal published only one issue, after which Marx and his new communist friends broke with the co-editor Arnold Ruge. Ruge also learned to despise the godless crowd: "They wish to liberate people . . . but for the moment they attach the utmost importance to property and in particular to money. . . . To free the proletariat intellectually and physically from the weight of its misery, they dream of an organization that would generalise this misery and make all men bear its weight."[7]

Among the crowd was Friedrich Engels, who would become a critical part of Marx's life and livelihood. The son of a wealthy factory owner, Engels led a double life. By day he worked in his father's business and earned a substantial salary as a capitalist. By night he read Hegel and communist literature. Although a German, Engels lived in England for several years, running the family textile business. After some time in Manchester, he wrote a scathing exposé of British poverty, *The Conditions of the Working Class in England in 1844.* Not that Engels volunteered his capitalist earnings to the poor or renounced his bourgeois habits. In fact, he seems not to have been psychologically torn by his double life. He felt rather comfortable fox hunting, sipping sherry, and fencing. He could raise a glass of the finest champagne and elegantly toast the proletariat. When he wasn't chasing foxes, he chased women, declaring: "If I had an income of 5,000 fr. I would do nothing but work and amuse myself with women until I went to pieces. If there were no Frenchwomen, life wouldn't be worth living."[8] Quite a leap from Socrates's "the unexamined life is not worth living."

In the 1840s Marx began to mold the doctrines that would change the world. Not everyone approved, of course. The Prussian government registered its opinion of Marx's writings by declaring him guilty of treason. When France deported him a year later, he fled to Brussels.

What were these perfidious writings that forced Marx and his family to move from one European country to another? In the 1840s Marx built the historical and philosophical foundations for a study of capitalism. What did these theories prove? That the foundations of capitalism were quickly crumbling, and that the masses would soon erupt in revolution and shake the owners until they tumbled from their pedestals.

Materialist Historian

Marx's philosophy and history used Hegel's terms, but he was no parrot. Marx may have used the same words, but he changed the order. To understand how he did so, let us first examine a major precept of his mentor.

Hegel taught that philosophy aims at knowledge of the unfolding of ideas. The human spirit and ideas guide history. The material world, the stuff we see and touch, and the institutions in society follow the path of ideas. The German sociologist Max Weber would also employ this thesis in his famous work, *The Protestant Work Ethic and the Spirit of Capitalism*. Quite simply, Weber alleged that the rise of Protestantism led to capitalism; that is, a belief about God transformed economic institutions.

According to Hegel, we can trace the path of history by dominant nationalisms: the Age of Egypt, Greece, Rome, and so on. A patriot, Hegel thought Prussia was the leader of its age.

Marx rejected Hegel's idealism. Following the German philosopher Ludwig Feuerbach, Marx looked to materialist forces in history. God, according to Feuerbach's *The Essence of Christianity*, is simply a projection of human desires, needs, and attributes. Man created God; God did not create man. The real stuff, man, led to the idea of God. (Feuerbach's writings led Marx to later denounce religion as the "opium of the people."[9] As long as people could project their longings onto God and a hereafter, they would passively accept material conditions and injustices in the real world.)

So far Marx sounds more like a dropout from the Hegelian school of thought than a Young Hegelian. But Marx retains the key to the Hegelian method, the *dialectic*. Hegel insisted that history, like reality, does not follow a smooth, gradual pattern. Nor does it consist of a series of independent accidents. History consists of struggle between opposing forces. Every idea includes its opposite. Philosophers often summarize Hegel's dialectic by stating that every thesis or idea is confronted by its antithesis. The battle between these ideas produces a synthesis, a new thesis. The new thesis then faces its antithesis. The world is ever changing. History never repeats itself—although windy historians may repeat themselves.

Compare the dialectic method to the Newtonian approach to economics, which sees unchanging cause-and-effect relations. The only thing immutable in Hegel's vision is the presence of change.

Marx fuses the dialectic method with materialism. Engels later termed the alliance *dialectical materialism* or *historical materialism*. If Hegel's head was in the clouds, Marx wants to rub our noses in the ground. History takes place on earth, he said. Forget about studying religion, ethics, or nationalism. Simply look out the window and see how man grapples for the bare necessities of life. There is no history without men. And there are no men without food. Thus, "the first historical act is . . . the production of the means to satisfy these needs."[10] Idealist historians might as well write the history of Oz.

Marx plots the course of history from slavery to feudalism to capitalism to socialism. The path lies not in the stars or the laws but in production—and more specifically in the relationship of people to production. Each system of production creates ruling and ruled classes. Each epoch is marked by a particular way of extracting income for the rulers. In Roman times, whoever owned a slave owned a claim on his output. In feudal times, lords owned a claim on the output of serfs. Under capitalism, owners of factories and land own a claim on the output of their wage laborers. The survival of the master class rests on the work of the serving class. Does this give the workers great bargaining power? No. The workers must cooperate with the ruling class, for the rulers control the means of production. The workers cannot just "take their marbles and go home." They don't own the marbles.

Thus, a mutual dependency exists. Nonetheless, the rulers strive to appear as if they do not need the workers as much as the workers need them. If successful, they extend their dominance.

How do they try to ensure their status? Here's where Hegel's concern for ethics, nationalism, and ideas enters. The ruling class develops the beliefs, laws, culture, religion, morality, and patriotism that support the production process. A patriotic worker whistles while he works and doesn't cheat the owner by taking too many coffee breaks. Today, car manufacturers and breweries love to link America with a "good, honest day's work." The American dream once burst forth in the jingle "Baseball, hot dogs, apple pie, and Chevrolet." Chevrolet actually displaced Mom. (Would the American oedipal dream include lust for Dad's car?)

Our ethical and legal system teaches us to feel guilty if we shirk our work. Why are owners entitled to profits derived through our sweat? Because they own the property, we respond. But why should we accept the legal system? Marx asks.

According to Marx, rulers who have a stake in the private property system hypnotize the masses. The power of suggestion and persuasion leads Americans to dream of stocks, bonds, and BMWs. Of course, the individual thinks the dreams are his own and internalizes the suggestions. Marx calls the supportive ideas, laws, and ethos the *superstructure*.

Marx's classic statement appears in the preface to his *Contribution to the Critique of Political Economy*: "The mode of production of material life conditions the general character of social, political and intellectual life. . . . It is not the consciousness of men that determines their being, but, on the contrary, their social being that determines their consciousness."[11]

The serf bows and shows fealty to the lord. The journeyman serves the master craftsman with pride. The wage laborer strives for promotion by working harder. They all toil and seek a better life within the reigning system.

Marx did not argue that the ruling class knowingly conspires to construct the superstructure. Owners may truly believe in their religion and not view it instrumentally. The superstructure emerges because the productive process skews and frames the perception of people. According to Marx, "Men make their own history, but they do not make it just as they please; they do not make it under circumstances chosen by themselves, but under circumstances directly encountered, given and transmitted from the past. The tradition of all the dead generations weighs like a nightmare on the brain of the living."[12] (Incidentally, Engels later admitted that Marx and he sometimes overstressed the causation from production to superstructure. Ideas occasionally had real consequences.)

If an ethos and a culture automatically arise to buttress the class system, why does Marx announce in the opening thrust of *The Communist Manifesto* that the "history of all hitherto existing societies is the history of class struggle"?[13] Why should anyone struggle? How does anyone know to struggle in the first place? The owners simply squeeze the workers, and the workers accept the squeeze as contentedly as a mesmerized Moonie giving away daisies at an airport. As long as the Moonie/worker gets token benefits, the economy rolls on, and the profits roll into the bank accounts of owners.

The rebellion takes place when the technology of the productive process changes. A new technology or method alters the quantity or quality of land, labor, and capital. Through discovery, invention, education, and population growth, the material forces of production are *dynamic*. With a new mix of material forces, the old productive process becomes obsolete. For example, slavery might have produced farm profits when the ratio of land to worker was high. But if tractors and reapers work more efficiently than slaves, or if the population of workers rises, slavery may be less profitable. The future lies in the new process.

Do not forget, though, that a whole political, ethical, and legal system rested on the *old* method. Ministers preached that serfdom led to God's kingdom. This was an eternal truth etched in the mind and on the stones of the medieval cathedral. Thus, the superstructure appears *static*.

The struggle occurs when the old ruling class barricades itself from the dynamic course of history by clutching the old ideas and blocking new economic developments. Marx writes that the hand mill begets the feudal lord, while the steam mill announces the industrial capitalist. But the feudal lord battles his successor, the industrialist. Later the guild master brawls with the factory owner. Forget tales of Sir Lancelot and Galahad. The real jousting with the sharpest lances took place not between knights but between lords and commercial forces.

The ruling class always faces a threat when land, labor, capital, or technology shifts. They may tumble down from the penthouse of the house of cards while screaming the "eternal truths" of their philosophy. History reshuffles the deck, and he who held the king may be beheaded.

A story might help here. Once upon a time, swift sentries warned a devout feudal lord of a flood. The lord rushed to his cathedral and prayed to God for salvation. As the water reached the steps of the holy building, a serf in a small boat rowed to the steps and asked the lord to come aboard. "No, thanks. I believe in God, and I believe in justice. God will save me." As the water rose, the lord walked up to the pulpit. This time a motorboat rushed toward him. As the water sloshed against the pew, the driver yelled, "I'll save you. Jump on!" Again the noble lord replied, "Do not worry. I believe in God. He will save me. I don't need noisy machines." Finally, the water engulfed the cathedral. As the lord clutched the very top of the highest spire, his body thrashed by waves, a helicopter flew overhead. The pilot screamed, "Please, my lord. Take hold of this ladder." Again the lord replied, "Do not worry. I believe in God. He will save me." Moments later, the water rose higher and the lord drowned.

In heaven (he was, after all, a good lord), he confronted God. "God," he said, "I believed in You all my life. I followed every parable my priest ever told me. When others doubted and turned to machines, I believed You would save me. But you let me drown—"

"Schmuck!" God interrupted. "Who do you think sent the rowboat, the motorboat, and the helicopter!"

He who doesn't go with the flow of historical materialism drowns in it. Marx depicted the flow:

At a certain stage of their development, the material forces of production in society come in conflict with the existing relations. . . . These relations turn into their fetters. Then comes the period of social revolution. With the change of the economic foundation the entire immense superstructure is more or less rapidly transformed. In considering such transformations the distinctions should always be made between the material transformation of the economic conditions of production which can be determined with the precision of natural science, and the legal, political, religious, aesthetic or philosophic—in short, ideological forms in which men become conscious of this conflict and fight it out.[14]

Because capitalism rested on a class system, revolution and victory for the workers was inevitable. Marx's masterpiece, *Capital*, portrayed "tendencies working with iron necessity towards inevitable results."[15] Only a classless society could avoid revolution. And in Marx's vision, a classless society would eventually arrive. Rotten capitalists would finally be annihilated. After centuries of theft, workers would finally be free.

If capitalism must with "iron necessity" collapse into socialism, didn't feudalism have to collapse into capitalism? Wasn't capitalism a necessary stop on the way to communism? If so, it was not a gratuitous slaughter, or a stroke of very bad luck for mankind, as many utopian socialists saw it. Marx was repulsed by unscientific romantics who depicted capitalism as a wicked accident contrived by evil men. In fact, Marx composed some of the most eloquent paeans to the capitalist, since his view was that capitalism liberated man from even worse conditions. Marx's *Communist Manifesto* had no time for fuzzy-headed nostalgia-mongers:

> The bourgeoisie, by the rapid improvement of all instruments of production, by the immensely facilitated means of communication, draws all nations, even the most barbarian, into civilization. The cheap prices of its commodities are the heavy artillery with which it batters down all Chinese walls, with which it forces the barbarians' intensely obstinate hatred of foreigners to capitulate. . . . The bourgeoisie, during its rule of scarce one hundred years, has created more massive and more colossal productive forces than have all preceding generations together.[16]

Marx may have criticized the bourgeoisie, but he saved his most poisonous attacks for fellow socialists who veered from his vision. No coalition builder, he was at his friendliest a coiled python. Marx would have hated the Green Party and dreamed of its members choking on their Grape-Nuts. Capitalism, he wrote, "rescued a considerable part of the population from the idiocy of rural life."[17] He would have sent "back to nature" advocates back to their history books to learn how terrible preindustrial life was. Marx acidly responded to Pierre-Joseph Proudhon's *The Philosophy of Poverty* with *The Poverty of Philosophy*. Intelligent people do not try to erase or "recall" stages of history and send them back to God's little factory for repair.

Capitalism is a necessary precondition for socialism. Because capitalism produces so much, it permits a less driven system, socialism, to follow. Precapitalist nations have no business hoping for communist revolutions to overthrow feudal lords or czars. Marx did not look to Russia. He did not expect communism to come soon even in Germany, since only 4 percent of the male labor force worked in factories at the time. The shackles would burst open first in England and France, strongholds of advanced capitalism. France would signal when Germany was ripe for communism: "When all internal conditions are fulfilled, the day of German resurrection will be heralded by the crowing of the Gallic cock."[18]

Capital and the Collapse of Capitalism

Marx did not just arrogantly wait for the cock to crow. Instead he arrogantly wrote his definitive dissection of capitalism, *Capital*. In the 1850s, Marx buried himself in piles of economics texts in the British Museum in London. His family starved while he analyzed the abstract suffering of the proletariat. The Marxes lived in a sleazy apartment in one of the poorest parts of London. A police spy investigating Marx provided an extraordinarily vivid portrait of the squalor his family endured:

> When one enters Marx's room, the eyes get so dimmed by coal smoke and tobacco fumes that for the first moments one gropes as if in a cave. . . . Everything is dirty, everything full of dust, sitting down becomes a truly dangerous business. Here stands a chair with only three legs, there the children play and prepare food on another chair which happens to be still whole.

As for Marx himself, "he is a highly disorderly, cynical person, a poor host; he leads a real gypsy existence. Washing, grooming, and changing underwear are rarities with him; he gets drunk readily. Often he loafs all day long, but if he has work to do, he works day and night tirelessly." Jenny, though raised on aristocratic fare, "feels quite at home in this misery."[19]

The Marxes lost three children to pneumonia, bronchitis, and tuberculosis in five wretched years in London. Most horrifying, undertakers would not extend credit. Jenny, driven to depression, once had to beg for the two pounds for a child's coffin. Although Marx was often nasty to outsiders, his children had brought out the humane side of his personality. He, too, was broken when they died:

> Bacon says that really important people have so many relationships to nature and the world, so many objects of interest, that they easily get over any loss. I do not belong to these important people. The death of my child has deeply shattered my heart and brain, and I feel the loss as freshly as on the first day.[20]

Marx, of course, blamed his plight on the bourgeoisie and promised to make them pay for his family's calamities and for his own ailments, including carbuncles.

Marx seldom blamed himself. He should have. Marx had an infantile sense of home economics. Someone once described an infant as a canal with a loud voice at one end and no responsibility at the other. If one counts gifts from Jenny's family and from Engels, and payments for articles in the *New York Daily Tribune*, the Marxes "earned" an adequate sum of money for a lower-middle-class family. In their poorest years, they enjoyed roughly three times the income of an unskilled worker. A radical German poet, also banished from his homeland, reported that an income similar to Marx's always bought him "the luscious beef-steak of exile."[21]

But instead of regularly feeding his family, Marx invested money in political journals and in piano, music, and dancing lessons for his children! Although the wife of a revolutionary, Jenny continued to print posh stationery calling herself "Baroness von Westphalen."

To compound his problems, Marx impregnated the maid (she was a gift from the von Westphalens). Again Marx denied responsibility. He told Jenny that Engels was the father. The maid left for a while, then returned with a rather swarthy, hairy child who was subsequently whisked off to foster parents.

It comes as no surprise, given such a home life, that during 1850 and 1851 Marx spent more time at the British Museum than at home. He read almost everything available on economics. He spent months filling notebooks with lengthy passages from about eighty writers. Engels tried to hurry him along, but Marx kept to a painfully slow, pedantic pace. Marx also had a tough time finding a publisher willing to accommodate his proposed format for *Capital*. Engels admonished the stubborn communist: "Show a little commercial sense this time."[22]

By the time Marx finished his research, writing, and editing, and recovered from several illnesses, the calendar read 1867. Volume 1 finally came out. An additional three volumes would appear posthumously.

To describe *Capital*, one might as well choose a page from *Roget's Thesaurus* and read random adjectives aloud. It includes 2,500 pages with citations to more than 1,500 works. Some pages are literary masterpieces. Some gleam with lucid logic.

And some are so technical, picayune, and boring they recall Truman Capote's swipe at writer Jack Kerouac: "This isn't writing. It's just typing."

Let us take *Capital* in three steps. First, we will discover the key to capitalism, Marx's idea of labor exploitation. Second, we will look at the laws of capitalist motion, which inevitably lead to its downfall. Third, we will look at the psychological costs of capitalism.

Marx does not take the easy route. He does not simply point to domineering businesses and proclaim that the era of entrepreneurs and perfect Smithian competition is over. Remember, he is a Hegelian; he wants to show that even the ideal form of capitalism must fail on its own. He starts with classical tools.

Like Smith and especially Ricardo, Marx "proves" that the value of a product is determined by the amount of labor needed to produce it. Machines are just past labor stored up in metallic form. A stereo that takes ten hours to make is twice as valuable as one that takes five hours.

If this is true, there can be no profits unless labor is exploited. The following simple syllogism would be sound:

1. The value of a product (price) is determined by the amount of labor.
2. Workers receive the full value of what they contribute to the product.
3. Therefore, the value of a product equals the amount workers receive.

But the selling price of a product is not just split among the workers. The owner seizes a share, his profits. Forget the invisible hand. The intrusive, visible hand of the capitalist grabs a piece of the action. Where does the profit come from? Premise 2 must be wrong. The workers must not receive the full value of their contribution. They must be exploited. (Critics of Marx argue that premise 1 is flawed.)

How do capitalists cheat the workers? Instead of paying

them the amount by which they enhance the value of the capitalist's business, the capitalist pays them only a *subsistence*—what it takes to keep them alive and working. The capitalist buys labor power as if it were any other commodity. Then he puts it to work X hours per day.

Let's use Marx's terms. Marx portrays capitalists providing factories and equipment, called *constant capital*. They also pay for labor, called *variable capital*. When production takes place, the capitalist must ensure that the value of the final product surpasses the sum of *constant* plus *variable capital*. The extra value (profit) comes from paying workers less than the value they produce. In other words, the value that workers add to the product exceeds the *variable capital* they get paid. Marx calls this loot robbed from the laborer *surplus value*.

For example, Jasmine works as a seamstress for the Radio City Music Hall stage show. Audiences generally don't like torn costumes. So her sewing boosts the value of a performance by $10. But she only gets paid $6. The bosses squeeze a $4 surplus from Jasmine for each daily performance. The ratio of surplus value to wage (4:6) is the *ratio of exploitation*.

Why doesn't Jasmine charge $10 and get her full value? Capitalism leads to unemployment and a *reserve army* ready to take Jasmine's place if she demands more money. She does not own the sewing machine, the costumes, or the stage. The bosses do. By controlling the means of production, they dominate the labor market.

How do the bosses set Jasmine's $6 wage? Bosses need to pay workers only enough for them to survive. Jasmine gets $6 because $6 will keep her alive. She receives a *subsistence wage*. If she got $1 per hour, six hours of work would provide a subsistence. But the bosses do not let her stop at six. They force her to work a longer day, mending more torn costumes. They spread her $6 wage over ten hours, for example. The result: She works six hours for herself and an extra four hours for the bosses. The four-hour surplus goes right into the bosses' pockets. They need not lift a thimble.

Why do workers get paid only a subsistence wage? We said earlier that the value of a commodity is determined by the amount of labor that went into it. Labor supply is also a commodity. Therefore, the price of labor is the amount of money needed to produce and maintain a human being: the subsistence level.

In general, bosses do not pay workers enough to buy what they produce. Workers struggle for just a portion. In our example, Jasmine cannot afford a $10 ticket to the performance, even though she adds $10 of value to it. Perhaps the bosses would let her buy a ticket for $5, but only if she promised to watch the performers from their waists up.

If profit comes from exploiting labor, we can define the rate of profit as the ratio of surplus to the sum of variable plus constant capital $(s/[v + c])$. The capitalist can boost profits if he squeezes a longer workday out of his employees. Or he can raise profits by exploiting the labor of women and children in addition to men. During the era when Marx wrote, hours did increase and more women and children had entered the industrial workforce.

Now we see how profits rest on exploitation. But why can't this go on? What are the laws of capitalism that finally deliver workers from despair and drive the capitalists to their knees? Marx did not merely announce that a social revolution would burst forth. He carefully depicted the *economic* inconsistencies of capitalism. We will examine five "laws" or "tendencies" that point to an economic implosion. Far from applauding capitalism, the invisible hand ultimately smashes it.

1. Falling Profit Rates and Accumulation of Capital. Like Adam Smith, Marx sees the capitalist confronting competition. If one company expands its scale of production, it may produce more efficiently. The innovative company forces its competitors to expand. They hire more workers. But this drives up the wage beyond subsistence. What do the bosses do? They substitute equipment for labor. If they do not, their profits plunge, for higher pay halts their exploitation. Competition coerces them to substitute.

But here the bosses outsmart themselves and stumble into a dilemma. Surpluses can only be squeezed from human beings. Capitalist machine sellers can charge the full, fair value for the products. (If a high-speed film-developing device increases a company's income because it can develop more photographs per hour, the equipment manufacturer will probably charge the photography company appropriately.) Look again at Marx's formula for the profit rate, $s/[v + c]$. By adding machines (c), the capitalists drive down their profits. On the other horn of the dilemma, if they resist adding machines, no one will buy their uncompetitive products:

> The development of capitalist production makes it constantly necessary to keep increasing the amount of capital laid out in a given industrial undertaking, and competition makes the immanent laws of capitalist production to be felt by each individual capitalist, as external coercive laws. It compels him to keep constantly extending his capital, in order to preserve it. . . .
>
> Accumulate, accumulate! That is Moses and the prophets! . . . Therefore, save, save, i.e., reconvert the greatest possible portion of surplus-value, or surplus-product into capital!"[23]

The same result occurs if one capitalist improves a machine. The owner who builds a better sewing machine can charge a lower price for admission. Since bosses must keep up with one another, competitors *must* save the surpluses extorted from labor and invest in the new sewing machinery.

The "boundless greed" of capitalists forces their destruction. To delay the loss in profits, bosses may try to exploit labor even more. How? They will speed the pace of work. And they will stretch the working day even further. Of course, these tactics only stretch the patience of laborers dangerously further.

2. Increasing Concentration of Economic Power. With capitalists driven to expand and develop, a battle rages. The largest firms, which produce more cheaply, triumph. The bloody battle "always ends in the ruin of many small capitalists, whose capitals partly pass into the hands of their conquerors, partly vanish."[24] Survivors soon dwarf the vanquished.

3. Deepening Crises and Depressions. "Childish babble . . . claptrap . . . humbug." Marx used these words to describe Say's argument for capitalist stability. As capitalists substitute for labor, unemployment rises. Who buys the goods when the bosses expand output? No one. The goods sit. Bankruptcies vault. Panic engulfs. Financiers dump their holdings. Investment dives. Investors dive off their balconies.

The cycle, of course, turns up again after prices drop. The survivors again pick up the pieces of broken businesses and hire desperate workers. Surpluses and profits reappear. But only to fall faster and farther the next time.

4. Industrial Reserve Army. Through substitution and depression, the capitalists throw more and more people out of the factories and into the streets. The "army" is no more militant than the Salvation Army—at first. As long as the army remains peaceful, it remains a good source of low-cost labor. An abundance of workers helps the capitalists stay in control—at first.

5. Increasing Misery of the Proletariat. Along "with the constantly diminishing number of magnates of capital, who usurp and monopolize all advantages . . . grows the mass of misery, oppression, slavery, degradation, exploitation."[25] Longer workdays and less vacation bring more misery for the downtrodden laborers. Marx's earlier writings argued that their absolute standard of living falls. But in *Capital*, written in the face of indisputable evidence that workers were better off than they had been, he retreats, claiming only that workers have a smaller share of the wealth than they did before.

Finally, after unemployment, crashing profits, inhuman despair, and misery, the proletariat will see their plight. The mask of the superstructure is ripped off. The ugly monster called capitalism is revealed. The oppressed lot rebel: "The knell of capitalist private property sounds. The expropriators are expropriated."[26]

The proletariat gain more than factories. They regain their humanity. The capitalists robbed more than proletariat pockets. They also robbed hearts and minds. To Marx, work plays a special role in human life. Human beings are impelled to *create* and enhance their lives through nature and through relationships with other people. The human personality cannot develop without creative work. Under capitalism, labor becomes just another commodity. People are forced to accept routine, dull jobs. They become animated tools. They feel *alienated* from themselves, the world, and each other. Alienation becomes a prominent theme in Marxist and in existentialist critiques of modern society.

In the *Communist Manifesto*, Marx and Engels urged the proletariat to capture the economy and liberate themselves:

> The Communists disdain to conceal their views and aims. They openly declare that their ends can be attained only by the forcible overthrow of all existing social conditions. Let the ruling classes tremble at a Communist revolution. The proletarians have nothing to lose but their chains. They have a world to win.
>
> Workingmen of all countries, unite![27]

With the publication of *Capital*, nearly twenty years later, the proletariats could back up pithy slogans with trenchant analysis.

But what happens after the revolution? Does everyone simply kiss and luxuriate in newfound humanity? Does everyone sit in a circle before a campfire, hold hands, and sing "Kumbaya"? Some contemporary Marxists might lead one to think so.

Surely, Marx scorned autopian socialism and sneered at

rustic simplicity. He was not sentimental. He disdained wistful longings for a "fair" distribution of income or a massive redistribution of wealth. Workers, even under socialism, would not get the "full value" of their work. The surplus would, however, go to the "people" for collective services.

What would communism really mean? We do not know. Marx deliberately avoided leaving "recipes" for the "cookshops of the future."[28] Without a recipe, Marxism as a governing system became the political equivalent of sausage: a cheap way to squeeze a committee's goals into a shape that can be fed to others.

Marx suggested that ultimately the state would "wither away." In the meantime a dictatorship of the proletariat would rule. The *Communist Manifesto* includes a ten-point plan that would carve "despotic inroads into the rights of property":

1. Abolition of property in land and application of all rents of land to public purposes.
2. A heavy progressive or graduated income tax.
3. Abolition of all right of inheritance.
4. Confiscation of the property of all emigrants and rebels.
5. Centralization of credit in the hands of the state by means of a national bank with state capital and an exclusive monopoly.
6. Centralization of the means of communication and transport in the hands of the state.
7. Extension of factories and instruments of production owned by the state; the bringing into cultivation of waste lands, and the improvement of the soil generally in accordance with a common plan.
8. Equal obligation of all to work. Establishment of industrial armies, especially for agriculture.
9. Combination of agriculture with manufacturing industries; gradual abolition of the distinction between town and country, by a more equable distribution of the population over the country.

10. Free education for all children in public schools. Abolition of child factory labor in its present form. Combination of education with industrial production, etc.[29]

Future Marxists would have to figure out how to implement the plan. Not entirely optimistic about the splintered socialist movements in Europe, Marx once declared that he was no longer a Marxist.

In the Bible, God prevents Moses from entering the Promised Land. But the Marxists, unlike the Israelites, had no Joshua to take them forward when Marx died, in 1883.

Looking at Marx

How can we comprehensively critique Marx's ingenious analysis? The task is intimidating. Over the past century, intellectuals have filled millions of pages with praise, insults, and blab. Here is a modest agenda for assessing Marx: (1) How does Marx's materialist history deform the idea of surplus labor? (2) What about the prophecies of misery, unemployment, and the fall of capitalism? (3) What did Marx give to modern economics? (4) What did he give to modern politics?

1. How does Marx's materialist history deform the idea of surplus labor? In Victor Hugo's *Les Misérables*, Jean Valjean continually confronts the same nemesis: Inspector Javert. And life keeps dragging Javert inexorably back to Valjean. The literary dialectic creates the dramatic struggle for each. Without the other character, life is too simple for each.

The trouble with Marx's history is that the master dialectician ignores the most dramatic dialectic: between idealist causes and materialist causes. For the most part, Marx portrays material factors as causal. They establish and periodically change the ideas or superstructure of a society. But in assuming this relationship, Marx too often slights idealist forces. And this flaw infects his economics.

The notion of surplus labor supports the whole Marxian theory of capitalism. Recall the simple syllogism. Why must labor be exploited? Because Marx embraces the "labor theory of value" by which capitalists collect profits. According to Marx, "not one single atom" of value comes from the capitalist.[30] Marx easily envisages Jasmine the seamstress or the blacksmith pounding at the anvil. They create value.

What does Marx miss? He ignores imagination and entrepreneurship. To create wealth requires more than tangible inputs. The development of streaming videos did not require new types of raw materials or more drastic ways of exploiting labor. The video industry required two things: invention and entrepreneurship—the willingness to take risks with investments. Why did Russians living under communism beg for American-made denim jeans? Not because the Soviet Union lacked the cotton or the workers to produce high-quality clothing. But because they lacked the imagination, motivation, and discipline. These intangibles separate the successful companies and countries from the others.

Marx's materialism unfortunately leads him to scorn every kind of capital, including *human* capital: the knowledge, knack, and management skills so crucial to profits. How can the labor theory of value account for flashes of brilliance or insight like in the following example?

Some years ago, as a man walked through the woods, a burr caught in his wool sock. The man's bank account now overflows with money. He invented Velcro. Are all his profits stolen from the workers?

In the next chapter we'll see that Alfred Marshall attacks Marx for ignoring the value to society of risk-taking and "waiting." By investing, the capitalist gives up the immediate gratification of buying goods. His return on investment pays him for waiting, for delaying his pleasure. If everyone consumes everything now, society will produce nothing new. Thus, profits play a crucial and perfectly legitimate role. (Incidentally, the marginalist "revolution," which Marshall helped lead, demonstrates that value comes from *demand*, as well as from production or supply. By the time volume 2 of *Capital* appeared posthumously, the marginalists had savaged the supply-side focus of Marx and the classicals.)

By assuming the labor theory of value, Marx snubs too many dynamic, idealist factors. Ricardo avoided this problem because he saw the labor theory of value merely as a tool for approximation, not as the definitive *cause* of value. When Marx tried to prove the theory mathematically, he fell into so many burrs, it's surprising he didn't discover Velcro in the nineteenth century.

2. What about the prophecies of misery, unemployment, and the fall of capitalism? Marx did not intend to prophesy. He aimed at scientific prediction, projecting the course of history based on identifiable tendencies. But as history swerved from his predictions, his posthumous followers created a pseudo-religion from his works. Thus his "laws" conformed to history. Having molded the laws, his disciples could proclaim the correctness of the prophecies. Although it started as atheistic science, Marxism in the twentieth century came to resemble a stained-glass window that selectively admitted the sun and seldom admitted error. Once the laws became religious scripture, the effort to test Marxism scientifically was lost.

Marx lived long enough to see some of his supporters extrude and exalt his laws, erect pulpits, and perform sacraments. The anarchist Proudhon warned Marx against bestowing a catechism:

> For God's sake, after we have abolished all the dogmatisms *a priori*, let us not of all things attempt in our turn to instill another kind of dogma into the people. . . . Let us have decent and sincere polemics. . . . But simply because we are at the head of the movement, let us not make ourselves the

leader of a new intolerance, let us not pose as the apostle of
a new religion—even though this religion be the religion of
logic, the religion of reason.[31]

Even if we cannot disprove Marx's predictions, we can observe a few developments in capitalist economies since his time.
First, the standard of living for workers has risen dramatically
in the past hundred years as home ownership and automobile
ownership rates have soared. By today's definition of "poverty,"
the rising bourgeoisie of Marx's time were impoverished and
"immiserated," to use Marx's term. And using the conventional
definitions of Marx's time, today's workers are ostentatiously
wealthy. No one denies a rise in the "absolute" standard of living of workers.

Yet the *Communist Manifesto* forewarned workers that "the
modern labourer . . . instead of rising with the progress of industry, sinks deeper and deeper below the conditions of existence of his own class. He becomes a pauper." But Marx soon
noticed that the pocketbooks of workers grew fatter. He even
admitted that in the ten years following the *Communist Manifesto*, agricultural wages soared by 40 percent.[32]

For this reason Marx switched definitions and warned that
workers would become poorer *relative* to capitalists. The apoc-
alyptic plight of the laborer fades: The rich get richer, *and* the
poor get richer. But the rich get richer more quickly.[33]

Marx squeezed the new definition into *Capital* by declaring
"subsistence" a relative term, dependent on contemporary lifestyles. Presumably in the twentieth century, bare subsistence
requires a color television, since the average "wage slave" in
manufacturing can afford one. By retreating to the relativist
argument, Marx surrenders passion and the feeling of desperation in the workers' plight. As long as the poor keep getting richer, the scenario even passes philosopher John Rawls's
test of social justice (which allows the rich to gain only if the
poor also benefit).[34]

Modern Marxists therefore emphasize psychological misery

and alienation. They may be right; workers may often be bored and disgusted. But Marx does not tell us, for example, how socialism will make trash collecting exciting. If happy laborers work better, then, at least under capitalism, owners have strong incentives to satisfy their employees.

Moreover, how should we define happiness in laborers? If wages are relative, why isn't happiness? Should we ask the absolute question: Are workers today happier than they were one hundred years ago? Or should we ask the relative question: Are they growing happier at as fast a rate as capitalists? Consider: The rich are getting happier, and the poor are getting happier. But the rich are getting happier more quickly. Once we begin construing happiness so that we can test "scientific" Marxism, it's a sad day for Marxists and non-Marxists alike.

Marx also prophesied the collapse of capitalism, a system that provides its own "gravediggers." But capitalism does not seem dead yet. The unemployment rate is slightly higher than it was in the beginning of the 1900s, but if we consider the percentage of the population working, and especially the addition of women to the workforce, employment is higher.

Furthermore, capitalism often produces a middle class that indirectly owns some of the means of production through the stock markets. In the late 1980s, millions of lower-middle-class Britons bought shares in "privatized" companies such as British Telecom, British Steel, and British Airways. Most union pension funds in the United States invest heavily in corporate stock.

Some of Marx's defenders point to the growth of government in capitalist nations as the surprising savior of capitalism. Social welfare spending protects the capitalists from deeper depressions and revolution. Marx's defenders are probably right. But remember, Marx predicted that the political system and superstructure would stay *static*, resistant to change. Inflexibility would destroy it. If, in retrospect, the superstructure bowed to save capitalism, then Marx was wrong on two counts.

Finally, Marxists explain capitalism's surprising success by pointing to foreign nations. Capitalists began exploiting foreign workers in lesser-developed countries, they say, and these exploited workers abroad sustained the domestic economies. Again, even if the argument has merit, it takes us far astray from Marx's analysis of capitalism's internal, dialectical ruination.

In sum, Marx devised a scientific system in *Capital*. He confidently predicted the path of capitalism. With slippery and generous interpretations, he may have been right on occasion. But one thing is certain: Marx so despised religious sentimentalists, he would have angrily rejected the effort to win the argument by intellectual charity.

3. What did Marx give to modern economics? In mocking the relevance of a colleague's theory, the economist Joan Robinson used to say: "Imagine a dog running through the meadow chasing a fox. The dog follows the fox's trajectory. My colleague's theory is the flea on the back of the dog."

To most mainstream economists in the United States and Britain, Marx's economic theories are fleas. Within the mainstream, the defiance of Marx is just as loud left of center as it is right of center. Paul Samuelson depicts the labor theory of value as either definitional or metaphysical chicanery.

During the Great Depression, George Bernard Shaw tried to persuade John Maynard Keynes of Marx's virtues. Keynes resisted:

My feelings about *Das Kapital* are the same as my feelings about the *Koran*. I know that it is historically important and I know that many people, not all of whom are idiots, find it a sort of Rock of Ages and containing inspiration. Yet when I look into it, it is to me inexplicable that it can have this effect. Its dreary, out-of-date, academic controversialising seems so extraordinarily unsuited for this purpose. But then, as I have said, I feel just the same about the *Koran*. How could either of these books carry fire and sword round half the world? It beats me. Clearly there is some defect in my understanding. Do you believe both *Das Kapital* and the *Koran*? Or only *DK*? But what ever sociological value of the latter, I am sure that its contemporary economic value (apart from occasional but in-constructive and discontinuous flashes of insight) is nil. Will you promise to read it again, if I do?

Shaw did. Keynes did. Did Keynes see the light or the Mecca? He did not:

"I prefer Engels of the two. I can see that they invented a certain method of carrying on and a vile manner of writing, both of which their successors have maintained with fidelity. But if you tell me that they discovered a clue to the economic riddle, still I am beaten."[35]

Since that genius Keynes was beaten, most modern econo-mists have given up the fight and have stopped studying Marx. According to Frank Hahn, a distinguished critic of laissez-faire capitalism, "Most *Marxists* have never even read Marx. Of course, you really can't blame them."

Still Marx lurks behind the arguments of several thousand radical economists who publish the *Review of Radical Political Economics* and have a strong voice at the University of Massa-chusetts, Amherst. The etymological root of "radical" is *radic*, meaning "root," as in "radish." Like Marx, radical economists believe that the very root of modern economic theory is rotten in its analysis of capitalism. Nonetheless, radicals do not want to be responsible for every sentence Marx uttered or for every prediction he pronounced.

A few radicals do still embrace Marx's labor theory of value. All radicals, though, stress the issue of *control* under capital-ism. The bosses strive to "divide and conquer," and maintain control in the workplace and in the polling booth. The Polish Marxist Michał Kalecki argued in the 1940s that govern-ments deliberately ignite inflations and recessions to smother the demands of workers. The contemporary radical Stephen

Marglin claims that businesses often welcome recessions. If Marglin is right, a lot of people operate under a Marxian "false consciousness." Consider Marglin's reading of the presidential election of 1980: Ronald Reagan promised lower inflation *without* recession. Foolishly, he thought the bosses disliked recessions. But the bosses voted for Reagan anyway. Why? They knew he would fail and inadvertently incite a recession. He did, and, under Marglin's thesis, they were happy to see their stock prices fall.[36]

The modern radicals fight many battles—against the models of their economist colleagues, against the government, against the capitalists, and sometimes against the memory of their mentor, Karl Marx. So far, their victories are hard to count.

4. What did he give to modern politics? The loudest cry in any debate about communism today comes from the Marxists who excoriate the politics of the former Soviet Union and its satellites. This is not the communism of Marx, they shout. Of course, they are right. For a start, Marx restricted communism to countries that had been industrialized (although in his last years, he cautiously considered an eventual revolution in Russia). Stalin had a difficult task in accelerating agrarian Russia into the industrial era. In accordance with the *Communist Manifesto*'s proposals 1 and 9, Stalin forced farmers to join collectives and state farms. During the winter of 1932–1933, he deliberately starved millions to death to break their resistance, especially in Ukraine.[37]

Before Stalin, Lenin had faced similar political troubles in reshaping the Russian mind. During his reign, the dictatorship of the proletariat emerged as a dictatorship of the party—a dictatorship that would not soon wither away.

At the end of the 1980s, Mikhail Gorbachev tried to cure a sclerotic economy that had suffered through, its defenders say, seventy years of bad weather. At times Gorbachev seemed ready to jettison Marx and accept some free-market mechanisms, including long-term leases of farmland and manufacturing shops to profit-seeking, private cooperatives. Gorbachev could not hold on, though, as the free market forces singed the communist hands that held on to the economy. Arguably, the fax machine played as big a role in ending the Cold War as any military technology, by permitting democracy organizers to spread their messages. Russian president Boris Yeltsin struggled to push the Russian economy forward but was thwarted by corruption, an emergent mafia, and an elderly population that found little advantage in a new economy. For pensioners, communism guaranteed them a sum—a paltry sum—but at least a dependable ration. Capitalism guarantees them nothing but turmoil. In contrast, younger Russians jumped at the opportunity to build new businesses, to travel freely, and to try their hand at entrepreneurship. This dangerous social split—a deeper schism than the "capitalist versus worker" rift that Marx and Lenin exploited—looked nearly impossible to heal. In July 1998, Yeltsin attended a burial ceremony in Saint Petersburg for Czar Nicholas and his family, whose remains had been burned and left buried for decades. Yeltsin denounced the heinous butchering of the czar by the Leninists, hoping to find an issue that young and old could agree upon. At the beginning of Vladimir Putin's long reign, he vowed to retain Soviet retirement promises that kept old people in grubby but sturdy concrete buildings. Now retired people make up nearly one-third of the population, and more than three-quarters of them believe the breakup of the Soviet Union was a bad thing.[38] In 2018, Putin blotted out his expensive pledge to keep up old Soviet retirement schemes and announced that he would raise the retirement eligibility age from sixty to sixty-five years for men and from fifty-five to sixty-three years for women. Though videos of his old pledges went viral on YouTube, he likely calculated that the older critics are dying off fast.

The Chinese worshipped Marx after their 1949 revolution. They soon became polytheists, placing Mao Zedong on the same altar. But in the late 1970s under Deng Xiaoping, the Chinese began to move quickly toward free enterprise in many sectors, chiding Marx and scolding Mao. Deng, who had been thrown into prison by Mao during the bloody 1960s Cultural Revolution, was a pragmatist, stating that "it doesn't matter whether a cat is black or white so long as it catches mice."[39] He permitted shopkeepers to keep their profits and farmers to sell their own crops. What did they call this movement? They transliterated the term "free market." Millions of Chinese think "free market" is a Chinese term. After some ten years of liberalization, however, conservative forces reasserted themselves in 1987 (although they did not dismantle the Kentucky Fried Chicken restaurant located on the other side of Mao's tomb in Beijing). The backlash was temporary, though. After Deng's death, new prime minister Zhu Rongji and President Jiang Zemin committed to sparking more private business and cutting the reach of publicly owned businesses. In 1998, Jiang even took on the army, whose fingers reach into every sector, from hotels to refrigerator plants to karaoke bars. Chinese businessmen have woven themselves into the world economy. Most of the toys at your local Target were made in China, as are components of your iPhone and pills in your medicine cabinet. Meanwhile, more Chinese wash their hair with Procter & Gamble shampoo than any other brand! The odds of Zhu's, Jiang's, and Xi Jinping's successors managing to foster more free enterprise, while still keeping the Communist Party in power, are daunting. In recent years, pro-market Chinese economists and businesspeople have complained that leaders are freezing them out of future planning. There is little doubt, though, that this is not your father's Communist Party.

The Soviet Union and China were the last of the large communist nations that claimed to be Marxist. As the Iron Curtain melted along the borders of Poland, East Germany, Czechoslovakia, Hungary, and Romania, more workers achieved the freedom to unite—against Marx's ideas.

Thus far, no country has conformed to the Marxism that his admirers envision. Even the kibbutzim of Israel evolved from tending to socialist farms to capitalist technology missions. Perhaps no country will ever fulfill the Marxist's dream, which promises more than the real world, filled with scarcity, egoism, and evil, can deliver. It is a dream that resembles a kind of heaven or paradise lost, better suited for angels than for proletarians. Unfortunately, the yearning grows so strong that good people have been mesmerized into supporting vicious regimes that preach but do not practice the Marxist gospel. George Bernard Shaw, who shook Stalin's hand, saw years of Soviet oppression before shaking his head.

To many people today, Marx reminds us that economic change can be excruciating, that power can transform into oppression, and that the subservient sector of a population should be protected from exploitation. But these warnings apply even more crucially in communist regimes. Marx's admirers laud the younger, less scientific Marx. Rather than a cogent economic theorist or a charismatic political leader, Marx becomes an ever-present voice for humanistic social justice. He becomes like Tom Joad in John Steinbeck's *Grapes of Wrath*:

> "I'll be ever'where—wherever you look. Wherever they's a fight so hungry people can eat, I'll be there. Wherever they's a cop beatin' up a guy, I'll be there. . . . I'll be in the way guys yell when they're mad . . . An' when folks eat the stuff they raise an' live in the houses they build—why, I'll be there. See?"[40]

Given the abuses and atrocities wreaked under the name of Marx, this is probably the best place for him.

CHAPTER VII

Alfred Marshall and the Marginalist Mind

The three snippets that follow, gathered from the worlds of literature and entertainment, can help us understand an important development in neoclassical economics:

In Evelyn Waugh's novel *Scoop*, a British newspaper owner confronts an editor whose vocabulary consists of two responses: if the owner says something true, the editor replies "definitely"; if the owner says something untrue, the editor replies "up to a point."

"Let me see, what's the name of the place I mean? Capital of Japan? Yokohama, isn't it?"

"Up to a point, Lord Copper."

"And Hong Kong belongs to us, doesn't it?"

"Definitely, Lord Copper."

The old vaudeville comedian Henny Youngman, whose jokes have elicited more moans than ptomaine poisoning, framed many a classic line worthy of philosophical discourse, including

"How's your wife?"

"Compared to what?"

In the peculiar cult film *The Adventures of Buckaroo Banzai*, the hero reminds his friends of a metaphysical tautology:

"No matter where you go, there you are."

"Up to a point," "Compared to what?" and "No matter where . . ." can be said to symbolize the powerful change in economic thought at the end of the nineteenth century called *marginalism*. Before we examine the impact of Alfred Marshall, the preeminent marginalist, let us see how these snippets can explain this new approach.

Imagine you are traveling through Europe. You begin in Greece and have a splendid time. On the way to Italy, you stop in Corfu, where you rent a moped and circle the charming island. In Italy you enjoy Florence more than any place you have ever seen. Your visit in Italy cost $800 but gave you thousands of dollars' worth of pleasure. You reach Venice and then consider crossing the border into Austria. Austria, you fear, will be disappointing compared to Italy. You prefer calamari to Wiener schnitzel. How to decide whether to go forward or go home?

First, consider Buckaroo Banzai's advice: "No matter where you go, there you are." You are now on the border of Austria. Forget where you have been—the pleasure you had in Italy is irrelevant! *Marginalism declares that the past is behind you.* The issue is whether to step forward, and the starting point is where you are now.

Second, think of Henny Youngman's joke. What do you compare when choosing whether to go to Austria? You ignore the past pleasure in Italy and ask, Will the benefits of going to Austria exceed the costs of going to Austria? If a day in Austria will cost $50 and give you $75 worth of pleasure, go. So what if in Italy the benefits outweighed the costs by tenfold? The issue at hand is whether to go forward. And you should go forward if the benefits outstrip the costs, even if they exceed by a lesser margin than those before.[1]

Third, remember the editor in *Scoop*. Up to what point do you continue moving forward? You continue as long as the benefit of one step outweighs the cost of one step, until the marginal benefit equals the marginal cost. When a $50 day in Austria gives $50 of pleasure, you rest. To keep going would be like the proverbial boy who says he knows how to spell "banana," but just doesn't know when to stop. One shouldn't get carried away with forward movement. Many businesses fail because they do not know when to stop expanding. When People Express airlines saw success in the early 1980s, it rapidly expanded the number of routes and aircraft it owned and ignored the warnings of many consultants. Within a few years the overambitious airline folded. In more recent times, Boston Market and Krispy Kreme doughnuts walked into a similar mess. And in 2019, Forever 21, known for jumping onto changing "fast fashion" trends, declared bankruptcy, admitting that many of its eight hundred stores couldn't last another week, much less forever.

The essence of marginalism is the insistence on incremental, gradual moves as the focus of inquiry. How do firms decide how many cars to produce? They continue producing until the revenue they receive from producing one more car equals the cost of producing that extra car. The marginal revenue/marginal cost rule has numerous applications in and out of economics. Some students study all night for exams. But if at midnight the cost of staying up an extra hour (in terms of fatigue the next day) exceeds the benefit of cramming a bit more, it's better to be between the covers of a bed than the covers of a book.

Alfred Marshall did not invent or discover marginalism. It was in the European air, hovering in the cigar smoke of faculty clubs and intellectual kaffeeklatches. Just as Newton and Leibniz stumbled on or invented calculus in the seventeenth century, the Frenchman Augustin Cournot and the Germans J. H. von Thünen and H. H. Gossen began exploring marginal analysis a decade or two before Marshall did. William Stanley Jevons, an Englishman, contributed many important ideas that Marshall developed further, as did Carl Menger, founder of the Austrian school of economics. Questions of originality can spawn grudges. One summer while vacationing in the Alps, Marshall found himself in a shouting match over interest rates with Menger's successor, Eugen Böhm-Bawerk. Mary and Frau Böhm-Bawerk managed to tug their husbands away from each other before noses could get bloodied.[2] Marshall will get prime attention here for four related reasons: First, he most clearly and comprehensively applied marginal analysis; second, he established the marginal tradition that dominates microeconomics today; third, he taught some of the most prominent twentieth-century economists, including John Maynard Keynes (and Keynes's father), A. C. Pigou, and Joan Robinson; and fourth, his life neatly contrasted with Mill's and reflected the intellectual movements of his day, as well as the spirit of marginalism.

The Early Years

Alfred Marshall was born in the London slum of Bermondsey in 1842. It was on the wrong side of the Thames, and often on the wrong side of the law. In Dickens's *Oliver Twist*, the vicious thug Bill Sikes dies there, amid cramped homes with "rooms so small, so filthy, so confined, that the air would seem to be too tainted even for the dirt and squalor which they shelter."[3] Marshall's father, a Bank of England cashier, was a weak figure only if compared with James Mill or Caligula. William Marshall was a stern, nasty tyrant with a jutting jaw and an austere, evangelical creed to match. Alfred's great-great grandfather was a minister known for his strength and intimidating physique, traits not passed on to the boy, who was more inclined to hypochondria and agnosticism.[4] William Marshall drilled Alfred on his schoolwork, often Hebrew lessons, until eleven at night. A kind aunt saved Alfred's sanity, for he spent long summer holidays with her. She did not care so much for Hebrew, but did buy him a boat, a gun, and a pony.

Alfred soon put down the gun and got off the pony, trading Cowboy Alfred for Cambridge Alfred. This was an act of defiance. William wanted Alfred to accept a scholarship to Oxford, where he could study Latin and prepare for the ministry.

But Alfred had a touch of the devil in him. While the father thought he was studying religion in his room, the rebellious son was often reading mathematics, which his father did not understand and therefore despised. For Alfred, mathematics was a symbol of liberation (perhaps, subconscious guilt led him later in life to hide his mathematical economics in footnotes and margins). As Keynes's majestic essay on Marshall put it: "No! he would not take the scholarship and be buried at Oxford under dead languages; he would run away—to be a cabin-boy at Cambridge and climb the rigging of geometry and spy out the heavens."[5]

At St. John's College, Cambridge, Marshall earned academic honors in mathematics and then pocketed money for coaching other mathematics students. In his final exams he scored second highest at the university. (Marshall was sandwiched between the top scorer, J. W. Strutt, who later won the Nobel Prize in Physics, and the third scorer, H. M. Taylor, who invented the Braille system for mathematics and chemistry.) Marshall gravitated toward science, too, and graduated in 1865, the year that the first stick-and-ball model of the molecule was displayed. Excited by such developments, Marshall intended to study molecular physics, but metaphysics got in the way. In 1868 he trekked to Germany to read Kant in the original. Soon he followed his Cambridge colleague Henry Sidgwick into agnosticism. Sidgwick, who sometimes wrote on political economy, approved of Christian ethics and ideals, showing every Christian virtue except faith. An admirer once said that of all forms of wickedness, "Sidgwickedness" was the least wicked. According to Keynes, Sidgwick spent half his life proving that God did not exist and the rest of his life hoping he was wrong. While Marshall did not share Sidgwick's tortured internal struggle, he did strive for a similar noble character.

To his father's disappointment, Marshall did not hear God's voice calling him to the pulpit, but he did hear cries of the poor urging him to study economics:

From metaphysics I went to Ethics, and thought that the justification of the existing condition of society was not easy. A
friend, who had read a great deal of what are now called the
Moral Sciences, constantly said: "Ah! if you understood Political Economy you would not say that." So I read Mill's *Political Economy* and got much excited about it. I had doubts as
to the propriety of inequalities of *opportunities*, rather than
of material comfort. Then, in my vacations I visited the
poorest quarters of several cities and walked through one
street after another, looking at the faces of the poorest people. Next, I resolved to make as thorough a study as I could
of Political Economy.[6]

Once Marshall had chosen economics as his calling, he
showed priestly devotion to it. In the Middle Ages, three great
disciplines reigned: theology, aimed at spiritual perfection;
law, aimed at justice; and medicine, aimed at physical soundness. Marshall offered a fourth great vocation: economics,
aimed at the material welfare of all. Though many economists
fought among one another, Marshall never faltered in his respect for his profession and his dedication to improving the
human condition.

Throughout his life Marshall fought for economics as a separate field apart from history and the "moral sciences." In
1890 he called a meeting in London and led the charge to
create one of the first professional journals, the *Economic Journal*. The hall was packed with prominent economists, philan-
thropists, journalists, and businessmen. Even George Bernard
Shaw attended.[7] While trying to carve a space in the curriculum for economics, he also tried to unify the practitioners. To
Marshall, economics was a cooperative calling. He had little
patience for internecine rivalries (he was especially touchy
when others criticized his work). He said that nearly everything the classical economists taught, when properly interpreted, was right—except when they were criticizing one

another. Economists must be guardians of reason and truth, above politically expedient allegiances:

> Students of social science must fear popular approval. . . . If there is any set of opinions by the advocacy of which a newspaper can increase its sale, then the student, who wishes to leave the world in general and his country in particular better than it would be if he had not been born, is bound to dwell on the limitations and defects and errors, if any, in that set of opinions, and never to advocate them unconditionally.[8]

Cambridge inertia proved potent. Not until 1903 did Marshall persuade the university to establish a separate economics course.

But from Marshall's first contact with economics in the 1860s, he began developing a system of it. He saved metaphysics for light vacation reading and spent his vacations in the Alps. Each summer he took

> a knapsack, and spent most of the time walking in the high Alps. . . . He left Cambridge early in June jaded and overworked and returned in October brown and strong and upright. . . . When walking in the Alps his practice was to get up at six. . . . He would walk with knapsack on his back for two or three hours. He would sit down, sometimes on a glacier, and have a long pull on some book—Goethe or Hegel or Kant or Herbert Spencer. . . . This was his philosophic stage. Later on he worked out his theories of Domestic and Foreign Trade in these walks. A large box of books, etc., was sent on from one stage to another, but he would go for a week or more just with a knapsack. He would wash his shirt by holding it in a fast-running stream and dry it by carrying it in his alpen-stock over his shoulder. He did most of his hardest thinking in these solitary Alpine walks.[9]

With a small gift from his uncle, Marshall sailed across the Atlantic in 1875 to spend a summer in the United States. He did more than hike, for within just a few months he stamped letters from New York, Boston, Cincinnati, San Francisco, and points in between. During his travels, he met with factory managers and union workers at stove foundries, horseshoe works, carpentry shops, and elsewhere, trying to discern New World hype from New World fact. Like a man visiting a zoo, he wrote his mother some charming letters about his encounters with the exotic Americans, who did not feel obliged to abide by English manners. Shortly after arriving in New York, he walked into a hat shop where his Victorian sensibilities were shocked when the proprietor asked his hat size and, before waiting for an answer, swiped Alfred's hat off his head, placed it on his own head, and quickly calculated Alfred's cranial measurements. "My friend was the perfect democrat," Alfred wrote, and then suggested to his mother that some "go-ahead Yankee will find space in his advertisements for a line: 'Our shopmens [sic] heads warranted perfectly clean.'"[10]

Marshall spent nine years at St. John's College teaching economics to young men while also instructing women at Cambridge's Newnham College, which had recently been launched as a residential house that hosted "Lectures for Ladies." Marshall may have been the first—and certainly the most important—academic economist to tutor women at the most sophisticated level. In that era, well-to-do women were directed to "home economics," which involved planning for a Sunday roast and budgeting for maids and gardeners (the word "economics" comes from the Greek *oikos*, meaning "management of the household"). In the process of his lecturing, Marshall gained a wife and thereby, like Malthus, violated his bachelor vows and lost his fellowship. Mary Paley, great-granddaughter of Malthus's intellectual archenemy, Archdeacon William Paley, was one of the five students who made up the Newnham College inaugural class that Marshall tutored. With his fellowship

withdrawn, Alfred and Mary, who had been named the first
woman lecturer in the history of Cambridge, moved to University College at Bristol and then Oxford before returning to
Cambridge in 1885, when Marshall accepted the chair in political economy. Alfred and Mary worked closely together, and in
1879 jointly authored *Economics of Industry*. Though Alfred's
name appears above Mary's on the title page, the sizes of the
fonts are equivalent, a generous nod by a much higher-ranking
scholar. Unfortunately, as Marshall aged, he would grow grump-
ier and more dyspeptic about such matters and not fully support
the elevation of female researchers.

In his prime, though, Marshall was an engaging if quirky
man with cheery blue eyes. His students tell of innumera-
ble conversations over tea at his home. As a teacher, he stressed
illustration and current events over an orderly textbook
approach. Marshall could find economic examples almost
anywhere, sometimes in ancient history, other times in contemporary plays being performed in Cambridge. He spoke
with a chuckle and often concluded sentences with a gleeful
falsetto. Sometimes he seemed a bit silly. One famous story
recalls a graduate student visiting Marshall's home in search
of a dissertation topic:

> "Come in—come in," he said, running in from a little pas-
> sage, and I went with him upstairs. "Have you any idea what
> to do?" he asked me. I said, "No." "Well, then, listen," he
> said, producing a small black book. He proceeded to read
> out a list of subjects, having previously ordered me to hold
> up my hand when he came to one that I liked. In my ner-
> vousness I tried to close with the first subject, but Marshall
> took no notice and read on.

Marshall rejected the student's second and third signals.

He kept reading out topics for another five minutes. Finally,
Marshall stopped and asked, "Have you found a subject you

like?" "I don't know," I began. "No one ever does," he said, "but that's my method."[11]

Despite such silliness, Marshall could be stunningly clever. According to Cambridge mythology, whenever a difficult mathematical treatise came out, Marshall would read just the first chapter and the last chapter. He would then stand in front of the fireplace and figure out the rest. He also had a touch of vanity and did not think that photos did justice to his noble gaze. While a graduate student at St. John's, Cambridge, I would eat dinners most evenings under the gaze of his portrait, painted in 1908 by the acclaimed artist William Rothenstein, who reported that Marshall "took sitting seriously," adding that "vain men make the best sitters."[12] Marshall preferred a portrait of another man. In the 1870s, before he had achieved much fame, he spotted in a shop window a small oil painting of a dark-complexioned, anonymous laborer, with a "strikingly gaunt and wistful expression," staring downward. Marshall bought the portrait for a few shillings. "I set it up above the chimney-piece in my room . . . called it my patron saint, and devoted myself" to trying to help such men, he said.[13]

The Gradualist Approach

Perhaps no one among the "hall of fame" economists contrasts more with the tempest-tossed mind of John Stuart Mill and the incendiary visions of Karl Marx than Marshall, whose life and thought were about as frenzied as an old basset hound on a Sunday afternoon. Interestingly, his inner and outer calm reflected his view of economics and, indeed, his view of the world. He had read enough German philosophy to know that he had a Weltanschauung. Never one for legerdemain, Marshall immediately tells us his creed when we open *Principles of*

Economics, first published in 1890: "*Natura non facit saltum*"—
nature makes no leaps.

Whereas Apollonian and Dionysian forces battled in Mill's
mind and revolutions exploded in Marx's, Marshall appeared
as steady as the Alps. Like his predecessors, he hosted idealistic visions of a better world. But he was never fooled into abandoning careful analysis:

> In every stage of civilization . . . poets in verse and prose
> have delighted to depict a past truly "Golden Age," before
> the pressures of mere material gold have been felt. Their
> idyllic pictures have been beautiful, and have stimulated
> noble imaginations and resolves; but they have had very lit-
> tle historical truth. . . . But in the responsible conduct of af-
> fairs, it is worse than folly to ignore the imperfections which
> still cling to human nature.[14]

Still, Marshall thought the world could improve—gradually.
Whereas classical economists followed a Newtonian scientific
approach searching for laws of nature, Marshall turned to a
more evolutionary approach. Charles Darwin and biology replaced Isaac Newton and physics. The "mathematico-physical"
sciences ruled in the eighteenth century—studying unvary-
ing natural phenomena—and economists followed. As the
nineteenth century wore on, however, biological studies—
concentrating on organic, evolving phenomena—ascended
into prominence. Economists, first led by John Stuart Mill, followed. Marshall took them even further.

Alfred Marshall's marginalism is evolution applied to economics. The businessman and the consumer make no great
leaps, but step by step they try to improve their situations. Individuals, companies, and governments all adapt to changing
prices. The fittest firms survive. Low profits drive out the
weakest. Competitive pressures force firms to cut costs. Although the final results do resemble Adam Smith's Newtonian economics, Marshall teaches us how to closely inspect

individual decisions along the way. Marginalism paves the way for the development of microeconomics. And microeconomics persuades us that actors will reconsider their positions and decide to take new steps if the benefits exceed the cost. Only if benefits and costs stagnate can we assume constant, Newtonian behavior:

> The main concern of economics is thus with human beings who are impelled, for good and evil, to change and progress. Fragmentary statical hypotheses are used as temporary auxiliaries to dynamical—or rather biological—conceptions: but the central idea of economics, even when its Foundations alone are under discussion, must be that of living force and movement.[15]

Marshall lived his life by a gradualist creed: he dared to be cautious. Sometimes he may have been too slow. While Marshall developed many of his ideas in the early 1870s, *Principles* was published so many years later that critics disparaged his claims of originality, although more recent scholarship shows that many of his principles did appear in lectures decades before they appeared in print.

Fortunately, *Principles* stayed fresh for a long time. Originally appearing in 1890, the text sold more and more copies every year, finally peaking in the 1920s. Marshall saw eight editions in his lifetime, and modern microeconomics textbooks still rest on this text. *Principles* differs from contemporary works in several ways, though. First, Marshall can't resist moral platitudes. Every so often Marshall slips in advice that might be better suited for "Dear Abby"; sometimes he sounds like the right man to resolve a feud between Abby and her sister, Ann Landers, but the wrong man to resolve a tough business dispute. Happily, Marshall does not always sound as if he's addressing a convention of Victorian schoolmarms.

Second, in contrast with modern textbooks, which aim at students and specialists, *Principles* often speaks directly to laypeople. Economists cannot hide in pure theory but must look at the world and try to improve it with the tools they develop. Marshall develops complex models, but he saves the complexity for footnotes and appendices. In the main text he uses simple, accessible English. Marshall warned that elegant models with "long-drawn-out and subtle reasonings" may become "scientific toys rather than engines for practical work."[16] If Marshall wanted toys, he could have stayed with his aunt and played cowboys and Indians. Instead he sought a noble profession and urged others to follow. And they did, although he sometimes complained about his early students. By the first publication of *Principles*, more than half the chairs in economics in the United Kingdom were filled by his pupils. And as the number of chairs increased, more Marshallians settled into them.

Although trained as a mathematician, Marshall feared that economists would calculate themselves into irrelevancy. Ricardo forever remained a hero to Marshall, because Ricardo thought like a mathematician without resorting to obscure symbols and secret formulae. Marshall translated Ricardo and Mill into calculus but never let his economic arguments rest on solely mathematical proofs. In a charming letter, Marshall put forth his system:

(1) Use mathematics as a shorthand language, rather than as an engine of inquiry. (2) Keep to them till you have done. (3) Translate into English. (4) Then illustrate by examples that are important in real life. (5) Burn the mathematics. (6) If you can't succeed in 4, burn 3. This last I did often.[17]

No wonder Pigou reported that Marshall read mathematical treatises in front of the fireplace. Perhaps Marshall's maneuvers assuaged his guilt for stashing mathematical curves under his childhood bed the way other boys conceal sketches of other kinds of sinuous shapes.

Marshall was a little less pert about economic method than the preceding letter suggests. Like Mill, Marshall avoided the classical trap of declaring rigid economic laws. History had a place in economics along with deductive theory: "The chief fault in English economists at the beginning of the century was not that they ignored history and statistics, but that they regarded man as so to speak a constant quantity. . . . I do not assign any universality to economic dogmas. It is not a body of concrete truth, but an engine for the discovery of concrete truth."[18] Marshall also realized that facts teach nothing by themselves. According to John Neville Keynes, Marshall employed "deductive political economy guided by observation."[19] By finding a golden mean between the ivory tower and the public house, between pure theory and earthly fact, Marshall defended economics from the biting attacks of sociologists and moralists.

Rather than becoming the Newton of economics, Marshall sought to be the Darwin. He would look at firms to see how they reacted to environmental changes. "The mecca of the economist lies in economic biology," he declared.[20]

Economic Time—Short and Long Runs

Rome was not built in a day, and man did not evolve from monkeys in a week. Paradoxically, Darwin taught that whereas a thousand years may be biologically insignificant, the brief lifetime of a mutant could determine the future of a species. Marshall realized that like biological time, "economic time" was not synchronized with Big Ben in London. Ten years does not simply permit a firm to do ten times what it could do in just one year. For some transactions, one year is a long time. For other moves, one year barely allows preparation.

During every step of economic analysis, clocks are ticking. During the first OPEC embargo in 1973, politicians grabbed economists by the necks, shaking them to and fro until they answered crucial questions: When will consumers respond to higher prices by conserving? When will General Motors, Ford, and Chrysler respond by producing smaller cars? When will oil companies respond by drilling elsewhere? Each of these eventually took place—but not at the same time.

Marshall tried to isolate particular tendencies and the time periods in which they operate. Time is "a chief cause of those difficulties . . . which make it necessary for man with his limited powers to go step by step; breaking up a complex question, studying one bit at a time, and at least combining his partial solutions into a more or less complete solution of the whole riddle." Marshall created an ingenious system of analysis. While looking at one factor, he threw all others into a "pound." There they waited while he vetted the solitary factor. He called the pound *ceteris paribus*, meaning "*other things being equal*: the existence of other tendencies is not denied, but their disturbing effect is neglected for a time. The more the issue is narrowed, the more exactly can it be handled."[21]

Prior economists had already advised a ceteris paribus assumption. But Marshall derived an explicit method and constructed rigorous theories according to it. Today's textbooks rest on Marshall's method.

Marshall's method contrasted sharply with the highly theoretical and mathematical "general equilibrium" analysis of the nineteenth-century Frenchman Léon Walras. While Walras's abstract apparatus receives little attention in undergraduate textbooks, his work was extended in modern times by some very intelligent theoreticians, including Nobel laureates Kenneth Arrow, Gérard Debreu, and Cambridge's Frank Hahn. (An interesting aside: despite the dazzling mathematics behind Walrasian analysis, Walras twice failed the mathematics portion of his college entrance exam.)

An example may help our understanding of Marshall's system. Assume the development of a new product called Yuppie Yogurt, which appeals to an obvious market, partly because it's actually produced on Wall Street. Even better, assembly workers drop pieces of Godiva chocolate into the yogurt cultures as they grow. The slogan "Eat Your Way to the Top Without Getting a Fat Bottom!" drives yuppies wild for yogurt. On any particular day, the supply of Yuppie Yogurt is fixed. If computers crash and more than the usual number of yuppies take snack breaks, some will go hungry. By the time the producer hears about an excess demand, packages more yogurt, and sends it out of the factory, the working day is over. In the time frame of one day, therefore, only demand fluctuates.

With more notice, producers can boost supply. The second time frame, which Marshall called the "short run," lasts long enough for producers to change the amount supplied. To supply more, they can hire more labor and buy more raw materials. But they cannot expand too much. Marshall's short run does not last long enough to build new manufacturing plants. What if Yuppie Yogurt manufacturers advertise on television, which sends demand flying? In the short run, they can buy more milk for the yogurt and hire more workers to add the chocolate. If demand falls, they can fire the workers and reduce their milk purchases.

Because plant capacity is fixed in the short run, producers do face the law of diminishing returns—that is, stuffing too many workers in a room reduces their productivity. Of course, producers will still employ the marginal rule and produce yogurt until the price they receive equals the cost of the last pint.

In the third time frame, the "long run," producers have enough time to build new plants, as well as vary labor and materials. If demand for Yuppie Yogurt persists, they can even extend Wall Street into New York Harbor—or erect a plant across the harbor. They may even replace the workers with pin-striped robots.

In the long run, new producers could enter the industry, and old producers who lost money could leave. Survivors would earn normal profits. Thus, supply becomes prominent in the long run.

How long are the short and long runs? It depends on the particular industry; the periods are defined by how long it takes to alter capital and capacity. Obviously, Marshall did not discuss Yuppie Yogurt. Instead he discussed fish; in the fishing industry, Marshall supposed that it would take a year or two to employ new ships. As technology improves, however, the long run (reaction time) may shrink.

Marshall had more to say about the size of firms. The classicalists often decreed that as a firm increased in size, its average costs remained the same: growth tended to neither help nor hurt a firm. By Marshall's time, most economists spoke of decreasing returns: at some point bigness led to inefficient operations. In his fish examples, Marshall noted that too much fishing may deplete resources and eventually force fishermen to sail farther from shore for their catch. Nonetheless, Marshall asked, what if bigness made certain industries more efficient? Larger companies often have access to cheaper credit and more efficient machinery. Today, Whirlpool can get a loan cheaper than you can; moreover, it can afford to buy a better assembly line than you.

Marshall identified two different sources for increasing returns to scale. *Internal economies* arise from division of labor, buying supplies in bulk, and using specialized, large machinery that smaller producers cannot afford to operate. Imagine a small company called Chuck's Crossings that transports aristocrats across the Atlantic on luxurious dinghies. The cost to the company is $3,000 per passenger. If Chuck can attract one thousand passengers, he can use the *Queen Mary 2* instead of dinghies. With a thousand on board, the cost per passenger is only $2,000. Thus, if Chuck can billow his sales, he can scrap the dinghies and sail more cheaply. (Eventually, if Chuck keeps expanding, costs will likely rise because of management inefficiencies and marketing problems.)

The seemingly dull business of freight shipping has changed in radical and exciting ways over the past fifty years. In the 1950s, when a ship steamed into port, one hundred stevedores would toil for a week unloading it. Now, with freight packed into containers, seven dockworkers can unload a major vessel in just a day. Those containers go directly from ships to trains to trucks with almost magical efficiency. This transportation revolution has stomped on distribution costs, making it economical for Americans to import bottled water from Fiji.

External economies follow from events outside the particular firm. If an industry tends to locate in a particular area, the communities may provide an orderly, constant market for skilled labor. The firms get an extra push because subsidiary trades emerge, offering the industry low-cost supplies:

> Good work is rightly appreciated, inventions and improvements in machinery, in processes and the general organization of the business have their merits promptly discussed: if one man starts a new idea, it is taken up by others and combined with suggestions of their own; and thus it becomes the source of further new ideas. And presently subsidiary trades grow up in the neighborhood, supplying it with implements and materials, organizing its traffic, and in many ways conducing to the economy of its material.[22]

One need consider only the rather incestuous relationship between Stanford University and Silicon Valley or Cambridge University and the collection of high-tech firms located in "Silicon Fen" to see important linkages between an industry and its suppliers. Cities like Wichita, Kansas, and Querétaro, Mexico, have become hubs for airplane and helicopter manufacturers. In an older example, Pennsylvania miners extracted coal, which was turned into coke and fed into nearby furnaces used in the steel industry. Sometimes the linkages are not so obvious. Consider: Broadway is a boulevard running north to south in Manhattan, and of course the moniker "Broadway" refers to the theater district, a square-mile neighborhood near Times Square where the theaters are located. But the district is not made up of just theaters. Within blocks of Broadway are rehearsal halls that can be rented by the hour and the offices of theatrical producers, casting directors, publicity firms, and vocal and dance coaches. The union of stagehand, lighting, and sound workers is right in the heart of it, too, a few yards from Joe Allen, a legendary tavern catering to the Broadway crowd. It would be hard for, say, Albuquerque to grow a similar complex of talent within a small neighborhood.

Marshall's observations apply beyond cities, however. Fargo, North Dakota, the butt of jokes and a sardonic movie, has become a fast-growing software powerhouse that boasts one of the lowest unemployment rates in the country. In the early 1990s, Fargo looked like just another Great Plains town fading away, as frigid winter winds blew through a dilapidated downtown. But some entrepreneurial souls figured out that modern telecommunications could permit them to design and sell software from anywhere, including a remote place in North Dakota. Microsoft bought Great Plains Software in 2001 and expanded the facilities, and today Fargo is a bustling hub of technological know-how. Belying its dusty, backward reputation, North Dakota spends more on research and development as a proportion of income than almost any other state.

If Marshall is right about increasing returns, then big is beautiful. If big is beautiful, competition could not long continue, for large firms would always defeat small firms. Chuck's Crossings would always be swamped by Cunard. And a monopoly would dominate each industry. How could Marshall, a prime proponent of competition, live with this theoretical implication?

He could because he thought that firms could not live forever. He resorted again to biology and borrowed an organic metaphor. Entrepreneurs can fertilize and deliver a bouncing baby firm. They can nourish and raise it to adulthood. But soon the entrepreneurs die. Succeeding managers will frequently be less talented. New firms, sired by other entrepreneurs, will flourish:

> Nature still presses on the private business by limiting the
> length of the life of the original founders, and by limiting

even more narrowly that part of their lives in which their faculties retain full vigour. And so, after a while, the guidance of business falls into the hands of people with less energy and less creative genius, if not with less active interest in its prosperity. If it is turned into a joint-stock company, it may retain the advantages of division of labor, of specialized skill and machinery: it may even increase them by a further increase of its capital, and under favorable conditions it may secure a permanent and prominent place in the work of production. But it is likely to have lost so much of its elasticity and progressive force, that the advantages are no longer exclusively on its side in its competition with younger and smaller rivals.[23]

According to Marshall, the lean and hungry will eat into the profits of the fat and lazy. While Marshall's theory seemed dated in post–World War II America with the rise of international conglomerates, it now appears rather contemporary. Stable, giant conglomerates of the 1970s, like Gulf and Western, ITT, AT&T, and IBM, all got thrashed in hotly competitive markets of the subsequent decades. RCA, which dominated media and electronics under longtime chief David Sarnoff, quickly unwound after his retirement.[24] Later, even the famous red-neon RCA sign on its Rockefeller Center headquarters was dismantled, though millions of New Yorkers had lived their lives under its glow.

New entrepreneurial efforts may be willing to take more risks than established companies that must answer to stockholders. Even if the start-up ventures usually fail (perhaps for taking foolish risks), just one success story from a garage can spoil the careers of dozens of vice presidents for long-range strategic planning who work in shiny, glass skyscrapers. During the last thirty years, a clear majority of the new jobs in the United States were created by companies with fewer than five hundred employees.

After waves of corporate mergers from the 1950s through

the 1980s, many firms reversed gears and aimed to create "meaner, leaner" businesses by streamlining and selling off divisions. National Distillers Corporation no longer produces liquor and changed its name to Quantum Chemical Corporation, after spinning off its spirits division to Jim Beam. In March 1989, *BusinessWeek* devoted its cover story to the question "Is Your Company Too Big?"[25] AT&T's biggest success in the 1990s was spinning off Lucent Technologies, which made sophisticated telephone equipment. While AT&T languished, Lucent share prices soared into the stratosphere, until crashing in the "tech wreck" of 2000. At the same time, many corporations such as Time Inc. and Warner Communications merged in hopes of efficiently sharing knowledge and assets. The subsequent Time Warner merger with AOL in 2000 was miserably timed and miserably executed. Since the publication of Marshall's *Principles* more than a hundred years ago, businessmen have continually struggled to balance flexibility and economies of scale in order to discover the optimal size of their enterprises.

The Marginalist Consumer

So far we have discussed the firm without examining the consumer. Marshall would not be happy with such one-sidedness, for he rebelled against the classical claim echoed by Ricardo and Mill that the value of a product reflects the hours it took to produce it. In a famous metaphor, Marshall proclaimed that supply and demand are equally powerful: "We might as reasonably dispute whether it is the upper or the under blade of a pair of scissors that cuts a piece of paper, as whether value is governed by utility or cost of production."[26] With Marshall's encouragement, then, let us combine supply and demand, using the marginalist tools.

The last time we left our Wall Street friends they were lust-ing for yogurt. Yuppie Debbie's demand for yogurt is based on the additional satisfaction each half pint of yogurt gives her. Marshall called this "marginal utility." Jevons insisted on calling it "final utility." Fortunately, they never lectured together, or a very boring debate might have followed.

Marshall and Jevons each asserted that Debbie's marginal utility would diminish with each portion of yogurt. That is, the first portion might give her $1 worth of pleasure; the second, only 90 cents; the third, perhaps 70 cents; the fourth, 64 cents; and so on. Finally, the idea of eating one more spoonful would repulse her. In deciding whether to buy yogurt, Debbie would compare the selling price with her marginal utility. If the selling price for each portion were $1, Debbie would buy only one (because a second portion costing $1 would give her only 90 cents of pleasure). If the price were 65 cents, Debbie would buy three. The third portion, costing 65 cents, would give her 70 cents of utility. But if she kept going and bought a fourth, it would give her only 64 cents of pleasure. Economists draw downward-sloping demand curves that trace the diminishing marginal utility. In each case, Debbie compares the marginal utility (benefit) of yogurt with the marginal cost (price).

Marshall then enunciated the "*law of demand:*—The greater the amount to be sold, the smaller must be the price. . . . The amount demanded increases with a fall in price, and diminishes with a rise in price."[27]

Of course, Marshall knew that price alone did not determine demand. He listed several other factors and placed them in the ceteris paribus pound. Most important of those he discussed are as follows: (1) the consumer's tastes, customs, and preferences; (2) the consumer's income; and (3) the price of rival goods. If Debbie read in the *Wall Street Journal* that eating Yuppie Yogurt helped one's racquetball game, she would immediately begin salivating, and her tastes would change. Even if the price stayed the same, she would buy more. But in explaining the law of demand, Marshall asked us to assume that tastes, income, and other prices remained steady. If so, the law of demand usually holds (a change in one of the impounded factors shifts the demand curve).

Marshall then deployed the marginalist principle again and asked the marginalist/Henny Youngman question: Where does Debbie step next? The rational consumer continually looks forward and compares the additional satisfaction available from one good with that of other goods. If $1 spent on yogurt yields $1 worth of pleasure, but that dollar spent on sushi would bring $1.20 of pleasure, Debbie should buy sushi. How long should she continue buying sushi? Remember that according to the law of diminishing marginal utility, as she buys more, the sushi becomes worth less to her. Therefore, she should continue buying until the pleasure from sushi equals the pleasure from yogurt. In equilibrium, a dollar spent on all goods begets the same amount of pleasure. If a dollar spent on product A gives more pleasure than a dollar spent on product B, the consumer should consume more of A and less of B until the marginal utilities are equal. In Marshall's words, the consumer is "constantly watching to see whether there is anything on which he is spending so much that he would gain by taking a little away from that line of expenditure and putting it on some other line."[28]

When Marshall visited American shops as a young man, he noticed many bargains. But what really is a "bargain"? Marshall said that when a shopper buys something for a lower price than she would be willing to pay, it is a "consumer surplus." Take this example: In 2018, Bruce Springsteen performed on Broadway in a one-man show that sold out every night and was filmed for a Netflix special. The average price of an official ticket bought at the box office was $500. But many of his fans would have paid much more. We know this because scalpers charged about $2,000 per seat.[29] Many of those fans lucky enough to purchase official box office seats for $500 enjoyed a $1,500 "consumer surplus," in Marshall's parlance. Marshall used his ingenious mathematical and graphical framework to illustrate this surplus, a technique that still shows up on economics exams.

Marshall developed a similar framework for suppliers. As a producer supplies more, her costs tend to rise. The law of supply is opposite to the law of demand: supply will rise only if the price received from consumers rises. The producer compares the marginal cost of producing one more unit to the marginal benefit, the price. (A supply curve slopes upward, whereas a demand curve slopes downward.)

In the same way that the consumer constantly compares the marginal utility of spending a dollar on various products, the producer constantly compares the marginal utility of spending a dollar on capital (machinery) with the marginal utility of spending that dollar on labor. If a dollar spent on a new machine yields more than a dollar spent on a new employee, the manager will invest in machinery and reduce her labor force. In equilibrium, the marginal return from capital equals the marginal return from labor.

Assume that the firm is in equilibrium. The assembly union gets a raise. What happens? The marginal return from labor (the marginal output divided by the wage) falls in comparison with the marginal return from capital. The manager would *substitute* a robot for a human assembler until the marginal returns equalize again. For this reason, Marshall blasted unions that supported make-work projects and featherbedding, for they only hurt their members.

Sometimes prices would lead the manager to fire robots and hire human assemblers if, for example, the cost of electricity rose or wages fell. Sometimes governments seem to inadvertently tip the scale against human beings. Let's ask a simple question: If you were a manager, why would you hire a human? Yes, they can be wondrously creative and caring, but they get sick. They daydream. And they take coffee breaks. The cost of capital equipment, meanwhile, from laptops to lathes, has plummeted for the past twenty-five years. Moreover, because interest rates have been remarkably low, the cost of leasing and financing new tools has fallen to the lowest levels since, well, before there were laptops and lathes. At the same time, federal tax policy has been tilted toward capital spending, with businesses able to immediately deduct the cost of new equipment. People, however, remain relatively expensive. Let's say that an applicant can deliver $50,000 of value to a firm—and she is willing to work for $50,000 a year. Great match, right? Not exactly. In addition to her salary, in the United States the employer also has to pay a 7.56 percent Social Security and Medicare tax and contribute to workers' compensation and unemployment insurance. And then there are health insurance costs. Suddenly, that hunk of metal robot is looking shinier.

The constant balancing act is not just between capital and labor, but among land, new machinery, used machinery, skilled labor, unskilled labor, and such. If land prices rise, a manager may build another story onto the plant rather than expand horizontally.

Marshall's *Principles* do not argue that all producers act marginally or rationally. But if a producer does not, her competitors will be more successful, and economic evolution will favor them. Eventually, the irrational firm will fail.

Whether consumers or producers, most economic agents live by the words of Evelyn Waugh, Henny Youngman, and Buckaroo Banzai, engaged in a never-ending comparison of marginal steps.

Is it the consumer or the producer who determines the price? Both. Like blades of scissors, the intersection of supply and demand gives us prices. While the classicalists overemphasized supply, Jevons overstressed demand. But Marshall's persuasive idea, that of an "equilibrium point of demand and supply, was extended so as to discover a whole Copernican system, by which all the elements of the economic universe are kept in their place by mutual counterpose and interaction."[30]

Marshall also took time to rebut the Marxian labor theory of value. He starts by stating that man cannot create material things—man can only rearrange matter to make it more satisfying to others. Capitalists contribute to satisfying others by contributing their money. Their return rewards them for waiting, for not spending it today on consumer goods. Marshall speaks so forcefully here that direct quotation is warranted. Marx and others

argued that labour always produces a "surplus" above its wages and the wear-and-tear of capital used in aiding it: and that the wrong done to labour lies in the exploitation of this surplus by others. But this assumption that the whole of this Surplus is the produce of labour, already takes for granted what they ultimately profess to prove by it; they make no attempt to prove it; and it is not true. It is not true that the spinning of yarn in a factory, after allowance has been made for the wear-and-tear of the machinery, is the product of the labour of the operatives. It is the product of their labour, together with that of the employer and subordinate managers, and of the capital employed; and that capital itself is the product of labour and waiting: and therefore the spinning is the product of labour of many kinds, and of waiting. If we admit that it is the product of labour alone, and not of labour and waiting, we can no doubt be compelled by inexorable logic to admit that there is no justification for interest, the reward for waiting; for the conclusion is implied in the premiss. . . .

. . . If it be true that the postponement of gratifications involves *in general* a sacrifice on the part of him who postpones, just as additional effort does on the part of him who labours; and if it be true that this postponement enables man to use methods of production of which the first cost is great; but by which the aggregate of enjoyment is increased, as certainly as it would be by an increase of labour; then it cannot be true that the value of a thing depends simply on the amount of labour spent on it. Every attempt to establish this premiss has necessarily assumed implicitly that the service performed by capital is a "free" good, rendered without sacrifice, and therefore needing no interest as a reward to induce its continuance; and this is the very conclusion which the premiss is wanted to prove. The strength of Rodbertus' and Marx's sympathies with suffering must always claim our respect: but what they regarded as the scientific foundation of their practical proposals appears to be little more than a series of arguments in a circle to the effect that there is no economic justification for interest, while that result has been all along latent in their premisses; though, in the case of Marx, it was shrouded by mysterious Hegelian phrases, with which he "coquetted," as he tells us in his Preface.[31]

The Elastic Economy

While developing his demand apparatus, Marshall refined one of the most important tools in all economics, elasticity. Almost every economic debate today, whether "macro" or "micro," confronts the elasticity issue. Every government policy must implicitly or explicitly deal with elasticity. What is this unavoidable, haunting specter? Elasticity is another name for responsiveness. How responsive are people to changes in prices? Do people adjust their purchases when prices rise or fall? Or do they continue buying the same amount? The answer, of course, depends on the product.

If the price of a product rises and people cut back their purchases, we say that demand is *elastic*. If they continue buying the same amount, demand is *inelastic*. More precisely, elasticity is the percentage change in demand divided by the percentage change in price. If a 10 percent change in price leads to an 11 percent change in purchases, demand is elastic. If it leads to a less than 10 percent change in purchases, demand is inelastic. If it leads to a 10 percent change, demand is "unit inelastic." (If demand is highly elastic, we should see a nearly horizontal demand curve, indicating that people will easily adjust their purchases. If demand is highly inelastic, we should see a nearly vertical demand curve, indicating that people will purchase the same amount regardless of price.)

Why is this important? Let's look at some simple examples. In nearly every James Bond movie, the following line appears: "Vodka martini, shaken not stirred." If Bond drinks one and only one vodka martini and does not substitute a gin martini or a glass of milk, his demand is inelastic. Regardless of price, he will drink one vodka martini. This puts bartenders in a good position. They can charge a million dollars for a drink. Lucky for Bond, other bars will compete for his business.

Trouble arises, however, when a monopoly meets inelastic consumers. If only one company supplied insulin, for example, it could charge an outrageous price. When monopolies face inelastic consumers, government regulators often step in. Thus, for example, the relationship between pharmaceutical companies and the government is precarious. On the one hand, the government wants companies to perform research to cure diseases. But companies need assurances that the government will not just seize their miraculous discoveries and leave them bankrupt. On the other hand, the government must ensure that needy, desperate patients are not gouged. In August 2016, just before the school year began, the pharmaceutical company Mylan announced a dramatic price hike for its popular EpiPen, which counteracts life-threatening food and insect-sting allergies. Parents were outraged. While Mylan had a monopoly on the injector mechanism, it did not have a patent on the drug inside (epinephrine). It turned out that the Food and Drug Administration had been slow to approve alternatives in a convoluted process that can cost applicants hundreds of millions of dollars and takes years to get a verdict. In 2018, new FDA commissioner Scott Gottlieb clarified and sped up the process, leading to a rash of competitors, including a generic version of the EpiPen released by the Israeli company Teva, which undercut the Mylan product price by about 50 percent.

The fear of price-gouging and of limiting supply leads economists to follow Marshall's advice that many monopolies—for instance, water and electrical utilities—be regulated. Since they are "natural monopolies" (it would be inefficient to have several water companies lay pipes on one street), Marshall suggests that the government encourage them to expand output through subsidies or at least guarantees that they will remain profitable.

Often demand for goods is highly elastic. If the price of iceberg lettuce rises, people will turn to Boston lettuce, romaine lettuce, or maybe the crabgrass on their front lawns.

What determines the degree of elasticity? First and most obvious, the number of substitutes available. The more alternatives, the easier consumers can switch. The demand for Robert De Niro may be inelastic. The only alternative seems to be Al Pacino, although some would say that he is an almost perfect substitute. Hollywood first offered the part of Rick in *Casablanca* to Ronald Reagan, not Humphrey Bogart. Not exactly substitutes, but Marshall never claimed that everyone was rational.

Second, the more time we have to find substitutes, the more elastic demand can be. From fall 1973 to summer 1974, gasoline prices rose by 45 percent. In that year demand fell by only 8 percent. After a few years, though, consumers showed much more elasticity. They bought smaller cars, rode mass transportation, and insulated homes. Airlines reduced their flight weight by cutting the number of pillows, blankets, and magazines. They also reduced the amount of food and fuel carried, and even thinned the exterior paint.

Third, Marshall argued that products unimportant in the household budget may be inelastic. If the price of toothpicks rose sharply, few would cut back. Toothpicks compose too small a percentage of the budget to worry about.

Consumer companies must constantly gauge the elasticity of demand, and sometimes they get it wrong. In 2020, the Clorox company sheepishly admitted that it had sold fewer Glad trash bags and freezer wraps than expected. When the company raised prices, shoppers shied away and stores cut back the amount of shelf space, shaving sales by 8 percent. The CEO reported, "Pushback was more than we anticipated," meaning that the company underestimated the elasticity of demand.[32]

Marshall's elasticity toolkit led to another insight: the *income* elasticity of demand. This measures whether people will buy more or less of something if their income changes. For example, during a recession, when people lose jobs, they may be less likely to buy "name brands" like Clorox and Kleenex and more likely to buy cheaper store brands or so-called plain wrap. Comedian Chris Rock jokes about his parents being so cheap that they would buy only unbranded food in a plain white box, rather than famous brands featuring flashy labels and iconic spokespeople: "The label just said one thing: 'rice.' No Uncle, no riverboat, just 'rice.'" And for breakfast? "White box, black letters: 'cereal.' There ain't no captain on this ship. Ain't nothing lucky about these charms." But what if Rock's father got a raise? Maybe he would spring for Uncle Ben's rice and Cap'n Crunch or Lucky Charms cereal. If so, his income elasticity of demand would be positive, and his family breakfast might be sweeter.

Following Marshall's lessons, economists call less-desirable, no-brand items "inferior goods." The coronavirus crisis delivered a quick example. Between February and March 2020, as consumers lost jobs and investors watched their stock portfolios crater, Walmart's sales of ramen noodles jumped by 578 percent.[33] Suddenly, Americans across the country were adopting the culinary proclivities of poor college students armed with only a teapot.

How does the elasticity issue sneak into every government policy? A few more examples will suffice:

1. Every few years, New York City's MTA raises the subway fare, arguing that higher fares mean more revenue to balance the budget. The argument assumes that demand is relatively inelastic. If too many people respond by taking buses, an Uber or Lyft, or a horse-drawn carriage, total revenue falls.

2. In 1998, the Clinton-Gore White House proposed jacking up cigarette taxes in order to cut teenage smoking. Vice President Gore asserted that for every 10 percent increase in cigarette prices, teenagers smoke 7 percent fewer cigarettes. Using these elasticity estimates, the White House proposed a $1.50 per pack increase, which it claimed would reduce smoking by 42 percent over a five-year period. Opponents argued that since lower-class Americans are disproportionately smokers, the burden of the tax would fall on their shoulders. At the same time that U.S. politicians debated the issue, Sweden actually cut its tobacco tax to make black market smuggling from neighboring countries less attractive.

3. Marshall's elasticity also applies to international trade, and was enhanced by a posthumous partner named Abba Lerner. Lerner was a pioneering Moldovan-born, British economist who hopscotched from university to university from the 1930s to the 1970s, poking holes in neoclassical economics and trying to patch the craters in socialist economic theory. Lerner used Marshall's elasticity formula to show that under certain conditions, if a country's currency dropped in value, its trade balance would improve. The "Marshall-Lerner condition" now appears in every international economics textbook and informs many foreign-policy shouting matches. From the early 1980s until the present, the United States has run large foreign trade deficits. In 1985, many economists blamed a "high" dollar—that is, American goods seemed expensive to foreigners, whereas other countries' goods seemed cheap to Americans. These economists suggested driving the dollar downward by buying up foreign currencies, thus making

American goods appear cheaper and thereby spurring foreigners to buy more (and making foreign goods appear more
expensive to Americans). The argument assumes that domestic demand for foreign goods is elastic. From spring 1985 until
fall 1987, the value of the dollar fell by 40 percent against the
currencies of other industrialized nations. But it was not until
the very end of 1987 that the trade deficit began falling. The
long delay in reducing this deficit indicated less elasticity than
expected. Economists also underestimated the willingness of
foreign companies to maintain their market shares by allowing profits to fall, for prices of goods imported into the United
States did not rise enough to fully reflect the dollar's fall.[34]
From 1995 to 2002, the United States took a reverse trip as the
U.S. dollar jumped by more than 25 percent. As a result, the
trade deficit worsened significantly. In 2019, when President
Trump officially named China a "currency manipulator" and
said that China's cheap-currency strategy was one of "the
greatest thefts in the history of the world," he was inadvertently opining on the Marshall-Lerner condition, a mathematical formula put together by the sons of a poor English cashier
and a Moldovan peasant.

Elasticity underlies nearly every practical economic dispute.
Marshall always warned that economists must confront the
real world. A neat, theoretical model may be persuasive on
paper but prove useless when actual elasticities are included.
By clarifying the concept, Marshall showed economists that
they must unite theory and practice.

The Big Picture

On macroeconomic issues, Marshall did not venture far. He
held to Say's Law and the "quantity theory" of money (see
chapter 10), and he taught them both to Keynes. Keynes held

to them for years before turning on Marshall and tossing them away, as we will later discuss.

Although Marshall thought the economy operated rather smoothly on its own, he admitted that business cycles bring ups and downs. Business optimism and pessimism accelerate and amplify the blips and dips. In the ascending phase, banks lend too boldly, even to novice businessmen. But when the economy finally slows, investors withdraw their funds, sending the economy down faster. "The fall of a lighted match . . . has often started a disastrous panic in a crowded theatre," Marshall analogized.[35] Happily, Marshall's old friend, time, heals all wounds, and the economy rises again. Though Keynes would agree that moods help swing the economy, he would later point out that after the fire goes out, the theater remains ruined for a long time. Depression can be a long-running act.

One macroeconomic distinction that Marshall and Yale professor Irving Fisher drew has still not been accepted by politicians today. Economists distinguish between real interest rates and nominal interest rates. Nominal interest rates are the lending and borrowing rates as usually posted in the windows of banks. Real interest rates subtract the rate of inflation from nominal rates: if bonds pay 8 percent, but inflation is 5 percent, the real rate is 3 percent. Politicians have been known to define the real interest rate as the rate you "really" have to pay when you go to the bank for a loan.

Despite the grand theoretical scope of the *Principles*, Marshall insisted that economics must be practical. He frequently served on royal commissions and testified before Parliament. He studied economics to help the poor. Years later, he said to the Royal Commission on the Aged Poor: "I have devoted myself for the last twenty-five years to the problem of poverty; and very little of my work has been devoted to any enquiry which does not bear upon that."[36] He supported public education and argued that "the best investment of the present capital of the country is to educate the next generation."[37]

Although Marshall supported a moderate redistribution of wealth, because it would heighten productivity and social happiness, he stopped far short of socialism, at one point calling it the "greatest present danger." Like philosophers and economists as far back as Aristotle, Marshall feared that collective ownership would "deaden the energies of mankind, and arrest economic progress; unless before its introduction the whole people had acquired an unselfish devotion to the public good." Revealing again his gradualist, evolutionary Weltanschauung, Marshall observed that "patient students of economics generally anticipate little good and much evil from schemes for sudden and violent reorganization of the economic, social and political conditions of life."[38]

To Marshall, "impatient" was nearly as devastating an insult as "dishonest."

Marshall thought that both the classical pessimists and the hopeful Marxists were wrong. The stationary state had not arrived yet. Population did not outstrip food. Landlords did not reign. Although poverty still degraded a portion of the citizenry, the

hope that poverty and ignorance may gradually be extinguished, derives indeed much support from the steady progress of the working classes during the nineteenth century. The steam-engine has relieved them of much exhausting and degrading toil; wages have risen; education has been improved and become more general; the railway and the printing press have enabled members of the same trade in different parts of the country to communicate easily with one another, and to undertake and carry out broad and farseeing lines of policy; while the growing demand for intelligent work has caused the artisan classes to increase so rapidly that they now outnumber those whose labor is entirely unskilled. A great part of the artisans have ceased to belong to the "lower classes" in the sense in which the term was originally used; and some of them already lead a more refined and noble life than did the majority of the upper classes even a century ago.[39]

Only Marx wrote a more glowing paean to capitalism.

But Marshall was no knave. He knew work had to be done. He begged his students to help make economics a tool for enhancing man's well-being. He was disgusted by the remaining poverty he saw, but he refused to let disgust guide his economic logic. Nature would make no quick leaps in wiping out destitution.

Marshall retired in 1908 but continued to refine and update his works. He retreated to his house on Madingley Road in Cambridge, where he endured an assortment of ailments, digestive and respiratory. He lived until 1924, a few weeks shy of his eighty-second birthday, remaining the grand old professor of Cambridge. He left his estate to Mary (who would live until 1944) and asked that she provide an annual lifelong gift to their gardener and maid, along with a generous grant to Newnham College, where he had established himself as one of the first Cambridge dons to educate women. He provided scholarships for economics students, specifying that one-quarter should go to Newnham women, and established the Marshall Library to support the economics faculty. Mary spent the next twenty years painting watercolor landscapes and pedaling her bicycle to the library to work as a volunteer librarian, until she retired at age eighty-seven. Visitors to the library today can see Alfred's patron saint, the portrait of the workingman that he bought at the little shop for a few shillings 150 years before.

While researching the first edition of this book, I decided to pedal my bicycle to the old Marshall house on Madingley Road. I wasn't sure what I would find roughly a half century after Mary's death. I knocked at the door, and a stern-looking older woman answered. If I hadn't known that the Marshalls were childless, I would have guessed that she was Mary's now-elderly daughter. I explained my mission, that I was writing a book on Marshall. The old lady paused, suddenly grinned, and then invited me into the parlor. It was in this room that Marshall would give students a copy of his *Principles* and inscribe it, "To ____, in the hopes that in due course he will render this treatise obsolete." Then we strolled out to the backyard, and the lady said, "The professor loved living along the fen. He thought the marshes would help his breathing. Alfred and Mary loved the garden and the students. They tended the garden and they tended the students together."

Keynes praises Marshall for a rare combination of gifts. The master economist must, like Marshall, be a mathematician, historian, statesman, and philosopher to some degree. "He must study the present in the light of the past for the purposes of the future."[40]

A man who shared Karl Marx's surname but had a better sense of humor was once scolded: "Sir, you try my patience." Groucho responded: "I don't mind if I do. You must come over and try mine sometime."

All economists would do well to "try" Marshall's brand of patience. He did not wait for answers, he searched for them. He did not wait for their adoption, he campaigned for them. But he never embraced his own ideas without cautious thought. And he never rejected the ideas of others without careful reflection. He wanted to unite classical and marginalist economics. He wanted to understand slopes and plateaus, change and equilibrium, evolution and stability. In the end, he did much of this, while reconciling a heart of soft gold and a mind as sharp and clear as a diamond.

CHAPTER VIII
Old and New Institutionalists

The idea of "old" and "young" in economics means very little. As Alfred Marshall taught, economics has a different kind of clock. An eighty-five-year-old firm may fail because it adopts new techniques without proper testing. Is it an old firm or a new firm?

What do we mean by "old" and "new" institutionalists? Clear definitions and distinctions are impossible. Generally, institutionalists look away from the usual economic categories: rents, profits, income, capital, labor costs, and such. Instead they focus on society's laws, ethos, and institutions for insight. The *old* institutionalists, who emerged in the early 1900s, criticized Marshall's eager students for sitting in their offices, drawing the blinds closed, and manipulating irrelevant mathematical curves rather than examining the real world, as their master had implored. In the hands of his proselytes, Marshall's abstract theory ignored too much, the old institutionalists charged. While the Marshallians naively and gleefully slid along their curves, institutions were evolving and economic theory was growing obsolete.

The *new* institutionalists are startlingly different from the old school. Like the old institutionalists, they look at society's institutions—but they use the very tools of Marshall that the old institutionalists assailed.

Veblen and the Old Institutionalists

Let's first look at the old school by examining its preeminent member, Thorstein Veblen. Except for Karl Marx, the economists we have discussed so far were rather mild-mannered. They probably would have made good neighbors, and one can imagine Adam Smith and Alfred Marshall as jovial Boy Scout leaders. Veblen is a refreshing, devilish exception. Along with his puckish persona, Veblen contributes a scalding critique to the history of economic thought.

Veblen's institutional approach bashes two pillars of neo-classical economics: (1) Marshall's law of demand, which says that people buy more of a good when the price falls; and (2) the assumption that laborers work only because they are paid and do not "work for work's sake."

Veblen also attacks the marginalists for assuming a smooth, gradual path to a point of equilibrium. Equilibria do not exist; the economy always changes, the old institutionalists charge. Equilibrium is a daydream of economists who do not live in the real world.

Veblen was probably a better critic than constructive theorist. He was not sure how to reconstruct economics, but he was sure that Marshall and his followers made a mess. Veblen thought that economists should be less turf conscious and more willing to meet with sociologists, anthropologists, and psychologists if they wanted to develop better theories.[1]

Who was Thorstein Veblen, this penetrating critic of neo-classical economics? He was born on a Wisconsin farm in 1857, the son of Norwegian immigrants. When he was eight, the family moved to Minnesota, where the cheese was less good but the crops more plentiful.

Like other American immigrants, the Veblen family was poor. But the children didn't know it. They had enough to eat, and their neighbors lived a similarly rustic, humble life.

Commentators almost always link Veblen's critical attitude to his family's impoverished, immigrant status. Throwing Veblen on the psychoanalyst's couch, they portray him as a pariah in the United States. In the close-knit immigrant communities of Wisconsin and Minnesota, English was a second language. The pariah theory argues that Veblen's outsider status gave him a unique and unbiased view of American economic life. He could see the cracks in the foundation of capitalism because his eyes pierced through the facade. Veblen himself employed a similar hypothesis in his essay "The Intellectual Pre-eminence of Jews in Modern Europe."

No doubt there is something to this, but such environmental explanations may reach too far. After all, his eleven brothers and sisters, equally Norwegian, never showed spectacular insight. In fact, Veblen was always a bit of a kook, albeit a shrewd one. He might have been just as kooky and incisive had he grown up in Norway. A precocious child, Veblen manipulated his parents so that his chores involved reading books in the attic, while his duller siblings toiled in the fields. At seventeen, Veblen attended nearby Carleton College Academy. Because Carleton was not a Lutheran institution, which would have catered to Veblen's Scandinavian culture, Veblen's rough social skills presented problems. He showed up for formal affairs in a coonskin cap, and during one class exercise Veblen delivered a sober speech calling for drunkenness. It didn't go down well with the denominational college. Nor did his serious speech calling for cannibalism. No surprise that the college pushed this heathen to finish his degree ahead of everyone else.

But Veblen graduated with high honors.

Veblen did not convert the college to alcoholism or to cannibalism. During his stay, though, John Bates Clark (later recognized as an eminent American marginalist) persuaded him to read economics. Veblen found it intriguing but decided instead to pursue an academic career in philosophy at Yale. He should have started with the myth of Sisyphus. After completing his doctoral thesis, he would spend a number of frustrating years wandering, loafing around the family farm while his siblings toiled, applying for jobs and waiting for rejections.

Eventually, Veblen's Ph.D. from Yale landed him a job at Cornell—teaching economics. His future mentor, J. Laurence Laughlin, had been "sitting in Ithaca when an anemic-looking person, wearing a coonskin cap and corduroy trousers, entered and in the mildest possible tone announced: 'I am Thorstein Veblen.'"[2] After two years, Laughlin moved to the University of Chicago, along with his protégé.

Now in his mid-thirties and married for a few years to the niece of the president of Carleton College, Veblen worked on his writing and teaching, as well as his philandering. Two of three came easy.

Let us start with the writing. This involved numerous reviews and articles on odd subjects such as "The Economic Theory of Women's Dress" and "The Barbarian Status of Women." His teaching involved mumbling, teasing, taunting, and daring his students to quit. He was happy that most did. This apparently sadistic, irreverent man would start the semester by smearing the blackboard with book titles and then announcing that next week's exam would cover all the books. He almost always gave Cs—to discourage the Phi Beta Kappa aspirants. As for philandering, the juicy details of his sexual escapades remain a secret.

Deriding the Leisure Class

Regardless of Veblen's manner and extracurricular activities, one thing is certain: his first book, *The Theory of the Leisure Class* (1899), demonstrated that the man who spoke in mumbles wrote pristine prose. Subtitled *An Economic Study of Institutions*, Veblen's book thrashed the neoclassical model of demand. According to Veblen, the neoclassicalists assumed that each consumer independently weighed the costs and benefits of purchasing an item. In an earlier article, Veblen put it in more sensational, mixed-metaphoric language: "The hedonistic conception of man is that of a lightning calculator of pleasures and pains, who oscillates like a homogeneous globule of desire of happiness under the impulse of stimuli that shift him about the area, but leave him intact."[3]

What is glaringly wrong with this model? An individual is not an independent globule. Each globule looks at other globules before deciding where to go. Except for a few trendsetters and sociopaths, most people want to either keep up with the Joneses or at least look over the fence to see what the Joneses are doing. An individual's valuation of utility depends partly on what her neighbors will think of a purchase. The ritziest host serves caviar at a party. The most insecure guest proclaims the splendor of the salty fish eggs. But how many guests *really* like caviar better than ice cream or chocolate-chip cookies?

Veblen's biting observations also apply to fashions. Pity the man who strolls down Wall Street in a polyester leisure suit. "How many polyesters were killed for that?" a wag may tease. But leisure suits were once stylish. Did the leisure suit change? No. Fashions changed.

Veblen conducts a lengthy anthropological study in *The Theory of the Leisure Class* alluding to the Ainu of Yezo, the Todas of Nilgiri Hills, and the bushmen of Australia. Relying partly on the research of Lewis Morgan and Franz Boas (Margaret Mead's mentor), Veblen discovers an "emulatory instinct." Sure enough, he says, the grass is always greener on the other side of the bush, and Todas do try to keep up with other Todas.

Self-preservation is, of course, the primal instinct. But soon after the process of evolution separated the chimps from the boys, the boys began judging their social status by property ownership. He who plundered amassed social esteem as well as wealth.

Eventually, *how* one acquired property became important.

If a person gathered property by toil and sweat, he was not admired. According to Veblen, the family that gained property *passively*, without a drop of perspiration, earned admiration and incited emulation in the community. The *leisure class* was born. Veblen pictured rich people lounging around their swimming pools, hoping others would catch them with little umbrellas in their drinks. He thought the walking stick was a great advertisement, because a man carrying a stick rather than a wrench must have time on his hands.

In the 1980s, Veblen was memorialized by an antiperspirant company that advertised the following golden rule of social climbing: "Never let them see you sweat." The sweaty man betrays his commonness. Effortless grace is the goal. The aristocrat shudders at sweat the way a soufflé chef shivers at a slamming door.

Veblen provides two dramatic examples of the leisure class working hard to maintain their nonworking status. First, "we are told of certain Polynesian chiefs, who, under the stress of good form, preferred to starve than carry their food to their mouths with their own hands." Second, a "better illustration, or at least a more unmistakable one, is afforded by a certain king of France, who is said to have lost his life through an excess of moral stamina in the observance of good form. In the absence of a functionary whose office it was to shift his master's seat, the king sat uncomplaining before the fire and suffered his royal person to be toasted beyond recovery."[4]

Along with "conspicuous leisure," Veblen also sneers at "conspicuous consumption." Our modern culture overflows with examples. Clothing used to have labels on the inside, hidden from view. Today, designer labels blaze from shirts, ties, blouses, and the seats of pants. Of course, it's free advertising for the designer. More important, it's paid advertising *by the consumer.* Ralph Lauren's name tells the world that the wearer can afford expensive clothing. (One wonders how the designer's original name, Ralph Lifschitz, would look on an expensive sweater.) In the movie *Back to the Future*, the 1950s schoolgirl assumes that the name of her friend from the future is Calvin, because he wears jeans bearing that name.

Automobiles obviously provide more than mere transportation. According to comedian Jackie Mason, the Cadillac is considered one of the finest cars throughout the United States—except in Beverly Hills and Cedarhurst, Long Island. In those two hamlets, all respectable citizens own a Mercedes-Benz. A Cadillac is repugnant. No one will accept blame for a Cadillac in his driveway: "Oh, it's not mine. . . . I don't know whose it is—maybe my tacky neighbor's? . . . Someone must have left it there last night. . . . I'll call the garbagemen now to remove it." Why do they like Mercedes? "The engineering," they insist. But these engineering aficionados probably don't even know how a toaster works, much less a $70,000 car.

According to Washington legend, Senator Everett Dirksen was the first man in D.C. with a telephone in his car and enjoyed calling up his rivals to remind them. One rival, Senator Lyndon Johnson, exploded in rage. He installed an even better system. Immediately after its arrival, Johnson called Dirksen. They spoke for a minute. Then Johnson barked: "Sorry, Everett, I'll have to put you on hold. I've got a call on my *other* line!"

At first, Veblen's piercing observations found their way more easily into sociology than economics. In 1950, though, Professor Harvey Leibenstein published an article titled "Bandwagon, Snob, and Veblen Effects in the Theory of Consumer Demand"[5] that applied Veblen's theory to economics. Usually, he said, Marshall's law of demand reigns, a lower price leads to more demand. But for some goods, "Veblen goods," a consumer's demand is determined by the use of the good *and the price that the consumer thinks other people will think she paid, the expected conspicuous price.* Not long ago, Ursinus College in Pennsylvania jacked up its tuition by almost 18 percent. Why? It wanted to boost its prestige. Surprisingly, it also boosted the number of applications by 35 percent. "It's bizarre and embarrassing," said the college president.[6] If the market price of Gucci handbags falls so that they become available in any department store, we may soon see fewer Gucci bags sold. They will have lost their Veblenesque appeal. You cannot be taken seriously at the country club with Kmart clothing. You might as well drive up to a valet parking attendant in Beverly Hills with a Cadillac.

The Creative Urge of Engineers

Producers know that envy and peer pressure force consumers to act. According to Veblen and his disciples, businessmen spend more time enhancing a product's expected conspicuous price than improving its usefulness. This, the institutionalists argue, is a shame and a waste of time and talent, resulting in slicker advertisements for shoddier products.

It is also a perversion of a natural drive. Like Marx, Veblen believed in the creative urge, the instinct of *workmanship*. Unfortunately, as conspicuous leisure and conspicuous consumption infect society, the creative desire suffers.

Veblen avoids Marx's class-struggle analysis.[7] To Veblen, the enemies are not capitalists, and the heroes are not laborers. He portrays a different cast of characters: The bad guys are businessmen (whether or not they own the companies), and the good guys are engineers. In the modern world, only the engineers accept the urge to create, improve, and produce. Businessmen, who boss them around, strangle creativity. Businessmen thrill at conspicuous consumption. They produce for one reason only: to make money. If they could make money without making a single product, they would be happier. Compare the dreams of engineers and businessmen. The engineer goes to bed each night with pens in pocket and CAD/CAM apps on his cellphone. He dreams of inventing the perfect, absolutely efficient motor. The businessman goes to bed in pin-striped pajamas. He dreams that the public suddenly finds his *old* product fashionable. That way he makes millions of dollars without investing one cent in new technology or innovative thought.

The history of IBM is filled with bitter battles, almost insane arguments, between founder Thomas Watson Sr. and his son Thomas Jr. In the 1950s, Watson Sr. wanted the company to stick to selling punch-card machines. His son, who hired newly minted engineers, urged the company to develop electronic computers. The old man worried that computers would make IBM's lucrative punch cards obsolete. The son, as president, bet nearly all the company's assets on computing. IBM survived the radical transformation, but their personal relationship almost did not.[8] The lesson: *It is better to make yourself obsolete than to wait for your competitors to do it for you.*

Veblen thought that the rise of scientific engineers in the twentieth century would bring the downfall of the philosophical bases of capitalism. Veblen expected machines to discipline modern minds and arouse suspicion in capitalist superstition and catechism. Because engineers and even lowly machine operators see scientific relationships, Veblen thought they would rebel against symbolism, ceremony, and abstract collective beliefs in God, country, and private property:

> What the discipline of the machine industry inculcates, therefore, in the habits of life and of thought of the workman, is regularity of sequence and mechanical precision; and the intellectual outcome is an habitual resort to terms of measurable cause and effect, together with a relative neglect and disparagement of such exercise of the intellectual faculties as does not run on these lines.[9]

Veblen predicted that the conflict between engineers and managers would ravage more than just philosophical underpinnings. The economy would also waste and wear down. Captains of industry strive to achieve high profits. Two lanes lead to this goal. The first involves restricting output in a monopolistic manner. The second involves lowering production costs. Since businessmen know little about mechanics, they neglect efficiency. Veblen blasted a *conscientious withdrawal of efficiency*. After the manager invests in old techniques, he prefers to hold back production and to hold back advances. In contrast, the engineer yearns to move ahead. The manager prefers cheap, cosmetic distinctions. The engineer wants to satisfy needs. The engineer wants to build a better mousetrap; the manager wants to trap the consumer. By stressing short-term financial gain, businessmen and financiers sabotage long-term economic growth.

Veblen offered only faint hope that government would rein in the robber-baron businessmen. In fact, it was too late, for businessmen had already lassoed and corralled public officials: "Representative government means, chiefly, representation of business interests."[10] Despite his critique of neoclassical economics, Veblen sometimes echoed Adam Smith, especially on trade restrictions:

Where the national government is charged with the general care of the country's business interests, as is invariably the case among civilized nations, it follows from the nature of the case that the nation's lawgivers and administration will have some share in administering that necessary modicum of sabotage that must always go into the day's work of carrying on industry by business methods and for business purposes. The government is in a position to penalize excess . . . traffic.[11]

Veblen viewed labor unions and their bosses with the same contempt he kept ready for government. Like businesses, he said, unions also block efficiency and sabotage the economy. Rather than aiding common workers, unions raise wages by stepping on the backs of the nonunion employees:

The rank and file . . . stand on the defensive in maintaining a vested interest in the prerogatives and perquisites of their organization. They are apparently moved by a feeling that so long as the established arrangements are maintained they will come in for a little something over and above what goes to the common man.[12]

In *Engineers and the Price System*, Veblen speculated that engineers might grow so disgusted with waste and wanton sabotage that they would overthrow their bosses and take charge of the factory floor and the boardroom. After all, the administrators needed them more than they needed the administrators. Technical specialists representing 1 percent of the population, and without one college credit of political science, might emerge as the "philosopher kings" of Veblen's republic: "It will no longer be practicable to leave . . . control in the hands of businessmen working at cross purposes for private gain, or to entrust its continued administration to others than suitably trained technological experts, production engineers without a commercial interest."[13]

Like Marx, Veblen had little idea what the new rulers would do. But he was sure they would not do worse.

Veblen writes as if engineers and businessmen represented two entirely different species, but this seems more farfetched as the years go by. According to a *Fortune* magazine survey, a very high percentage of corporate chief executive officers started in engineering labs,[14] and engineers make up a large percentage of today's MBA students. The CEOs of Amazon, Netflix, and Google earned engineering or computer science degrees. The founders of Microsoft and Facebook were college dropouts, but I will assume that Bill Gates and Mark Zuckerberg would have been clever enough to pass their courses at Harvard. When the coronavirus struck in 2020 and American hospitals were desperate for ventilators, Elon Musk, who holds an undergraduate degree in economics and in physics, directed his engineers at Tesla to build ventilators from car parts that were on the shelf. Within a week, they had repurposed hoses, valves, and sensors to build prototypes, powered by the car's infotainment system. A video screen that might otherwise display rap music selections was showing oxygen levels and heartbeats. It was a stunning sharing of business, science, and engineering acumen.

Veblen also assumes that engineers who take power will not surrender to self-interest. But why won't they act as nastily as the oligopolists they replace? Are engineers really more beneficent and permanently committed to the creative urge? In 2019, Boeing fired its CEO after software deficiencies triggered crashes of the 737 Max jet. Boeing had rushed and bungled the rollout of the new jet and the training of pilots. The CEO had been an aerospace engineer at Boeing since his early days as a college intern.

Veblen did not assemble a detailed model of the economy. He did not think he or anyone else could. So he spent much of his time tearing down the neat theories of his predecessors. While Alfred Marshall placed nonmonetary factors in a "pound" called ceteris paribus, Veblen displayed the courage to enter the pound and vet the forces that Marshall assumed would remain steady, such as tastes. Veblen snickered at economists who ignored the unpredictable, human side of economics. Henry Ford recalled seeing John D. Rockefeller only once: "But when I saw the face, I knew what made Standard Oil." One cannot quantify a face or predict how a grimace from the boss can change productivity on the shop floor.

Veblen is still fun to read and read about. His most distinguished student depicted Veblen writing with "one eye on the scientific merits of his analysis, and his other eye fixed on the squirming reader." Learning from Veblen was like doing a vivisection without an anesthetic. Not everyone could take it,[15] but no one could forget it. Veblen still haunts us. Every time some big-shot executive conspicuously whisks off in a tinted-windowed stretch limousine while we poor slobs wait in the rain for a bus, Thorstein Veblen unleashes a sinister laugh.

Galbraith and the Lure of Advertising

Veblen inspired many outstanding disciples, including Wesley Mitchell, John R. Commons, and the sociologist C. Wright Mills. But the follower most famous to the public for keeping alive Veblenite jokes and jibes was John Kenneth Galbraith. In his long career Galbraith took many controversial economic positions. His colleagues acknowledge two areas in which he indisputably reigned supreme: height and humor. Born in rural Canada, Galbraith drolly identified with Veblen's bucolic background. He wrote that a good farmer needs a strong back and a weak mind. In his memoir, Galbraith recalls the kind of summer day that inspires an adolescent's hormones. While strolling through an orchard with the fair lass who filled his pubescent dreams, Galbraith pointed to the lush field where the family cows were grazing. As they winsomely gazed, they noticed a white bull "serving" a heifer that was in season. As the lass looked on with interest, Galbraith summoned the courage to say: "I think it would be fun to do that."

The lass did not blink at the subtle suggestion. She replied: "Well, it's your cow."[16]

Galbraith, who died in 2006 at age ninety-seven, spent most of his long career in the United States, serving as Harvard professor, presidential adviser, novelist, and social commentator. He wore many of these hats simultaneously. For this, many economists deride his works for superficial, dilettantish economics. To wear many hats, you need both a big head and a lot of brains. Only that genius Keynes could get away with it, they insinuate.

Not that Galbraith boasted of superhuman talents. When President Truman telephoned Galbraith to request his help in regulating wages and prices, a young Galbraith reportedly recoiled, "Surely there are at least ten other economists far more qualified, Mr. President."

"Damn right there are! But none of them will take the job!"

Galbraith took the job and developed a political and economic philosophy favorable to big government. In three major works, *The Affluent Society* (1958), *The New Industrial State* (1967), and *Economics and the Public Purpose* (1973), Galbraith savaged modern capitalism and its chief apologists, neoclassical economists. Galbraith's writings mocked the same objects that Veblen mocked. How could anyone believe in Smithian competition in the face of enormous, rapacious corporations? For him, the theory of Marshallian competition ranks high on the same fantastic list as Tinkerbell, Santa Claus, and Snow White. Only intellectual dwarfs who couldn't see above their windowsills would deny the awesome power of General Motors, Galbraith insisted.

How could anyone still believe the myth called "consumer sovereignty," that consumers determine what subservient firms will produce? Galbraith argues that causation works in the reverse direction: that firms mold consumers to serve their sales needs.

Imagine the following scenario. You walk into a supermarket to buy Cocoa Puffs cereal. You are "cuckoo for Cocoa Puffs," as the advertisement screams. Ken Galbraith strides in to buy generic, healthful, sugarless, tasteless Bran Dust cereal to keep him going. You turn to Galbraith in the cashier line and say: "I've *got* to have Cocoa Puffs in the morning. *I* really like them."

Galbraith objects loudly. He distinguishes "needs" and "wants." You cannot *need* Cocoa Puffs. All needs emanate from within. There is no natural drive to consume Cocoa Puffs. You merely want the cereal, and wants are less important than needs. Then, Galbraith denies that *you* determined your desire for Cocoa Puffs. Madison Avenue advertisers persuaded you to want Cocoa Puffs. Advertising and salesmanship "cannot be reconciled with the notion of independently determined desires, for their central function is to create desire—to bring into being wants that previously did not exist."[17]

Galbraith thinks he has exploded Marshall's "marginal

utility of demand." For the market does not read the *consumer's* true demand for goods, formed in his heart of hearts; it reads the artificial desires implanted by manipulative advertisers. Galbraith calls this the *dependence effect*.

Galbraith does not stop at a mere assertion. He also infers a powerful conclusion: since firms invent and instill wants, and wants are not urgent, the government should limit private consumption and use resources to improve public facilities. Galbraith denounces the fancy limousine that roars through decrepit parks and slums, and asserts that private America flourishes in disgusting, selfish affluence, while public America starves. Americans do not *really* want this imbalance. Corporations mesmerize them.

Galbraith foresees an even more despicable future unless the government adopts principles of democratic socialism and planning. He predicts more unemployment as technology displaces workers, more pollution, and more houses filled with "new, improved" useless gadgets. Who really needs the motion-activated toothpaste dispenser, anyway? Was the squeeze tube too complex?

Galbraith's salvo strikes the nerve center of neoclassical economics. If he exposes marginal utility analysis to be as impotent as the Wizard of Oz, Marshall turns out to be a brainless Scarecrow.

But who flies in from the East to play the Good Witch and pour water all over Galbraith's theory? Friedrich von Hayek.

In "The *Non Sequitur* of the 'Dependence Effect,'" Hayek repels Galbraith's charge that all important wants come from within.[18] He contends that only a few needs truly emerge naturally. Does Galbraith mean that only food and sex are important in life, and that all other concerns are trivial desires? Hayek asks why environmental influences should negate the importance of desires.

If Galbraith's logic is right, culture is trivial. Nobody in the eighteenth century ever woke up and said, "Boy, I wish there were a Mozart symphony." Mozart composed and then aroused in others a desire for his music. Is his music a mere toy of the rich? Or is it a significant, enhancing contribution to mankind?

For years the Public Broadcasting System promoted Julia Child, "the French Chef," later memorialized in a Meryl Streep movie. Prior to her show, did any viewers wake up in the middle of the night craving a tall, goofy woman with a funny voice to teach them to cook? Of course not (nightmares notwithstanding).

What we call civilization is largely a reflection of external factors vying for the brain's attention and affections.

Galbraith pleads for more public schools. Presumably, the schools would spend much time teaching "unimportant," "externally contrived" things like literature and music.

No doubt, modern homes bulge with silly toys, appliances, and conversation pieces. But what possible remedy can Galbraith provide without appearing either tyrannical or contradictory?

A simple ban on consumer goods is tyrannical. Instead, Galbraith could urge a ban on the advertising of consumer goods. During the 2020 presidential race, Senator Bernie Sanders suggested taxing targeted advertisements on Facebook and other media.[19] Taking Galbraith's advice, leaders could implore the public to spend their money more wisely and less conspicuously. Leaders could persuade people to contribute private wealth for public goods. But this advice contradicts Galbraith's own principle! By promoting more prudent consumption and more public goods, the leaders would instill new "externally contrived," "non-urgent" wants. Advertising, whether by politicians or salesmen, is still advertising.

This critique of Galbraith does not imply that politicians should not advocate for public schools. But Galbraith should not push politicians toward this without conceding the flaw in his "dependence effect" theory.

Galbraith probably exaggerates the power of advertising, which is a complex issue. No doubt an advertising battle among virtually identical products that features only musical jingles and jiggling models is a waste of resources. However, many advertisements deliver some useful information amid much flashiness. Does the flashiness simply get the audience's attention while the information actually sells the product?

A famous study of advertising and eyeglasses showed that in states that permitted opticians to advertise, eyeglasses sold at prices about 25 to 30 percent lower than in states that prohibited advertising.[20]

Do people fall for mere sparkle? American marketing history is filled with failures named Edsel, *Ishtar*, and Heinz EZ Squirt rainbow-colored ketchup. Corporate marketing departments struggle to keep up with the fancies of the American public, much less lead them. The *Wall Street Journal* reported that sneaker manufacturers test-market their goods in inner cities, because urban youth often ignite cultural fads. In 1986, a sneaker called British Knights, or BK's, leaped into prominence. Sales soared until, for no apparent reason, local street gangs dubbed them "Brother Killers," at which point sales plummeted.[21]

Even if a splashy commercial convinces a consumer to buy, for example, a particular brand of shampoo, will the consumer buy it a *second* time if she finds the shampoo makes her hair brittle? Most print and online advertisements display products that survive on *repeat* buyers, customer loyalty, and so on. The goods are not one-shot profit-makers. The producers cannot afford to sell just one time and leave their customers bald or otherwise unsatisfied. On the other hand, ads for "big ticket" goods such as automobiles scream out for the consumer to test-drive the product. Only the dimmest wit in the world buys a Buick from what they see on the television screen.

These points do not defend dishonest advertising or deny its existence. But most advertisers are not fly-by-night outfits eager to cheat for a fast buck. Galbraith himself has written that firms concentrate more on market share than on quick profits. Lousy products lose market share fast.

Many people are, like Galbraith, uncomfortable with the

choices modern capitalism gives modern consumers. Many are psychologically uneasy that they have such a wide range of choice. With choice comes responsibility for the selection one makes, and existential angst. Do we choose Crest, Aquafresh, Close-Up, Ultra Brite, or Colgate? We can try to blame the advertisers for our ultimate choice. Of course, toothpaste is trivial. Let's consider the more important principle involved. If Galbraith is right, can people take credit for momentous issues, for choosing Churchill over Goebbels, or the NAACP over the KKK? The Galbraith critique superficially concerns advertising. More important, it concerns what man really is. Are we any more free than Pavlov's dogs? If we are not, Galbraith is right, and neoclassical economics fails.

Galbraith happily aligns himself with Thorstein Veblen. He shares many traits, including a sardonic view of modern culture and capitalism. But he shares another trait, vagueness. Neither develops a paradigm or method that economists can carefully test or even emulate. The institutionalists seem content to criticize and to observe. Their work is carried on today in the *American Journal of Economics and Sociology* and *Journal of Post Keynesian Economics*. Contributors to the latter are also greatly influenced by the Italian economist Piero Sraffa, the Polish Marxist Michał Kalecki, and the late Cambridge economist Joan Robinson.

The Daring Joan Robinson

Joan Robinson was one Mao collar away from winning the Nobel Prize in economics in the 1970s. Born in 1903 to an elite family in Surrey, she had briefly studied with the elderly Alfred Marshall but probed for flaws in his model. She married an economist named Austin Robinson, but quickly sped ahead of him academically, and later romantically. In 1933, simultaneously with Harvard's Edward Chamberlin, she published important findings on "imperfect competition," identifying cases in which just a few companies might exercise extraordinary power in the marketplace (oligopolies), or where products that fell into the same category might have slight differences that made them less competitive against each other. Gertrude Stein said that "a rose is a rose is a rose," but today Robinson might say that "coffee is coffee, but if Starbucks can charge five times more than Folgers, they're not selling the same thing." She and her Harvard competitor Chamberlin referred to such cases as "monopolistic competition," and pointed to the power of advertising in distinguishing brands. Robinson's most famous term, *monopsony*, recently cropped up in a U.S. Supreme Court case, *Apple v. Pepper*. In the decision, Justice Brett Kavanaugh said that Apple, which takes a 30 percent cut of an app's revenues, may have undue power because it is the only buyer of Apple-compatible apps and could be sued as a monopsony. Whereas a monopoly is a single dominant seller, Robinson called a single dominant buyer a monopsony. She came up with the Greek-infused word while having tea with a professor of classics. She was still in her twenties when she wrote *The Economics of Imperfect Competition*, and quickly became part of John Maynard Keynes's inner circle, while her ideas began to enter standard textbooks. The Keynes circle was marked by bon mots and nontraditional explorations of economics and other matters. To bring these characteristics together, we might retell Keynes's story of walking into a study and surprising the married Robinson and his protégé Richard Kahn, as they rolled over each other on the floor. With a wink, Keynes assured his wife that "the conversation was only on *The Pure Theory of Monopoly*."[22]

So why did Robinson, who lived to age eighty, helped remake microeconomics, and was quoted by a sitting Supreme Court justice, miss out on a Nobel Prize? Milton Friedman and Paul Samuelson, arch intellectual rivals, both would have applauded such an honor. A few reasons come to mind. First, she resisted the path of economics hurtling toward "mathematization," stating, "I never learned mathematics, so I had to think." As a scholar in the 1960s, Nobel laureate Joseph Stiglitz studied under Robinson, but their relationship grew "tumultuous," and he soon decamped to a mathematically driven mentor. Second, she seemed to recant support for her earlier work on imperfect competition. Third, her post–World War II politics seemed to infect her economics. Although other respected economists wrote on Marxian economics, Robinson flew to Moscow, Beijing, and even to North Korea, not only to investigate economic policies but to praise their repressive results. She wrote sympathetically about Mao's Cultural Revolution and called North Korea's Kim Il-sung "a messiah rather than a dictator," lauding "the Korean miracle." In 1964, after a visit to North Korea, she predicted that "as the North continues to develop and the South to degenerate, sooner or later the curtain of lies must surely begin to tear."[23] In fact, since the 1960s, South Koreans have grown about twenty times wealthier than their cousins to the North and stand one to three inches taller. With such role models as Mao and Kim, it is no surprise that Nobel Prize–winning development economist and philosopher Amartya Sen described Robinson as "brilliant but vigorously intolerant." Perhaps the final straw in Robinson's application to the Nobel Committee came when she began dressing up as a Maoist peasant to deliver her lectures. The committee might have been willing to finally grant a prize to a woman, but not a blue-eyed one from Surrey lecturing from under a coolie hat.

New Institutionalists and the Economics of Law

In his lifetime, John Kenneth Galbraith saw the height of the old institutionalists and the rise of the new institutionalists. He surely liked the old folks better. They criticized free market economics for ignoring institutions and blasted free market economists for leaning blindly on Marshallian assumptions about human behavior.

The renegade new institutionalists reverse nearly everything that Veblen and Galbraith set out to do. They don't announce that institutions belie Marshallian economics. Instead, they wield Marshallian scalpels and scissors with which to dissect institutions. They are not a carefully delineated group. Most are economists, some are lawyers with economic training. They are united by curiosity about social institutions and confidence in neoclassical economics.

The new institutional economists start with a basic question: What structures need to be in place for an economy to begin developing? In the 1960s, Douglass North, a former merchant marine who admitted to being a middling undergraduate at the University of California, Berkeley, directed economists to a new focus of study, namely, history. He and his colleagues called the specialty *cliometrics* (after Clio, the Greek muse of history) and uncovered old data, from bills of lading on eighteenth-century ships to receipts for bales of cotton and flasks of whiskey. During the 1960s and 1970s, the University of Chicago's Robert Fogel, who would later share the Nobel Prize with North, produced controversial, counterintuitive statistical studies questioning the importance of railroads and the economics of slavery. To explain economic development, North himself targeted property rights and the ability of citizens to freely choose their vocations. He theorized, for example, that England and the Netherlands led the Industrial Revolution because the guild system was weaker in those countries, which allowed workers to move more easily among jobs.

If we think about institutions from the very beginning of economic history, I would argue that progress comes when people engage in trading transactions where both sides gain. These are nonzero-sum transactions. In a zero-sum situation, one person's gain is another's loss; for example, I just stole your chariot. Even before the golden age of Greece, Thucydides, the historian of the Peloponnesian War, pointed out that without commerce, nomadic groups kept to themselves, never planted beyond their shifting parcels of land, and never improved their standard of living. What makes nonzero-sum deals possible? In a book called *Rush*, I point to four factors: First, a legal construct with *enforceable contracts*, whether enforced by a tribal leader, a court system, or social stigma. Second, a willingness to wait for results—that is, *patience*. Third, an *interest rate structure* that allows people to gauge the value of waiting for rewards. Fourth, and perhaps more important, *repeat transactions*, or expecting to deal with someone again. This is what I call the *Rule of Repeats*. When someone expects to do business with you again, they are far less likely to cheat you. Repeat customers at restaurants are bigger tippers than transient ones. The Rule of Repeats turns strangers into partners and counterparties. Trade prods people to treat strangers better and to expand communities, which largely explains why trading societies are less violent than premodern peasant societies and why contemporary homicide rates in Europe are perhaps one-tenth the rate they were in the year A.D. 1300, and life expectancy is almost three times greater.[24]

Joseph Schumpeter, a man with a flashy style, a bizarre sense of propriety, and a penetrating mind, taught that modern economic growth relied on the entrepreneur. Schumpeter, who came from the same Austrian school as Hayek before settling at Harvard in the 1930s, shared few views with Veblen but must have shared some of the DNA markers for heresy. He once challenged a librarian to a duel over the right of his students to get better access to books, and bragged that he had three great ambitions in life: "I wanted to be the greatest economist in the world, the greatest horseman in Austria, and the best lover in Vienna. Well, in one of those goals I have failed." Schumpeter strolled into faculty meetings wearing riding boots, and with his capes, spats, and silk shirts, he could have stepped out of an old Hollywood movie as Errol Flynn's aristocratic sidekick. But Schumpeter was not just a dandy. He was also the most learned economist of the twentieth century. Even John Maynard Keynes, whose accomplishments drove Schumpeter to jealous depressions, could not compete with Schumpeter's erudition, which included a command of the economics literature in German, French, English, Italian, Latin, and ancient Greek.

Before immigrating to the United States in 1932, Schumpeter held and was ousted from two notable jobs: Austrian finance minister and chairman of the Biedermann Bank. It is not hard to figure out why he was ousted. As chairman of the bank, he rented a castle, lavished a big salary on himself, and, when told to tone down his manner, rented an open-air carriage and rode along the main boulevard of Vienna at noon with a pretty blond prostitute on one knee and a brunette on the other.[25] Schumpeter's economic growth model did not depend on castles and big banks. Instead, he crowned the entrepreneur as the driver of economic waves that crash against the status quo, bringing new ideas amid gales of "creative destruction." (His ideal entrepreneur closely resembled his grandfather and great-grandfather, who owned textile mills.) Schumpeter thought Veblen was wrongheaded about business-people and accused Veblen of belonging to the "depredation theory of entrepreneurial gain," which sees these key players as pointless parasites.[26] Unlike Galbraith, he wasn't worried about big businesses, because he figured that sooner or later they would be vanquished by upstart entrepreneurs. In the meantime, large firms that dominate could afford to plow their excessive profits into innovation. Schumpeter would not be surprised that 90 percent of the firms that were in the Fortune 500 in 1955 would be moribund themselves in 2020, either merged, bankrupted, or too shrunken to show up on a list.

Although Schumpeter encouraged pure economic theory and helped found the Econometric Society, he knew too much about human society to hide behind arid mathematical symbols. Indeed, his depiction of the entrepreneur in *The Theory of Economic Development* appears to stem more from Max Weber and Friedrich Nietzsche than from Adam Smith and David Ricardo: "First of all, there is the dream and the will to found a private kingdom," he wrote. "Then there is the will to conquer: the impulse to fight, to prove oneself superior to others.... Finally, there is the joy of creating."[27] Despite his respect for Weber, who posited that the Protestant work ethic (especially Calvinism) spurred capitalist growth, Schumpeter publicly quarreled with his elder. In one altercation in a coffeehouse, Weber denounced the Russian Revolution while Schumpeter praised it as a "fine laboratory" experiment. Finally, Weber stormed out, screaming, "I can't take any more of this!" and leaving Schumpeter calmly asking for another drink with a bemused expression on his face.

Though few college students have seen Schumpeter's *Theory of Economic Development*, thousands continue to study his *Capitalism, Socialism, and Democracy*, which we will discuss in the final chapter. In that book Schumpeter poses his most famous query: "Can capitalism survive?"

Starting in the post–World War II era, a new institutional approach invaded the world of law. Although antitrust law always involved economics, economists forced lawyers and judges to examine nearly all legal decisions through the eyes of Alfred Marshall and his followers. No area of law can hide from economic analysis, and no law professor today can teach competently without some economic training. Law journals and court judgments bulge with discussions of marginal benefits and marginal costs. The discussions are not just academic. Several prominent experts in law and economics sit on federal courts, influencing the lives of millions of people. No one can hide from economists. Even jailbirds must worry that some graduate student will perform an economic analysis of jail cells, perhaps proving that a particular diet of bread and water optimizes rehabilitation rates.

In 1916 Louis Brandeis wrote that a "lawyer who has not

studied economics . . . is very apt to become a public enemy."[28] Unfortunately, the United States produces thousands of public enemies each year.

Let us explore four very important areas in which economists have dramatically transformed traditional legal analysis of *negligence*, *property*, *crime*, and *corporate finance*.

Negligence

Most accidents fall under the category of *negligence* law, also known as *tort* law. Every time someone slips on a banana peel left on the supermarket floor, a lawyer hopes for a lawsuit on the grounds of negligence. "The supermarket shouldn't have left the peel on the floor," a tweedy litigator will argue. He will probably win.

Should a person or business be held liable for *every* accident on its premises? Try another example. A storm shipwrecks Gilligan, the skipper, and the passengers of the S.S. *Minnow* on a palmy isle. Only two people live on the island. But they share the island with two hundred monkeys. The 202 inhabitants produce banana liqueur for export. The monkeys peel and squeeze the bananas. In the process, they hurl the peels across the island. Suppose Gilligan wanders around the island and slips on a banana peel. Is the banana business negligent? Most courts would say no.

What are the key differences between the supermarket and the deserted island? First, the probability of a human walking down the fruit aisle of the market is high, whereas the chance of a shipwrecked person wandering around the island is small. Second, the cost of supervising the supermarket is low, whereas the cost of monitoring monkeys on an island is high.

Using these concepts, Judge Learned Hand established a brilliant economic analysis of negligence law in a 1947 case.[29] Hand identified three key factors: the probability of injury

(P), the extent of injury or loss (L), and the cost of preventing the accident (C). According to Hand, *a person is negligent if the probable injury to the victim exceeds the cost of avoiding the accident.* Thus in algebraic terms, a defendant is negligent if $P \times L > C$.

In the supermarket, the probability of someone slipping on a banana peel left on the floor is high; let's say 20 percent. The injury is severe; let's say $20,000 in medical bills, lost wages, and inconvenience. Thus $P \times L = \$4,000$. If the supermarket could have prevented the accident for less than $4,000, it was negligent. A $3 broom in the hands of a stock boy would have done the trick.

On the balmy and palmy isle, the probability of a ship-wrecked wanderer slipping on the banana peel is very low, perhaps 1 percent. Even if the injury causes $20,000 damage, the probable loss or expected loss is only $200 (.01 × 20,000 = 200). The liqueur producers would be negligent only if they could have prevented the accident for less than $200. Of course, they could have prevented the accident by placing fences, signs, and security cameras all around the island. But this would be expensive. Further, the monkeys might have injured themselves on the fences. According to Hand, producers should not waste money protecting against an accident highly unlikely to occur. If a judge declared them negligent, he would encourage them to waste valuable resources.

To maximize social welfare, courts should encourage people to spend money on safety only as long as the marginal benefit surpasses the marginal cost. Thus Hand's formula brings Marshallian logic to the law.

We could try to avoid *all* accidents. We could wrap ourselves in foam rubber and never leave our homes or turn on an oven. But most of us agree to take some risks. Hand helps us to know when the risks are foolishly high or trivially small. In the fifty years following Hand's opinion, lawyers and economists have improved his original formula. Nonetheless, the original formula still correctly conveys the flavor of modern negligence law.

Property

Over the past few decades, law and economics scholars have forced judges to recognize the effects of their legal decisions on real property. Judges who ignore economics sometimes command people to take actions that result in precisely the opposite of the judges' intentions. Let's look at two examples in which scholars have compelled lawyers, judges, and legislators to rethink their analyses: Coase's Theorem and rent control.

In 1960, Professor Ronald Coase of the University of Chicago presented a powerful tool for economic analysis.[30] In short, Coase showed that the initial assignment of a property right may not determine how the property is ultimately used. Let's apply Coase's Theorem to nuisance law. Assume that Frank Sinatra owns a nightclub. Sleepy Simon lives next door. Whenever Sinatra belts out a high note, it rattles Simon's teeth and jars him from his bed. Simon brings Sinatra to court, claiming that he has a right to snooze soundly. Sinatra claims a right to hit the high notes. The judge sides with Simon and closes down Sinatra's saloon. According to Coase, the story is not over. Coase's Theorem predicts that Sinatra will sing again if he values his saloon more than Simon values sleep. If Sinatra values his saloon at $1 million and Simon values his sleep at $100,000, Sinatra may bribe Simon into withdrawing his complaint. If Sinatra offers more than $100,000, Simon would accept. With $100,000, Simon could install soundproof walls or buy fancy earplugs. Coase's Theorem states that once a property right is clearly defined, the property will be put to its most valued use. Once the judge clearly assigns to Simon the right to sound sleep, Sinatra can buy that right or bribe Simon into giving up his sleep or moving elsewhere. Even if the judge gives Simon the right to silence Sinatra, Sinatra may sing again if he treasures the right to hit high notes.

So, Sinatra and Simon will settle at a price between $100,000 and $1 million. (If Simon insists on receiving more than $1 million, Sinatra will not pay and will not sing. If Sinatra offers less than $100,000, Simon will turn it down.)

What if the judge had ruled for Sinatra and decided that he had a right to hit the high notes, regardless of his neighbor's sleep? Is it possible that Sinatra would *not* sing even though he had won the case? Yes. If Simon valued his sleep more than Sinatra valued his singing, Simon might buy Sinatra's silence. According to Coase, then, the judge's initial assignment does not determine what ultimately takes place. It determines only who might buy and who might sell. While adoring fans may pay Sinatra to sing, his neighbors may pay him not to.

Coase applies this same analysis to polluters. After all, a soaring human voice may be considered by some as just another form of pollution. A factory that releases smoke may irritate its neighbors. But if the factory values its right to pollute more than its neighbors value the right to clean air, or if the factory is willing to pay the neighbors to move to another location, the factory may continue to pollute. The upshot: judges act foolishly if they assume that by assigning a right, they determine what will finally take place.

Sometimes it is impossible to know in advance whether a neighbor's behavior will be a positive or negative "externality." With great fanfare, in 2003 Los Angeles unveiled the swooping, stainless-steel Walt Disney Concert Hall, designed by the renowned Frank Gehry. At first, neighboring residents assumed that this $274 million marvel would boost their property values. Then the sun came out, and Gehry's stainless steel reflected laserlike rays into apartments, propelling interior temperatures, baking sidewalks to 140 degrees Fahrenheit, and burning the skin of pedestrians like ants under a magnifying glass. Employees observed trash bins combusting and traffic cones melting. Concert hall officials sandblasted the gleaming exterior, trying to turn their negative externality into a positive again.

Like Learned Hand's negligence theory, Coase's Theorem

has been attacked and refined. The prime point of attack is the assumption that people can bribe each other without large transaction costs. Especially in pollution cases where large numbers of homes are affected, it's unlikely that families can organize efficiently to bargain with the polluter. (When an externality affects masses of people, they might lobby the government to tax the behavior—that is, levy a "Pigou tax," as discussed in the earlier chapter on Malthus.) Despite these complications, though, Coase's Theorem appears to be a brilliant and innovative insight into the way legal decisions may actually affect individuals. His approach was so novel that his most learned colleagues thought it had to be wrong. George Stigler recalls Coase presenting the argument to twenty-one members of the University of Chicago faculty, all of whom dismissed it as foolish heresy. After a two-hour debate at the home of Milton Friedman's brother-in-law, Coase had won over each of them. Stigler recalled that it was such an "exhilarating moment" that "he lamented afterward that we had not had the clairvoyance to tape it."[31]

Economists have carefully analyzed another real property issue, municipal rent control laws. Legislators who know how to get votes but not how to govern prudently frequently pass economically perverse regulations. In the 1970s, officials possessed by a utopian vision promoted rent control laws aimed at providing affordable housing by restricting the landlord's ability to raise prices. Some would call this a noble goal but a lousy policy.

Quite simply, rent-control laws nearly always create a shortage of housing. At low prices, people demand housing. But the laws convince landlords to constrict supply. At first, you may think that landlords have no choice once they construct a building. In fact, landlords can reduce supply. They can skimp on maintenance and repair. Or they can convert the rental units into condominiums, cooperatives, Airbnb rentals, or commercial office space. A wrecking ball cares little for history or sunk costs. One econometric study of U.S. cities estimated the long-run price elasticity of supply to be 0.20, which means that if the government forces rents down by 10 percent, landlords will take 2 percent of the rental units off the market.[32] In the long run, landlords do alter the number of units in response to price changes.

Stockholm, Sweden, has compiled a waiting list for rent-controlled housing that includes nearly six hundred thousand people—more than half the population! Once you sign up, you will wait between nine and twenty years for a phone call. Spotify, which launched its music-streaming business in Stockholm, wrote an open letter to policymakers threatening to vacate the city if the rules weren't relaxed and if more housing wasn't encouraged.[33]

In 1979, Santa Monica, California, adopted the toughest rent control laws in the United States. The laws prevent landlords from cutting back supply by forcing them to pay for a new rental unit for each one converted or destroyed. As a result, property values acted perversely. Ten years after the laws were passed, an empty lot could sell for $600,000, whereas an apartment building on an equal-size adjoining lot might command $200,000 less.

No surprise that *Forbes* magazine reported that

abandoned small apartment buildings sit forlornly next to homes costing $500,000 or more. Run-down rental units share streets with chic merchants selling everything from high-fashion clothing to automobiles for the rich and famous.[34]

Even if landlords do not cut supply, they may furtively raise rents, by demanding bribes or "fixture fees" especially from new tenants. "The apartment costs $400 per month. But the window shades, which you *must* buy, cost $10,000," says the landlord.

Does anyone gain from rent control? In the short run, two groups profit. First, politicians, who sound like heroes slaying the evil landlords. Second, tenants who already occupy units at the time rent control is invoked and thus continue to enjoy bargain rents. As a result, these tenants seldom move. This reduces mobility and freezes out new residents of the city. Because of rent control laws enacted in 1980, a high percentage of University of California, Berkeley, students commute to classes from neighboring towns or take long freeway drives from outlying regions. New York City boasts many large apartments occupied by older couples who once shared them with their children. Instead of moving to smaller apartments when the children moved out, they stayed. So a large family moving to the city hasn't a prayer. Most people know that the way to find an apartment in Manhattan is through the obituary pages, not the real estate pages.

Ultimately, rent controls tend to depreciate the housing stock, as maintenance falls and supply diminishes. Usually, such controls are a poor way of helping the poor—and a good way of destroying a city.

Crime

So far we have seen how economists examine tort and property law. But no area of law is untouched by rapacious economists. Economist Gary Becker applied Marshallian economics to family law and to criminal law. The issues are fascinating. Becker's crime model posits criminals who apparently weigh the costs and benefits of committing offenses. If we have a crime problem, Becker implies, it's because crime *does* pay. Economists have tried to calculate what deters criminals. Two variables seem most important: (1) apprehension rates and (2) severity of punishment. The deterrent effect differs for different types of crimes. For some crimes, police should concentrate on catching the criminals. For other crimes, apprehension rates do not scare offenders. Instead they are frightened and deterred by severe punishments.[35] The Beckerian analysis has not been unanimously adopted. Many statistics contradict each other. Nonetheless, it ranks higher than Evelyn Waugh's silly theory that almost "all crime is due to the repressed desire for aesthetic expression."

Criminals often figure that crime pays because they care little about the future. They are willing to dodge bullets, flee police, and pocket a quick payoff rather than make an investment in the future (school, job training). Criminologists and economists who study crime have not focused enough on time horizons. In an economic model I developed back in the 1980s, I concluded that when time horizons shrink, the value of acting honestly diminishes, leading to economic collapse.[36] With due respect to one's Sunday-school teacher, honesty is not always the best policy if your goal is to get rich with the least amount of effort. Two forces normally dissuade even amoral egotists from cheating or stealing, especially in business. First, the fear of punishment. Second, the fear that a bad reputation will repel others from dealing with you *in the future*. But what if you do not care about the future? Crime goes up. (The same dynamic explains why tourists passing through tend to tip waitresses less than regular restaurant patrons.) Sometimes society shrinks the time horizon, making crime look more inviting to more people. How? When governments are about to collapse, for example, South Vietnam in 1975, Indonesia in 1998, or Iraq after 2002.

Another way for society to shrink time horizons is to let interest rates rise. Higher interest rates force us to discount the future more. That is, a dollar next year is worth less today if interest rates go up. The "Buchholz Hypothesis" suggests that higher interest rates induce people to commit more crime because they reduce the value of people's future. During the Great Depression, nominal interest rates dropped, which could solve the mystery of why crime rates actually descended amid economic misery. From the 1960s through the 1970s, interest rates began a steady climb, accompanied by higher crime rates. Violent crime peaked around 1980, as did interest rates, only to climb again in the late 1980s. In the 1990s and 2000s, we enjoyed a rapid drop in interest rates that tracked the plunge in violent crime, with both the crime rate and U.S. Treasury yields plunging and staying near historic lows.

Surely interest rates are not the only factor. Demographics, police work, and punishment rates play a huge role. But when society tells potential felons that tomorrow counts for less, we should not be shocked when they take advantage of today.

Economists who examine the criminal narcotics trade criticize misguided government policies that fail to solve the dreaded problem. During the last thirty years, the federal government has tried to curtail the supply of drugs by destroying crops and sealing U.S. borders. Although the Drug Enforcement Administration seizes tons of narcotics each year, for several reasons this supply-side focus does little good.

First, drugs such as cocaine are derived from plants that grow easily in many parts of the world. There are just too many fertile fields to burn or monitor. Second, because the street value of cocaine, for example, exceeds the import price by tenfold, boosting the price at Miami docks would add very little to the price on Chicago streets. Third, even if interdiction or burning fields did raise the street price, regular cocaine users do not care much about cost. In Marshallian terms, addicts have an inelastic demand. And perversely, higher prices might spur addicts to mug and rob even more in order to pay for their drug habits. (New consumers of narcotics may be more sensitive to higher prices.)

To win the drug war, or at least achieve a truce, the federal and state governments must focus on the demand side. That means severely penalizing drug users. They may be insensitive to price; but they may be more sensitive to jail time. Of course, better counseling and treatment should also be available. These measures should be accompanied by harassing and punishing street vendors. Until Americans give up a desire to use drugs, the war against drugs cannot be won in fields south of the border or on docks on the southern border. It can be won only in the streets of American towns and cities.

No one denies that economists have enriched legal scholarship. Critics do ask, however, if lawyers mesmerized by economics have gone too far. After all, the law should aim for justice. Does efficiency equal justice? Should we repeal inefficient laws, even though they are just? What if whipping prisoners were efficient? Defenders retort in two ways. Extremists actually argue that justice equals efficiency, which recalls the pre–nervous breakdown Mill. The early editions of Richard Posner's treatise *Economic Analysis of Law* claimed that efficiency is "perhaps the most common" meaning of justice. "We shall see that when people describe as 'unjust' convicting a person without a trial, taking property without just compensation ... they can be interpreted as meaning nothing more pretentious than that the conduct in question wastes resources." This rather dim observation by a brilliant man was lightened up, however, in the third edition of the treatise, in which Posner admits, "There is more to justice than economics."[37]

The more reasonable retort has two parts. First, in many legal decisions, especially involving business law, judges do strive for efficiency. The law and economics school can help them. In past decades, judges tried to act efficiently, but ignorance clouded their sight. Second, in cases where issues of justice arise, a moral judicial system should at least know the likely consequences of its decisions. From a moral point of view, we should distinguish between just actions and just actors. A just man is one who chooses correctly after contemplation. A laboratory rat can choose the right action, but that action is not just unless it has been contemplated. A judge who simply ignores consequences is no more just than a laboratory rat. Even if a judge refuses to enforce an efficient result, he should know that he is ignoring efficiency. Lest we reach clouds too lofty, let us put aside this tangential argument with Posner and Kant and move on to an interesting development in corporate finance.

Corporate Finance

The law and economics scholars contrast with the old institutionalists because the new people use Marshallian tools to investigate institutions. In one narrow area, however, the old and new sound alike. In 1932, Adolf Berle and Gardiner Means, a law professor and an economist, respectively, at Columbia proclaimed a mortal split between owners and managers of firms.[38] Since the owners (including stockholders) no longer run the firm but delegate authority to paid managers, firms no longer act efficiently. Galbraith later insisted that managers would pursue their own goals such as enhancing their own prestige by increasing the size of the firm.

Though denying the dire effects, new institutionalists admit that owners must monitor their managers. To monitor costs money, sometimes called "agency costs."

To lower agency costs, owners often give managers incentives to raise profits. Most senior corporate officials receive part of their compensation in the form of stock. If they raise profits, the stock will rise, and they will earn more. In addition, executives frequently receive "stock appreciation rights," where the company pays a cash bonus if the stock price climbs. This trend took off in the 1990s when the share of top executive compensation tied to stock prices zoomed from less than 10 percent to almost 70 percent by 2003. More and more companies are also promising stock incentives to nonexecutive employees. The corporate scandals that took place in the late 1990s at Enron, Tyco, and Fannie Mae did show, however, that shady executives may manipulate stock incentives by backdating options or artificially propping up share prices for short-term gain, with little regard to the firm's long-term health.[39] A few years ago, executives at Wells Fargo were exposed for pressuring their employees to open millions of fake new bank accounts in the names of existing customers without the customers' consent. The operation tricked the stock market into thinking that the bank had acquired more customers, lifting its share price, as well as the bonuses of executives. There is much room for fine-tuning the incentives that shareholders give management. Stock options, crooked executives, and lazy boards can be a treacherous trio for shareholders to face.

Crookedness is not limited to the executive suite, of course. The General Mills Green Giant brand once had a problem with insect parts showing up in bags of frozen peas. The Green Giant mascot was not so jolly to see the legs and thoraxes, and neither were consumers. The company set up an incentive program to reward employees for detecting bug parts. The incentives must have been too alluring, however, since some employees began sneaking insect parts from home gardens into the factory, planting them among the peas, and "finding" them to collect a bonus.[40]

In the 1980s, strong incentives to cut agency costs arose with the increasing popularity of the *leveraged buyout* (LBO). In many leveraged buyouts, the managers borrow money, buy up all the stock, and take over the ownership for themselves. The new debt pressures them into trimming costs and selling off less productive assets. Vice presidents hand in their keys to corporate jets. Thus, the mortal split is mended. Agency costs plummet because the managers have an extremely large stake in the company's performance. Hertz, Levi Strauss, and Black Entertainment Television took part in the first wave of LBOs. Not long after Black Entertainment Television's LBO, founder Robert Johnson became the first black billionaire in the United States. In recent years, PetSmart and Dell have "gone private." Leveraged buyouts do have their critics. Although stockholders who sell their shares to the managers usually receive substantial premiums over the pre-LBO market price, critics question whether the buyout price is determined in a fair manner. Maybe the managers have inside information that they haven't divulged that should make the price even higher.[41] Furthermore, critics point out that the mammoth debt burden can dramatically increase the risk of bankruptcy if the economy falters. While this is true, new creditors of these companies are generally sophisticated insurance companies and institutions that carefully examine risks.

Many plays and films are now financed so that producers pay stars and directors a percentage of the gross proceeds only *after* costs are paid. Thus, everyone has an incentive to reduce costs. No one has an incentive to squander and splurge on lavish extras. Hollywood financiers call these "contingent deferments."

In corporate finance, the old institutionalists pointed to a problem. Fifty years later the new institutionalists pointed to solutions.

Almost every institution and social phenomenon has economic implications. According to a 1988 study, the historical treatment of prisoners of war closely correlates with the costs and benefits of killing or sparing a vanquished adversary. The Middle Ages, the authors conclude, were not always horrible for prisoners of war, since captors often treated captives well enough to command high ransom prices.[42] The bad news for prisoners of war seized during the Middle Ages: if demand for them or for their labor fell, heads would roll.

Even the existence of time has economic implications. How would people behave if they knew that the world would end tomorrow? How would they behave if a new legal system, a system that would not enforce contracts or punish criminals, was going to be imposed next week?

People act civilly toward one another for many reasons. One reason is that they want reputations for being trustworthy. This is especially important in business. But if time is short and reputations in the coming regime will not be based on present behavior, some people might renege on promises and take advantage of others. A healthy market economy demands a certain level of civility and sanctity of promises. A society that perceives no future would see economic collapse.[43]

* * *

There is clearly more to economics than prices, profits, rents, and costs. Laws, morals, fashions, and philosophies all contribute to an economy. They may support it, or they may tear it down. Veblen and Galbraith expanded the definition of economics and forced colleagues to open their eyes to broader phenomena. Economics is not as easy as Marshall made it look.

The new institutionalists admit that economics isn't easy. But they show how robust Marshall's tools are. For they use his methods to understand the complex institutions that help mold the economy.

Brandeis warned that lawyers ignorant of economics menace society. What is the legacy of the old and the new institutionalists? They finally explained that economics is as big as society itself.

CHAPTER IX

Keynes: Bon Vivant as Savior

Cambridge is perhaps the most beautiful university in the world. Every year hundreds of thousands of tourists meander through medieval courts, punt on the River Cam, and snap photographs, as students play cricket and croquet on lush lawns. Sometimes the students put down their cricket bats to play practical jokes on the visitors. A few years ago, some merry sons of Cambridge painted a papier-mâché ball to look like a heavy concrete ornament found on one of the many bridges spanning the Cam. As a boat filled with Japanese tourists streamed by, the boys pushed the ball off the bridge and screamed. The tourists shrieked and leaped overboard—cameras in hands. Aside from terrorized tourists, Cambridge can be idyllic. Fellows and students donned in gowns still stroll into sixteenth-century halls to dine beneath portraits of Henry VIII, Elizabeth I, and alumni such as Newton, Darwin, and Wordsworth.

Here it was that Cockcroft ran through the streets hugging passersby and shouting, "We've split the atom! We've split the atom!" Here it was that Watson and Crick revealed the secret of life in their DNA model.

No one embodied the Cambridge spirit of culture, fun, and public duty so much as Maynard Keynes. No one was more brilliant or charming. No economist in his century influenced politicians or the course of economics more. Bertrand Russell, one of Britain's most distinguished philosophers, announced that Keynes had "the sharpest and clearest" intellect he had ever known: "When I argued with him, I felt that I took my life in my hands, and I seldom emerged without feeling something of a fool."[1] One feels sorry for Charles Rye Fay, a classmate of Keynes's. The first freshman Fay met upon arriving at Cambridge was Keynes, and poor Fay thought that all his classmates would be just as superior to him. He later reflected that the first person he met at college turned out to be the smartest he would meet during his entire life. Incidentally, Keynes was smart enough to know that he was smart. Few accused him of modesty. In fact, Keynes did not return Fay's admiration, later writing that his friend was unfit as a traveling companion: "He is too ugly. Ugliness of face, hands, body, clothes and manners are not, I find, completely overbalanced by cheerfulness, a good heart, and an average intelligence."[2]

Despite his origins in the secluded paradise of Cambridge, Keynes and his ideas ranged throughout the world. If Ronald Reagan wore an Adam Smith necktie, every president from Franklin D. Roosevelt to Richard Nixon could have slipped on a Keynes cravat, especially Kennedy and Johnson. Ironically, after Nixon announced, "We are all Keynesians now," Keynes's influence began to wane. Milton Friedman, the fiercest critic of Keynesian economics, admitted that "in one sense, we are all Keynesians now; in another, no one is a Keynesian any longer."[3] During the 1980s and 1990s, Keynes's allure began to fade. Robert Lucas, the Rational Expectations pioneer we will discuss in chapter 12, said that the Keynes name began to elicit whispers and giggles at economist gatherings. And yet when the stock market and economy tumbled into a banking crisis in 2008 (and a coronavirus panic in 2020), whose name came back into vogue? Lucas admitted, "Well, I guess everyone is a Keynesian in a foxhole."[4]

What does it mean to be a Keynesian? Two basic propositions will suffice here: (1) the private economy may not reach full employment; (2) government spending can spur the economy into filling the gap. Every time a politician ardently advocates priming the pump, government programs to get the country moving again, or slashing taxes to boost consumption, he exalts Keynes.

Keynes was not concerned solely with employment, though. His *Collected Writings* number more than two dozen volumes and span many subjects, including currency questions, trade restrictions, rebuilding after the world wars, and graceful essays on such figures as Einstein and Newton. The distinguished Oxford historian Hugh Trevor-Roper names Keynes as among the major contributors to historical method.

Escape from Victorianism

Keynes was born in 1883 into a Puritanical Victorian home. John Neville Keynes, his father, was a well-known logician, economist, and Cambridge University registrar, whose mind impressed Alfred Marshall, but whose nerves had always required soothing. Like many students in any era, Neville's anxiety showed up on exam days, and he would complain about headaches, toothaches, and chest pains. While his son would learn to walk with kings and princes, Neville would rather stroll among the stacks of the library and pursue calming hobbies like chess and stamp collecting. While his son would, with sneaky glee, toss around words like "sodomy" and "catamites," Neville resisted Ibsen's plays because he was offended that Nora would desert her husband and children in *A Doll's House*.[5] The daughter of a minister, Maynard's charming mother, Florence Ada, was taller and psychologically sturdier than her husband. She later served as mayor of Cambridge, and kept their marriage strong for sixty-seven years. Neville's family had an ample cushion of money, and so they could afford to indulge in theater-going, library-building, and other high-minded pursuits of the Victorians. The marriage started with a sort of bang, however, because Maynard was conceived not long after their honeymoon, in June 1883.

An aunt had explained to young Maynard that "'Keynes' rhymed with 'brains.'" Although Keynes was fond of his parents, he spent much of his life escaping from their moral and philosophical influences. Keynes liked to have fun and cared little for the Puritan attitudes embodied in Sir James Stephen, grandfather of his friend Virginia Woolf, who reputedly once smoked a cigar and found it so pleasurable that he never smoked again. Still, Keynes felt quite comfortable as a member of the high intellectual bourgeoisie. In a pun on the British expression "wet" (meaning "weak political devotion"), Lenin referred to him as a "bourgeois of the highest water," while Keynes joked that when the communist revolution came, he would be found beside the bourgeois banner.

At Eton, he amassed numerous prizes for mathematics, and performed well in the theater and humbly on the cricket pitch. Entering King's College, Cambridge, he flourished even more boldly. More important, he developed friendships and liaisons, both intellectual and physical, with other highbrows and was invited to join the university's most select and secretive society, the Apostles. The society included eminent older members, or "angels," such as Russell, G. E. Moore, and Alfred North Whitehead, as well as Keynes's peers, many of whom would later achieve fame in literature and the arts, such as Lytton Strachey, E. M. Forster, and Leonard Woolf. The Apostles threw themselves into the radical philosophy of morality that Moore spelled out in *Principia Ethica* and agreed with him that "goodness" could not be prescribed, written in stone on Mosaic tablets, or beaten into a child by the hickory stick of a schoolmarm. Instead, goodness was an "intuition," a claim that seemed to liberate the Apostles. Generally, the Apostles discussed three topics: philosophy, themselves, and aesthetics. Not that they were particularly pleasing aesthetically. Most, including Keynes, lacked what Virginia Woolf called "physical splendour." The most blistering commentary on Keynes's looks comes from an assistant master at Eton, who described him as "distinctly ugly at first sight, with lips projecting and seeming to push up the well-formed nose and strong brows in slightly simian fashion."[6] Friends at Eton had called him "Snout." As Keynes grew to a stooping height of six feet, six inches, he grew into his pseudo-simian face, though he remained convinced of his ugliness. It did not help when Virginia Woolf went beyond the primate species and said that Keynes resembled "a gorged seal" and later a "queer swollen eel." These descriptions seem gross and grossly unfair. A 1931 video shows him looking quite human, with an accent and bearing that Henry Higgins would approve of.[7]

The Apostles bred an ugly arrogance, and Keynes himself had many ways to look down on his inferiors. Not only did the Apostles consider themselves far superior to the masses; they thought they soared above all of Cambridge and Oxford. "I get the feeling that most of the rest never see anything at all— too stupid or too wicked," Keynes wrote to Strachey.[8] Still, no one can deny that the Apostles were a formidable group who often engaged in sparkling conversation. Here, as well as in the Cambridge Union Society, Keynes learned to be the consummate debater and raconteur, who later surpassed colleagues, competitors, and politicians in seminars and summits.

Many of the Apostles, including Keynes, later emerged as the Bloomsbury Group, whose anti-Victorian, bohemian attitudes powerfully affected the development of British culture. In addition to his achievements in economics, Keynes would spend almost as much time collecting books, founding the Cambridge Arts Theatre, and serving as a trustee for the National Gallery, buyer for the Contemporary Arts Society, and chairman of the trustees of the Royal Opera House. A report of his theater activities shows a deep concern for microeconomics: he "was fascinated by statistics of bar-profits, and programme money, and matinee ices, and cups of coffee."[9] As an academic, arts patron, finance manager, and government officer, he seemed to be everywhere. Over the years, he would have a finger, a foot, and every other appendage in every camp, from beagling with landed lords to buggering with itinerant actors. In today's more specialized academic world, one might seriously ask whether Keynes would choose economics, given his dilettantism.

Keynes did not come to Cambridge to study economics but mathematics. Though he performed satisfactorily, he struggled. "I am saddening my brain, destroying my intellect, souring my disposition," he wrote to a friend.[10] After passing his mathematics exam, he read his first economics book, Marshall's *Principles of Economics*. Keynes began writing papers for Marshall, who scribbled encouraging words in the margins. In the greatest understatement since Smith started writing a book to "pass away the time," Keynes wrote about economics: "I think I am rather good at it." He added, "I want to manage a railway or organise a Trust, or at least swindle the investing public." A few days later he reported, "Marshall is continually pestering me to turn professional Economist. . . . Do you think there is anything in it? I doubt it."[11]

Keynes's studies with Marshall lasted only eight weeks. Nor did he take a degree in economics. He proved rather good at on-the-job training, however.

In 1905 Keynes began studying hard for the Civil Service Examination. As he reviewed mathematics, philosophy, psychology, et al., his prejudices again emerged. After reading a book by a non-Cambridge philosopher, he lamented, "What a home of diseased thought Oxford is." Keynes came in second of 104 candidates. Ironically, economics and mathematics were his worst subjects! "Real knowledge seems an absolute bar to success," he reported. About economics, Keynes decided that the examiners did not know enough. He would teach them.[12]

Since the first-place candidate snatched a job at the Treasury, in 1906 Keynes grabbed the second-best position, at the India Office in London. He never made it to India. His first task was to ship ten young bulls to Bombay. Keynes quickly became bored silly, or more accurately, bored flippant, reporting to Strachey that he was working on the annual report on the moral and material progress of India and planned a "special feature" in "this year's edition . . . an illustrated appendix on Sodomy."[13]

Keynes returned to King's College, Cambridge, repelled by tedium and attracted by Marshall's offer of a lectureship. As an economics teacher, Keynes leaned on one of the few texts he had actually read, Marshall's. In the early years his economics did not venture far beyond Marshall and the classical tradition. As he read more, though, his reputation for insight and lucidity grew, resulting in an appointment as co-editor of the influential *Economic Journal*. Keynes held this post until 1945 and established a sterling reputation for careful editing and good humor. Once he told a foreign contributor that while "exempli gratia" may be abbreviated "e.g.," he could not abbreviate "for instance" as "f.i." Two years later, in 1913, he published *Indian Currency and Finance*, one of the few fruits of his India Office years. Joseph Schumpeter called it the "best English work on the gold exchange standard."[14] Of course, Schumpeter, who sometimes seemed envious of Keynes, may have been insulting English economists as much as complimenting the book.

War and a Dangerous Peace

World War I brought Keynes back to government in the Treasury Department. The war posed a test to the Bloomsbury Group and their aloof, iconoclastic, and apatriotic persuasions. Almost all the male members, including Keynes, claimed exemption from military service as conscientious objectors. As usual, Lytton Strachey injected humor into the serious matter. Though he stated that all physically fit intellectuals should be prepared to defend the shores of England, he added one proviso: no intellectuals are physically fit. Sometime later, Strachey made his proudest contribution to the war effort: he knitted a navy-blue wool scarf for the neck of a sailor he desired. Finally, when Strachey was haled before the war tribunal to test his conscientious-objector status, officials asked the classic question: What would you do if you saw a German officer attempting to rape your sister? Strachey paused. "I would attempt to interpose my body between them," he said, winking.[15]

After the war, Keynes represented the Treasury at the Paris Peace Conference. Again he grew disgusted with government, but not because of boredom. Keynes witnessed Woodrow Wilson being bamboozled by British prime minister Lloyd George and the Frenchman Georges Clemenceau into squeezing a defeated Germany beyond reason and beyond her ability to rebound, except in frightening belligerency. Keynes came close to predicting another world war. Unable to endure the diplomatic nightmare he was watching, he resigned and quickly penned *The Economic Consequences of the Peace,* one of the most acid polemics of his time, judged even by Bloomsbury standards. He was perhaps inspired by his friend Strachey's brutal takedown of societal paragons in his bestselling 1918 work, *Eminent Victorians*, in which Strachey even poked at Florence Nightingale, the founder of modern nursing. In his Versailles postmortem, Keynes said that President Wilson's reputation had the world and Keynes in awe: He noted how the crowd pressed around the president's carriage, trying to catch a glimpse of this man of destiny who would bring healing. Instead, Wilson appeared like a Presbyterian minister with "no plan, no scheme, no constructive ideas whatever . . . his mind was too slow."[16] When visiting Washington, D.C., which he called "very oriental," Keynes changed metaphors and described Wilson as "an invisible sultan spending most of his time in his harem," by which Keynes surely meant seclusion, not the arms of wives and concubines.[17] Clemenceau seldom spoke at Versailles, Keynes reported, but then "a sudden outburst of words, often followed by a fit of deep coughing from the chest produced their impression rather by force and surprise, rather than by persuasion." The Germans were a sad lot with drawn, dejected faces, and were led by a small, noble-visaged man who bore a high collar and the gleaming eyes of "an honorable animal in pain." This was Carl Melchior, a lawyer for the once-powerful Warburg Bank, representing vanquished Germany. The negotiations were tetchy and treacherous. One day, Melchior and Keynes snuck away from the rage and the bank ledgers and stepped into a small room. Keynes was quivering with excitement and fear, for breaking ranks and protocol. Each begged the other to see the honesty and humanity in the other. How did these two men end up in a room, the result of a gunshot in Sarajevo, mustard gas in trenches, and twenty million dead? "I begged him to believe that I, at least, at that moment was sincere. He was as much moved as I was. . . . In a sort of way I was in love with him."[18] Along with searing portraits of the world's leaders, Keynes carefully argued to the French and Americans that Germany could not afford the reparations demanded of her. He ominously warned, "If we aim at the impoverishment of Central Europe, vengeance, I dare say, will not limp. Nothing can then delay for very long the forces of Reaction . . . before which the horrors of the later German war will fade into nothing, and which will destroy, whoever is victor, the civilisation."[19] Book sales soared, breaking records in England and the United States, and so did Keynes's reputation and ego. In a parodic poem, one magazine commented on "The Candour of Keynes": "Still we feel . . . That possibly some of the Ultimate Things / May even be hidden from Fellows of King's."[20]

Not much was hidden from Keynes. In the next decade he continued to teach, edit, write, advise governments, and serve as chairman of a life insurance company. He corresponded with the most prominent politicians, academics, and artists of his time. In 1925, he married Lydia Lopokova, a Russian ballerina who had danced with Nijinsky and had headlined Diaghilev's traveling troupe. She was known for her lively style, louche manners, and memorable malapropisms. She once told a fellow dancer that he danced like a cantaloupe. She meant antelope. It turned out that she had learned English in the Catskill Mountains of New York. At a British embassy reception in Washington on the evening of Franklin Roosevelt's reelection, she kept turning to others and asking, "Do you like Rosie?"[21] Lydia puzzled and troubled Maynard's Bloomsbury friends, who wondered what a world-class intellect could see in a middling dancer whose brain seemed to pirouette more dizzily than her legs. Besides, she was female, and Maynard had seemed to be spending more time with young men. He even paid for his brilliant friend Ludwig Wittgenstein to visit them for six days during their honeymoon in Sussex, during which time Wittgenstein acted like, well, Wittgenstein. Lydia comments brightly, "What a beautiful tree!" The fiendishly fey philosopher replies, "What do you mean?" Lydia cries. No matter, Keynes and Lydia stuck together through the honeymoon and twenty years beyond until his death in 1946. At the wedding, his friends bet on whether Lydia would get pregnant soon, and Keynes's friend Clive Bell, an art critic and the brother-in-law of Virginia Woolf, took the long side of the bet, saying, "Maynard is too fast on the trigger."[22] In the end, Maynard and Lydia did not raise children but instead raised money for the opera, ballet, theater, and other artistic causes across Britain.

Luck and a good measure of skill aided Keynes as he earned a fortune trading stocks and commodities. He not only spoke the King's English, but he was also fluent in rubber, cotton, tin, and gold.[23] Perhaps because he was secure in his intellect and so well connected among those whom sociologist C. Wright Mills would call the "power elite," Keynes took big chances in his portfolio and, when he felt bullish, borrowed from banks to buy more shares than his cash on hand would permit. He would sit in his bed each morning, sift through the newspapers, take phone calls from brokers, and then place his orders. Though he went nearly bankrupt in the late 1920s and late 1930s, when he died in 1946 he left behind a solid portfolio worth £400,000 (about $20 million in today's dollars), in addition to a prescient art collection featuring coveted works by Picasso and Braque. He frequented auctions and once accompanied the head of the National Gallery on a clandestine trip to Paris. To disguise his deep pockets from other bidders, the gallery chief shaved his mustache and donned spectacles. On another trip, Keynes reported, "I've got a Cezanne in my suitcase" and then added that because it was too heavy, he had to temporarily leave it in a "ditch, behind the gate."[24] His collection, including the work retrieved from the ditch, is worth about $100 million today and was donated to Cambridge's Fitzwilliam Museum. Some critics challenge economists to "put up or shut up"—that is, if they know about money, why aren't they rich? If economists were judged by this test, Keynes would rank second only to David Ricardo. Too many economists tie for last place to mention any others.

The Great Depression and the Fall of Classical Economics

In economics, Keynes focused mostly on monetary policy, writing his *Tract on Monetary Reform* in 1923, followed by a two-volume *Treatise on Money* in 1930. The *Treatise* tied together much of Keynes's earlier work on investment with new insights on the connection between savings and investment. But despite the comprehensive nature of the *Treatise*, 1930 brought challenges to economics so perplexing that he could no longer rest on his published work and enchanting charm. Though Keynes's luck seemed never to run dry, the world's luck did, and nations were awash in the debt and despair of the Great Depression.

Recall the scary Malthusian scenario, with the world seemingly splitting, leaving victims scrambling for survival. Once upon a time not far removed and in a place familiar to us, it nearly happened. From 1929 to 1933 in the United States, the invisible hand of the free market slapped prosperity in the face. Unemployment rocketed from about 3 to 25 percent, and national income plummeted by half. Residential construction stopped. Many lost their homes and businesses. The stock market crash of 1929, with brokers jumping to their deaths, became both symbol and cause of further economic decline. The Roaring Twenties sputtered to a halt, leaving income in 1933 lower than that in 1922. Workers scrambled for the few jobs available. Soup kitchens sprang up. And psychological depression accompanied economic depression.

The popular song lyricist Yip Harburg, who would later promise a brighter place for Judy Garland in the song "Over the Rainbow," echoed the frustration and despondency of the Depression in his classic "Brother, Can You Spare a Dime?" The song chronicles the generations that labored to help carve a prosperous civilization from the American wilderness. Yet now the singer who helped build a railroad that raced "against time" has no job. Can one beg with pride and dignity? Yes. For he has not lost his job because of any personal failure. An economy run awry has robbed him.

Economic historians have long debated the cause of the Great Depression, but there is no simple answer. The more important question is, what transformed a recession into a nightmare? The United States had lived through dips and drops before, but never so severe. Most economists stress a coincidence of bad events: investment opportunities dried up after accelerating in the 1920s; consumers decided to decrease spending and repay loans; nations panicked into protectionism; and the Federal Reserve system responded with tighter, not looser, policies.[25]

When Ronald Reagan battled President Carter in 1980, he wittily defined some economic terms: "A recession is when your neighbor loses his job. A depression is when you lose your job. And recovery is when Jimmy Carter loses his job."

Maynard Keynes might agree, but with a slight change in

the last definition. Recovery from the Great Depression comes when old fuddy-duddies in the British Treasury (and the American government) lose their jobs. To Keynes, the old men of the Treasury were drunk on the old wine of the classical economists, which to his taste had turned to vinegar. Keynes blasted the Treasury view, which prescribed patience and promised recovery in the long run. What is the point of having such a government? *"In the long run* we are all dead," he wrote in his *Tract on Monetary Reform.*

In truth, the Treasury men were not simply bound by inertia and old age. They did have some smart, young theorists to back them. The chair of the London School of Economics, Lionel Robbins, had visited Vienna a number of times and had begun to embrace the views of the so-called Austrian school of economics, led by Ludwig von Mises and his student Friedrich von Hayek. Robbins found Hayek's views electrifying and exotic, compared with the Marshallian analysis that dominated in England. He offered the thirty-two-year-old Hayek a position in London, and together the duo set out to battle Keynes. Even though Hayek was awed by Keynes's brainpower and bewitching voice, he was stunned by Keynes's ignorance of non-English economics and European history. In an interview in the late 1970s, Hayek recalled that Keynes "knew nothing but Marshallian economics. . . . He hated the nineteenth century and, therefore, knew little about it." According to Hayek, Keynes was enamored with his own theories and "had contempt for most other economists."[26] In *Prices and Production* (1931), Hayek lays out his own business-cycle theory, which contends that central banks spark downturns because they first spark a boom. By pushing interest rates lower than the "natural rate" (a term from Knut Wicksell) in the Roaring Twenties, the central bank mistakenly spurred businesses to borrow too much and to overspeculate on too-risky ideas. The economy raced on an amphetamine high and then crashed. Future Nobel laureate Ronald Coase heard Hayek's first London lectures and called his effect "magical." But what to do about the Depression? Keynes and Hayek amicably toasted each other at dinners, while exchanging friendly missives and bitter reviews of each other's work. Keynes could be a vicious debater and called Hayek's work "frightful muddles" that "end in bedlam." Regardless of insults, the two men offered radically different prescriptions. Keynes said that the government should jump into the breach and throw more money at workers and businesses. Hayek and Robbins advised waiting for the excesses to unwind and for prices to readjust. Herbert Hoover would later call this the "liquidationist" method, while Milton Friedman would deem the London axis a dismal and dark view that did the world "a great deal of harm."[27] The Cambridge-versus-London wrestling match took place on the blackboard, in journals, and in newspapers. On October 17, 1932, Keynes and his supporters signed a letter to London's *Times* making their case, and two days later Robbins and Hayek rebutted. In a time of crisis, however, "do nothing" was not an attractive policy. With jobless numbers soaring and British exports collapsing by 50 percent, Robbins and Hayek retreated from the fight. They each bore wounds for a long time. More than forty years later, Robbins admitted, "I was on the wrong side," and fifty years later Hayek remarked, "The moment there is any sign that the income stream may actually shrink, I should . . . try everything in my power to prevent it from dwindling."[28] After the battles with Keynes and after World War II, Hayek turned more toward political and legal philosophy, producing striking and enduring works like *The Road to Serfdom* and *The Constitution of Liberty*. Though he died in 1992, Hayek might be considered the grandfather of cryptocurrencies, for he advocated nongovernment money long before the first Bitcoin, and even before the first Internet connections were flipped on.[29] While King George VI would grant Keynes the title of baron and place him in the House of Lords, Hayek would receive the Presidential Medal of Freedom from George H. W. Bush.

Back in the 1930s, Keynes knew that writing letters to editors would not win the day. He justified the advice he gave to politicians in his 1936 masterpiece, *The General Theory of Employment, Interest and Money*, which smashes the Treasury view and presents a new framework for macroeconomic analysis. As Keynes predicted in the preface, conventional economists would fluctuate "between a belief that I am quite wrong and a belief that I am saying nothing new." Paul Samuelson, whose introductory economics text has taught Keynesian economics to generations, cleverly summed up the ambiguity of *The General Theory*: "It is a badly written book, poorly organized; any layman who, beguiled by the author's previous reputation, bought the book was cheated of his five shillings. . . . It is arrogant, bad-tempered, polemical and not overly-generous in its acknowledgments. It abounds in mares' nests and confusions. . . . In short, it is a work of genius."[30]

Keynes begins by mercilessly attacking his predecessors and Cambridge colleagues (especially A. C. Pigou), sometimes directly, sometimes through caricatures. During the prosperous years before the Depression, Pigou used to confidently say, "It is all in Marshall," as if few questions in economics remained to be solved. (Despite his shy manner, Pigou did devise many original ideas, and in recent years he is making a comeback. In the following chapter we shall see how his model helps explain the economic rebound from the Great Recession of 2008.) Unlike Keynes, Pigou disliked discussions of economic controversies once he had put down the chalk and left the classroom. Keynes's friend Ludwig Wittgenstein was even less accessible. After class he ran off to movies, preferably those starring Carmen Miranda, who was famous for dancing with tropical fruit on her head and singing the "Chiquita Banana Song." Whether Wittgenstein found a deeper meaning in this rite, we do not know.

The General Theory tries to settle some scores with Hayek, likening him to Ibsen's "wild duck," who dives to the bottom of a mucky lake and gets tangled up.[31] Harry Johnson described well Keynes's sarcastic, terroristic intellectual strikes in *The General Theory*: "It posits a nameless horde of faceless orthodox nincompoops, among whom a few recognizable faces can be discerned, and proceeds to ridicule a travesty of their published, presumed, or imputed views."[32] The most nincompoopish belief was in Say's Law, which Malthus had attacked a century before. Recall from an earlier chapter that Say's Law states that producing goods generates enough income to workers and suppliers for all the goods to be purchased. Therefore, no general gluts can take place. People have enough money to buy everything that has been produced. (Of course, a merchant may produce too much of a particular product. But this would not be a general glut. The price would fall to eliminate the particular surplus.) If one believes in Say's Law, however, one must not believe in long-term unemployment and great depressions. Only a schizophrenic could believe in both. And even Keynes would not accuse his colleagues of schizophrenia. He gave them the benefit of the doubt and called them stupid.

The nincompoops ignored an important leak in the smooth, cyclical flow from producers to consumers to producers and so on. What happens when households save? As they build up their bank accounts, won't merchants find themselves staring at piles of unsold goods? Keynes thought so. The nincompoops had an answer. Was it right? Keynes thought not. He argued against two prime propositions:

1. According to the classicists, households consume part of their income and save the remainder. If consumers decide to save more, demand for goods and services slips, *but* this is offset because merchants simply invest more. Why would merchants invest more? When people save, they do not usually stuff bills under their mattresses. They put money in the bank. The banks lend the money to merchants. Now, if people bring more savings to the bank, the bank will lower the price it charges borrowers, which is the interest rate. And if the bank lowers the interest rate, merchants will borrow more for investment because more projects will appear profitable compared with

the cost of borrowing. *Thus, whenever consumers boost their savings and reduce their consumption, merchants will be induced to boost their investment.* A flexible interest rate will, in Marshallian splendor, tie investment and savings together. We might say that consumers provide the supply of savings (which rises as interest rates rise, because saving becomes more attractive), while merchants provide a demand for those savings (which falls as interest rates rise).

If a recession seems imminent because people cut back on their purchases and instead raise savings, the model predicts that interest rates will fall, which inspires merchants to spend more on investment, which puts money in people's pockets and sustains the flow.

2. Flexible wages and prices buttress Say's Law. Suppose that all merchants limp. They cannot walk to the bank as fast as consumers do when the consumers raise their savings. Thus, merchants cannot invest quickly enough to make up for the decreased consumption. A slight recession may result. But wages and prices would fall in response to a fall in demand for goods and services. As wages fell, unemployed workers would be rehired. As prices fell, surplus goods would be sold. The recession would be over quickly.

An art aficionado, Keynes refused to admit that the neat, logical, classical picture belonged to the realism school. It might be vaguely reminiscent of the truth in an impressionistic way. But the world was not so pretty, especially in 1936.

Keynes launched a two-pronged attack on the classical school. First, he denied the automatic link between savings and investment. Households and businesses save and invest for completely different reasons. A family may save from habit or for a particular purpose such as old age or for an automobile. Businesses may change their investment plans based on politics, confidence, technology, foreign exchange rates, or who wins the World Series. To expect interest rates to bring harmony is silly. If household savings exceed business investment, gluts will emerge, and bosses will fire employees, leading to even less consumption. During 1997 and 1998, Japanese households cut back their spending even though the central bank slashed short-term interest rates to just 0.5 percent. As income falls, savings may drop enough to equal investment, but not necessarily at full employment.

Second, Keynes scoffed at fluid, flexible wages and prices. When politicians prophesy that prices will float to their correct levels, they sound like magicians chanting prophecies that "*abra* will rise, *cadabra* will fall." Monopolies and union contracts surely impede adjustment. During a recession, real wages should fall, according to classical theory. But workers usually refuse to accept lower nominal wages, Keynes thought.

In a recession, Keynes argued, businesses slash investment. Yes, savings eventually equal investment. But why? Not because investment rises (as the classicists say), but because laid-off employees cannot afford to save. Further, because wages and prices take a long time to adjust, prolonged recessions or depressions are possible.

Sure enough, savings did equal investment in the early 1930s. There was none of either. The classical show was over.

The Keynesian Solution

It was time for a new show. The spotlight would shine on aggregate demand. The marquee would read "Depressions Occur When Total Demand for Goods and Services Is Less Than Total Income." (A large marquee would be needed, but remember that during depressions, vacancies rise.) Through his analysis, Keynes warns of inadequate demand for goods and services by households and businesses. If they do not purchase enough, merchants will fire workers and slash output. This is Keynes's capsule description of a depression.

Let's build the simple Keynesian model step by step, discussing first households and then businesses. Since more products are bought by households, households are the most important component of overall demand. What determines how much households spend? Although family size, tastes, and expectations are significant, Keynes appoints income the chief determinant. If income rises, people will buy more. If income falls, they will buy less. This seems logical. In fact, Keynes assumes that each time a person gets an extra dollar, he will spend most of that dollar and save the rest. Keynes calls the spent part the *marginal propensity to consume.* Say a dollar falls from heaven into your pocket. You buy a candy bar for 80 cents and put the rest in the bank. Your marginal propensity to consume is 0.80 (algebraically, the change in consumption divided by the change in income). Your marginal propensity to save is 0.20.

Businesses also buy goods and services. By investing in equipment and inventories, they form the other substantial part of aggregate demand. What does investment depend on? Keynes thought investment was much more volatile than household consumption. Expectations, interest rates, confidence, weather, and politics could all distort investment plans. In the simplest Keynesian model, we assume that so many factors count that businessmen do not change their investment plans in response to short-run changes in incomes. (Recall that households do change their consumption in the short run.)

What does this model mean? To have a healthy economy with full employment, households must consume enough and businesses must invest enough that sales of goods equal the amount produced. If people consumed all their income (MPC = 1), Say's Law would produce full employment. But since people save, business investment must make up for the savings. If it does not, output exceeds sales, inventories build, and employers lay off employees. The problem is deficient demand for goods and services. The culprit in a recession is savings.

Several years before *The General Theory*, Keynes urged citizens to spend more. In a *Redbook* magazine article, "Can America Spend Its Way into Recovery?," Keynes proclaimed: "Why, obviously!" Few listened. Nor did they hear when he wrote in *The Listener*:

> When anyone cuts down expenditure, whether as an individual or a town council or a Government Department, next morning someone for sure finds that his income has been cut off, and that is not the end of the story. The fellow who wakes up to find that his income is reduced or that he is thrown out of work . . . is compelled in his turn to cut down his expenditure, whether he wants to or not. . . . Once the rot has started, it is most difficult to stop.[33]

Whereas past critics of capitalism eagerly pointed a bony, prosecutorial finger at evil robber barons and sordid profiteers, Keynes calmly claims that well-intentioned savers, including harmless old ladies, inflict more harm than any wicked industrialist.

The harm, or "rot," compounds itself, though. This is the remarkable Keynesian *multiplier* (actually borrowed from his colleague Richard Kahn). The point of the multiplier is that any change in spending by one person starts a snowball effect, and the ultimate change in national spending far surpasses the initial change.

Let's say that Maynard Inc. decides to raise investment by $100 by building a new men's room. Total spending rises by $100. But Maynard Inc. has to pay plumbers, architects, and interior decorators. What do they do with the money when they come home from work? They spend some and save the rest. The part they spend may go to grocers, video game sellers, and Girl Scouts for cookies. These recipients now have more income, part of which they spend. The chain reaction continues. Although the initial injection was only $100, total income may rise by $300. If so, the multiplier is 3.

Keynes provides a simple formula to calculate the multiplier. Since he exalts consumption, it's not surprising that the key is the marginal propensity to consume:

$$\text{Multiplier} = 1/[1-\text{MPC}] \text{ or } 1/\text{MPS}$$

The higher the degree of consumption, the higher the multiplier. The chain reaction moves more quickly if recipients spend more money. Again, saving slows the process.

Startling conclusions follow. First, small drops in investment, perhaps due to depressing weather or despondent corporate officers, may severely pressure the economy as a whole. If people save one-third of their additional income, the multiplier is 3. Therefore, if business cuts investment by $50 million, national income plummets by $150 million! *Business pessimism is a self-fulfilling prophecy!* Dreary dreams become suicidal nightmares. No wonder presidents and vice presidents spend so much time cheerleading. Even Dwight Eisenhower, whose reticence provoked some to call the White House the "tomb of the well-known soldier," begged the public to buy during the 1958 recession. Buy what? "Anything!" In 1982, Ronald Reagan's advisers labeled a dip in the economy a "growth recession." They claimed that the economy slowed while preparing to soar ahead. Critics mocked by calling Reagan's pet dog a "growth horse." In the 1991 recession, President George H. W. Bush tried to inspire shoppers by going to a mall and buying socks. Because Bush was mocked for his efforts, his successors have been more cautious about public displays of shopping during downturns, with presidents Obama and Trump preferring to show good cheer and poise by swinging golf clubs.

The startling implications of Keynes's advice are not all bad, though. In fact, some are nearly magical. If deficient demand incites recessions, the antidote must be to arouse more spending. Further, if we know the MPC, we know the multiplier. Therefore, we can inject spending into the economy, which will multiply throughout and cure the recession by filling the original gap between output and sales.

Who is "we"? *The government.* Nothing prevents the private sector from flowing into dire straits and foundering at sea, while laborers thrown overboard are tempest-tossed. But the national government can either cut taxes or spend money directly to save the ship. If deficient demand brings a recession gap of $12 billion, and the MPC is two-thirds, the multiplier equals 3. Thus, a $4 billion government spending program should spur the economy into closing the gap.[34]

In fact, Keynes estimated the United States' multiplier at about 2.5 and advocated massive public spending programs in letters to President Roosevelt as well as in magazines. In a 1933 letter he advised "a large volume of loan expenditure under government auspices. It is beyond my province to choose particular objects of expenditure. But preference should be given to those which can be made to mature quickly, on a large scale, as, for example . . . railroads. The object is to start the ball rolling."[35]

Keynes knew that economists and politicians would attack his activist fiscal policy. British and U.S. Treasury officials cherished a balanced budget, and if the governments followed Keynes, deficits would emerge. So what? responded Keynes. During recessions, balanced budgets are stupid, for there are two sides to a budget: tax revenues and outlays. Since in recessions incomes fall, governments collect less in taxes. If the government is obsessed by a balanced budget, it must either cut spending or raise taxes. But each of these squeezes the economy further by the multiplier process! Over the course of the business cycle, budgets should be balanced, Keynes urged. During prosperity, people pay more money in taxes, and budget surpluses should result. But during recessions, the government should allow deficits. The dunces at the treasuries took a long time to understand this.

Throughout his presidency Ronald Reagan vigorously pressed for a constitutional amendment requiring a balanced budget, despite $200 billion deficits at the time. Reagan toiled to force spending reductions, not raise taxes. Most economists, remembering Keynes's advice, objected to the proposal, to the extent the law would have required balanced budgets during downturns. By 1997, though, a public backlash against spendthrift politicians combined with a surging economy produced a balanced budget without a constitutional amendment. (Further discussion of this will come with the Public Choice critique of Keynes.)

Keynes also knew he would face philosophical opposition. After all, more government means less freedom, the laissez-faire tradition taught. But Keynes, who ridiculed Marx and mocked his friends who were fooled by Stalin, thought he was trying to save capitalism, not bury it.

> I defend [the enlargement of government] . . . both as the only practicable means of avoiding the destruction of existing economic firms in their entirety and as the condition of the successful functioning of individual initiative. . . . For if effective demand is deficient, not only is the public scandal of wasted resources intolerable, but the individual enterpriser who seeks to bring these resources into action is operating with the odds loaded against him.[36]

Sometimes it's important to put principle aside and do what's right. Keynes often responded wryly to philosophical objections:

> If the Treasury were to fill old bottles with banknotes, bury them at suitable depths in disused coalmines which are then filled up to the surface with town rubbish, and leave it to private enterprise on well-tried principles of *laissez-faire* to dig the notes up again . . . there need be no more unemployment and, with the help of the repercussions, the real income of the community, and its capital wealth also, would probably become a good deal greater than it actually is. It

would, indeed, be more sensible to build houses and the like; but if there are political and practical difficulties in the way of this, the above would be better than nothing.[37]

Although government spending under Roosevelt never reached Keynes's suggested levels or the worst fears of Keynes's critics, from the 1936 publication of *The General Theory* to the Nixon years, Keynes's influence grew. Paul Samuelson recalled that the "*General Theory* caught most economists under the age of 35 with the unexpected virulence of a disease first attacking and decimating an isolated tribe of South Sea islanders. Economists beyond 50 turned out to be quite immune from the ailment."[38]

Harvard University, under the influence of Professor Alvin Hansen's popular seminar on Keynes, became the principal American outpost for Keynesians, educating such eminent economists as Samuelson, James Tobin, and Robert Solow. During the Kennedy and Johnson administrations, the Council of Economic Advisers became an outpost for Cambridge, Massachusetts, Keynesians, as well as prominent participants from Yale and the University of Minnesota. These economists, along with their European counterparts, developed Keynesian economics, adding rigor where Keynes left intuition and insight.

With Keynesian economics in their grasp, politicians could blaspheme the invisible hand and battle the business cycle. When the economy slowed, they could boost federal spending or cut taxes, leading to temporary deficits until the economy rebounded. If demand rose too quickly, outpacing the supply of goods and therefore pressuring prices upward, they could raise taxes or cut federal spending to rein in demand. A neat symmetry. If it were not apparently true, it would be deemed magic. Confidence in fiscal control grew. Politicians gleefully passed the Employment Act of 1946, which boldly went where no measure had gone before, declaring Congress's responsibility to "promote maximum employment, production, and purchasing power."

The Keynesian star shone most brilliantly in 1964, when Kennedy-Johnson advisers perceived a sluggish economy and confidently prescribed a shot of economic adrenaline. Estimating a recessionary gap of about $30 billion and a multiplier of 2.3, they cut personal and business taxes by about $13 billion. No discretionary economic policy ever worked better. All the vital signs responded vigorously. Higher demand propelled output, creating jobs for thousands. It appeared that economics had finally shaken off Carlyle's insulting tag, the "dismal science."

In the 1970s, though, when Keynesian policies seemed to falter, Carlyle's affront haunted, and the multiplier hobbled. In 1973, the Arab oil embargo targeting the United States, the U.K., Canada, Japan, and other countries sparked "stagflation," raging inflation simultaneous with a stagnant job market. The crisis confounded Keynes's model, because it was designed to fight just one of those opposing foes. In the next chapter and in chapter 12, we will take a closer look at the intellectual forces that seemed to dethrone Keynes.

Despite the setbacks for Keynes's paradigm, even today every political leader knows that when the economy and job market begin to sniff the fumes and fire of a deep recession, they can turn to a "break the glass" emergency plan that still has Keynes's name on it. For example, during the financial meltdown of 2008, President George W. Bush, who was as anti-Keynesian as any president in his lifetime, mailed out $600 paper checks to every American adult and $300 to every child. When the Great Cessation struck in 2020, President Trump and Congress sent $1,200 checks to adults and $500 to children. The Great Cessation does present a different case, however. Unlike a typical recession sparked by excess risk-taking, bloated inventories, and central-bank miscalculations, the coronavirus suddenly forced healthy businesses to shutter. Immediately prior to the viral invasion, the U.S. economy looked solid, with tame inflation, lean inventories, and unemployment rates near record lows. The stimulus checks were not intended, in Keynesian style, to stir up dispirited consumers; they were intended to help people pay their bills and offset the sheer inability to earn money in a shutdown.

Discretionary fiscal policy depends on the wisdom of politicians. Since few sleep soundly while relying on such a scarce resource, the economy has been equipped with automatic tools to dampen the swings in the business cycle. Automatic stabilizers such as progressive taxes and unemployment insurance counteract downturns and inflationary accelerations. If the economy slows down and income begins to fall, people automatically move into lower tax brackets. When workers are laid off, unemployment insurance permits them to maintain spending. When they are rehired, the payments stop. These stabilizers act counter-cyclically, dampening volatility. They thereby stabilize national sleep patterns also.

Maynard Keynes suspected that the volatility of investment would eventually lead to even more government influence over the level of national investment, if not the kind. In murky passages he spoke sometimes of "socialisation of investment"; at other times he praised the structure of the status quo. No wonder he gained a reputation for economic duplicity. In some of his writings, almost every word was ambiguous. His associates told many stories about his rather tidal positions. One joke reported that "when a Royal commission solicits opinions from five economists, they get six answers—two from Mr. Keynes." If Harry Truman begged for a one-handed economist, he certainly didn't want Keynes, who was an octopus on policy matters.

But the reputation is somewhat unfair. Keynes probably wrote and spoke more words to more audiences than any other economist. Since situations differ, prescriptions should. Keynes once said that economists should be practically minded, like dentists. How many would rush into the chair of a dentist who always drilled the same tooth regardless of the patient? Whenever dentists slip or slice accidentally, they calmly say the one word that is supposed to heal all oral wounds: "rinse." There is no "rinse" in macroeconomics (although Schumpeter thought that a recession acted like a good cold shower and ultimately invigorated an economy through new ideas and risks taken by entrepreneurs). When teased about his fickle reputation, Keynes responded, "When my information changes, I alter my conclusions. What do you do, sir?"

Still, fickleness may be a symptom of sloppiness. All economists know that time is a scarce resource. Keynes probably devoted a lower proportion of his time to economic theory than almost anyone else in this book. On the other hand, he probably got the highest return on investment. He often preferred attending the theater to reading another economist's theoretical work. Given the success of his Cambridge Arts Theatre and the aridity of most academics, we can't blame him. Apparently, Keynes did not look to economic theory for the same intellectual enrichment and fascination he found in practical applications and in other disciplines. Given these proclivities, he probably sacrificed a more integrated, consistent analytical framework.

As fickle as critics found Keynes, so Keynes found the stock market. Chapter 12 of *The General Theory*, "The State of Long Term Expectation," is important for two reasons: first, Keynes explains why the hope of mathematical precision in economics is folly; second, he describes the innate volatility of investment. Keynes stressed that much investment is incited by "animal spirits," irrational forces impelling entrepreneurs and speculators forward. But these forces are not consistent:

> A conventional valuation which is established as the outcome of the mass psychology of a large number of ignorant individuals is liable to change violently as the result of a sudden fluctuation of opinion. . . . The market will be subject to waves of optimistic and pessimistic sentiment, which are unreasoning and yet in a sense legitimate where no solid base exists for a reasonable calculation.[39]

Keynes cleverly speculates that the way to make money in the stock market is not to be the best corporate analyst, but to be the best at guessing what *others* think is good. With an ingenious metaphor, Keynes likens professional investment to

> those newspaper competitions in which the competitors have to pick out the six prettiest faces from a hundred photographs, the prize being awarded to the competitor whose choice most nearly corresponds to the average preferences of the competitors as a whole; so each competitor has to pick not those faces which he himself finds prettiest, but those which he thinks likeliest to catch the fancy of the other competitors, all of whom are looking at the problem from the same point of view.[40]

The passage recalls Woody Allen's line about cheating on his metaphysics examination by looking into the soul of the student sitting next to him. Keynes managed a great deal of money for his own family and for King's College. Ironically, he learned that he was better at investing in a bottom-up way—assessing individual companies—rather than making broad predictions about which way the overall economy would lurch next. In other words, Keynes was not so Keynesian in his personal portfolio, and it served him well: "I get more and more convinced that the right method in investment is to put fairly large sums into enterprises which one thinks one knows something about and in the management of which one thoroughly believes."[41]

From this, Keynes does not deduce reason to despair about macroeconomics, just cause for uncustomary modesty in economics:

> We should not conclude . . . that everything depends on waves of irrational psychology. On the contrary, the state of long-term expectation is often steady. . . . We are merely

reminding ourselves that human decisions affecting the future, whether personal or political or economic, cannot depend on strict mathematical expectation, since the basis for making such calculations does not exist; and that it is our innate urge to activity which makes the wheels go round, our rational selves choosing between the alternatives as best we are able, calculating where we can, but often falling back for our motive on whim or sentiment or chance.[42]

A View of the Future

By the time World War II struck, Keynes was tired and often sickly. He had been diagnosed with a lingering infection of the heart valves, and the organ was stressed by the burden of powering his exceedingly large frame and excessively demanding calendar. One night in 1942, though, he found himself sleeping on a rooftop with Hayek. After dropping bombs on London, the Luftwaffe launched the Baedeker Blitz, attacking smaller cities, villages, and cultural landmarks. Since Cambridge was a suspected target, the university asked faculty to defend its buildings against the expected fires. Civil defense forces learned from the London bombings that if they could sweep incendiary devices off rooftops, the explosives would do less damage at the ground level. One night it was Keynes's turn to man the rooftop of King's College Chapel, completed by Henry VIII in 1515. Hayek had been visiting his old rival, and so Keynes directed Hayek to climb with him, past the gargoyles to the limestone parapets of the rooftop, where the two men gazed at the black sky, searching for the menacing glow of incoming bombers. The planes never showed up. But all night long, the economists held their brooms and, no doubt, held forth on the future of the free world.

After the war, Keynes soldiered on, counseling the Treasury and crisscrossing the Atlantic by rickety airplane and heaving troopship, trying to persuade U.S. government officials to loosen their lending terms to the U.K. When the war ended, he helped lead frustrating, endless negotiations in the United States, only to be greeted in the House of Lords by starry-eyed aristocrats who accused him of surrendering to the Yanks.

In the midst of the war in 1942, King George VI had named him to the House of Lords and given him a title, Baron of Tilton. Some days later Keynes stood in his Tilton garden before a nonflowering fig tree and (alluding to the New Testament) punned, "Barren fig tree. Baron Keynes." In that rare moment he was wrong about his lack of progeny. Keynes, who died of heart failure in the arms of Lydia and his mother in April 1946, would have been thrilled to see his ideas triumph—but not too surprised. Against the Marxists and with the religionists, Keynes fervently held that the truth shall make you free. Having spent much of his life advising governments, he witnessed the power of mind. He passionately affirmed this in the famous final passage of *The General Theory*:

The ideas of economists and political philosophers, both when they are right and when they are wrong, are more powerful than is commonly understood. Indeed the world is ruled by little else. Practical men, who believe themselves to be quite exempt from any intellectual influences, are usually the slaves of some defunct economist. Madmen in authority, who hear voices in the air, are distilling their frenzy from some academic scribbler of a few years back. . . . But, soon or late, it is ideas, not vested interests which are dangerous for good or evil.[43]

The Public Choice school now battles Keynes's contention, warning that special interests effectively capture and hold good ideas and good policy hostage.

Despite his famous "long run" quip, Keynes thought quite hard about the future. In a graceful 1930 essay reminiscent of Mill, "Economic Possibilities for Our Grandchildren," Keynes shined his crystal ball.[44] The news was good, he said, Malthus was wrong. In the next hundred years, man could solve the raison d'être of economics: scarcity. Because each generation stands on the shoulders of its parents, perfecting their achievements and living their dreams, our grandchildren and great-grandchildren might climb high enough to satisfy all their material desires, including luxuries. The streets might soon be paved with gold. After all, despite bumps along the business cycle and wretched wars, the Western economies had swiftly ascended for two hundred years.

More striking, as human existence grows more gentle, human hearts may soften. Keynes claimed that we needed the self-interested *homo economicus* to evolve economically. Having satiated material desires, humans may heighten their desire for kindness and affection.

We may not live happily ever after, however. With cupboards full and new cars shined, what would we do? Keynes asked. Today, retirees often yearn for work and complain of tedium. What if the whole world retired? How many Paul McCartney and Mick Jagger "final tours" would it take to entertain an entirely pensioned population? Existential angst might pervade a sated world. Often joy comes in striving for goals, not achieving them.

Perhaps this explains Keynes the dilettante, Keynes the art collector/investor/benefactor/curator. Maybe he diversified his portfolio of activities just in case he was too good at economics and brought us too close to heaven. He wanted something to do just in case he made it through the long run.

CHAPTER X

Milton Friedman and the Monetarist Battle Against Keynes

Responding to a beggar, W. C. Fields quipped: "Sorry, my good man, but all my available funds are tied up in cash." To Keynes, this would be a problem not just for the beggar; by keeping wealth "tied up" in cash or in checking accounts, he would say that Fields was helping to deepen the Depression.

Since his view was that stingy misers perpetuated the Depression, Keynes advocated government spending to lift consumption. To Keynesians, the national economy is like an automobile. The accelerator pedal is marked "higher government spending / lower taxes"; the brake is marked "lower government spending / higher taxes." A government that drives deftly and carefully can bring economic growth and stable prices.

This chapter tells the story of an intellectual movement that attacks the Keynesian model by asserting that (1) governments are usually lousy drivers, and (2) the economy's brake and accelerator have little to do with fiscal policy. This movement, called *monetarism*, admits that the economy does have an accelerator and a brake, but insists that the accelerator should be marked "higher money supply" and the brake "lower money supply." The monetarists also disagree with the Keynesians about who sits in the driver's seat. According to the Keynesians, Congress, which authorizes spending and taxes, is the driver.

In contrast, the monetarists portray the Federal Reserve Board, which oversees the banking industry, as the driver.

A titanic struggle took place between Keynesians and monetarists from the 1950s through the 1970s. Led by Milton Friedman, Karl Brunner, and Allan Meltzer, the monetarists were initially greeted with derision, even though their intellectual forefathers included Locke, Hume, Mill, and Ricardo. But as they kept producing cogent studies and courageous graduate students, they wore down Keynesian opposition and earned more respect and prominence until finally, during the Carter administration, Congress required the Federal Reserve to take the monetarist arguments seriously, and the chairman of the Federal Reserve Board decided to follow monetarist advice.

Where does the struggle stand today? It's a tie. We will see that the federal government treats the national economy as an automobile with four pedals—two accelerators and two brakes! Remember poor Harry Truman begging for a one-handed economist. Today's leaders seem to be stuck with four-footed economists. To make matters worse, the pedals don't seem as potent as the strict monetarists and orthodox Keynesians had promised.

What Is Money?

To understand today's macroeconomics, we must trace the course of the Keynesian-monetarist battles and learn how the monetarist model operates. This requires us to learn a bit about banking and the Federal Reserve Board. Some of the concepts may seem tricky at first, but the effort necessary to understand them is worthwhile, for the story of how the monetarist theories earned respect is one of the fascinating epics in contemporary intellectual history.

Monetarists accuse Keynes of ignoring money and the money

supply, which sounds absurd. After all, how could a man who made a fortune in stocks and commodities and who revolutionized macroeconomics ignore money? That would be like accusing Melville of ignoring whales. Surely, monetarists have something in mind other than the everyday idea of money.

What is money? Anything can be money, including shells and beads; cigarettes often serve as money in prisons. In today's macroeconomic lingo, we follow the Federal Reserve Board definitions of money supply. The most popular measure is called M1 and equals (1) the amount of currency held outside the banks plus (2) the amount of funds in checking accounts ("demand deposits") at commercial banks. (Note that corporate stocks and bonds are not considered money. Broader measurements of the money supply include less-liquid assets such as savings accounts and money market mutual funds.)

Why would anyone be foolish enough to argue about the money supply? The more money, the merrier, right? Wrong. In slapstick movies, bumbling gangsters drop suitcases filled with bills, and bystanders dive past one another hoping to grab a few. The bystanders always smile, and the bad guys wail. Why do economists cry with the gangsters? A problem does not arise when just a few suitcases burst open. But if lots of luggage were to suddenly flood a town with bills, inflation might follow. If the amount of money overwhelms the capacity to produce goods, consumers, with more money to spend, bid up prices. The town is no wealthier than it was before; more bills do not bring a higher standard of living any more than if everyone added two zeroes to his or her salary. Remember that wealth is measured by the goods and services it can buy, not by numerals. Since one U.S. dollar can buy thousands of pesos, a Colombian millionaire might be considered poor compared with a low-income American. Giving all the Colombians suitcases packed with pesos would not help. More paper does not bring more merriment.

What's the correct money supply level? The easy answer:

enough to buy all the goods produced, so that full employment is reached without a rise in prices. But the easy answer avoids the crucial question. How much money should be in circulation in order to have full employment and stable prices? To answer this question, we must know how fast people spend the money they receive. Do people tend to hold on to their money for a long time before spending it, or do they spend money quickly? How fast does money change hands and circulate through the economy? If money moves quickly, the country does not need as much as it would if people were to leave it lying around in their sock drawers for months before spending it. Academic careers and national economies hinge on this simple issue. The rate at which the money stock turns over each year is called the *velocity* of money. Economists compare this with GDP and speak of the *income velocity of money, V.* Thus, *V* equals the level of GDP divided by the money supply.

For example, if the GDP is $24 trillion and the money supply is $12 trillion, *V* must equal 2. If money turns over two times during the year, on any particular day people are holding about six months' worth of income (in the form of currency or checking accounts).

Why is this important? How could anyone debate this with anything but gentlemanly insouciance? If velocity is stable, and if the central bank can control the money supply, the government has a powerful tool with which to speed up or slow down the economy. The accelerator and brake pedals marked "money supply" directly control the engine. If velocity is unstable, however—if people vacillate between holding a lot and holding little of their funds in currency and checking accounts—controlling the money supply is not very helpful, and the accelerator becomes unhinged.

To simplify the sides in the battle, monetarists believe that velocity is stable, while Keynesians see it as unstable. No wonder monetarists tap the money supply as the most powerful pedal in the government's car, while Keynesians exalt fiscal policy, and a rigid subset of Keynesians see monetary policy as being no more important to the engine than a windshield wiper.

Before exploring the history of monetarism and the evidence for and against it, we must first summarize how the Federal Reserve Board manipulates the money supply. Three tools are most important. First, the Fed controls the percentage of deposits that banks are permitted to lend (the reserve ratio). Assume that the Fed sets the reserve ratio at 20 percent, so banks can lend 80 percent of the money deposited with them. Then assume that our friend Chris deposits $10 in a checking account. This counts in the money supply. (Remember, the money supply equals checking accounts plus currency.) If Lynn now borrows $8 from the same bank, the money supply rises by $8. If she deposits the $8 in a checking account, and Brad borrows $6.40, the money supply rises further, by $6.40. Now, if the Fed tells banks they may lend only 75 percent rather than 80 percent of their deposits, the banks will have to call in some of their loans, which shrinks the money supply. The more banks lend, the larger the money supply.

Second, the Fed sometimes lends funds to banks. By raising the interest rate on these loans (the discount rate), the Fed discourages banks from lending and reins in the money supply.

Third, and most important, the Fed buys and sells government securities (open-market operations). The public, including corporations and individuals, holds about 20 trillion dollars' worth of government bonds, which pay interest to holders each year. To understand this tool requires concentration, and it helps to use visual aids. Take out a dollar bill and a piece of paper. Mark the paper "BOND." Designate one end of the table "Public," the other "Fed." Remember, bills held by the Fed are *not* considered part of the money supply. If the Fed wants to expand the money supply, it can buy bonds from the public. By buying, the Fed receives a bond (which is *not* part of the money supply) and gives the seller a check (or dollar bills) in return. When the check is cashed or deposited, it becomes part of the money supply. (When it was held by the Fed, it was not considered part of the money supply.) In contrast, if the Fed *sells* a bond to an individual or institution, it receives a check (or dollar bills) drawn on an individual's account. The money supply contracts, for the bond that the seller receives is not money, whereas the funds that the Fed receives cease to be money once the Fed owns them.

The Monetarist Model and Keynes's Critique

Even before the Federal Reserve System was set up in 1913, classical and neoclassical economists outlined the impact of changes in the money supply. Yale professor Irving Fisher took a crucial step forward in 1911 by deriving a simple mathematical framework from John Stuart Mill's analysis. One popular version of the "quantity theory" is $MV = PQ$. This simple equation allows us to understand a great deal about the monetarist critique. First, recall that M is the money supply and V is velocity. PQ represents nominal GDP (P is the price level, and Q is the amount of goods and services produced, which is the real GDP). No one disputes this equation. By definition, the amount of money multiplied by the number of times it changes hands equals the nominal value of goods and services purchased. But economists can argue endlessly about the behavior of these variables.

The most crude caricature of monetarism contends as follows: (1) velocity is constant; (2) the amount of goods and services that can be produced is fixed in the short run; therefore, (3) if the Fed raises the money supply by 5 percent, we will see a 5 percent rise in prices. The crude quantity theory essentially erases V and Q from the equation and concludes that any change in M will be felt only in P.

Even this cartoon has some merit, though, especially in

explaining hyperinflation. The German Weimar Republic presents the model case. Between 1921 and 1924, the printing presses worked full speed, blasting the money supply into the stratosphere. It did not just double, triple, or quadruple. It rose by more than 25 trillion percent! The price index followed, soaring in a year and a half from 1 to 200 million. Everyone was a billionaire! And nearly every millionaire was hungry. Closets burst with bills while cupboards were bare. In America, Samuel Goldwyn said that "an oral contract is not worth the paper it's printed on." In Germany, money wasn't worth the paper it was printed on. The German economy was destroyed. In recent years, Venezuela joined the hyperinflation club, reaching a 10 million percent annual pace in 2019. Middle-class citizens found themselves scavenging through dumpsters for food, and 10 percent of the population fled the country. Though Venezuela sits atop the world's largest oil reserves, a corrupt government skimmed the wealth from the people and tried to compensate by handing out worthless pieces of paper currency.[1] The moral here is that cheap money does not come easy.

Modern quantity theorists, monetarists, claim that their intellectual forefathers were too humble about money. In the short run, money can sway not just prices but also economic activity. In the long run, however, a change in the money supply changes only prices. The monetarists also add an anti-Keynesian tenet: government spending will not affect prices or output unless the money supply also changes. Only money matters.

We have three important tasks here: First, we must see why monetarists sound so arrogantly confident about money. Second, we must see why Keynesians speak so flippantly about money. Third, we must see why monetarists speak flippantly about government spending. After that, we can examine how the debate stands today.

Let's look at the transmission mechanism that directly links the money supply with GDP. Assume that the monetarists are right: velocity is stable. If the Federal Reserve increases the money supply by buying bonds, it places more money in the hands of the sellers. But people want to maintain a stable level of money holdings. According to monetarists, people hold money mostly for daily transactions. Since they now have extra money, they will spend it on goods, services, and real assets. GDP climbs.

If the Federal Reserve instead touches the brake and sells bonds, people have less money. Since they want to maintain a stable level of money, they cut back spending, slowing GDP.

Essentially, monetary policy plays with the liquidity of the public. Provided people persistently desire a stable level of liquidity, monetary policy can predictably and powerfully affect GDP. The Federal Reserve can toy with the public to promote different levels of spending.

How could Keynes and his followers disagree with this model? Ironically, Keynes once believed it. Even more ironic, the foremost monetarist since World War II, Milton Friedman, once did not. Keynes started as a monetarist and matured into a Keynesian. Friedman started as a Keynesian and matured into a monetarist. His friends may have nicknamed Keynes "Snout" when he was young, but neither he nor Friedman was born pigheaded.

Let's follow Keynes's turn from monetarist principles. Part of the Cambridge oral tradition that Keynes imbibed was the "Cambridge Equation," as taught by Marshall. This equation operated similarly to Fisher's model. According to Keynes, Marshall "always taught" that the demand for money was measured by "'the average stock of command over commodities which each person cares to keep in ready form.'"[2] During the German hyperinflation, Keynes stressed the power of the quantity theory in his *Tract on Monetary Reform*, which demonstrated how rapid inflation, encouraging people to spend money at a faster rate, forced prices up even further. By the time of the *General Theory*, however, the Great Depression convinced Keynes that monetary policy was impotent.

The chief target of Keynes's criticism was velocity. Why assume that velocity is stable? So what if the central bank raises the money supply and liquidity? Why assume that people will spend the extra money? Maybe they will keep it under their mattresses. If they do, lower velocity would offset higher money. GDP would still flounder. Keynes thought this particularly possible in a depression. Whereas quantity theorists maintained that people hold money for daily purchases and perhaps for "rainy days," Keynes introduced a third motive, "speculative." People may hold extra liquidity just to speculate in stock and bond markets. If interest rates bounce about, speculative demand for money will also bounce. Thus, even if the money supply rises, the desire to hoard may rise also.

In a letter to President Roosevelt, Keynes presented a clever metaphor while scoffing at monetary forces: "Some people seem to infer . . . that output and income can be raised by increasing the quantity of money. But this is like trying to get fat by buying a larger belt. In the United States today your belt is plenty big enough for your belly."[3]

Keynes not only insulted the power of money; he and his followers depicted a different transmission mechanism for money. Monetary policy does not work directly through consumption, but through interest rates and investment, they suggested. Two long, treacherous leaps must be taken if the economy is to feel anything from monetary maneuvering. If the Fed raises the money supply, people must not hoard (step one). Even if people do spend the money, according to Keynesians, they may purchase stocks and bonds—financial assets rather than real assets. This will lower interest rates. Only if businesses or households borrow from banks and then buy goods and services will GDP budge (step two). While waiting for these two big, risky steps, many monetarists could fall into the gorge below.

Strides in the reverse direction are just as long and perilous. If the Fed shrinks the money supply, people may not care that they have less cash in their sock drawers. Even if they do respond by selling off financial assets (which raises interest rates), borrowers may not be discouraged by higher borrowing costs (if, for example, they are obligated to continue a building project). GDP could continue to hum along.

In sum, the Keynesian critique cuts deepest when (1) velocity or money demand is fickle, and (2) borrowers do not care about interest rates.

Friedman laments that Keynes's influence "led to a temporary eclipse of the quantity theory of money and perhaps to an all-time low in the amount of economic research and writing devoted to monetary theory and analysis. . . . It became a widely accepted view that money does not matter, or, at any rate, that it does not matter very much."[4]

The eclipse even shaded Friedman's early views. Despite his graduate studies at the University of Chicago, a long-standing home for Keynes critics, a young Friedman penned a 1942 article on inflation that scarcely mentioned monetary forces. Eleven years later, the article appeared in his book *Essays in Positive Economics*, together with seven new paragraphs. Friedman explained the additions: "As I trust the new material makes clear, the omission from that version of monetary effects is a serious error which is not excused but may perhaps be explained by the prevailing Keynesian temper of the times."[5]

Milton Friedman and the Counterattack

No one was better suited by temperament or intellect to lead the monetarist counterrevolution. A ferocious debater who argued his case so forcefully that he unnerved academic opponents, Milton Friedman was not intimidated by conventional wisdom. On the eve of the counterrevolution, his diminutive physical appearance matched his professional stature. Galbraith recalls that during the 1950s and 1960s, anyone who "dwelled too persistently" on the role of the money supply was considered a "crank." Through his courage of heart and brilliance of mind, Friedman's professional stature grew, earning him a Nobel Prize in 1976 and Galbraith's recognition of him as "perhaps the most influential economic figure of the second half of the twentieth century."[6]

Friedman considered himself a lucky man and named an autobiographical work about himself and his wife, Rose, *Two Lucky People.* He was born broke in Brooklyn in 1912, his Austro-Hungarian immigrant parents toiling in sweatshops. A few years later, they crossed the river to Rahway, New Jersey, a place best known for its state prison. His mother, Sarah, opened a small clothing store, while his father, Jeno, peddled wares and did odd jobs around town. Young Milton and his three sisters did not grow up in luxury, but times got even tougher when their father died during Milton's senior year in high school. How could he consider himself lucky? Because he was born in a free country. To get through Rutgers University, he waited tables and worked as a store clerk, meanwhile earning a scholarship. At Rutgers he first studied mathematics and accounting. A high school teacher had inspired him to see the beauty in math by comparing the Pythagorean theorem to Keats's "Ode on a Grecian Urn." Then Milton discovered economics—and not a moment too soon. Economics needed some help, for he entered the university in 1929, just as the stock market crash was breaking apart modern capitalism like an urn that had toppled off a high shelf.

Under Rutgers professor Arthur Burns, later a Federal Reserve Board chairman, Milton learned the orthodoxies of the classical economists. He moved on to graduate school at the University of Chicago, where he was lucky enough to have a professor who seated students alphabetically, putting him in a seat next to a young woman named Rose Director. Though their marriage lasted sixty-eight years, somehow Milton seemed to suggest that had he been born Milton Zuckerman, he would not have found his bride.

Milton Friedman was short (about a foot and a half shorter

than Keynes), but he was sure. There's an old adage that one should "punch up, not down"—that is, pick fights with those of higher social stature. (National Public Radio once asked me to recommend an opponent I should face in a debate on the economy. I suggested that they ask Nobel laureate Joseph Stiglitz, chairman of the president's Council of Economic Advisers. Stiglitz agreed, and we had a mostly genial discussion.[7]) Friedman picked his first fight as a graduate student in his early twenties with some pretty famous foes. He sent an article to Keynes's *Economic Journal* criticizing Pigou's elasticity-of-demand calculation. Keynes rejected the article, siding with Pigou, though Keynes would soon savage Pigou in *The General Theory*. Instead of in the *Economic Journal*, Friedman's article and Pigou's rebuttal were published in the *Quarterly Journal of Economics*. Then in another battle, Friedman wrote a book that showed the American Medical Association propping up doctors' wages by keeping out competition. The association found advanced galleys of the book and protested, demanding the publisher cancel the book. The publisher refused, and Friedman's career as a fearless analyst was born. Friedman argued that in "all professions . . . aristocratic, or at least restrictive movement had taken hold," hurting consumers and propping up barriers to entry for new competitors. In 1900 only 4 percent of the labor force worked as "professionals," but by mid-century states had passed more than 1,200 statutes for jobs as diverse as physicians and embalmers.[8] From cradle to grave, Americans passed through the hands of licensed professionals.

During World War II, Friedman worked for the government as a statistician, attempting to apply mathematics to the testing of metals. He learned that theoretical models must be linked with empirical testing. At one point, he designed on paper a superstrong metal alloy for jet engines. Econometric tests yielded very robust results. Friedman marched into the chemists' laboratory with his winning formula. He boasted that his turbine blade could spin for two hundred hours without a rupture. They followed his recipe and produced a metal with all the strength of a ripe banana. He learned not to trust theoretical statistics without real testing.

After the war, the bespectacled Friedman began teaching at the University of Chicago. He admired Keynes's work. Even after smashing many Keynesian ideas, Friedman continued to generously laud the Englishman, calling him both a great economist and a great man. Friedman's intellectual generosity was a constant trademark, just as notable as his ferocity in debate. But smash he did.

In a series of pathbreaking studies, Friedman salvaged the quantity theory from Keynes's attack. Keynes left only one dusty, disreputable escape path open: Friedman would have to show that the private sector was stable. Velocity and consumption must not undulate like the hips of a Hawaiian hula dancer for monetarism to make sense.

In 1956, at a time when Keynesians dominated academia, Friedman published a set of essays that improved and tested the quantity theory of money. Instead of just tying money to prices, Friedman aimed at redefining the demand for money (the reciprocal of velocity). Demand for money is stable, he submitted, because it depends on long-term factors such as health, education, and the income an individual expects over a lifetime. Since these do not wildly waver, velocity does not. Keynes slighted long-term influences.[9]

The next year Friedman turned to consumption. The simple Keynesian model assumed that as current income rose and fell, so did consumption. If income fell in a particular year, people would spend less. This seems obvious on the face of it. Again, though, Friedman advocated a longer view. After all, a man who receives his paycheck on Fridays does not starve all week and feast all weekend. Rather, he maintains a steady flow of consumption because he holds expectations about long-run income. Friedman's Permanent Income Hypothesis posits a smooth path, veering only when expectations about future income flows change. Consumers will not let a bad week or month or year alter their patterns. They will simply use up some of their savings. In an exceptionally good year, they will just save more. Only if they perceive a major shift will they alter their course.[10]

Friedman was not alone in pointing to long-run concerns. Franco Modigliani, a Keynesian and 1985 Nobel laureate, performed similar studies at this time on a Life-Cycle Hypothesis with similar results.[11]

The prime conclusion of Friedman's work? Consumption is impressively stable.

If Friedman and Modigliani are right, temporary government policies have only weak effects on the private economy. How can we test this? A highly successful 1964 tax cut boosted consumption and sent the economy roaring ahead. Since the program slashed payroll tax *rates*, consumers viewed it as permanent. In 1968 the Johnson administration feared inflation and deficits resulting from Vietnam War expenses and burgeoning social spending. Congress passed an explicitly temporary tax surcharge to slow the economy. Sure enough, consumers responded not by spending less, but by drawing more from their savings in order to maintain their high consumption levels. In 1975, a temporary tax rebate also proved ineffective. Again, in 2001, a $600-per-couple tax rebate proved far less powerful than cutting tax rates.

Temporary policies have failed outside the United States as well. The Japanese Ministry of Finance tried to pump up consumer buying during the mid-1990s with temporary tax cuts, which did nothing but annoy the recipients. Families were so angry at the government for *permanently* raising sales taxes that they thought a *temporary* income tax cut was a chintzy concession. Instead of spending the money, they simply put it in the bank. Japan scrolled through more than a half dozen prime ministers during the long-lasting recession of the 1990s.

Although Friedman designed supporting theories for monetarist claims, he soon required empirical, historical studies to answer critics who ranged from the skeptical to the mocking.

Friedman had long held the philosophical position that the true test of a theory is whether it correctly predicts events. Elegant molds are wrong if they are useless in the real world, he maintained. In 1963, he and Anna J. Schwartz released a massive report, *A Monetary History of the United States, 1867–1960.*[12] Friedman knew that the strongest case for Keynesians was the Great Depression. He wasted little time before declaring that the Depression testified to the power of *monetary policy*, not, as Keynes believed, to its impotence. In other words, he stole the best witness from the Keynesians. Between 1929 and 1933 the quantity of money had plunged by one-third, and the Federal Reserve did not even publish this data. Friedman and Schwartz pointed fingers at the Federal Reserve Board, which had refused to provide liquidity to banks when panic-stricken customers banged on doors demanding their deposits. A little support from the Fed would have instilled a lot of confidence among customers, they said.

In sum, *A Monetary History* claimed that monetary mischief accompanied every severe recession and every significant inflation over the past century. There were no Keynesian recessions or inflations. One by-product of Friedman's work was to deflect blame for inflation from the usual suspects, like labor unions.

As Friedman and other monetarists such as Meltzer and Brunner chipped away at the Keynesian orthodoxy, the Keynesian response varied. Some Keynesians countered with their own studies, some admitted that monetarists had a point, and others continued to laugh. At a conference in the late 1960s, Robert Solow of MIT commented on a Friedman paper: "Another difference between Milton and myself is that everything reminds Milton of the money supply; well, everything reminds me of sex, but I try to keep it out of my papers."

As the 1960s progressed, though, monetarism gained more strength, for velocity was showing a remarkably stable pattern. In fact, during the three decades following 1948, velocity behaved predictably, growing at just over 3 percent per year. The crusade that Friedman had fought with just a few believers seemed to be getting divine help.

After proving the power of money and breathing new life into the quantity theory, monetarists sought to challenge the Keynesian claim that government spending could spur the economy. To slay this dragon, they needed to show that the Keynesian multiplier was nil.

Monetarists announced that Keynes dodged the big question: Where does money for fiscal spending come from? If the money supply stays constant and the government spends money, somebody else must have less to spend. There's no such thing as a free lunch. If Congress raises taxes to pay for programs, consumers cannot buy as much. If Congress borrows money by selling Treasury bonds to the public, businesses cannot borrow as much for investment. Interest rates rise and investment falls. Government spending must *crowd out* private spending. Keynes's elementary multiplier ignores this.

Keynesians cannot deny that crowding out takes place. But, they counter, crowding out does not completely offset government spending, especially during recessions. The real issue is the extent of crowding out. In the 1990s, a model sympathetic to Keynes's, from Data Resources, estimated a multiplier of about 1.6 the first year of government stimulus but steadily dropping after that. And recently, the evidence for Keynes's model has grown more meager. During the 2008 Great Recession, President Obama nudged Congress to pass a stimulus plan that included $340 billion in new federal spending. A postmortem by Valerie Ramey of the University of California, San Diego, concluded that such spending probably generated less than $340 billion in GDP growth.[13] In retrospect, it is striking that in *The General Theory*, Keynes used a multiplier example ten times greater than current estimates.[14] In 2020, the trillion-dollar emergency package in response to the coronavirus didn't aim to spur spending (in fact, the government had closed down most shops) but instead aimed to give families enough cash to limp along until it was safe to come out of their homes.

The stagflation of the 1970s made Milton Friedman frustrated, but it also made him famous. In December 1967, he delivered an address to the American Economic Association in which he contended that higher inflation could not spur more jobs. This seemed kooky to listeners who were reading or even writing typical textbooks. But a few years later, economists would reread his speech and realize that Friedman had left unerasable skid marks on the history of economic thought.[15] In the 1960s and 1970s, undergraduates were taught that "everyone" knew that more jobs could be created, if only society would allow slightly higher inflation. This tradeoff seemed documented by a curve named for the New Zealand economist A. W. Phillips. Under the Phillips curve analysis, if you were not willing to tolerate a little more inflation in exchange for more jobs, you were not just stupid but miserly. Friedman did not buy it. He showed, along with future Nobel laureate Edmund Phelps of Columbia, that if government tried to "buy" more jobs by unleashing inflation, it would only get higher prices. In fact, inflation might even destroy jobs. The 1970s stagflation proved a disaster for U.S. households but a ringing endorsement for Friedman's analytical powers. Lawrence Summers, the eminent economist and former Treasury secretary, recalled that Milton Friedman had been a "devil figure" to his family of progressive, Keynesian economists. But between the time Summers was an undergraduate in the early 1970s and a young professor a decade later, "Friedman's heresies had become the orthodoxy," and Friedman was no longer a demon but a man whom Summers looked to with "great admiration."[16]

Modesty in Victory

Imagine that you are Milton Friedman. You have just demonstrated that money not only talks, but that it walks and runs the economy along. The next step would be to persuade the Federal Reserve Board to raise the money supply in recessions and to lower it when inflation appears imminent, right? When business seems slow, you would point to the printing presses and shout to the Fed governors, "Don't just stand there! Do something!" Not our Milton. Instead he shouts, "Just stand there!"

With perhaps uncustomary humility, Friedman claims that economists do not know enough about monetary policy to manipulate it wisely. Sometimes it takes six months before monetary policy affects nominal GDP, and sometimes two years. The Fed usually hurts the economy when it tries to fine-tune, because it cannot know how long the lag will be. In 1968 the Fed feared a recession. It pressed down hard on the monetary accelerator. But the economy did not feel the effects until after the downturn had passed. The result was high inflation, for the effects came during the recovery. In 1974 the Fed slammed on the monetary brakes to halt inflation. A recession followed in 1975. When Gerald Ford jumped into the driver's seat at the White House, he cleverly accepted the automobile metaphor and told Congress to restrain its high expectations, for he was "not a Lincoln but a Ford." Wise advice, since the economy poked along like an Edsel.

Friedman's advice that the Fed not react to economic news sounds like Admiral Hyman Rickover's advice when he grew weary of Pentagon bumbling. The Pentagon should split into three divisions, he stated. The first division should do all the work. The second and third should spend all day writing longhand letters to each other. Even with this plan, the Pentagon would work harder than Friedman wants the Fed to work.

Friedmanites propose that the Fed be replaced with a robot that would delicately press the monetary accelerator at a fixed growth rate regardless of economic conditions. Whether 3, 4, or 5 percent, a constant growth would erase a major source of instability, the caprice of the Federal Reserve. If the economy dips, the constant addition of liquidity would feed spending.

During upswings, inflationary sparks would not have enough fuel to inflame.

What a difference from Brookings Institution economist Arthur Okun's confident hyperactivist Keynesian position of the 1960s! The 1962 *Economic Report of the President* did not stop at combatting inflation or recession. Sophisticated economists would fine-tune the national economy. Fiscal policies would smooth out an ever-growing prosperity:

> Insufficient demand means unemployment. . . . Excessive demand means inflation. . . . Stabilization does not mean a mere leveling off of peaks and troughs in production and employment. . . . It means minimizing deviations from a rising trend.[17]

While no honest economist could write such braggadocio today, most economists disagree with Friedman's monetary rule. Their motto: To err is human, but to really foul things up takes a computer. Even if Friedman is right and velocity appears stable over a long period, it certainly deviates in the short term. If velocity falls for several months while money continues on a fixed trend, the economy will tumble. Perhaps not for long, but jobs do hinge on the Fed's performance in those instances. The tough questions regarding an activist Fed remain unresolved: How long does it take for the Fed to detect velocity swings ("recognition lag")? How long does it take for its action to affect the economy ("impact lag")? Does the Fed know what it should do?

In academia, victory comes when your peers get bigger laughs pointing at your critics than at you. By the late 1970s the monetarists moved from being the butt of jokes to the head of the class. Central banks throughout the world began closely monitoring the money supply. German central bankers at the Bundesbank became orthodox monetarists and in 1999, with the introduction of the euro, prodded the new European Central Bank to follow their tradition. Mainstream economics absorbed many monetarist propositions and shed its flippancy about money and its worship of fiscal forces. Economists can no longer be cleanly bisected into monetarist and Keynesian camps. Recall Richard Nixon's remark "We are all Keynesians now." Even Friedman admitted that Nixon was right, with reservations, of course. The intellectual cycle has come around again, for Modigliani has confessed, "We are all monetarists now," with reservations, of course.

The 1985 edition of Samuelson's *Economics*, written with William Nordhaus, conceded that "early Keynesianism has benefited from 'the rediscovery of money.' Money definitely matters. In their early enthusiasm about the role of fiscal policy, many Keynesians unjustifiably downgraded the role of money." Samuelson and Nordhaus did not mention the names of any perpetrators.[18]

A perhaps apocryphal story illustrates the point: A successful businessman visited his old economics professor. While chatting, the former student noticed an exam on the professor's desk and began reading. Shocked, he announced, "This is the same exam you gave me fifteen years ago! Aren't you afraid the students are just going to track down old tests?" The professor laughed. "No, that's okay. I do keep the same questions. It's the answers I change each year."

Velocity Vexes the Victors

Having persuaded Modigliani and Samuelson that money matters a great deal, by 1981 the monetarists were singing "Who's got the last laugh now?" from the old Gershwin tune.

But the monetarists soon stopped singing. Margaret Thatcher in Great Britain and Ronald Reagan in the United States urged the central banks to follow a monetarist anti-inflation path, cutting the money supply and ignoring a rise in interest rates. Sure enough, inflation dropped at an impressive rate, falling in the United States from more than 12 percent in 1980 to less than 4 percent in 1982. Few economists had expected money to work so forcefully. As forecast, however, a severe recession accompanied that (since at first monetary policy alters output and prices, not just prices, as it does in the long run). Unemployment in the United States topped 10 percent and began declining only in 1983. To wring inflation from an economy is not fun.

Monetarists believe that the Federal Reserve took too crude a course, slamming the monetary brakes too hard. Furthermore, they assert that the Fed under chairman Paul Volcker allowed the money supply to swing wildly. But even monetarists admit that a more gradual policy would still have induced a recession.

If the anti-inflation course proved the power of money, why aren't monetarists still whistling a happy tune? Why did the counterrevolution not end in an unambiguous shutout? Well, a funny thing happened on the way to economic recovery. Remember the hub of monetarism, stable velocity? Just as monetarists reached exalted status, people began reexamining their sock drawers. From 1948 to 1981, velocity maintained a steady 3.4 percent growth each year. Suddenly, in 1982 the sock drawers filled up. Velocity plummeted by nearly 5 percent. From 1982 to 1988, the course of velocity was thoroughly confusing. If velocity falls, and the money supply does not grow at a higher rate, GDP must fall also.

How did the Federal Reserve respond to the collapse of velocity? Far from following a monetary rule of 3 or 4 percent growth, the Fed stomped on the monetary accelerator. Ignoring a target of 3 to 8 percent growth, the Fed launched M1 to more than 15 percent during 1986 to offset tumbling velocity.

A fixed monetary rule in 1986 might have been disastrous. Even Beryl Sprinkel, a Friedman protégé and the first orthodox monetarist to chair the Council of Economic Advisers, admitted in the 1987 *Economic Report of the President*:

In the context of moderate real growth, very low inflation, and falling inflation expectations and given the uncertainty about the behavior of velocity, the de-emphasis of M1 in favor of other variables . . . appears to have been an appropriate judgment. . . . No evidence suggests that the Federal Reserve has erred on the side of monetary restriction.[19]

The Thatcher government also jumped on the monetary pedal in the face of lower velocity. Rather than using a fixed mechanism, many central banks today track a rule-of-thumb equation known as the Taylor Rule, named after Stanford's John Taylor, a friend of Friedman's and a former colleague of mine at the White House. The Taylor Rule says that central banks should adjust short-term interest rates by weighing two different gaps: (1) the gap between actual inflation and target inflation, and (2) the gap between actual GDP and target GDP. Let's say, for example, that the economy has been weak but now is heating up, and inflation is crawling higher. The rule tells the Fed to hoist up interest rates by one half a percentage point if (a) inflation goes up by one point or (b) GDP gets one point closer to its potential. Former Federal Reserve chair Ben Bernanke kept close tabs on the Taylor Rule during his reign from 2006 to 2014, but concluded that, like all equations, it had flaws in practice: "I don't think we'll be replacing the FOMC [Federal Open Market Committee] with robots anytime soon. I certainly hope not."[20]

During the 1990s and 2000s, velocity took a wild, round-trip flight, first jumping unexpectedly and then plunging hard and fast. No one knows whether velocity will return to a stable pattern. Several hypotheses have been advanced to account for the drop. Friedman and other monetarists explained that the dramatic fall in inflation and interest rates in the 1980s and 1990s reduced velocity. Since the deregulation of banking in the 1990s, people are keeping more assets in interest-bearing checking accounts and can zap funds instantaneously through

PayPal, Venmo, and their competitors. Because such accounts hold more money, velocity falls. Some tests show, however, that velocity would have fallen despite such innovations. In addition, housing refinance tools have given home owners a new source of liquidity. To paraphrase Churchill, velocity has become a riddle wrapped in a mystery inside an enigma. And it is getting the last laugh. Despite fickle velocity, central banks throughout the world agree that either a soaring or a collapsing money supply should sound loud alarms. In a speech honoring Friedman's ninetieth birthday in 2002, Ben Bernanke, on behalf of the Federal Reserve, toasted Friedman and apologized for failing to heed his principles and letting the money supply crash during the Great Depression: "You're right, we did it. We're very sorry. But thanks to you, we won't do it again."[21] No doubt, Bernanke thought that his toast was a gentle gesture to an elder warrior and that his words would fade with the last sip of champagne that evening. In 2006, Friedman died of heart failure. Two years later, the world's financial system shattered, money supply growth dropped, 15.4 million Americans were thrown out of work, and a puffy-eyed Bernanke was living on trail mix, spending twenty hours a day trying to live up to his promise to Friedman.

During the late 1990s and early 2000s, the global real estate market had inflated into a thin-skinned bubble, as governments encouraged banks to lend money to home buyers who weren't safe bets, while banks stopped asking buyers for substantial down payments. In 1995, for example, the U.S. Department of Housing and Urban Development required government-chartered firms like Fannie Mae and Freddie Mac to buy riskier mortgages from banks in order to boost the homeownership rate. Since the banks were going to unload the risky mortgages anyway, lending officers did not bother to vet the loans as carefully as they should have. Some home buyers received mortgages without even showing their tax returns (others received "NINJA loans": meaning, "no income, no jobs, no assets"). By 2006, one in four California mortgages was considered subprime, and home prices had doubled within the prior five years. Borrowers got more access to more credit, with less reason to worry about paying it back. Economists call this a "moral hazard" problem, while laypeople call it a lack of "skin in the game." When the bubble popped in 2008, banks went, well, bankrupt, and Wall Street's 160-year-old brokerage house Lehman Brothers evaporated, sparking panic selling and a nearly 60 percent dive in the S&P 500 stock index. (The name Lehman Brothers became infamous, even appearing in the kids' cartoon movie *Despicable Me* as the predecessor to the "Bank of Evil.") To survive the crisis, Bernanke, himself a scholar of the Great Depression, yanked out his Friedman playbook and slashed interest rates from 5 percent to nearly zero. Other central banks followed, with the Bank of England cutting rates to their lowest since the founding of the bank in 1694. The U.S. Treasury Department forced banks to accept government loans so they would have enough capital to endure the downturn. But even those steps were not enough. With interest rates near zero, many skeptics said that the Fed had run out of policy bullets and could do no more. At that point, Bernanke deployed a rarely used tool outlined by Friedman known as QE. Up until the Great Recession, most well-read people would have identified QE as a British cruise ship named after the queen. Bernanke applied monetarist thinking and directed the Fed to buy up mortgages and bonds, injecting massive sums of money into the hands of sellers. The technique was called quantitative easing, or QE. By 2010, the Fed had gobbled up more than $2 trillion worth of securities, equal to about 15 percent of the size of the entire economy. Critics denounced the Fed, claiming it would spark hyperinflation and a disintegrating U.S. dollar. It did neither. By forcing money into the economy, the Federal Reserve avoided another Great Depression. In September 2009, U.S. GDP turned positive again, though it took four more years for housing prices to bounce back to prior levels. What kind of recovery was this?

Amid the financial and economic drama in 2008, I began citing an old name from the past and argued on National Public Radio that the economy would enjoy not a Keynesian recovery, but a Pigouvian recovery, named for Keynes's discarded, insulted colleague.[22] Pigou died in 1959 and could not put up much of a fight for his ideas even in his prime. After a ringing start as a youthful star professor, the final forty years of his career had been a slow decrescendo, deafened by the pounding, hypnotic drumbeat of Maynard Keynes. The son of a distinguished army officer whose wedding was described as "royal" by the local newspaper, Pigou was born in 1877 and grew up in a privileged household. He was, like other eldest sons in the family, sent to the tony Harrow School, where he won academic and athletic prizes and was described as a "god among mortals," a remarkable achievement considering that one of his schoolmates, who took home the fencing prize, also achieved some success.[23] The schoolmate's name was Winston Churchill. Arthur grew to be tall, fair-haired, and ramrod straight, at least in his posture and moral positioning. He studied with Cambridge's leading political economists, and at age thirty was elected to take over Marshall's coveted professorship. Pigou worshipped his mentor's textbook. New economics books were not particularly appealing; he'd rather lead vigorous young men on hiking treks across the Alps. His students noted his quick ability to switch from a weighty equation to a "hair brained spree" and back again to grave matters if Keynes stepped into the room.[24] Pigou absorbed the reigning sexism of the day and had a reputation for favoring male students over females, and scoffing at politicians and foreigners, including Americans. But he made many exceptions. He worked closely with his younger colleague Joan Robinson, supported her faculty promotion, touted her writings, and invited her to convalesce at his lakeside cottage after a nervous breakdown. He would also let former students honeymoon at his picturesque cottage.[25] When World War I broke out, Pigou was stranded in Zermatt, Switzerland. His brother was a Royal Navy man and rose to the rank of captain. While Keynes ended up at the Treasury, Pigou declared himself a pacifist and found himself driving an ambulance near the front lines, perhaps near such notables as Ernest Hemingway and Ray Kroc, founder of McDonald's. Pigou was a conscientious objector to killing, but not an objector to saving lives. He was as focused on moral philosophy as he was on downward-sloping demand curves, and he published essays titled "The Ethics of Nietzsche" and "The Ethics of the Gospels." During the war, he wrote an article in the *Nation* warning that a crushed Germany might regroup and rearm to lodge an even bigger battle ahead. Though his prediction of a second war was later reflected in Keynes's *Economic Consequences of the Peace*, critics ripped Pigou for cowardice and Germanophilia. Seared by the reaction, he learned to stay quiet about politics. He was no coward, though, and earned ribbons and medals for civilian valor. After the war he would take those awards and bestow them on the young men who had hiked with him, recognizing their service in hill walking and "distinguished incompetence."[26]

When Keynes released *The General Theory* in 1936, Pigou was struggling with cardiac issues, which could not have been helped by the public mauling of his ideas and his work. Repeating his name throughout the text, Keynes made Pigou the poster child for old-fashioned, fuddy-duddy economists who could not grasp his new paradigm. Reeling from the arrows, Pigou said that Keynes imagined himself to be an Einstein (note the "*General*" Theory), except Einstein did not dismissively smirk at Isaac Newton and call his followers "a bunch of incompetent bunglers."[27] For the next thirty years, Pigou grew more elusive and more reclusive. But silently in his own little corner of his King's College room, Pigou persisted. Something niggled at him.

In early 2009, in the midst of the Great Recession, I flew to Cambridge as a visiting fellow to dig into the Pigou story. After a petition and intervention from Alfred Marshall's Cambridge college, St. John's, I received permission from the King's College librarian to access Pigou's private papers. As I entered the oaky rooms and flipped through dusty manuscripts, I quickly learned a few things about the man. First, he was very private. Second, he ordered his papers burned after his death. Third, he was notorious for indecipherable penmanship. I looked down at the jots on his papers and thought, Alan Turing couldn't break this code! Still, I was able to gather bits from the work he tried to do to fend off Keynes, if not in a quick rebuttal, then in the long run.

In 1941, after a reclusive stretch, Pigou finally came forth with the secret to solving the *2008* Great Recession. Around the time Lehman Brothers imploded, headlines blared about crashing commodity prices, including oil and food. Many economists warned that falling prices would bring on a Greater Depression. After all, the world suffered slumping commodity prices in the 1930s. Pigou had another take. He argued that falling prices can potentially make us feel wealthier because our savings can buy more. If our savings are worth more, we have a "greater sense of power, sense of security."[28] If shoppers feel as if they have more buying power, they can lead the country out of recession. An automobile owner might feel better if he swerves into his local gasoline station and sees a posted price starting with a $2 handle instead of a $4 handle, for example. During 2009, collapsing gasoline and home heating oil prices were pumping more than $300 billion of extra buying power into the pockets of Americans, roughly $300 per month for a typical family. Cheaper turkeys and chickens were flocking their way to supermarkets, too. Meanwhile, Amazon was offering free shipping, and nearly everything seemed to be on sale, except the Lincoln Bedroom at the White House (though possibly to large political contributors). The Pigou Effect basically takes the money supply and divides it by the price level. With Bernanke printing more money and prices falling, the consumer might have the wherewithal to defeat recession.

Unfortunately, this Pigou Effect flopped in the early 1930s. Keynes announced, "Ding-dong, the free market is dead," and Pigou's theory slumped into a corner of our dusty textbooks.

But why did the Pigou Effect fail ninety years ago? Because central bankers yanked the electrical cord out of their printing presses and sat on their hands. During the 1930s, both the money supply *and* the price level dove into a sinkhole. In the United States, the money supply shrank by 30 percent, as 40 percent of banks bolted their doors. This was the sin that Bernanke apologized to Friedman for. With Bernanke at the helm, though, the Pigou Effect had a chance.

When enough people begin bargain-hunting, you can start hunting for a Pigouvian recovery. By spring 2009, the Housing Affordability Index was soaring, restaurant owners began reporting the strongest sales in a year, and the jobless rate in half America's states, including New York, California, and Texas, was drifting downward. In the U.K., like the suspect glimpse of a possibly extinct ivory-billed woodpecker, newspapers tentatively reported sightings of home sellers "gazumping"— nudging up their asking prices after receiving an informal offer from a buyer.[29] By the end of 2009, the U.S. growth rate leaped to a 5 percent pace.

Pigou finally had his moment, in the long run. If we were to give a prize for the greatest comeback in the history of economic thought, the tall, shy hiker once stranded on Zermatt would win it, not just for his Pigou Effect but also for his work on externalities that inspires the virtual Pigou Club based at Harvard today.

A Synthesis and a Look at Supply

Since Keynes's death, the world has witnessed an enriching intellectual struggle. The persistent hammering by Milton Friedman kept alive a tradition that reached back centuries.

Mainstream economics can neither deny its past nor refuse all Keynes's innovations. Federal Reserve economists closely monitor both M2 and the Keynesian concept of potential GDP in a way that has been described as "putting Keynes's head on Milton Friedman's body."

In the previous chapter, we asked whether Keynes would choose to study economics today. Here we may ask whether Keynes would have remained purely a Keynesian if he had lived to see the research and resurgence of the monetarists. Given his pragmatic, piercing mind, he would surely admit that some of the fundamental things apply, as time goes by.

The generations of bright economists who followed Friedman and Samuelson, including luminaries such as Martin Feldstein, Michael Boskin, Greg Mankiw, Paul Krugman, and Lawrence Summers, have been spared the bloody Keynesian-monetarist debate. They all find a role for both monetary and fiscal policy.

Rather than wrangle over policies that try to control aggregate demand, they have turned to the question of aggregate supply, asking how the federal government can induce firms to lift productivity. Higher productivity translates into a higher standard of living. But rising productivity requires rising investment in plants, equipment, research, and education. American economists aligned with both major political parties have blamed imprudent tax policies for sluggish productivity growth.[30]

Most of these economists carefully distinguish themselves from the zealous pamphleteers and politicians of the early 1980s whom Herbert Stein called "punk supply-siders," some of whom promised that income tax cuts would unleash such a tremendous burst of economic activity that tax revenues would quickly and automatically rise. The Laffer curve, named for the cocktail-napkin sketch of University of Southern California economist Arthur Laffer, illustrates that high tax rates could dampen activity and, ultimately, tax revenue. If, for instance, a government placed a 100 percent tax on an extra hour's income, would an individual have much reason to work that last hour? Actor Michael Caine moved from London to Los Angeles in the 1970s to avoid an 83 percent tax on his next movie. He boarded the plane after hearing the incoming chancellor of the exchequer's speech about squeezing the rich "till the pips squeak." Instead of 83 percent, the British Treasury got nothing from the actor, until Margaret Thatcher cut taxes and he moved back home.[31] While the argument was sometimes exaggerated—most people do not have the choices of an Academy Award winner who starred in *The Man Who Would Be King*—the infectious enthusiasm of the supply-siders inspired economists to push harder in their research on the ill effects of high taxes and low savings rates on the economy.

Edward Prescott, a 2004 Nobel laureate, contends that high tax rates explain why the French, Germans, and Italians spend so much time relaxing at coffee bars and spas. He finds that western Europeans "work one-third less than North Americans and Japanese," because France, Germany, and Italy tax collectors take 60 percent of their income, while Americans, Canadians, and Japanese tax labor at 40 percent. He points out that during the early 1970s, French used to work nearly 50 percent harder—but their marginal tax rate was far less.[32]

Even those economists who disdain supply-siders oppose a return to the 70 percent tax bracket of 1980 (or the 91 percent marginal tax rate of the early 1960s!), which inspired people to avoid taxes through gimmicks, shelters, and loopholes. During the last half of the 1980s, more than fifty countries cut their top rates, including such bastions of egalitarianism as Sweden and Australia. (Lebanon was one of two that hiked rates. Did it not have enough trouble?) When President Clinton persuaded Congress to raise taxes on the rich, he meant moving the top rate from 33 percent to 39.6 percent. Despite campaign rhetoric denouncing the 1980s as a giveaway to country-clubbers, he did not suggest returning the rate to the 70 percent that welcomed Ronald Reagan when he moved into the White House. Note also that while Clinton pushed up tax rates in the United States, he spent seven years urging the Japanese government to slash its income taxes in order to resuscitate its rather lifeless economy.

President George W. Bush reversed the Clinton tax hikes, and the push-pull between politicians continued with Presidents Obama and Trump reversing and squawking at their predecessors. Nonetheless, several prominent Democratic governors have made a point of cutting taxes in their states, beefing up their supply-side bona fides. Corporate tax rates have also been part of the debate. Obama's chief economist, Jason Furman of Harvard, stated in 2014 that after the Reagan reforms in the 1980s, peer countries "leapfrogged over the United States leaving us with the dubious distinction of having the highest corporate tax rate in the world."[33] Furman and Obama proposed snipping U.S. business tax rates, though Trump took rates down further than his predecessor's target.

Taxes will always be with us, pulling and pushing us through business and personal decisions. No one is immune. In 1998, Mick Jagger canceled the British leg of the Rolling Stones "Bridges to Babylon" world tour, complaining that the British laws would levy a $19 million tax on his band if they played on British soil. By playing a single concert in the United Kingdom, the Rolling Stones would have been forced to pay taxes on all the income they earned from their foreign concerts, too. If instead they stayed away from their home turf, they would escape British taxes. So they did, disappointing 350,000 fans. Jagger did not hide behind a publicist, by the way. He explained his economic decisions to the press cogently, as you would expect from someone who attended the London School of Economics in the early 1960s.

More recently, I would argue that the so-called gig economy is a strong supply-side force. For the past ten years, like characters in a Samuel Beckett play, Wall Street, Main Street, and the Federal Reserve have been waiting for inflation to bubble up. Several forces have been tamping it down, and one of them is a supply-side shock. What is a positive supply-side shock? Consider a simple story. Let's say that you live in a remote village that gets its fuel from a single oil well. Then a neighbor, call him Jed Clampett, fires a shotgun while hunting varmints, and as a result, up from the ground comes bubbling crude. Suddenly, the village has twice as much oil, and the price will go down. Now, what happens if this same type of phenomenon (not the varmint-hunting) erupts in other sectors?

College economics students learn about the "production function," a simple formula showing that output is a function of land, labor, capital, and technology. The more inputs, the more stuff people can create. The Internet and globalization are effectively increasing the magnitude of these factors. Wait a minute, how can we have more land? Are we talking about reclamation, China building new islands in the sea, or fourteenth-century Holland diking up swamps, which inspired the adage "God created the world, but the Dutch created the Netherlands"? No, we are talking about companies like Airbnb that take idle rooms and dump them onto the market. This effectively increases the supply of land available and curbs the price of vacations. Airbnb, which boasts more than 7 million listings worldwide, has increased the number of available vacation rooms by more than 25 percent in U.S. cities.

With that massive influx, the hotel industry's favorite measures, average daily rates and revenue per available room, have lagged GDP growth. In 2019 Marriott announced it was going head-to-head with Airbnb by launching a home-rental business.

How can physical capital magically grow? It's not magic, but upstarts like Dozr and Yard Club have boosted the supply of equipment by creating a kind of Uber for earthmovers and dump trucks. We used to see yellow Caterpillar trucks sitting idle at construction sites awaiting the start of some scheduled task. Now those trucks are available to work elsewhere during off-hours. Steamrollers don't complain to the union foreman if they work more than fourteen hours. We have more capital because existing capital is used more intensively.

The Internet, through financial technologies and software firms like Square, PayPal, and Salesforce, fosters a freer flow of funds and a faster connection among buyers and sellers. Former Fed chair Bernanke has pointed to a gush of global savings that slosh across borders. Consumers play a role when equipped with handy tools from online platforms. Amazon's nifty feature "Customers who viewed this item also viewed" teaches buyers to consider substitutes when they are shopping for an item. Without leaving the garage and without expending a dime on search fees, a shopper looking for, say, a Honeywell portable air conditioner that costs $500 may discover a Black & Decker that will do the job at $470. By increasing the visible supply of alternatives, Amazon's feature tamps down prices paid. Research by Obama's former Council of Economic Advisers chair Austan Goolsbee and Peter Klenow found that online inflation is 1 percent lower than the standard consumer price index calculation.[34]

These forces do not explain the entire story, because inflation is, as Milton Friedman taught, a monetary event. The strong dollar, up by 20 percent between 2014 and 2020, made foreign goods appear cheaper to Americans and created a hurdle for domestic firms that try to raise prices. Further, the destruction of wealth during the Great Recession spurred households to rebuild their balance sheets, pushing up the saving rate to about 7.5 percent, twice the pre-crisis level, and reducing the velocity of money circulating in the economy. Taken together, the supply-side shocks might have dampened inflation by about 1.5 percent. That 1.5 percent makes an enormous difference, because sleepy inflation allowed the Fed to keep interest rates low, which supported stock market prices and, combined with generous depreciation rules, prodded firms to invest in even better equipment and technology, which lifted productivity. That is why U.S. workers finally began to see wage gains.

This supply-side shock is not a deliberate government plan

like President Reagan's individual tax cuts in 1981. It is more like Jed Clampett's well-timed buckshot. But it is potent and helps the overall standard of living to bubble up.

We are all Keynesians now, thanks to Keynes. We are all monetarists now, thanks to Friedman. We all care about supply, thanks to the gig worker next store. And we are all eclectics now, thanks to a turbulent world.

Beyond Mere GDP

Milton Friedman's sparring went beyond monetary debates. While free market economists are sometimes derided for lacking compassion, Friedman proposed a "negative income tax" back in 1962 to help poor people and to replace the convoluted welfare system. His design inspired today's Earned Income Tax Credit. In international economics, Friedman committed heresy, arguing in 1953 that exchange rates should float, rather than be fixed by governments. Now trillions of dollars trade each day in foreign exchange and global bonds markets, pressuring governments and central banks to act more efficiently. In the years before his death, in 2006, at the age of ninety-four, Milton and Rose Friedman together argued vigorously in favor of creating competition among schools by offering parents the freedom to choose schools, thereby replacing the monopoly of local schools.

Milton Friedman's proudest moment, beyond the Nobel Prize, beyond the theoretical and empirical triumphs, came in 1970. The subject had little to do with the economy: It was the military, which drafted hundreds of thousands of young Americans to a bloody war in Vietnam. President Nixon appointed Friedman to a commission that would consider whether to scrap the draft and replace it with an all-volunteer force. At the outset, the commission was evenly split between supporters and opponents of a volunteer army. Army General William Westmoreland grimly testified that he did not want to command an army of mercenaries. Friedman stopped him: "General, would you rather command an army of slaves?" Westmoreland drew himself up, his steely eyes and bronze oak-leaf clusters flashing, and declared to the bespectacled Friedman, "I don't like to hear our patriotic draftees referred to as slaves." Friedman replied, "I don't like to hear our patriotic volunteers referred to as mercenaries. But if they are mercenaries, then I, sir, am a mercenary professor, and you, sir, are a mercenary general; we are served by mercenary physicians, we use a mercenary lawyer, and we get our meat from a mercenary butcher." Friedman recalled, "That was the last that we heard from the general about mercenaries."[35] Like the dissident, persistent juror in the play *Twelve Angry Men*, Friedman brought forth from the commission a unanimous vote for the volunteer army, and for freedom.

CHAPTER XI

The Public Choice School: Politics as a Business

I saw a startling sight today," Mark Twain said, "a politician with his hands in his *own* pockets."

Can a new school of economic thought rise up on Twain's snide jibe? In 1986, the Nobel Committee awarded the economics prize to James M. Buchanan, a founder of the Public Choice school of economics. The Public Choice theorists ask us to reconsider and reject orthodox public finance theory on grounds that Twain would understand. A realistic view of politics damns Keynesian economics more certainly than any multiplier statistics mustered by monetarists, they submit. Public Choice supporters trust politicians no further than they can nudge or catapult them.

The Public Choice school thinks that it can explain many economic and political problems: why we suffer from persistent budget deficits; why special interest groups proliferate; why bureaucracies continue to expand despite presidential promises to trim them; and why government regulators often protect businesses more than they do consumers. Most economists see politics as an irritating, incomprehensible, noneconomic obstacle to good policy. In contrast, Public Choice economists insist that politics must be studied with the tools of economics. *Politics is, they charge, an economic activity.* Economists should not just throw up their arms and look disgusted. They should ask why bureaucrats and legislators frequently frustrate good policy.

If one looks hard enough, one can find many forerunners of Public Choice theory, including Adam Smith, James Mill, the Swedish economist Knut Wicksell, and just about anyone who has cursed bureaucrats. Nonetheless, the real explosion of scholarly work came after World War II. As government has grown, so have its critics.

Like that piercing critic Thorstein Veblen, James Buchanan often felt like a pariah in mainstream academic circles. Born in Murfreesboro, Tennessee, in 1919, Buchanan could not afford to attend a prominent university. Instead he chose Middle Tennessee State Teachers College in his hometown. MTST's future Nobel laureate earned money for college fees by milking cows each morning and evening. After four years of bovine life, Buchanan entered the University of Tennessee, where he earned a master's degree in economics. World War II interrupted his academic path, and Uncle Sam sent him to the Naval War College in New York.

John Kenneth Galbraith started with a similar bucolic background, among cows and meadows in Canada. However, while Galbraith moved smoothly into mainstream academics, a post at Harvard, and Swiss ski vacations with dashing James Bond actor Roger Moore, Buchanan struggled and quickly learned to despise the "Eastern elite." To his last days, Buchanan winced at the intellectual snobbery and discrimination he faced in New York as a Southerner. He told a story of training as a U.S. Navy cadet during World War II, as part of a group of six hundred who were divided alphabetically. Of the twenty cadets promoted to officer rank, Ivy Leaguers were awarded thirteen of the slots. Buchanan's platoon of "A" and "B" surnames was bereft of Ivy grads. Therefore, the commander passed over Buchanan's comrades and imported an "R"-surnamed man to lead the "A" and "B" platoon. The "R" stood for "Rockefeller." Buchanan recalled that the discrimination "radicalized" him, and at that point, he might have been willing to join a Marxist squad. Instead, he served at Pearl Harbor in an underground command center mapping out movements of the Pacific fleet.

He aided Admirals Nimitz and Spruance, the latter leading the epic Battle of Midway, the turning point of the war. Buchanan took pride that Spruance called him "mighty fast and fairly accurate."[1] After the war, Buchanan went west, earning his doctorate at the University of Chicago. A pivotal moment came by chance. After completing a German-language exam, he roamed the library stacks and happened to pull down Knut Wicksell's unread and untranslated dissertation on the politics of taxation. It excited Buchanan, and shortly after he fled south to Florida State and then the University of Virginia, where he established the so-called Virginia School of political economy.

Buchanan saw much of his work as a reaction to the idealistic musings of ivory tower scholars from the East. While convoys of Harvard economists flocked to Washington during the Kennedy and Johnson administrations, Buchanan quietly assailed their ideas from the hills of Virginia, publishing *The Calculus of Consent* with Gordon Tullock in 1962.

According to Buchanan, the "'eastern academic elite can't leave the mindset' of their role as lofty and wise elders who deliver Olympian pronouncements to government. 'They always think of themselves as advisers to Washington.'"

And as for Buchanan? "I call myself part of the Great Unwashed [who are] just trying to figure out what's going on."[2] He aimed to look at "politics without the romance."

Even his friends admitted that Buchanan was not a back-slapping guy. With the habits formed from hearing the first rooster crow in the field, he was known as the first guy to show up at the office in the morning and the first guy to sharpen his pencil. Considering his austere personality and distaste for bon vivants awash in Perrier, one can imagine few situations more tense than Buchanan in the same room with the elegant John Kenneth Galbraith.

Rather than trace the history of the Public Choice school, let's see how the school regards several of the most pressing issues in political economy. The thrust of Public Choice is glaringly simple: If businessmen are self-interested, why not assume that government officials are "political entrepreneurs"? What do they maximize? Their power and their ability to gain votes. Economists spent two hundred years developing a model of human behavior. Why throw it away when confronting government?

The Paradox of Special Interest Groups

No one is safe when Congress is in session—including the members. Lobbyists hound them and their aides, pushing for favors, tax breaks, grants, and protection. Buchanan's friend Mancur Olson, a University of Maryland professor whose personal politics were more liberal, contended that systematic incentives to sap society's efficiency drive special interest organizations, whether unions, clubs, or corporations.[3]

Why don't special interests patriotically lobby Congress to boost efficiency and national wealth? It doesn't pay. Consider the Committee for Thorough Agricultural Political Education of Associated Milk Producers, which ranks high on the list of donors to congressional campaigns. Milk producers love price supports, guarantees that they will "earn" a minimum price per gallon. Economists hate price supports. And consumers suffer because of them. (Incidentally, children drink a disproportionate share of milk. Since children make up a large proportion of the poor, poor children probably suffer most.) Suppose the committee members compose 1 percent of the U.S. population. If they were to successfully lobby Congress to pass a general measure that would raise overall U.S. productivity, they would receive only 1 percent of the benefits. Yet they would have exerted 100 percent of the effort to pass the bill. They could end up spending $50,000 on legislation that creates $1 million of new wealth for the country, but they would receive just $10,000 as their share. Only if the bill breeds new income greater than one hundred times the lobbying costs does patriotic lobbying make sense. Consequently, organizations have little interest in promoting a more efficient society through politics. It just doesn't pay.

Now consider the milk committee looking out for itself. It can profit by taking from others through price-support schemes. From whom does it take? Consumers, of course. Let's say that milk-price supports cost the committee $50,000 in lobbying fees but raise producer income by $10 million. The producers bear 100 percent of the lobbying burden but receive 100 percent of the benefits. Even during the Great Recession, when global real estate markets cascaded downward, Washington continued to attract business tenants. Politics can be a wonderful investment. No wonder producers often are more eager to decorate offices in Washington than to install new equipment in their factories. No wonder they hire plenty of lawyers: the payoff is better. Legendary thief Willie Sutton explained that he robbed banks because "that's where the money is." To many organizations, the money is in Washington.

These political activities usually hurt society. Do the coalitions care? The milk committee in our example bears only 1 percent of the total injury. Only if GDP drops by one hundred times their payoff, does an injury to the economy dissuade them. "A society dense with special-interest organizations is like a china shop filled with wrestlers battling over its contents, and breaking much more than they carry away," says Olson.[4]

If price supports rob the pocketbooks of consumers, why don't consumers organize to defeat the schemes? It doesn't pay. In our example, the total cost to consumers is $10 million. If the population equals 330 million, it costs each consumer about 3 cents. Yet it benefits each producer by $3. A milk producer will show one hundred times the interest of a milk consumer in the issue. Moreover, it's much easier to organize producers.

Lobbyists for sugar growers, who represent only about .0002

percent of the American population, manage to keep the U.S. sugar price at levels often triple the world price through tariffs and price supports that have been imposed since the time Ben Franklin was sprinkling the stuff in tea and arguing that the "sugar islands" of the Caribbean should be free from colonial occupation.[5] Not only do contemporary U.S. growers, including sugar beet farmers, benefit grandly, but producers of corn sweeteners (sugar substitutes) collect handsome profits competing with artificially high sugar prices. Log Cabin brand syrup contains no maple syrup, just corn syrup. The makers of Life Savers and Jelly Belly jelly beans built factories outside the United States to avoid high sweetener prices. Scientific studies show that some artificial sweeteners can cause cancer in laboratory rats. Artificial price supports can cause cancer in a nation's body politic.

This problem emerges again and again in democracies. Motivated organizations trample on the interests of consumers, who individually have a small stake in the outcome. Ultimately, the individual consumers are hurt badly as national efficiency and income fall. But whom do they blame? No obvious villain appears, because the special interests snatch such small bites from the common weal.

For consumers to blame themselves makes little sense. To keep track of Congress's actions costs money. It is rational to ignore special favors bestowed to others when they cost you only 3 cents. After all, it would cost more than that just to telephone your congressman to find out how much such a favor costs you. Economists call this "rational ignorance," a term coined by Anthony Downs, who served time as a consultant to the U.S. Department of Housing and Urban Development. We can't know everything. We haven't the brain capacity, time, or money to learn. The problem with socialism is that it takes up too many evenings. But being an "educated voter" is exhausting under any system.

Until the advent of Uber and Lyft in the 2010s, New York City and Boston residents knew there was a shortage of taxicabs.

These cities actually limit the number of licensed cabs, which drove up the income of drivers and drove down the morale of the cities. Still, the city governments refused to support the grumbling of the general public over the ranting of taxi owners. Then when app-based cars started arriving, allowing passengers to rate drivers and requiring drivers to maintain a rating of at least 4.7 (out of 5), many taxicab commissions declared war on the upstarts, even though they provided better service and often cheaper prices. In San Francisco, a city supervisor complained that cabdrivers were "losing about $15 per shift or even more." Here is another way to look at it: San Francisco residents and tourists were finding the city a more convenient place to live, work, and visit. The Public Choice school does not simply point out that the "squeaky wheel gets the grease." More important, Olson and his colleagues teach us *why* tight coalitions make a much more powerful noise than a diffuse, unorganized public.

Olson takes his arguments into far more controversial territory by drawing broad historical laws. He assumes that stable societies are more susceptible to special interests. He then claims that "long stable" societies will grow more slowly than relatively new societies. As time passes, leeches multiply and suck the lifeblood from a nation. If so, revolutions and wars can invigorate economies, since special interest groups lose their stranglehold. He cites Great Britain as a stable, retarded nation and postwar Japan as an economic miracle. My research shows that it is not just time that attracts bureaucracy, but also prosperity itself. America's bureaucracy grew rapidly during the Johnson and Nixon/Ford years, when the number of U.S. government employees jumped by 46 percent. This period was preceded by one of the most prosperous periods in history, the post–World War II boom. The pattern even shows up in China during the Middle Ages. In *The Price of Prosperity*, I document the prosperity of the early Ming dynasty and how Chinese sailors used magnetic compasses hundreds of years before Italian seafarers. But with the A.D. 1433 death of a leading palace eunuch who supported trade, the bureaucrats expanded their roles, banned competitive shipbuilding, sneered at merchants, and closed down printing presses to amass more control for themselves.[6] The economy began to slow and slouched to an ignominious close when the last Ming emperor hanged himself from a tree.

Few economists follow Olson all the way to his conclusion about the rise and fall of nations. Even so, the arithmetic of special interest groups seems to add up.

Is the special interest paradox hopeless? Not necessarily. After all, each group suffers when Congress awards favors to the others. If a president or congressional leader could get a mandate for across-the-board budget cuts or broad policies against subsidies, price supports, and protection schemes, the increased efficiency in the economy could offset for these groups the elimination of special favors. Sadly, historical examples are few. And it seems more likely that the politicians will continue to deliver tough-sounding rhetoric while special interests spout words of magnanimity—but nothing really happens.

How the Regulated Can Control the Regulators

Why does the government regulate many industries? The quick answer, found in high school texts, is that these industries are monopolies or oligopolies, and the consumer should be protected from gouging. The answer implies that businesses hate regulation.

Following the lead of Nobel laureate George Stigler, Public Choice economists have added another possible answer: *Businesses want regulation because it protects them from the risks of dynamic competition.* They actually lobby for regulation. This is known as the "capture theory" of regulation, for the regulated entities "capture" the regulators.[7]

How does this work? Consider a state's Board of Barbers.

The board insists on certain rules and standards—for example, that all barbers sterilize their combs and reject any customers who look like dogs. The board's interference may raise costs slightly, but the barbers may persuade the board to adopt other rules that benefit them grandly, especially by restricting entry. The board may hinder new barbers from moving to the state by demanding that they spend a year in Jamaica cutting Rastafarian dreadlocks or that they intern at minimum wage for three years at an accredited dandruff clinic. Each of these regulations, aimed at protecting barbers from competition, may be offered under the guise of protecting the public against inexperienced practitioners. In fact, the public gets scalped. The state of Arizona demands that hairstylists take sixteen hundred hours of classroom instruction—at a cosmetology school approved by the government. How many hours of training does Phoenix demand of a policeman? Six hundred hours. Evidently, it takes almost three times as much training to pick up a comb than a .40 caliber Glock.

In 2014, New Jersey banned Tesla from selling automobiles in the state because the company sold directly to consumers, rather than setting up traditional middleman dealerships. Despite Tesla achieving the highest rating ever bestowed by *Consumer Reports* that year, the state Motor Vehicle Commission prohibited willing buyers from purchasing the car of their choice. Since the commission was composed of political appointees and representatives of dealers, and because dealers traditionally contribute financing to election campaigns, it was not difficult to spot the logic in the ban (later lifted by the governor). For a period of time, though, dealers, whose honesty rating in a Gallup poll beat out only auto mechanics and lawyers, held sway over the mass of voters.

Regulation seldom levies only good or only bad upon an industry. Milk regulators may require stainless-steel vats, which cost more than plastic ones. The rule may irk milk producers, but the price supports and subsidies they receive surely outweigh such trivial irritants.

Why do regulated industries succeed in capturing the supposed guardians of the public interest? Recall the rational ignorance–special interest paradox. The industry has an incentive to gather all the academic testimony it can on its behalf. Economists actually advertise in the pages of law magazines, offering their expert research. Regulatory officials often feel that they might as well give in to the industries, since the "public" doesn't seem to care much. Finally, a more cynical explanation looms: regulators often have incestuous relations with the regulated. Commissioners come from the private sector and return to the private sector after their tenure. Making friends is one route to making money. In 1970 Ralph Nader referred to the "Interstate Commerce *Omission*" as a federal agency that kept the trucking industry cozy.

The capture theory has not captured the minds of all economists. The theory presents a narrow, one-sided view of politics. Sometimes politicians can reverse the hold and take businesses hostage. Surely, the light bulb industry did not applaud state regulations banning incandescent bulbs in the 2000s; nor did fast-food franchises celebrate local rules that banned plastic straws. During the 1970s and 1980s, many dominant businesses unsuccessfully battled a deregulation wave that forced them to compete against new upstarts. When Frank Sinatra sang "Come Fly with Me" in concerts in the 1960s, very few Americans could afford to climb into a commercial airplane. The federal government's Civil Aeronautics Board guided a cozy cartel of big carriers that kept prices sky high and divided up the globe among one another. Even start-up cargo carriers were grounded, and FedEx was not permitted to fly big jets until airlines were deregulated in 1977 and 1978, at the urging of Cornell economist Alfred Kahn. Incidentally, Kahn was plagued with a condition rare in Washington: blunt honesty. Serving President Jimmy Carter, Kahn had the nerve to state that certain policies could spark a depression. When the White House scolded him for uttering the word "depression," he decided to substitute the word "banana" and told reporters that between 1973 and 1975 "we had the deepest banana." Then when the banana lobbyists objected, he called the downturn a "kumquat." The point here is that sometimes individuals can buck the bureaucratic rules and corollaries embedded in Public Choice theory. Likewise, a demagogic politician might rise to power on the promise to crush greedy robber barons who have conspired with government officials. He could promise a capon in every pot and force down the price of capon with punitive regulations that harm the fowl industry. The indignant politician who arouses the public's anger and interest provides the chief rebuttal witness to the Public Choice hypothesis.

Public Choice economists do not say that all regulations help industry and harm consumers. They do not argue for pure laissez-faire economics. They do, however, urge people to compare the free market result with a realistic model of government regulation, rather than a mythical vision that assumes a benevolent government always striving to serve the public interest.

Big Promises, Bulging Budgets, and Bureaucracies

Olson and Stigler portray special interest groups swinishly struggling to stick their snouts in the public trough. Why does the government feed them? Why does the government supply the goods and services that different groups demand? Public Choice theorists answer these questions by examining bureaucracies and politicians.

Gordon Tullock and William A. Niskanen Jr. watched bureaucrats as closely as biologists study laboratory rats—which indicates the level of admiration the two authors had for their subjects. According to Niskanen, bureaucrats compete in a rat race similar to the one that businessmen participate in. The bureaucrat, like the businessman, is a self-interested rat, but his self-interest shows through in different ways. The business-man battles to maximize profits. Of course, government bureaucrats cannot maximize their own profits except, perhaps, through bribery. Instead, they try to maximize a different set of variables: salary, perquisites, power, prestige, opportunities after retirement, and so on. How does the bureaucrat maximize these? By inflating the budget and size of the bureau. Niskanen depicts bureaus as budget-maximizing organizations. Bureaus may expand far beyond an efficient size. And they expand by squeezing the taxpayer. More money means more power, so bureaucrats do not have strong incentives to trim costs. Skimpy bureaucracies lead to grumpy bureaucrats.

Even if elected officials vow to slash the bureaucracy, they seldom muster the power to do it. Jimmy Carter and Ronald Reagan both promised and both failed. Government payrolls continued to climb during their administrations. They learned to sympathize with the czar who admitted, "I do not rule Russia. Ten thousand clerks do." Although a political leader can order certain actions, only the bureaucracy can implement them. Sometimes bureaucrats may subtly refuse, hinder, or delay implementation, hoping the leader will retire, lose an election, or die. Often the men and women dressed in gray win. Supporters of the Trump administration call the Washington complex "the swamp" because they believe it is filled with shady characters maneuvering in the muck to strangle businesses and undermine the president.

Niskanen's theory has some problems. He lumps all bureaucrats together the way Marx lumps all workers together, as if they all have overriding confluent interests. They don't. One can draw a more complex model of bureaucracies. Who counts, after all, as the head of the bureau? The cabinet secretary? The senior civil servant? Might they sometimes gain political advantage by cutting the bureaucracy? During the first Reagan administration, Secretary of the Interior James Watt tried to emasculate parts of his agency. A more telling case concerns Caspar Weinberger. During the Nixon administration, he earned the tag "Cap the Knife" for his thrifty oversight of the Department of Health, Education, and Welfare. Later, as secretary of defense under Reagan, Cap the Knife transformed into "Cap the Ladle," turning the Pentagon into a gravy train. He couldn't find the tools to cut Jell-O, much less a trillion-dollar budget. What accounts for Weinberger's reversal? Why did Niskanen's theory work only half the time? Probably because Weinberger believed that one department was bloated while another had to expand to meet his president's goals and intimidate the Soviet Union, which capitulated and collapsed not long after.

Niskanen's model of bureaucracy is much more than half-baked, but it probably needs more time in the cooker.

Now let us turn to Public Choice theories on elected politicians.

"Congress is so strange," a Russian immigrant once observed. "A man gets up and says nothing. Nobody listens. Then everybody stands up and disagrees." On the contrary, James Buchanan sees too much *agreement* in Congress. Politicians love to lash out at government for waste, fraud, and abuse. In the 1988 Democratic presidential campaign, Governor Michael Dukakis assailed the IRS for faulty tax collections; Gary Hart attacked a profligate Pentagon; and Rev. Jesse Jackson denounced tax loopholes for the rich. On the issue of cutting budget deficits, they nodded their heads in blissful accord.

At the same time that politicians unanimously decry waste, though, they vote to spend more money on programs that inflate the budget. From 1958 to 2020, the United States enjoyed a balanced budget only six times. According to Buchanan, politicians' rhetoric collides with their voting records. They sound like statesmen yet vote like weasels. The most important deficit in Washington may be located along the spines and between the ears of the politicians. As Teddy Roosevelt put it, you could carve men with stronger backbones from bananas.

Buchanan does not simply vilify politicians, though he does

that well. He searches for the forces that pressure politicians into acting hypocritically. In reality, the problem lies not in the particular individuals in Congress; the problem is systemic. The political system fosters budget deficits, Buchanan claims.

Let's start by recalling the lesson of Keynes: During periods of prosperity, the budget should reach a surplus, as employment and tax revenues rise. During recessions, the budget should fall into a deficit, as employment and tax revenues fall. Over the course of the business cycle, the budget should balance. If that is the plan, Buchanan forces us to grapple with its failure. Why did the United States witness prosperity while seeing so few budget surpluses? Buchanan died in 2013, but he wouldn't have been shocked to find out that in 2019, despite record low unemployment rates and a record high stock market, the United States managed to blow the annual deficit to $1 trillion, about 4.5 percent of GDP. Compare that to the budget of the tiny Cayman Islands in the Caribbean. With the country's population of just sixty-eight thousand and a culture where people can easily keep tabs on leaders, the government was able to stash away for the future a budget surplus equal to about 4 percent of its economy.

Buchanan's answer to the riddle is rather simple and takes us back to Jeremy Bentham. Politicians want to please their constituents. People like pleasure and hate pain. Government programs are pleasurable; taxes are painful. Guess what people want from their representatives? High spending and low taxes, which usually translates into budget deficits.

Let's fire a quick retort at Buchanan: If persistent budget deficits hurt the economy, don't people feel pain and desire a balanced budget?

Buchanan replies that budget deficits do hurt, but the pain is indirect and diffuse. Compare the direct pain of a budget surplus to the indirect pain of a budget deficit. If we start with a balanced budget and wish to create a surplus, we may (1) raise taxes or (2) cut spending. Both strategies inflict pain directly. Higher taxes usually reduce private consumption. Slashing spending hurts beneficiaries of programs. Any benefits in terms of a healthier economy arrive later and only indirectly help the victims of higher taxes or lower spending. The victim must imagine how she will benefit in the future.

Now consider the budget deficit. We can create a deficit by lowering taxes or raising government spending. Both put smiles on the faces of taxpayers and beneficiaries. Deficits allow people to spend more on themselves. Yes, deficits may dislodge the economy, but, again, the effects are indirect: people must imagine the future and ask whether they will be affected.[8]

Buchanan's explanation rests on people misjudging indirect future effects. Too many people follow Albert Einstein, who said, "I never think of the future. It comes soon enough." Buchanan would prefer that they follow the words of Amanda Wingfield in Tennessee Williams's *The Glass Menagerie*: "The future becomes the present, the present the past, and the past turns into everlasting regret if you don't plan for it!"

Because deficit spending ignores the future, it harms future generations, Buchanan asserts. In fact, he raises a moral question: Don't deficits resemble taxation without representation? Congressmen today enhance their constituents' present welfare by jeopardizing the welfare of their grandchildren. The unborn cannot vote. Yet each child is born with financial liabilities.

Buchanan's point about future generations receives an intriguing rebuttal from the Rational Expectations school of thought, which we will address in the next chapter. Essentially, Rational Expectations theorists argue that people correctly weigh the future and magnanimously consider their offspring. As you might expect, this new school of thought incites even more controversy than the Public Choice school.

The strongest rebuttal to Buchanan comes from the obvious fact that the federal budget deficit did disappear in 1997 and surpluses did begin piling up. How did this happen, and does it doom the Public Choice model? In 1990, 1993, and

1997, Congress passed legislation cutting the growth rate of federal spending, and in 1990 and 1993 it raised taxes especially on upper-income Americans. More important, though, revenue growth exploded, as a long and strong economic expansion pushed down the unemployment rate to levels that Americans had not seen since the 1960s. More workers on the job meant more people earning income and paying taxes. Likewise, corporate profits generated higher corporate tax revenues and sent the stock market rocketing. Between June 1995 and June 1998, the Dow Jones index of stocks doubled. As stock investors sold their appreciated shares and "took profits," they paid capital gains taxes. All in all, an impressive performance for the U.S. economy at a time when politicians actually restrained themselves from going on a spending rampage.

Because the 1990s ended with a budget in surplus, should we tear up our portfolio of Public Choice research papers? "Just wait," the Public Choice scholars advised, and they were not surprised to see the budget surplus frittered away over the following few years. Even at the end of the 1990s, congressmen started to feel that old hankering for ham. A highway bill signed by President Clinton in 1998 contained a huge amount of old-fashioned pork spending. One researcher calculated that for the price of the $200 billion highway bill, the United States could *literally* pave the streets with gold (gold-plating, that is). Instead of gilding the highways, the bill gilded the political careers of congressmen, who bragged about bringing their districts new funds for bridges, tunnels, ferries, and bicycle paths. Five months after passing the bill, 98 percent of incumbent congressmen won reelection. The 1999 budget bill included such corporate goodies as a $300,000 grant to study whether Kellogg's Raisin Bran should qualify for a federal nutritional program.

Almost as soon as President Bush took office in 2001, Congress opened up the wallets of the American people, turned them upside down, and shook them hard. A $180 billion farm bill bailed out dried pea and lentil farmers, while resurrecting defunct programs for those mohair goat herders and beekeepers. A new $286 billion highway bill funneled almost $1 billion to 119 special projects in Alaska. A village with fifty residents received $223 million to build a mile-long bridge linking it to the bustling town of Ketchikan on the mainland. Another $231 million would build a bridge in Anchorage, specified in the legislation as "Don Young's Way." Who is Don Young? The chairman of the House Transportation and Infrastructure Committee.

The budget surplus of the late 1990s does show that Americans are not quite as ignorant and passive as the Public Choice advocates believe. Squeaky individuals like Ross Perot and bipartisan advocacy groups like the Concord Coalition effectively riled up voters throughout the country during the mid-1990s. Politicians suddenly felt scared that they would lose their jobs if they did not cut spending. A Republican Congress kept the heat on a Democratic president, until both sides of Pennsylvania Avenue compromised on spending cuts. The government would have kept on spending tax dollars if common voters had not voiced their anger at perennial deficits. The lesson is that sometimes "people power" does beat "public choice."

In fact, during the 1990s, budget-balancing broke out all over the industrialized world. Canada, Sweden, and Australia, which faced bankruptcy threats at the start of the decade, slashed government programs in order to regain their financial credibility. In Europe, European Union members signed the Maastricht Treaty, which obligated each of them to squeeze their deficits—or else lose their eligibility to join the new single-currency program. Only Japan completely missed the boat, as a terrible recession bloated the budget to alarming levels. For the Western world, though, the spirit of the times demanded fiscal austerity and permitted few flights of Keynesian fancy. Unfortunately, the Great Recession of 2008 upended many of these efforts, and mature countries throughout Europe have failed to regain command over their own budgets. A world map of government debt shows that wealthy, aging countries like Japan and France have worse public finance profiles than poorer places like Russia and Mexico.

Social Security and Medicare

The Social Security and Medicare debate offers another tasty example of a clash of interest groups fighting over the public fisc. Social Security got its start during the Great Depression, as a plan to help senior citizens maintain their dignity when they retired. In exchange for paying a new tax on their wages, the government would keep old people from falling into poverty when they could no longer work. Since most people died before age sixty-five, not many retirees actually collected at first. Two developments demolished the arithmetic. First, people started living much longer. Typically Americans retire in their sixties but now live to almost eighty. Second, the baby boom generation flew off the population charts after World War II. As a result, during the next few decades the United States will have many more retirees but relatively fewer workers to support them. In the 1950s, roughly 15 full-time employees paid into the program for every one who received a check; by 2035, about 2.3 full-time employees will support each retiree. Currently, about 15 percent of the population receives Social Security retirement payments. That number will jump to more than 20 percent in the decades ahead. So who is going to support the baby boomers gone to pasture? Where will we come up with the estimated $34 trillion to pay promised benefits?

Many Americans wrongly believe that Social Security taxes have already been invested and have been earning interest that will pay those bills. Sorry. In fact, Congress created Social Security as a "pay-as-you-go" system—that is, most of today's tax dollars go right out the door to pay for today's retirees. The rest go into the federal budget to pay for other programs.

True, there is a "Social Security Trust Fund," but it is a stack of IOUs that the U.S. Treasury has given the Social Security Administration. With the baby boomers hitting peak retirement age, Congress will either have to cut spending, raise taxes, or find some as-yet-unidentified pot of gold. Medicare beneficiaries face a similarly empty cupboard. No wonder Generation Xers feel the threat of huge tax hikes ahead, while baby boomers wonder whether they should have been kinder to their children and grandchildren. Perhaps this is why a public opinion poll showed that more eighteen- to twenty-four-year-olds believe in UFOs than in Social Security. After all, there still will be unidentified flying objects in the year 2100; Social Security is another question.

Wisps of hope sometimes appear when politicians speak freely about overhauling Social Security. Until the late 1990s, it was known as "the third rail of American politics." Anyone who suggested reform sizzled with the jolt of 49 megavolts of deadly power (49 million receive Social Security retirement benefits today). When Barry Goldwater mentioned the topic (in Florida!) during his 1964 presidential campaign, his advisers could hear the Lyndon Johnson landslide rumbling. Though during the 1980s, Republicans whispered about Social Security in private; they were afraid that Democrats would pounce on them if word got out. Two forces have liberated policymakers to discuss reform. First, the budget debates of the 1990s encouraged politicians that there is a "political market" for attacking deficits. Second, Americans began pouring their personal savings into the stock market during the 1990s, with success, except for the big slump in 2000–2002 and in 2008–2009. They learned that over time, equity investments tend to outperform bond investments. If so, why shouldn't their Social Security taxes earn higher returns? The average two-earner family sees only about a 1 percent annual return on their contributions, compared to an average of 9 percent for the stock market. If the government invested Social Security payroll taxes in the stock market, Americans might enjoy richer retirements, without taxing young workers so heavily.

Though Congress has not yet tackled Social Security, in 1998 some prominent Democrats such as Senators Patrick Moynihan and Bob Kerrey jumped onto the heretofore conservative bandwagon and proposed that workers be able to target some portion of their Social Security payroll tax for the stock market. Sure, there are risks, Moynihan argued. But it is a better risk than watching the entire system collapse as it becomes both arithmetically and politically impossible for young people to shoulder the burdens that baby boomers placed on them. President Bush attempted and failed to create widespread support for personal Social Security accounts, but at least he could discuss the proposal without being clobbered by voters and opponents. His successors, Obama and Trump, kept quiet about reform, averting their eyes even as future "balloon payments" inflated.

Medicare, too, calls out for major reform, and is even more precariously financed than Social Security. Our health care system does not give retirees a big enough incentive to watch where the money goes. Having a Medicare card feels like you are wielding someone else's credit card—literally, the credit card that belongs to other people's children. This is the *moral hazard* problem. Did you ever rent a car and decide to wash it before returning it? Have you ever been on vacation at a fancy hotel and, instead of dipping in the pool, asked the concierge to get you a sponge, a long hose, and a bucket? Of course not. In fact, people treat rental cars less gingerly than their own, daring to parallel park in the tightest spots and stomping their foot on the accelerator to launch themselves up the freeway access ramp. Likewise, if Medicare is paying 80 percent of your bills, you might decide on a whim to drop by the podiatrist's office for a pedicure. Instead of buying a $20 heating pad, you might spend $300 to talk to an orthopedic surgeon. These dynamics are not found only in Medicare. Employer-paid health insurance can lead to the same waste. A Rand Corporation study showed that when people are "free riders" on someone else's policy, they rack up 45 percent more in medical bills. More striking, they don't end up any healthier! Intensive-care patients in Miami spend twice as much as those in Minneapolis but do not come out any healthier.[9] Note though, that when people pay out of their own pocket, for example, for laser eye surgery and for cosmetic treatments like Botox and teeth whiteners, prices plunge, as medical providers rush in to create white-hot competition.

Political Cycles

Some Public Choice scholars have expanded James Buchanan's approach and stated that politicians manipulate the macroeconomy to boost their reelection chances. According to proponents of this "Political Cycle" theory, during election periods politicians force down unemployment by inflationary policies. Inflation will eventually come but only after the election. A recession will cure inflation. And unemployment will be forced down again in time for the next election. Although many politically conservative theorists sympathize with this theory, a Polish Marxist, Michał Kalecki, was the first to present it, in 1943. The theory gained respect during the Nixon years, when monetary tools appeared to follow polling results rather than sound policy.

There seems no end to the embarrassments that emerge from Richard Nixon's White House tapes. Nixon's views on monetary policy were both shrewd and cynical. During his presidency, the Federal Reserve Board was headed by Arthur Burns, a pipe-puffing dandy who parted his hair in the middle and wore a pocket watch. Burns more than looked the part; he had sterling credentials, too: a Columbia professorship, a term as Eisenhower's chief economic adviser, and a stint as head of the National Bureau of Economic Research. Nixon cajoled and hectored, trying to convince Burns to goose up the money supply before the 1972 election. Nixon blamed his 1960 presidential loss to John F. Kennedy on a sluggish economy and did not want to risk a repeat. When Burns reported to Nixon that he had persuaded the Federal Open Market Committee to cut the discount rate, Nixon cheered, "Great, great . . . just kick them in the rump a little." Nixon knew that monetary policy worked with lags, and he urged Burns to stimulate the economy more than a year before the election. But by February 1972, he told the Fed chief, "I really don't care what you do in April."[10] Sure enough, the money supply exploded in 1971, growing at a more than 13 percent pace, compared to one of just 7.4 percent in 1970. The stimulus sent the roaring economy to a blistering 7.7 percent growth rate during the election year. Unfortunately, inflation would soon roar, too. Nobody knows whether Burns caved to White House pressure or just misread the needs of the economy. But the episode does teach a valuable lesson: do not let the president close to the levers of monetary policy.

Since the Nixon-Burns days, the evidence for political cycles has grown skimpier. As we will discuss in the next chapter, fast-moving "bond vigilantes" make it tougher for central bankers and politicians to conspire. While serving in the White House of President George H. W. Bush, I saw missives from Treasury Secretary Nicholas Brady blazing across my desk on their way to Federal Reserve chairman Greenspan. Brady and the president believed that Greenspan had let the money supply droop in 1991 and 1992. Greenspan proved himself quite independent of Bush. He eventually slashed rates, but too late to help Bush. In 1997, Prime Minister Tony Blair and Chancellor of the Exchequer Gordon Brown built credibility for the British Labour Party by declaring the Bank of England independent of the chancellor, with Brown calling it the most radical reform since the bank's establishment in 1694. Their move immediately boosted the pound sterling in the eyes of global investors, while expected inflation rates dropped by more than half a percentage point.[11] In contrast, in 2019 when Turkish president Recep Tayyip Erdoğan fired the central bank chief before his term expired, endangering bank independence, the value of the Turkish lira immediately dropped by 2.5 percent and inflationary expectations jumped higher. Subsequent research around the world confirms that when central banks can break free from election-focused politicians, they can help deliver lower inflation rates for citizens. While President Donald Trump has made economists uncomfortable by hounding Federal Reserve chairman Jerome Powell and publicly arguing for lower interest rates, he has not proposed a takeover of the institution's independence.

The Public Choice school literature expands each year, and the research questions are intriguing. Why has the number of congressmen stayed at 435 although population continues to grow? Which congressional districts receive the most government grants? How do campaign contributions affect political programs?

Most economists regard the Public Choice school with skepticism. Even the strongest opponents, however, admit the truth of the school's most important lesson: do not assume that government takes economically prudent steps in the face of political opposition. Economic textbooks written in the thirty years following World War II pointed to market imperfections such as monopolies and pollution. Then they confidently stated that imperfections may be cured or avoided by government action. Then they described how government may theoretically act to assure efficiency. End of page. Public Choice theorists force us to ask: Will government actually do its theoretical duty, or will political pressures and incentives spoil the neat scenario? Just as the market may have imperfections, so may government. We must compare the realistic results of the market economy to a realistic prediction of the results of government actions. For too long textbooks compared a blemished view of the private economy with a squeaky-clean view of government. At long last we may admit that the only squeak in Washington comes from the subways, not from the Capitol.

Why Didn't Keynes Anticipate the Public Choice School?

The Public Choice school is a late-twentieth-century phenomenon, though it has trace roots in the ideas of Adam Smith, who warned of politicians colluding with big business; Knut Wicksell, who feared that a majority would gang up to impose taxes on a minority; and even a stammering Oxford mathematician named Charles Dodgson, who tried to write optimal calculations on voting systems but had more success with a fable called *Alice in Wonderland*, written under his pen name, Lewis Carroll. Why didn't more economists develop any suspicions about the political system? In particular, why didn't that genius Keynes, a promoter of government intervention, warn us about systemic government flaws? Either Keynes was politically native or nefarious—either he unwittingly promoted a faulty system or he knew but kept quiet. By looking once again at Keynes, a man caught between Victorian values and modern society, we can better understand the uniquely twentieth-century character of Public Choice theory.

Keynes's Prescriptions for Government Intervention

Keynes succinctly stated his position on the proper role of government: "not to do things which individuals are doing already . . . but to do those things which are at present not done at all," for instance, promoting full employment by augmenting consumption and investment.[12] Keynes harbored no desires to destroy capitalism. He thought Marx contributed nothing to economics and only trouble to politics. Yet he saw deficiencies in the capitalist system that could be mended by government action. In his very political and partisan 1929 pamphlet *Can Lloyd George Do It?*, Keynes vigorously urged public works to relieve unemployment and blasted the "Treasury view," which embodied neoclassic claims that government spending would only crowd out private investment rather than create jobs. The Marxist economist Paul Sweezy depicted Keynes's approach as a "habit of treating the state as a *deus ex machina* to be invoked whenever his human actors, behaving according to the rules of the capitalist game, get themselves in a dilemma from which there is apparently no escape."[13]

Keynes knew that a priori judgments on the "correct" size of government were silly. Nonetheless, he argued that the state would have to guide consumption through income taxes and the interest rate. As early as 1925, Keynes realized that the modern state would need new types of administrative agencies: "I believe that in the future the government will have to take on many duties which it has avoided in the past. For these purposes Ministers and Parliament will be inserviceable."[14] New agencies ultimately answerable to Parliament would, Keynes thought, carry out or at least influence two-thirds to three-quarters of total investment.

Keynes confronted his readers and audiences with few warnings. In a letter responding to Hayek's *The Road to Serfdom*, which argued that increasing political involvement in economics finally leads to totalitarianism, Keynes tenaciously held that "we almost certainly want more" planning, not less. "But the planning should take place in a community in which as many people as possible, both leaders and followers, wholly share your own moral position. Moderate planning will be safe if those carrying it out are rightly oriented in their own minds and hearts to the moral issue."[15] Nonetheless, Keynes spent little time explaining how the public can tell whose heart is "rightly oriented" or whether the public would even prefer rightly oriented types to those who would promise more benefits.

Cultural and Intellectual Influences on Keynes

Can cultural and intellectual factors explain Keynes's lack of caution? Our earlier study of Keynes described his Victorian upbringing. Roy Harrod, an Oxford economist and Keynes's first biographer, refers to the "presuppositions of Harvey Road," Keynes's home in Cambridge. Though Keynes sometimes rejected these presuppositions for himself, he imputed them to others. What were they? They sound like a Boy Scout pledge: economy, moral soundness, public duty, and discipline. Keynes believed that the British clerisy generally followed these tenets.

For himself and that cabal of intellectual elites at Cambridge known as the Apostles, however, the old morality was mortally wounded by G. E. Moore's *Principia Ethica*. Moore, a Cambridge philosopher, provided Keynes and a select group of friends with a new religion that savaged Aristotle, Jesus, Mill, and Kant. According to Moore, the highest goods were states of consciousness, not particular acts. Keynes interpreted Moore to say that the enjoyment of beautiful objects and of human intercourse took precedence over traditional moral acts. Keynes admitted that they bastardized Moore (ironically, Joan Robinson accused modern Keynesians of bastardizing Keynes), stating, "What we got from Moore was by no means entirely what he offered us.... We accepted Moore's religion ... and discarded his morals." Keynes also admitted that he and his friends saw little connection between having good states of mind and "doing good." Their attitude recalls the Quakers who, it is said, came to the United States to do good and ended up doing very well. The pseudo-Moore approach appeared aristocratic. How did they know which states of mind were good? If a disagreement arose, they usually concluded that some people simply had heightened senses of judgment, "just as some people can judge a vintage port and others cannot." Would general rules of morality ever bind them? No. "We repudiated entirely customary morals, conventions and traditional wisdom. We were . . . immoralists."[16] Perhaps this explains Keynes's 1905 letter revealing his interest in economics: "I want to manage a railway or organise a Trust, or at least swindle the investing public."[17]

In 1938, Keynes revealed that his "religion," despite some regrets, was "nearer the truth" than any other. The issue is not whether the religion was good or bad or a bastardization of Moore. The real issue: *Did Keynes contradict himself by embracing for himself a religion that exalted self-interested states of consciousness while assuming that others would foolishly cling to the moribund morality from which he had happily escaped?* He was either an elitist who assumed that others would not see the light, or he had contraverted himself. Keynes had little trouble conceiving of himself as part of an elite. Who could disagree? Regardless, Keynes provided little reason for assuming that politicians and bureaucrats would not act to enhance their states of consciousness at the public's expense in the same way that he apparently would.

Why didn't Keynes worry about runaway politicians and bureaucrats? Two reasons are central. First, Keynes seemed to hold a Weberian view of politics and bureaucracy: The politician, although not bound by an absolutist Kantian ethic (*fiat justitia, ruat caelum*—do good even if the heavens fall), is still bound by an ethic of responsibility—that is, consequentialism (*salus populi suprema lex esto*—the public good is the supreme law). He cannot ignore the consequences of flouting the public interest for private gain. Keynes also embraced Weber's vision of the bureaucrat who faithfully and dispassionately follows orders. States Weber: "The honor of the civil servant is vested in his ability to execute conscientiously the order of the superior authorities, exactly as if the order agreed with his own conviction."[18] Of course, as Weber stressed, this was an ideal type, and such purity was not likely to be found in reality. Nonetheless, Keynes often seemed to assume he was dealing with ideal types.

Second, Keynes absorbed the Harvey Road presupposition that the government would be ruled by an intellectual aristocracy, which would soar above crass self-interest and instead engage in highbrow debate about pressing social issues (over vintage port, no doubt). Keynes's contact with government officials, Bank of England directors, and leaders of other prominent British institutions frequently resembled Oxford-Cambridge reunions. Though these representatives may not have been Apostle material, they were competent preachers for the cause of public good. No wonder Keynes proclaims in *The General Theory*: "The power of vested interests is vastly exaggerated compared with the gradual encroachment of ideas."[19] But Keynes never asks the classic question: Who will guard the guardians? Nor does he ask whether Cambridge and Oxford could produce enough Apostles, priests, and choirboys to fill all the positions he envisions and faithfully spread the gospel as the government expands.

Perhaps Keynes's impressions of government were sound, considering the British civil service prior to World War II. If so, we can blame him only for not *predicting* that state officials would begin to act selfishly. Keynes saw many cases in which government officials refused to act in a politically expedient way. Time after time he saw civil servants stick to old beliefs and spurn new, attractive positions. In 1925, the British government, at the expense of unemployment, returned to pre-1914 gold parity. A few years later, Keynes denounced the government for refusing to boost public spending. Why did politicians resist? Certainly not because high unemployment made them more popular, more powerful, or more wealthy. Keynes thought they had good motives but terrible economic convictions. Essentially, political leaders and civil servants believed the laissez-faire doctrine they had been taught. The highest hurdles were stubbornness and inertia, not overween-ing ambition. In letters and articles written in the depths of the Great Depression, Keynes accused ministers of clinging to maxims and watchwords that dated from before World War I. In the path of economic growth stood "nothing but a few old gentlemen tightly buttoned-up in their frock coats, who only need to be treated with a little friendly disrespect and bowled over like ninepins." The civil service also blocked progress. And Keynes announced that civil servants were more impor-tant than ministers for constructive action. In fact, "little that is worth doing can be done without their assistance and good will. . . . The Civil Service is ruled today by the Treasury school, trained by tradition and experience and native skill to every form of intelligent obstruction. . . . They cramp our energy, and spoil or discard our ideas." The serfdom nightmares of Hayek and Buchanan would seem silly to Keynes, for ministers and civil servants "spend their time, not in forging chains for us—far from it—but in finding plausible reasons for *not doing things which public opinion almost overwhelmingly demands*" (em-phasis added).[20]

Thus, Keynes sees government officials deliberately avoid-ing opportunities to increase their power and maximize votes through public spending. He never came close to warning of future abuse, other than drolly declaring that once the be-frocked gentlemen abandoned the defrocked and defunct laissez-faire position, they would "quite likely enjoy it . . . when they have got over the shock."[21] Public Choice proponents de-clare that they liked it too much and too often.

Keynes also demonstrated his academic rearing with his firm faith in rational deliberation. If political or academic foes disagreed with him, they must be thinking incorrectly. He could change their minds through persuasion. Keynes admitted that his faith was excessive and blamed Moore's in-fluence. Keynes confesses: "We completely misunderstood hu-man nature, including our own. The rationality which we attributed to it led to a superficiality not only of judgment, but also of feeling . . . intellectually we were pre-Freudian. . . . I still suffer incurably from attributing an unreal rationality to other people's feelings and behaviour (and doubtless my own, too)."[22] (Although, compared with today's Rational Expectations theorists, Keynes looks like a swami mystic!)

Because he usually assumed noble motives and rationality, Keynes almost always attributed bad policy to bad logic (or at least habit based on bad logic, as with the "old gentlemen"). *The Collected Writings* bulge with letters accusing officials of implementing stupid and illogical programs, but never of venal or selfish acts. He called the stringent peace forced on the Germans after World War I a "serious act of political unwisdom." When the chancellor of the exchequer restored the pegged gold value, Keynes asked why Churchill would "do such a silly thing" and blamed misinformed experts. In 1928, he sent a pithy missive to Churchill along with an article:

Dear Chancellor of the Exchequer:
   What an imbecile currency bill you have introduced!

Churchill graciously replied that he would reflect on Keynes's enclosed article.[23]

Sometimes Keynes grew exasperated at officials who did not deduce correctly. On these occasions he would accuse opponents of lunacy, or he would desperately grope for reasoned explanations. Still, he did not question motives. As early as 1911 he wrote to his friend Duncan Grant: "You haven't I suppose ever mixed with politicians at close quarters. They're awful . . . Their stupidity is inhuman."[24]

Along with a faith in rational discourse, Keynes embraced faith in the power of persuasion. The golden rule of his faith was that he could persuade better than anybody else. The golden rule frequently proved right. Starting in the 1920s, Keynes often fired off letters to editors of newspapers and magazines, including the *Manchester Guardian*, *The Nation*, and *The Times* of London. According to Lionel Robbins of the

London School of Economics, Keynes replied to the tricky issue of removing temporary tariffs by stating: "I have never yet spoken on the problem."[25] Hayek frequently tells of an encounter a few weeks before Keynes's death in 1946. Keynes assured him that if his theories, designed for the 1930s, ever became harmful, he would quickly change public opinion. According to Hayek, Keynes believed that "he could play on public opinion as a virtuoso plays on his instrument."[26] Keynes himself reflected on his exaggerated assumption of human rationality and a "small but extraordinarily silly manifestation . . . namely, the impulse to *protest*—to write a letter to *The Times*, call a meeting in the Guildhall, subscribe to some fund. . . . I behave as if there really existed some authority or standard to which I can successfully appeal if I shout loud enough—perhaps it is some hereditary vestige of a belief in the efficacy of prayer."[27]

In sum, Keynes's experiences and influences persuaded him that politicians and bureaucrats, though sometimes stubborn and often stupid, work for the public good as they perceive it. Furthermore, they err on the side of *inaction*. Finally, even if empty-headed, the public is open-minded and can be persuaded to the correct position. These principles drove Keynes away from Public Choice precepts. But if cultural and intellectual influences are not deterministic influences, we can still hold Keynes accountable for accepting them so fully.

A Political Invisible Hand

Perhaps Keynes did not question the motivation of politicians and bureaucrats because he implicitly embraced a political invisible hand that ensured a confluence between political self-interest and the public good. For example, a politician may advocate policy X only because it is popular and will maximize votes. But it may be popular because the public correctly perceives its desiderata. Thus, the public gets what it wants, and what it wants is good. And the politician gets what he wants, even though he cared little about the act he performed.

Prior to World War II, a political invisible hand might have been viable. If so, Keynes's political naivete would have been *irrelevant*, for the government would flout the public good only out of conviction (as in the "Treasury" view) but not out of greed or venality. Greed would lead officials to the correct policy, or at least the popular policy. Machiavelli, whom Leo Strauss identified as the first modern political philosopher, redefined the term "virtue." Whereas to the medieval Scholastics virtue signified moral perfection, to Machiavelli it implied virtuosity, perfection in achieving a set of ends, regardless of justice, magnanimity, etc.[28]

Keynes's portrayal of George, Clemenceau, and Wilson at the Paris Peace Conference raises the issue of the political invisible hand. Few books depict so vividly such varied characters. In Keynes's view, the world sent two virtuosos and one virtuous man to the summit. Clemenceau was "aesthetically the noblest" and most determined to press for a hard peace. Intellectually the subtlest, George was a "Welsh witch," a goat-footed, half-human "visitor to our age from the hag-ridden magic enchanted woods of Celtic antiquity." Wilson was a "muddle-headed old Presbyterian," yet morally the noblest. Despite such striking contradictions, each character in this play was motivated to promote his national interest, as expressed by his public. Clemenceau wanted to smash Germany's ability to again surpass France. George wanted to impress the English citizenry with severe terms. Wilson wanted to achieve a magnanimous peace, much desired in the United States. Unfortunately, Clemenceau and George, the two virtuosos, were able to persuade Wilson that an austere peace was not austere but magnanimous. At the end, states Keynes, George realized the plan was too cruel, but "it was harder to debamboozle this old Presbyterian than it had been to bamboozle him."[29] Although each came to the meeting with completely different motivations, Clemenceau and George were led by a political invisible hand to serve their nations' interests, as the respective publics defined it. The virtuous Presbyterian would have done so anyway.

If the political invisible hand loses its grip, however, Keynes's political naivete finally appears damning, and he might be blamed for not predicting this fatal slip. Why? Because ordinary, systemic forces lurk behind the slip. It is not simply a shocking, demonic act.

Why would political self-interest diverge from the public interest? As government expands into microtransactions through regulations, subsidies, tariffs, and grants, information costs rise not only for government but also for the public. That is, citizens who want to be informed about public spending and policy must invest more time and effort gathering information. For most citizens, the investment will be economically irrational, because the information costs exceed the benefits to them. One may spend an entire day investigating a program that awards one hundred people $1 million. Yet the per capita value of eliminating or augmenting the program may be about the same as the price of a bag of potato chips. The citizen who is not among the one hundred and does not investigate is probably rationally ignorant. *Thus, a trend toward government expansion is a trend toward separating the acts of politicians from the knowledge of the public.* Officials can do more, both good and bad, without the public's knowledge. Such acts slip through the fingers of the political invisible hand.

The U.S. government accounts for more than one-fifth of the gross national product. Furthermore, federal agencies and regulations permeate society. Since so many groups have access to the federal government, the costs of exploiting the political system have plunged. No one needs to stand on a soapbox and persuade a majority of fellow citizens or of the legislature to act. A social meeting with a few commissioners will do. A box of four seats at Yankee Stadium will do far more than a soapbox in Central Park.

Originally, checks and balances among branches of government and interest groups were supposed to prevent influence peddlers. James Madison's *Federalist* no. 10 argued that a constitution should make it unprofitable for a faction to exploit the political system for economic gain. But pervasive federal power has weakened Madison's plan.

The political invisible hand loses its grip in a complex world. Democracy is not a precise political analogue of a free economic market. As Nobel laureate Kenneth Arrow taught, voting for a candidate is not equivalent to buying a product. Economists cannot design a logical political system that mirrors the market.[30] In a democracy, voters do not buy a particular product like a microwave oven. They buy a package—a candidate who they hope will usually vote as they would. In truth, the voter is not sure what she will get. Democracy is somewhere between a supermarket and a grab bag.

By advocating for a substantial increase in public spending and intervention, Keynes indirectly weakened the grip of the political invisible hand, which exposes the danger in trusting the motives of officials. In Keynes's time, public knowledge and long-standing rules helped enforce the good motives of civil servants. If Keynes envisaged any checks on political abuse, it was through the campaign process in which an administration would have to answer to opposition charges.[31] This check certainly makes sense. Nonetheless, it ignores the power of unelected bureaucrats to expand their influence regardless of the ruling elected regime, as well as the fact that attacking small programs (on a per capita basis) may not make for catchy campaign slogans.

The charge against Keynes resulting from his implicit assumption of a political invisible hand has both microeconomic and macroeconomic dimensions. On the microeconomic side, officials can twist spending programs and regulations for political self-interest when information costs to voters are high compared with benefits derived. These costs rise as the government expands operations. Moreover, to the extent that people do not see the harm from indirect effects of microeconomic transactions between the government and others, they discount the benefits of obtaining knowledge about government action. On the macroeconomic side, public finance will be prejudiced toward low taxes and high government spending, again to the extent that voters undervalue the indirect costs and benefits of fiscal and monetary policy. The argument is probably stronger for the microeconomic abuses, as those depend more on rational ignorance than on irrationality or illusion.

Verdict on Keynes

If Public Choice theory is correct, Keynes was politically ingenuous. Even if Public Choice theory is only partially correct, Keynes still seems blind to the issues raised. Even his admirer Harrod conceded this.[32] Yet based on Keynes's experiences with the British civil service and the historical context, we can blame him only for not predicting political abuse of his program. Moreover, critics of Keynes should carefully separate the political and Public Choice critique from the critique of his economic theory. To point an indignant, distrusting finger at politicians does not successfully argue that Keynes's economics was wrong. This would be like denying that water puts out fire because firefighters are too lazy to leave their dart games. To the extent that Keynes's economics was correct, he gave us water to extinguish economic fires. But he should have sounded a few more alarms.

CHAPTER XII

The Wild World of Rational Expectations and Behavioral Economics

Ready for a truly wacky-sounding theory? How about a theory that does not believe in involuntary unemployment? How about a theory that promotes dart throwing as a method of choosing stocks? How about a theory that does not believe that the government can hurt or help the economy very much? What a bizarre ending to our study of economic history! We began with the mercantilists, who said government generally helps the economy. Then Smithians said government hurts. Keynesians said government helps. Monetarists said government can help but often hurts. Public Choice economists said that government usually hurts. Now the Rational Expectations (or New Classical) economists laugh at all their predecessors and proclaim that government intervention is an illusion, like a magician's trick, which cannot change reality very much.

To reach this startling conclusion, New Classical economists follow some tricky logic. When they finish, however, they have a neat model that is admirable for its theoretical beauty. Their critics, though, look scornfully at the pristine but unrealistic model, better suited for an art gallery than for the Council of Economic Advisers.

The old guard of economists—the Tobins, Samuelsons, and Friedmans—find their life's work belittled by these newcomers, who trace their origins to a 1961 paper by a young Carnegie

Tech professor named John Muth. The youthful Rational Expectations movement attracts a significant proportion of young model-building scholars, charmed by its mathematical precision and opportunities for new discoveries. Old Keynesians fear that the new scholars will leave them behind, just as they surpassed the classical teachers who refused to follow Keynes during the Great Depression. The challenge to mainstream economics is to mine Rational Expectations for bits of truth and then add these to mainstream theory.

Let's find out why no one completely dismisses Rational Expectations theory. Its first tenet states that all markets clear, meaning that prices always adjust simultaneously to get rid of any surplus or shortage. No gluts may exist. If fish produce too much caviar, the price will fall. If demand for labor falls, wages will plunge. Now, most economists agree that markets eventually clear, but monetarists and Keynesians allow for longer transitions. Keynesians point to "sticky wages." Monetarists point to lags in the transmission of monetary policy. Baloney, say the Young Turks.

Second, they contend that people consider all available information in making economic decisions and continually update their models or expectations of the economy. Compare old-fashioned adaptive expectations with rational expectations. If people act adaptively, they look at the past behavior of variables and only gradually adjust their outlook. If prices have risen at 6 percent per year for the past few years, yet rise 10 percent this year, people might expect prices to rise 7 percent next year under the adaptive model, which heavily emphasizes past data. They wait for experience to knock them on the heads rather than change their expectations on the basis of new information. What if they heard that the federal government had unleashed the money supply and fiscal spending for a wildly expansionary policy? Under adaptive expectations, they would not vary their predictions until they had seen hard evidence.

Suppose that the cartoon character Wile E. Coyote waits on

the corner of Hollywood and Vine for a bus to take him home. Past experience teaches him to take two steps away from the bus stop at 5:30 p.m. every day, because every day at that time a five-ton anvil accidentally drops fifty stories from the roof of the Acme Anvil Company. One day Wile E. waits at the corner. The anvil falls fifteen minutes late and squashes him at 5:45. If Wile E. has adaptive expectations, what will he do the next day at 5:45? He will stand at the bus stop again, thinking that the anvil seldom falls at 5:45 p.m. Squashed again. Finally, after a week of flattening (as can only happen to cartoon characters), he may get the idea that the Acme schedule has changed.

What if Wile E. had rational expectations? After the first hit, he would walk up to the anvil factory as soon as he popped back into three dimensions and find out what was going on. He would reformulate his schedule. He would forget the past data if new information made them obsolete.

John Muth, the shy, awkward man who sparked rational expectations, was raised in the Midwest and built his reputation on hogs. By studying hogs, Muth learned economics from the ground up and never seemed interested in the glory achieved by some of his glittering colleagues, who included Nobel laureates Herbert Simon, Franco Modigliani, Merton Miller, and John Nash, the subject of the book and movie *A Beautiful Mind*. Modigliani praised Muth's mind but said that the bearded, slightly hunchbacked researcher "took pains to appear as an oddball."[1] At one point, while teaching at Indiana University's business school, his MBA students marched into the dean's office waving a petition to have Muth fired because he befuddled them with his brilliant but seemingly impenetrable mathematics.

What in the world did hogs have to do with higher math? Before Muth came along, most people believed that hog markets suffered wild, irrational booms and busts. When bacon was expensive, every farmer seemed to respond by raising more hogs. Then all the hogs would simultaneously stampede onto the market, sending bacon prices into a tailspin. Now faced with low prices, farmers would purportedly stop raising hogs, which once again led to a shortage and expensive bacon. "Hog-wash!" Muth concluded. He dug up data on hog prices, and showed that farmers were not so stupid as to assume that to-day's high prices would guarantee high promises tomorrow.[2] Farmers were rational, Muth said, disproving John Kenneth Galbraith's view that farmers had strong backs and weak minds.

If people have rational expectations, they will not make systematic mistakes. They may be fooled or surprised once, but they will work to prevent a second error. As *Star Trek*'s engineer Scotty put it, "Fool me once, shame on you; fool me twice, shame on me."

Tossing Darts at Brokers

The stock market provides the most persuasive evidence of rational expectations. Academic economists report that the stock market almost instantaneously absorbs information. In other words, once information becomes public, share prices instantly reflect it. If yesterday you read online that Tiffany's expects a good year, you're too late to take advantage of the information. Tiffany's stock will have risen immediately on the basis of next year's outlook, and information that everyone has is useless. In another example, suppose you cleverly observe that millions of college students flock from Boston to New York right before Thanksgiving. You discover that Kiddy Airlines carries many of the students. In September, two months before the Thanksgiving rush, you buy Kiddy stock, expecting that in November the price will skyrocket. Dumb move. The price of Kiddy stock already reflects the expected profits during Thanksgiving. Everyone knows that Thanksgiving is a good time for Kiddy. And prices are based on the expected profits and dividends, not just on current financial data.

If this model, called the Efficient Market Hypothesis, is

correct, you cannot beat the average return on stocks by religiously following companies, reading financial returns, or tracing past price movements. The market already efficiently estimates the future returns. Stocks cannot be "overvalued" or "undervalued" (unless just about everyone misunderstands some characteristic of the company, or there is undisclosed information). The market price becomes an infallible icon, until new information justifies a new price. (Nonetheless, the stock market "crash" of October 1987, the collapse of technology stocks in 2000–2002, and the financial meltdown of 2008 probably indicate that primordial "animal spirits" still lurk beneath the crisp white shirts of stock traders.)

You'd probably do just as well to choose a stock by throwing a stockbroker against a dartboard as to listen to his advice—and you'd save money. Here's a plan, consistent with the Efficient Market Hypothesis, for doing as well as famous stock advisers: Place two bowls of dog food in front of your dog—one with the name IBM glued on the front, the other with Mobil. Now buy stock in the company that the pet goes to. If she isn't hungry, place your money in a corporate bond fund.

The snorting bull market of the 1990s, which pushed the Dow Jones average from 3,500 in 1993 to 11,700 in January 2000 to 27,000 in 2020, left money managers in the dust, as passive "index" funds outperformed almost every professional stock picker. By the time people pay for advertising expenses, research costs, and commissions, the vast majority of mutual funds return a little bit less than a big dartboard. Paul Samuelson long ago suggested that "most portfolio decision makers should go out of business—take up plumbing, teach Greek." Of course, according to the Efficient Market Hypothesis, a bad portfolio manager would not muck things up too much (since it takes extraordinary ineptitude to perform *far* worse than the proverbial dart thrower), whereas a bad plumber could do some real damage!

Plenty of brokers and publicists rave about their predictions. Careful studies uncover little reason to believe them.[3] Sure, some may enjoy lucky streaks. But Las Vegas bettors sometimes beat the odds also. The point is not that brokers usually lose money. The point is that they do not consistently beat the average. Even when some superstar analyst discovers a winning way to interpret data, others follow, and the method becomes obsolete. So why pay extra money in commissions and financial advice for an average return? You might as well obtain a well-diversified portfolio that balances various risks, or invest in a broad market index that moves with the market average. Faced with this logic, in 2019 major brokerage houses like Charles Schwab cut their commissions on stock trades to zero.

Rational Expectations theorists, including the 1995 Nobel laureate Robert Lucas and Thomas Sargent, state that government has little power over markets. They start with the stock market and then analogize to wider markets in the economy. What if the government tries to temporarily raise the price of Kiddy Airlines by buying shares? The original price represents the current, "correct" feeling about future earnings and dividends, which would give a fair rate of return. If the government buys stock and bids up the price, shareholders will immediately sense that the stock is artificially overvalued and will sell. If the government dumps its stock, forcing down the price too far, investors will buy, sensing that the stock deserves a higher price. In the end, no matter what the government does, the price will return to its "correct" value unless new information convinces investors that a new price is justified.

Before applying the analogy to macroeconomics, let's examine two important points. First, note that the Efficient Market Hypothesis does not include inside information, secret knowledge of future profits or losses that company officials may have. Investors with nonpublic information may achieve higher-than-average gains. This seems logical but unfair. The poor slob without a seat on the board of directors will not reap the same gains as insiders. For this reason, insider trading is illegal. The Securities and Exchange Commission monitors stock trading by insiders and establishes penalties for illegal activity, including prison terms and the "disgorging" of profits. Of course, not everyone gets caught, nor do the laws cover everyone with inside information. Should they? In 2004, Martha Stewart, a cultural icon known for such dangerous work as decorating her home with Christmasy pine cones and coaching television viewers on how to torch crème brûlée, spent five months in prison and more time under house arrest because her stockbroker's assistant told her that a pharmaceutical company president had sold his own shares in the company. The president had inside information that the FDA was going to turn down its drug approval application. Stewart was convicted, not for selling her shares in the company but for lying to the FBI about her conversation with her broker's assistant. Her case was memorialized in the film *Martha Stewart: Behind Bars.*

Suppose Fido Inc. surreptitiously plans to take over the Spot Corporation by buying its stock. Fido managers will run Spot more efficiently, thus boosting the value of Spot's assets. For this reason, Fido is willing to pay a higher price for the stock. Spot shareholders who sell their stock will earn lots of money. The takeover plan is a secret. Only the presidents and vice presidents of Fido and their attorneys know. Naturally, if Fido's chief officers personally buy Spot stock before the takeover attempt is publicized, they can be arrested for insider trading. But what if the employee of a printing press that prints the forthcoming publicity documents buys Spot stock before the public announcement? Should he be considered an insider and punished? According to the Supreme Court, no.

Ironically, when Vincent Chiarella, the printer acquitted by the Supreme Court, was asked whether Ivan Boesky, who was convicted of insider trading a few years later, should be punished, he said, Throw the book at him.[4]

A second important point about the Efficient Market Hypothesis brings up another irony. *Stock picking is ineffective because so many people engage in research and stock analysis.* The current prices "correctly" reflect expectations *because* so many people buy and sell on the basis of available information. You have little chance of consistently interpreting the information in a superior way. If no one but you researched, however, you could outpredict a random approach. Therefore, the advice of Efficient Market believers to select randomly becomes itself obsolete if everyone takes the advice!

Economists on Wall Street

Until fairly recently, Wall Street managers and economists found little to talk to one another about. After all, economists like Samuelson were dousing portfolio managers with frigid water, telling them to take up plumbing. While Princeton professor Burton Malkiel wrote a book espousing the Efficient Markets Hypothesis titled *A Random Walk Down Wall Street*, Wall Street titans told economists to take a hike. The movers and shakers replied that academicians were simply too timid to bet on winners and losers in the financial markets. And most of them, outside of Keynes, did not succeed when they did get the nerve to roll the dice.

While some economists were deriding Wall Street's stock-picking powers, others were devising inventive ways to design portfolios and to put a value on companies and stock options. These were extremely difficult technical challenges, requiring advanced mathematics and economics. The problem for the researchers, though, was that in the 1960s and 1970s, no single discipline wanted them. Economists thought their work was too technical, and mathematicians thought their research too mundane. No matter, in 1990 the Nobel Committee awarded the Nobel Prize in Economics to three pathbreaking financial economists who actually sought to help Wall Street rather than tear it down.

In 1952, a young graduate student named Harry Markowitz

began a revolution in finance by publishing a paper called "Portfolio Selection." The paper built an analytical framework for a simple aphorism, "Don't put all your eggs in one basket." At first this seems so obvious that you might be inclined to deliver the Nobel Prize to Mother Goose's or Aesop's heirs. Five hundred years ago, Shakespeare's merchant of Venice told us that

> My ventures are not in one bottom trusted,
> Nor to one place; nor is my whole estate
> Upon the fortune of the present year;
> Therefore my merchandise makes me not sad.

Still, this folk wisdom was little more than a wives' tale or a rule of thumb until Markowitz put his mind to work. In fact, the great Keynes rejected the notion, arguing that a big investment in a company you know well is safer than many smaller investments. Markowitz did not simply show that more is better—that a portfolio is safer with stocks of five airlines. He demonstrated that the *kind* of stocks should be diverse. Your investments should truly be diverse—that is, not correlated with each other. Better to own stock in Delta Airlines and Johnson & Johnson rather than in two airlines or two pharmaceutical companies. Despite initial doubts, Wall Street has been following Markowitz's lessons for the past fifty years.

It's not easy to be a pathbreaker, though. Markowitz tells how Milton Friedman worried Markowitz when the graduate student had to defend his dissertation. Markowitz had been telling himself, "I knew this deal cold. Not even Milton Friedman can give me a hard time." A few minutes into his defense, though, Friedman piped up: "Harry, I don't see anything wrong with the math here, but I have a problem. This isn't a dissertation in economics, and we can't give you a Ph.D. in economics for a dissertation that's not economics. It's not math, it's not economics, it's not even business administration." Then others spoke the same complaint. Markowitz sat in the hall to await the committee's decision. Minutes later, a senior professor walked into the hallway, looked him in the eye, and said, "Congratulations, Dr. Markowitz!"[5]

Markowitz's co-laureates in 1990 were William Sharpe of Stanford and Merton Miller of the University of Chicago. Sharpe designed the Capital Asset Pricing Model, which warrants at least one chapter in every book on corporate finance, as well as the concept of *beta*, which helps investors figure out how risky a particular stock may be. In particular, beta tells you whether a stock will move in sync with the market as a whole. Starbucks has a beta of 1.0, which means that if the New York Stock Exchange rises by 10 percent, Starbucks shares will likely climb 10 percent too. That makes sense, since a strong market signals a strong economy, and consumers can afford to buy fancy coffee if they are feeling richer. Other kinds of stocks may have a low beta. People will keep buying candy even if the economy sours. No surprise, then, that Tootsie Roll has a lower beta of just 0.51, meaning that if the overall market falls by 10 percent, this candy company will slip by about half that proportion. When people look to diversify their portfolios, they keep track of the beta calculations to make sure that all their stocks do not go up—and down—together.

Merton Miller achieved his fame by studying the way corporations organize themselves. Prior to Miller's work with Franco Modigliani, many corporate treasurers thought that their firms would look more profitable if they funded their operations by issuing more bonds and selling fewer shares of stock. That way, a smaller number of shareholders would split the profits among themselves. Miller and Modigliani showed, though, that no matter how you slice up the ownership, the total value of the firm depends on the future earnings. If, for example, the firm got loaded up with debt (issued a lot of bonds), lenders would demand higher interest payments, which would offset the benefit of having fewer shareholders.[6]

Miller offered a colorful analogy that begins with a tub of

whole milk. The farmer could sell the cream separately, which fetches a higher price. But then he would be left with only skim milk, which sells for less. The cream plus the skim would bring the same total revenues as the whole milk. A tub of milk is a tub of milk, no matter how you mix it. Likewise, a stream of corporate profits is a stream of profits, no matter who you pay it to.

By focusing their economic training on financial markets, the three 1990 Nobel laureates enriched Wall Street, and didn't do so badly themselves! Sharpe and Miller have consulted with many of the leading firms on Wall Street. John C. Bogle, chairman of the famous Vanguard Group of mutual funds, admonished investors not to ignore the economists: "While there is a lot of witchcraft in the academic lore . . . the most solid academic thinking, however complex, abstruse . . . will find its way into actual practice, and into the investor marketplace as well."[7]

Alas, even Nobel laureates must learn humility. The two 1997 Nobel laureates, Robert Merton and Myron Scholes, who won for their work in valuing financial derivatives, joined a high-flying investment group called Long-Term Capital Management. Their fund crashed in August 1998, disrupting financial markets throughout the world. The firm had recklessly borrowed far too much money and placed massive bets that world interest rates would move closer together. They bet wrong and racked up billions of dollars in losses. Long-Term Capital proved not so durable after all, losing its capital within days. Can we blame Merton's and Scholes's Nobel Prizes? Possibly. After all, the banks that lent Long-Term Capital so much money felt confident such luminaries and their illustrious partners would not misjudge risk. Einstein may have been the greatest scientific mind of the century, but you probably would not have wanted him to change your radiator fluid. Likewise, just because people have Nobel Prizes does not mean that you should hand over your money to them.

The Lucas Critique

Before disputing Rational Expectations theory, let's follow its striking implications for the macroeconomy. Remember that rational actors continually update their model of the economy. Therefore, the first lesson is that econometric models are obsolete because they are based on past data, and statistical models cannot predict the effect of a new government policy. For example, if the government finds a stable, historic relationship between baseball games and GDP and therefore attempts to raise GDP by increasing the number of baseball games, economic actors will see this policy as new information and refine their model. Thus, their old behavior provides a poor basis for creating new policy. This implication is known as the Lucas Critique.[8] Robert Lucas, a professor at the University of Chicago, proved to be *too* good a teacher of rational expectations. When the Nobel Committee in Stockholm announced his prize in October 1995, his ex-wife's lawyer revealed that *she had foreseen* his possible winning. Seven years before, she inserted a clause in their divorce settlement to claim half his Nobel Prize money, should he win. That clause, based on her rational expectations, was worth $500,000.

Following the Lucas Critique, Robert Hall submits that mainstream models of consumption that rely on past income, wealth, interest rates, and inflation fail to predict as well as a simple model with only two factors: last year's consumption and a random variable. Hall argues that the only difference between next year's and this year's consumption levels can be explained by random surprises—that is, new information.[9]

The second lesson trashes the government's stabilization policy: only a surprise strategy has any effect. Suppose the economy tumbles into a deep recession marked by high unemployment. Mainstream economists would likely urge an expansionary policy. According to most economists, higher aggregate demand would lead to higher output and more hiring, and the economy would climb out of the doldrums.

Not according to Rational Expectation theorists. They argue that actors have learned that the federal government always leaps in to cure recessions by boosting demand. Rather than allow their prices to fall during the recession or raise their output, therefore, firms will simply raise their prices. *They anticipate government policy.* Since higher demand is just around the corner, they have learned not to let prices fall in a recession. It is as if the government passed a law that whenever unemployment reaches 7 percent, the Federal Reserve Board will press on the monetary accelerator. As evidence for their argument, theorists show that recessions prior to World War II saw prices fall, whereas post–World War II recessions, under the anticipation of demand-side responses, saw more stable prices. The Employment Act of 1946 guaranteeing maximum employment virtually notified firms that Uncle Sam always comes to the rescue. In sum, if Uncle Sam does what he is expected to do, he ends up doing nothing. Only surprise moves will affect the level of output.

Imagine how this theory shocks Keynesians and monetarists. Their advice appears as useless as the comedian Gracie Allen's absurd offer to solve the California–Florida border dispute.

Here's another shocker. If this theory is right, the Federal Reserve Board should find it easy to reduce the inflation rate. Why? Under mainstream approaches, a contractionary policy will first lead to a recession and finally to a reduction in inflation. Under rational expectations, though, if a credible Federal Reserve Board announces that the money supply will grow at zero percent, people will automatically expect lower prices and reduce their prices and wages. They will automatically accept a lower inflation rate based on the Fed's policy. Since they do not have adaptive expectations, they need not see a wrenching recession before they reduce their price predictions.

Now that Rational Expectations has thoroughly insulted Keynesians and monetarists, let's briefly look at the barbed arrows they shoot at Public Choice economists. James Buchanan maintains that politicians foster deficit spending and therefore cheat future generations. Bruno Frey, another Public Choice economist, maintains that political cycles exist in democracies, with politicians manipulating inflation and unemployment in order to win elections.

Both these claims clash with Rational Expectations theory. First, take the Political Cycle theory. Say politicians try to toy with policy tools in order to lift election chances. According to Rational Expectations, voters will catch on after the first attempt. They will figure out that a booming economy in an election year presages high inflation, and they will take steps that will spoil the false prosperity, for they will quickly learn that the government will slam on the brakes after the election. This explanation makes sense and probably explains the rather flimsy evidence for consistent political cycles. As for persistent budget deficits, Harvard economist Robert Barro argues (on behalf of Rational Expectations theory) that investors and savers calculate future burdens into long-term interest rates.[10] Higher long-term interest rates surely affect the performance of the economy in the present. Thus, future aspirations and expectations are actually represented in today's capital markets. Barro's argument actually descends from David Ricardo (and is called *Ricardian equivalence*); he noted that public debt and taxes are quite similar, since rational people know that the debt will have to be repaid at some point in higher taxes. Therefore, government bonds used to finance deficits push up future expectations about taxes. A Public Choice economist like James Buchanan would respond by noting that future generations have no *political* voice yet, even if they have an indirect voice in the bond market. After all, Buchanan sees the issue as a moral question as much as an economic one.

In recent years the Japanese Ministry of Finance has cited

Ricardian equivalence to explain why it cannot spur the economy by simply writing checks to the public. Since Japan is so indebted (its debt-to-GDP ratio tops the international comparison charts at about 200 percent), the Finance Ministry believes that Japanese households hoard extra income, because they know that someday they, or their children, will need to pay back the staggering debt.

Incidentally, Rational Expectations theorists can muster evidence that people catch on to political tricksters. Consider Margaret Thatcher in the early 1980s, who pledged to reduce the British budget deficit and even raised taxes in the middle of a recession in order to keep her promise. Might her two re-elections show that Britons had figured out and rejected the freewheeling policies of the old Labour Party?

The Rational Expectations professors get an assist in the real world from "bond vigilantes." What is this notorious-sounding gang? They don't carry guns or knives, but they can make a country's finance minister tremble in his boots. Bond vigilantes are traders and investors who buy and sell government bonds based on a country's economic performance and outlook. They can play a useful role in disciplining reckless governments. In the early 1990s, bond and foreign exchange traders looked at Sweden and saw a weak economy, a huge trade deficit, a bloated government sector, and a currency that was so strong that Swedish exporters could not compete abroad. In a few years, public debt had doubled and the deficit had multiplied tenfold. Sweden was teetering. Vigilant traders foresaw the country hurtling toward a future in which it could not afford to repay its debts to the rest of the world.[11] Skandia, a giant Swedish financial firm, announced it was "boycotting government bonds in light of the record budget deficit and fast-rising debt."[12] Bond and foreign exchange traders outside Sweden began dumping Swedish assets and driving up interest rates, and frightened the government into radically restructuring its finances. Faced with so many forward-looking traders, the government slashed the deficit from a mind-boggling

12 percent of GDP in 1994 to 2.6 percent in 1997, and then to an actual surplus in 1999. Since the mid-1990s, Sweden has looked like a ferocious competitor in international markets. Give the bond vigilantes some grudging credit.

The Mainstream Strikes Back

Finally, it is time to lash back at Rational Expectations theory, and it does deserve some lashes. Almost every economist feels insulted by the upstarts. We will first discuss some theoretical difficulties and then turn to real economic events.

Rational Expectations theorists can be an intimidating, frustrating lot to argue with. Like Koran-thumping fundamentalist Shi'ites, they have a quick, adamant answer for any question. Their works contain many freaky assumptions, such as instantaneously adjusting markets and superhuman capacities to absorb information. If we grant these assumptions, the theory appears impenetrable. How can we attack? To demolish an economic model, we must do more than laugh at unrealistic assumptions. As Milton Friedman (following Karl Popper) argued, the true test of a model is in its *predictions*, not its scrupulously faithful depiction of the actual economy.[13]

Around the same time that Rational Expectations theory started gaining traction, Joseph Stiglitz and George Akerlof (2001 Nobel laureates) were pointing to a frequent problem in business deals, namely that one party often knows much more than the other. For example, if you shop for a used car, the dealer is far more likely to know whether the car is a lemon than you are. An insurance company selling you fire insurance is far less likely than you to know whether you smoke in bed, or what you smoke. These "information asymmetries" complicate rationalist models.

In macroeconomics, Rational Expectations theory predicts that government stimulus does not spur the economy and that government contraction does not hurt. Let's start with the latter. How does 10.6 percent unemployment in 1982 sound? Following a monetary squeeze in 1980 and 1981, the economy plummeted into a recession. Following a similar crunch in 1975, the economy also slid downhill. It took severe unemployment rates to drive down inflationary expectations in those periods. Lucas and his cohorts might respond by deeming the monetary collapse a "surprise." "Who knew whether the Fed would stick to its tight intentions?" they might ask. Despite the rebuttal, it took quite a few long, depressing fiscal quarters before people adjusted their inflationary expectations. Rational Expectations theory is hollow if it can escape criticism by calling every economic event a surprise.

How about the government spurring the economy? If Rational Expectations theorists are right, tax cuts will not affect consumption when they are implemented. As soon as the tax bill is signed, people will adjust their consumption, even if the actual cut comes years later. Yet the Kennedy and Reagan tax cuts showed consumption stable and then rising after implementation. Alan Blinder, a Keynesian from Princeton, finds this snub of fiscal policy by the Rational Expectations theorists especially annoying: "Barro once said to me that there isn't any evidence in the world that fiscal policy is effective. Just open your eyes and see episodes of tax-cutting and government spending increases. How about World War II? That had big effects on output." Blinder also blasts the claim that markets always clear: "That also has to be ridiculous. Somehow, some people are able to look at the world and not see involuntary unemployment. I think I see it all over the place during cyclical downturns. I also think I see unsold goods all over the place, like automobile lots."[14] Can Rational Expectations defenders explain with a straight face the Great Depression as twelve years of "new," surprising information?

Why do most economists tend to agree with Rational Expectations theorists when they talk about the stock market yet explode in disagreement when speaking of the macroeconomy?

The fact is, the stock market is a more efficient market than most others. It is quite liquid—one can buy and sell easily. Transaction costs are few. An investor may even use a discount broker to handle his or her purchases. In contrast, real markets for goods and services show more complexity and rigidity. Can you quit your job as easily as you can sell stock? Can a corporation fire employees, close down a plant, or build a new plant as quickly and easily as one can buy and sell shares? Of course not.

In real markets, *contracts* play a large role. They increase the level of certainty regarding the nominal price of labor, capital, and equipment. But they reduce the degree of liquidity and flexibility. Even if Kiddy Airlines expects prices and salaries to fall, it may be bound by three-year union contracts to keep up salaries. *Even if its managers have rational expectations, contracts lock them into an adaptive path.* Critics of Rational Expectation actually ask two questions: (1) Do people have rational expectations rather than long-standing habits? (2) Even if they do have rational expectations, can they act as adroitly as they think? To the extent either answer is no, Rational Expectations theory incorrectly portrays the economy.

Behavioral Economics

Psychologists have also eagerly piled onto the stack of bodies trying to bury Rational Expectations. You can understand the eagerness of psychologists to jump in. After all, if people were perfectly rational, you would not need so many psychologists. With a great faith in reason, Immanuel Kant actually suggested that the insane should be tutored by philosophers. The insane reason badly. Therefore, experts in sound logic and reasoning would help them most. Since Kant's time, we have learned that when people are so deluded that they cannot reason clearly, they likely have gross emotional problems or, perhaps, chemical imbalances. Sitting them in a room with a Kant or Descartes might drive the philosopher crazy, rather than help the patient. Just as Kant may have overstressed the capacity of rational thought, so, too, might some economists. Let's say you are shopping for a new camera and discover that the ABC store sells the same model as the XYZ store but charges $200, which is $10 cheaper than XYZ's price. Most people will drive an extra mile to save the $10. Now let's say you are buying a new car and discover that the ABC dealership charges $30,080, which is $10 *more* than the XYZ dealer. Most people would ignore the difference. But $10 is $10, the psychologists point out—why should $10 off a camera lead you to drive a few blocks, while $10 off a car's price doesn't register on your brain waves?

Two Israeli researchers, who started developing their ideas while serving in the armed forces in the 1950s, compiled a virtual encyclopedia of irrational economic behavior based on interviews and real experience. Daniel Kahneman, who decades earlier (as a twenty-one-year-old lieutenant armed with only a bachelor's degree) had designed a psychological screening test for the Israeli army, and Amos Tversky showed that people will quickly switch from risk-averse to risk-seeking. They both knew a great deal about risk and fear. As a boy, Kahneman had escaped Nazi guards and their French collaborators while hiding in France with his family. Not all his family made it out alive, and at one point his father was sent to an internment camp, just one stop before execution. Though his father avoided the gas chamber, the family was constantly on the run and knew what it "felt like being hunted. We had the mentality of rabbits." This was not an abstract metaphor for the boy, since the family lived for some time in a chicken coop.[15] Tversky, who was a few years younger than Kahneman, was a true war hero. In 1956, he was a nineteen-year-old paratrooper in the Israeli Defense Forces when a young soldier placed a grenade at the base of a barbed-wire fence and then "froze" in place, literally lying on top of the explosive, unable to free himself. Knowing that the bomb would explode within seconds, the future expert on risk ran to the young man, picked up his body, and threw him to safety, just as the explosive burst, injuring Tversky. For that, the Israeli government awarded him the highest military honors.

Kahneman knew, of course, that people do not generally think like rabbits, but he was also fairly certain that they did not think like *homo economicus*, the thoroughly rational textbook model. After completing his service with the Israeli army, he focused on the connection between stress and the human body, and he published a novel study showing that when people are required to concentrate more intently, their pupils dilate.[16] Though he was trained as a psychologist, not an economist, it did not take long for him to surmise that if stress can change the size of one's pupils, it might also impact one's financial decisions. The two Israelis joined together and began developing their theories while working with Israeli fighter pilots. Here is an example of quirky but common economic thinking: A survey revealed that people would prefer to let inflation rise rather than permit the jobless rate to climb from 5 to 10 percent. Yet when instead asked whether they would prefer higher inflation rather than letting the employment rate fall from 95 to 90 percent, they said no.[17] The two choices are the same; only the phrasing and answers are different.

Likewise, another experiment asked participants how they would prefer combating an Asian disease outbreak. Program A would save two hundred people. Program B would have a one-third chance of saving six hundred and a two-thirds chance of saving nobody. Seventy-two percent of the respondents prized the certainty of Program A. People like certainty. Behavioral economists have discovered that people hate to lose and sometimes feel paralyzed into standing in place. Stock market investors hate to sell their shares at a small loss, even when they are warned that big losses could come. They may become emotionally attached to their stocks, their homes, and their jobs.[18]

A modest man who died of cancer in 1996, Tversky said that he examined things that every used-car salesman and advertiser already knew. How questions are semantically or mathematically framed can mean the difference between a bestseller and a flop. Tversky appeared on the front pages of newspapers in 1988 when he disproved the "hot hand" theory of basketball, demonstrating that a player making a basket did *not* have a greater chance of getting the next ball through the hoop. He examined every basket that the Philadelphia 76ers had scored in the past year and a half. (In 2018, however, other researchers reexamined the data and reached the opposite conclusion.)[19] Tversky's best work, though, was with his friend Kahneman, who said in his Nobel Prize autobiography essay, "Amos and I shared the wonder of together owning a goose that could lay golden eggs—a joint mind that was better than separate minds."[20]

For quite a few years, Richard Thaler, currently a professor at the University of Chicago, had described economic anomalies in *The Journal of Economic Perspectives*, which kicked off many classroom and faculty meeting discussions. But when the Nobel Committee awarded its 2002 prize to Kahneman, behavioral economics instantly became a star subject, attracting many more graduate students and corporate benefactors. Books like Daniel Ariely's *Predictably Irrational* and Kahneman's *Thinking, Fast and Slow* hit bestseller lists. Popular works tickled readers who learned of studies that found, for example, job interviewers who were handed a warm mug of coffee before meeting a job candidate were more likely to like the individual than interviewers who received a cool drink. Ariely and Kahneman both cited a study showing that when test subjects were exposed to words related to old age, like "bingo" and "ancient," they walked out of the room more slowly. The exposures to mugs and old-age terms somehow "primed" and "framed" their encounters and biased them. A more serious topic for economists is intertemporal choice, how people value the future. Behavioral economists suggest that people discount the future too much. They want instant gratification, which may lead them to ignore their shrinking retirement savings and their expanding waistlines. Behavioral economists point out that about one-third of American workers have ignored their company's 401(k) retirement savings plans, many of them leaving free money on the table if the employer matches their contribution. Using the research of behavioralists, in 2006 Congress passed and President Bush signed a law making it easier for companies to set up automatic enrollment. Previously, workers had to actively choose to participate. Now, eligible workers are automatically enrolled, unless they actively opt out. Rational Expectations thinkers do not spend much time worrying about inertia; behavioral economists do.

Intertemporal surveys can certainly confound. David Laibson, a Harvard behavioral economist, says that if you ask people whether they want chocolate or fruit today, they will say "chocolate." But if you ask them what they will order next week, they'll respond "fruit."[21] We will read John Grisham's thrillers on the beach today; someday we will wade through Proust. To the behavioral economists this is a problem. Nonetheless, a study showed that when you ask those old people who displayed discipline whether they are happy that they ate less chocolate and more bran-filled granola, they shout no! In retrospect, they wish they had "lived it up" even more!

Should the psychological games and quizzes that Kahneman and Tversky uncovered lead us to throw away all economic theory and replace the Federal Reserve Board with the American Psychological Association? Do oldfangled supply and demand curves simply trace the magic wand of mesmerizing magicians? Probably not. Mainstream economics need not assume that everyone is rational all the time—instead it assumes that economic forces will, over time, push people and institutions toward more rational behavior. In the 1930s, Joseph Schumpeter admitted that the assumption that "conduct is prompt and rational is in all cases a fiction." But he added that the fiction is "sufficiently near to reality, if things have time to hammer logic into men."[22] Remember the Rule of Repeats, which suggests that people eventually catch on to the reputations of others. The boy who cried wolf may have been a great behavioral psychologist—the first few times.

In the 1950s, the polymath decision-theorist Herbert Simon coined the term "bounded rationality" and noticed that many people do not aim to maximize but instead are "satificers," a mashup of "satisfy" and "suffice." Doing "good enough" is good enough for many people because they are too busy to suss out or digest all available information. You might decide to take up golf and be content to average 100 on a 72-par course because you don't have the time or passion to improve. But does satisficing work in a competitive marketplace over a longer period of time? Sears was once the premier retailer in the United States, placed its name on the tallest skyscraper in the world, and advertised that it was "where America shops." By the 1990s, Sears was known for drab styles and mediocre service. Because its executive officers acted like satisficers, while the bosses at Costco, Walmart, and Target invested in new supply-chain technologies, Sears executives had a front-row seat in bankruptcy court. Their golf game might have been better than their retail game.

The late, not-so-great chef but wonderful food writer Anthony Bourdain warned the public in his bestselling and salty *Kitchen Confidential* not to eat fish at a restaurant on Mondays, because the dried-out fillet was likely delivered on Friday. Even worse, he said, was the fancy-sounding, gummy fish surprise that chefs would whip up in a blender for Sunday brunch to get rid of the rotting stuff, with names like scrod terrine, mackerel mousseline, and trout galantine. After Bourdain's widely discussed exposé, the verbal menu tricks did not work so well, and restaurateurs had to do better.

In the financial markets, while the behavioral economists may be right that many people grow irrationally attached even to their losing stocks, professionals do not get giddy over their losers. Eventually, the sharpshooting, bloodless pros trample the amateurs, teaching the amateurs one of two lessons: get out of the game, or get rid of your emotional attachment.[23]

Another investment example will help here. During the early 1980s, some researchers discovered that shares in small companies seemed to outperform stocks in big companies, delivering greater profits to investors. That sounded like an irrational result, confounding the Efficient Market Hypothesis. Yet since the time of those findings, so many people have piled into small stock funds that during the 1990s they lagged behind bigger stocks. Rational investors looking for a bargain corrected the irrational historical trend.

Behavioral psychologists and economists have occasionally stumbled in methodology as well, and in 2012 Kahneman himself fired a missive across the social sciences, warning that disciplines were losing credibility because too many experiments published in journals could not be replicated, including the famous old-age walking study that he cited in his bestselling book. In Kahneman's open letter, he called priming the "poster child for doubts about the integrity of psychological research."[24] Often, an initial study would grab headlines, get reposted on social media, and then fail to hold up on further testing. A multi-university report showed that only thirteen of twenty-one oft-reported behavioral studies that appeared in the journals *Nature* and *Science* yielded statistically significant results when replicated. They included a 2012 study claiming that when people are primed to act more analytically, they are less likely to believe in God. In the initial study, the researchers showed a few dozen Canadian undergraduates a photo of Rodin's *The Thinker* (analytical) and then asked if they believed in God. A separate group of undergraduates were shown a photo of a neutral statue. Sure enough, the Rodin-inspired group was less devout than the neutral group.[25] The paper was cited hundreds of times, including in an article titled "Why Obamacare Could Produce More Atheists."[26] Beyond the small sample size, the inquiry suffered from a common plague among such reports: the subjects were college students. Too many studies that purport to demonstrate broad biases rest on a narrow sliver of society that lives in dorm rooms.

These two young schools of thought, Rational Expectations and Behavioral Economics, often battle each other. We could use valid insights of behavioral economists to barbecue the bold Rational Expectations school of thought till it was burned crispy. But we can also fillet the behaviorists, who have pointed to particular biases and anomalies but have yet to put together consistent, robust paradigms. Each deserves better. If we relax rational expectations and assumptions about full information and magically clearing markets, we are left with several ideas that mainstream economists are currently trying to graft onto their standard frameworks. People do catch on to political and economic tricks after a while. People will refine and discard previous expectations faster than a gradual adaptive model would depict. The challenge is to include these insights while recognizing the problems of contracts and imperfect information.[27]

In their radical voice, Rational Expectations theorists sound like they just leaped off the pages of Marvel comic strips. If one assumes that people always act fully rationally, why not also credit them with X-ray vision and the ability to fly? Surely, the planet Krypton never had stagflation. In the radical form, Rational Expectations theory gives us a model too perfect for the real world. We certainly can't ignore the discrepancies. As James Tobin put it, using this pristine theory to explain the world is like looking for a lost purse only under the streetlamp.[28] The problem is that the lost purse usually lies in the dark. And while you futilely bend down in the mesmerizing light of the streetlamp, you'll probably be bopped on the head by reality.[29]

CHAPTER XIII

Dark Clouds, Silver Linings

We have made a long run since Adam Smith. So long and so fast that it's like roller-skating past centuries of masterpieces in the Louvre with just enough time to flash a puzzled Mona Lisa smile. Pity the poor economist. He is expected to cull the "truth" from the twisted tour of history and then confidently counsel presidents.

The truth is that economics befuddles even the sharpest mind. To speak boastfully invites punishment. Brash economists would profit by taking Prometheus's place and having eagles pick at their livers until they learned humility. Why does economics stump so many and scare off even more? Unlike biologists, economists cannot conduct scientific experiments with carefully monitored control groups. Of course, not all natural sciences have control groups. Astronomers can no more harness a sample of moons than economists can manipulate a random sample of homemakers. But at least astronomers do not have to worry that planets will suddenly act whimsically, as consumers might. Astronomers have a pretty good record of predicting when Halley's comet will return. Economists have a pretty lousy record of predicting household savings rates. In a joke from the Soviet Union, a man asks, "Was communism invented by biologists or politicians?" "Politicians, of course. Biologists would have tried it out on rats first." Unfortunately, rats cannot help economists very much, either. Rats may have circulatory systems similar to human beings', but economics is more a matter of mind than of anatomy.

Economics is not, as Adam Smith and some of his rationalist successors tried to depict, a science of precise laws. Tendencies, maybe. Higher output usually means lower prices, except when Veblenesque goods enter the scene. A higher money supply usually means lower interest rates, except when fears of inflation push interest rates higher. Stock prices usually represent rational predictions of future cash flows, except when "animal spirits" panic or excite investors into dramatic swings. Investors usually take risks until the marginal benefits equal the marginal costs, except for Schumpeterian Übermensch entrepreneurs, who perceive values better than the market. These imprecise forces that disrupt the scientific approach are not necessarily irrational (that is, crazy). They may be nonrational and unpredictable, as in quantum physics, where electrons do not act crazily—they simply defy our current methods of modeling. As economists, we haven't figured out everything. On the other hand, to deliberately flout the tendencies discovered by the "Hall of Fame" economists is to flirt with economic calamity. Price supports, protectionism, and laissez-faire pollution policies can quickly deliver high prices, high taxes, and filthy air. Despite a reputation for contentiousness, few educated economists would advise any of them.

It's not easy being an economist. As usual, Keynes found the most sparkling words to describe the master economist, who "must be as aloof and incorruptible as an artist, yet sometimes as near the earth as a politician."[1] All the king's headhunters and all the king's men couldn't fill this job description.

None of the economists we have surveyed was able to flawlessly balance general/particular, future/present, or heaven/earth. None proved equally prodigious at microeconomic and macroeconomic analyses. They had their limits. Some of them even knew that.

They all knew one thing, however: they could not ignore the

interplay between government and the economy. Adam Smith blasted the government for supporting the trade restraints of the guilds. Malthus contended that Poor Laws promoted poverty. Ricardo warned that protectionism could sink England into the abyss of a new dark age. Marx argued that government worked only as a tool of exploitation and oppression. Keynes tried to shake government employees from a deep and dangerous sleep. And so on.

Despite the lonely cries of extremists, we have learned that governments are not necessarily evil or good. They are neither saviors nor satans, although their policies may at times have salvific or satanic consequences.

Nonetheless, each of the economists we have studied, despite their many differences, warned us that governments always face political pressures to take measures that can ruin good economies. U.S. congressmen can spend their entire careers consoling and consorting with victims of good economic policy. Free international trade hurts some domestic producers. Low inflation hurts borrowers. Falling interest rates hurt bond buyers. Technological innovation hurts some workers. Taxes on pollution hurt corporations.

Do not be inveigled into thinking that the victims of good economics exactly offset the beneficiaries. Good economics is not a zero-sum game, taking from Petra to pay Paula. As a matter of fact, we may define "good economics" as policies that produce positive gains, even though victims may be created.

Because even good economic policies often produce victims, economists have a very tough time persuading democratic governments to take good advice. Good economics may not be popular economics, especially in the short run. The benefits of lower inflation and higher investment may take some time to shine through—especially to shine through television images of fallen farmers and depressed homeowners (who enjoyed soaring asset values during the inflationary 1970s, suffered tougher times in the 1980s, and enjoyed a surge in the late 1990s and early 2000s). Unfortunately, the media generally prefers short bursts of wrenching, violent images to lengthy exposures of pleasing, peaceful images.

Good economics does not do well in fifteen-second sound bites. In fifteen seconds, a shill from any number of lobbyists can clobber an unbiased economist. What economists really need are lessons in sloganeering and pamphleteering. What news programs need is the patience to listen to difficult arguments.

Let's be honest, though. To a large extent, the media only reflect the demand of viewers for titillating tidbits. Apparently, people enjoy gruesome news stories, just as they enjoy horror movies. Some of the fault for inane news programs lies in ourselves. We cannot sympathize with market economics and then slam networks for pandering to the public.

As a public, we have at least three psychological barriers to economic literacy. First, we prefer brief, flashy bursts of information. Second, we prefer immediate results and quickly grow impatient. Keynes had it wrong. In the long run, we, or at least our descendants, are not dead. If we surrender to every urge today, we leave nothing for tomorrow. If we do not save, if we only borrow, if we dance too merrily tonight, tomorrow will be a very long and arduous day. Societies prosper only when they think of a long run. This is not to say that a society of misers always thrives. While the medieval obsession with a heavenly afterlife probably drained the energy to innovate and excel on earth, we in our century have exalted tonight as the chiliastic moment rather than tomorrow or the day after tomorrow.

Third, despite our short-run focus, we find it difficult to recognize the "good times" even when we have them. Economic happiness is not an explosion of wealth. The Industrial Revolution, the most dramatic economic event in the history of mankind, came at a rate of only about 5 percent per year. A 5 percent rise in the living standard does not sweep a pauper into the master bedroom of the palace. Nor does it replace gruel with foie gras. Year-to-year changes come slowly. But when he nears death, the pauper may find that his standard of living has multiplied fourfold. Life is seldom blissful and often just tolerable. Even if a higher living standard could bring happiness, it usually comes too slowly for us.[2] When it finally comes, we're at just the right age to sing nostalgic songs about the good old days. As we travel through time, we peer through the front window with nearsighted glasses, yet we glance through the rearview mirror with rose-colored glasses. It's hard to move forward that way. And it's hard for economists to point us in the right direction.

Newspapers seldom declare heydays. Only history books can. In retrospect, the middle 1960s were the heydays of economics. Sustained economic growth spanned years. Keynesian theory appeared powerful. Yet contemporaneous reports of that period highlighted despair and economic uncertainty. The good times passed by without too much notice, as if we had a right to expect prolonged economic success. Only a recession would have made the front pages. As Schopenhauer noted, peaceful years appear in history books as brief pauses scattered here and there, while wars and revolutions dominate. More pithily put by Beccaria, "Happy is the nation without a history."

Samuel Goldwyn warned us not to make any predictions, especially concerning the future. Let's ignore him. For despite jeremiads of a coming apocalypse bringing global hunger, despair, and misery, we do have reason for optimism. No guarantees, no overwhelming odds, just reason. Recall that national income depends on labor, capital, natural resources, and technology. Recent developments in each of these factors of production point toward economic growth in the long run.

In the United States, as well as other Western democracies, labor seems better acquainted with management than a decade or two ago. Through the influence of Japanese management techniques, workers in large plants play a larger role in designing and refining the production process. Furthermore, unions recognize that their prosperity rests on the success of the company, not on the extraction of high wages without concomitant increases in productivity. American unions seem willing to accept lower wages during recessions rather than layoffs, allowing their fortunes to rise and fall with the company's. In return, management finally understands that workers should have a large stake in the performance of the company. Many employees now receive stock options as part of their compensation. A more cooperative relationship promotes economic growth.

Capital markets are more efficient than they were twenty years ago. International financial capital moves more fluidly across national boundaries. Inefficient governments and corporations feel strong pressure to mend their ways, lest they fail to attract investors. Firms find it easier to raise funds to build new plants and buy new equipment. Once upon a time, a firm could draw a circle around the geographical area from which it could get financing. A century ago, the radius was perhaps ten miles. If the locals did not save enough money, the firm could not borrow anything from a bank. Throughout the century the radius has expanded. It now equals the radius of the earth. Today a Pittsburgh company can float a bond in Australia, even if all its Pittsburgh neighbors save their money in mattresses rather than in mutual funds.

Technology represents the most fascinating and unpredictable part of the production function. Who knows when the next Turing or von Neumann will emerge and where they will take us? They brought us modern computers, but even they would be surprised by how quickly and powerfully the Internet has woven the world together. A schoolgirl in Jakarta is just one click away from a virtual tour of Disney World or a NASA briefing on the next mission to Mars. A man with prostate cancer in the Congo can download research from Johns Hopkins and show it to his doctor. Physicists and chemists furiously work on superconductivity, a project that nearly eliminates the barriers that friction presents to us. Superconducting materials and nanotechnology will transport our bodies and our messages at mind-boggling speeds. Biologists scramble (carefully, we hope) to exploit recombinant DNA to improve the sources of nutrition and erase the blight of disease. On an institutional level, we see a burgeoning of cooperation between university research centers and corporations. Ventures joining the genius of both types of institutions accelerate the already lightning pace of science.

And of course, our natural resources multiply whenever technology grants new methods of extracting, recovering, or replenishing the earth's bounties (and the resources of space).

Surely, we should not ride into the future on a wave of reckless optimism. With each possibility of positive development comes risks and drawbacks. Recalling our production function, labor unions do not always hold hands with management. Factory innovations may displace some workers; prolonged strikes may take place. Capital markets may be thwarted by insider trading and other scams. Natural resources may be exploited selfishly by irresponsible firms. And so on.

Finally, we must consider all those other political, psychological, and institutional factors that mold our minds. Technology can blossom, but tribal taboos can halt progress. For example, if we thought that sand was holy, we might not have glass or semiconductors, much less vacation homes in Miami Beach. Surely, ancient and medieval restraints on lending restricted economic progress centuries ago. In addition, as Nobel laureate Robert Solow discovered, economic growth demands an educated populace. Paul Romer of Stanford has urged economists to spend as much time on "idea gaps" as on deficiencies in factories and roads. Romer argues that most technologies do not just pop up by accident or get delivered to man as Prometheus brought fire. Since so many people benefit from discoveries like the transistor and chemotherapy, societies should encourage scientists and engineers, whether by tax breaks or by patents, which give discoverers a temporary monopoly on profits. Sometimes ideas do begin with flash insights or even the work of tinkerers. Take a look at any airport terminal and watch thousands of people rolling their luggage with ease. Although a new Boeing 737 looks much the same on the outside as the first model built in 1967, passengers look different. When the initial Boeing 737 rolled off the assembly line, passengers dragged or carried their luggage in hand. "Lug" was a verb, and it was an unpleasant thing to do. Wheeled luggage was not patented until 1972. Since that time, wheels and hideaway handles have saved untold visits to chiropractors and drugstores. A few years ago, I had a flash insight that would make arithmetic more intuitive to children. I arrayed the numbers 1 to 100 in a special zigzag matrix called the Math Arrow. It turned out that no one had presented numbers in such a way, and when it raised test scores for first-graders, mathematicians wondered whether it could replace the number line in classrooms.[3] Nonetheless, it is not easy to persuade school bureaucrats to entertain a new idea. Many of the most important discoveries are not sudden flashes but instead might come from years of full-time laboratory experimentation. For seven years, Jonas Salk toiled in laboratories before bringing forth the life-saving polio vaccine in 1955.

Beyond innovations, insights, and inspirations, economic growth also requires, as Joseph Schumpeter taught (prior to the establishment of a Nobel Prize in Economics), an entrepreneurial drive. Who knows whether mental and spiritual forces will push us forward or twist us around and send us reeling toward barbarism? How free do entrepreneurs feel under the ever-too-watchful eyes of the Taliban or "Dear Leader" Kim in North Korea?

Schumpeter speculated about capitalism's future in his masterful *Capitalism, Socialism, and Democracy*. To Schumpeter, the greatest threat came not from economic factors such as falling profits but from political factors. In fact, capitalism's very successes would destroy capitalism. By creating a highly educated class with plenty of leisure time, capitalism would allow a new generation to begin questioning its moral framework. They would begin asking questions about income inequality, justice, pollution, and so on. Finally, their acidic questions would burn through capitalism's weak moral foundation, and they would turn nations to socialism, which would promise material welfare *and* moral support for those yearning for justice on this earth. In his now famous query, Schumpeter asked, "Can capitalism survive? No. I do not think it can."[4]

During the late 1960s, as long hair, bongo drums, psychedelic colors, and drug use spread, Schumpeter's predictions seemed to be coming true. Third World nations, newly liberated from Europe, turned to socialism. By the early 1970s, Ph.D.s were driving taxicabs and blasting the establishment.

But what did the 1980s bring us? Yuppies, short hair, striped shirts, and a parade of underdeveloped nations trading *Das Kapital* in for *Dress for Success*. Even the Soviet Union strove to revive its sclerotic economy. Nobody urges centralized planning anymore. Here are just a few headlines from *New York Times* feature stories: "Yugoslavia's Capitalist Tilt Becomes a Headlong Plunge"; "Adam Smith Crowds Marx in Angola"; "A Radical Diagnosis of Latin America's Economic Malaise: A Book Promoting Entrepreneurship Takes the Region by Storm."[5] Finally, read a few lines from the *New York Times* story "The Global March to Free Markets: As the World Economy Becomes More Competitive, Capitalists and Communist Countries Alike Are Turning to Adam Smith":

> In Moscow, entrepreneurial comrades are running their own beauty parlors and auto repair shops, while in China many farmers are eschewing the communal system in favor of selling produce they grow themselves. . . . It seems that no matter where you look, governments have been turning to market mechanisms—Adam Smith's ingenious invisible hand—to pep up their economies. Economists say there is unusual agreement among capitalist and Communist countries about the importance of giving freer rein to the market: that overarching mechanism that helps articulate consumer desires, encourages inventiveness, and disciplines inefficient producers.[6]

The 1990s and early 2000s broadly reinforced these trends, even though Russia and the Far East stumbled. When the

Communist Party won democratic elections in Poland in 1995, for example, they committed themselves to capitalist rule. Only their pedigree was communist. Romania, which once practiced a more austere communism than the USSR, signed a free trade pact with Turkey in 1998. Sandinista leader Daniel Ortega tossed aside his old Marxism and ran for president in Nicaragua under a pro-capitalist banner (only to relapse into authoritarian repression and earn condemnation from Amnesty International). When Labour governments replaced Conservative governments in Great Britain and Canada, they outdid their predecessors by keeping tight budgets and privatizing national industries. One of Prime Minister Tony Blair's first acts was to liberate the Bank of England from political rule so that it could determine monetary policy without feeling the pressure of squeamish politicians. No wonder Margaret Thatcher declared that Blair would do just fine.

Even if a return to market mechanisms does not magically turn poverty into wealth, at least governments have jettisoned rigid, ideological abhorrence of market economic systems. Most important, the wondrous communications technologies that brought us the Internet make it nearly impossible for despots to keep their people in the dark or in silence.

Of course, material prosperity will not cure some of the problems that Schumpeter thought would plague the educated class. Inequality and poverty may still remain. How can they best be assuaged? Taxes and redistributions that tend not to discourage invention and entrepreneurship would help. Many economists advocate for consumption taxes to ultimately replace income taxes.

One problem may not be solved by markets or shrewd governments, though. Can human beings keep up with the pace of new inventions that make traditional jobs and roles obsolete? Can human beings educate themselves fast enough to handle the computer and post-computer age? Most probably can. But as society grows more complex, more and more will fall through the various safety nets—those with psychological, physical, and intelligence handicaps will falter. The world is materially easier but psychologically more difficult to live in today than it was two hundred years ago. Life in the twentieth-century city is as tough on the human spirit as life on the farm ever was. It's quite easy to lose one's footing in the modern world, to be whirled around a factory and spat out a homeless waif, like Charlie Chaplin in *Modern Times*.

Our biological clocks may no longer be synchronized with our lifestyles. Two hundred years ago, women bore children by the age of twenty. By then they knew what the world had to offer, what kind of jobs they could hold, what kind of future they could expect. They could teach their children to survive. How many twenty-year-olds today know what they can or will do when they are twenty-five? The modern world presents us with so many more opportunities that we cannot be good predictors of our own lives, much less our children's. Our children are no longer raised by people who know the world, not because parents have gotten stupid or lazy, but because the world has gotten too big to master. Parents must eventually learn to teach their children how to handle uncertainty—not how to ensure stability.

In reciting glum news, we have ignored many other possibilities, including natural disasters. California may float off into the Pacific Ocean. Plagues may strike down millions. Drought may starve millions more. Wars may rob the youth from many nations. It is easy to paint a dark portrait of the United States and of the rest of the world.

The economist must study all these events. They all impinge on his easel, splattering blotches all over the carefully crafted, elegant portrait he wants to unveil to the world.

For most of man's life on earth, he has lived no better on two legs than he had on four. Give the economist a little credit for explaining and depicting the brief, shining moments when there has been a difference.

Acknowledgments

This book explains modern economic theories by exploring the lives and ideas of the greatest economists. Because many of the economic problems of our day also challenged our forefathers, the echoes of Adam Smith and his descendants still speak to us today. To provide a better understanding of their theories, I have used contemporary examples that I hope the reader will find entertaining as well as illuminating.

As any economics student learns the first day, economics is about scarcity and choice. I have chosen to omit many brilliant economists and to focus on the Anglo-American tradition. Thus, Walras, Jevons, Menger, and others receive less attention than they would in a lengthier book. I can only hope that the reader is inspired to pursue these individuals in other texts. To paraphrase Bacon, I aim not to inform *ad tedium*, but to stimulate the mind briefly yet fruitfully.

I want to apologize to those economists mentioned in this book who are living today. The title, *New Ideas from Dead Economists*, is not meant to refer to them, their personalities, or their public speaking abilities—although I cannot be held responsible for resemblances. They should take comfort in the honor of being mentioned alongside Smith, Ricardo, Keynes, and others.

I would like to thank a number of individuals and institutions for stimulating my mind and energies. Martin Feldstein and Lawrence Lindsey encouraged this project and asked Harvard students to read a first draft. My students at Harvard listened to numerous digressions on the history of economic thought. Ronald Coase and Milton Friedman provided helpful comments on Alfred Marshall. Not only was Friedman one of the century's greatest economists, but he was extraordinarily generous with his time, writing me letters outlining his views and introducing me to Coase, who knew John Maynard Keynes and his rivals, A. C. Pigou and F. A. Hayek. Geoffrey Meeks of Cambridge University and Sir Harry Hinsley, past master of St. John's College, Cambridge, allowed me to wander and ponder the same cloisters of Cambridge, frequented by so many of the heroes in this book. Before writing chapters on Malthus, Marshall, and Keynes, I searched among the medieval courts and halls for memories and mementos of these individuals, and their legacy spurred me onward. In 2009 I returned to Cambridge and spent time at King's College researching Pigou. I also thank Michael Moohr, who sparked my interest in the history of economic thought.

Another word about Martin Feldstein, who passed away in 2019 and was, as a prominent headline stated, "one of the most influential economists of his generation," having tutored Federal Reserve governors, Treasury secretaries, and chairmen of the White House Council of Economic Advisers. Former Federal Reserve governor Jeremy Stein called him the "pre-eminent bridge-builder in the economics profession."[1] Marty was bold enough to challenge President Reagan's Treasury secretary while serving as the CEA chair, and he was kind enough to offer to write a foreword to this book when I was a mere graduate student. Mathematicians often speak of their "Erdos number," meaning their degree of separation from the prolific and collaborative Hungarian Paul Erdos. Someday, perhaps starting now, economists will share their Feldstein number. I am proud that this book suggests a number 1.

Finally, I thank my family, whose support and good humor

gave me hope that I would find a few lessons and a few laughs among the "dismal" scientists. And perhaps the economists wouldn't have been so dismal had they known my cheerful and loving wife, Debby, and our delightful daughters, Victoria, Katherine, and Alexia, to whom I dedicate this book.

Notes

Preface to the Revised Edition

1. Albrecht Glitz and Erik Meyersson, "Industrial Espionage and Productivity," *American Economic Review* 110, no. 4 (April 2020), pp. 1055–1103.

2. Maxim Pinkovskiy and Xavier Sala-i-Martin, "Parametric Estimations of the World Distribution of Income," National Bureau of Economic Research, Working Paper 15433 (2009), p. 57, fig. 32.

I. Introduction: The Plight of the Economist

1. William Manchester, *The Last Lion: Winston Spencer Churchill* (New York: Dell, 1983), p. 35.

2. T. S. Kuhn, *The Structure of Scientific Revolutions*, 2nd ed. (Chicago: University of Chicago Press, 1970).

3. With the rise of quantum physics and its corollaries such as Heisenberg's principle, even the "hard" sciences are losing their muscle tone.

4. John Maynard Keynes, "Alfred Marshall," in *Essays in Biography*, in the *Collected Writings of John Maynard Keynes*, vol. 10 (London and New York: Macmillan/St. Martin's Press for the Royal Economic Society, 1972), p. 173.

5. See Todd G. Buchholz, "Biblical Laws and the Economic Growth of Ancient Israel," *Journal of Law and Religion* 6, no. 2 (1988) 389–427.

6. For a fascinating history of the usury doctrine, see Benjamin Nelson, *The Idea of Usury* (Princeton, NJ: Princeton University Press, 1949).

7. Georges Duby, *The Age of the Cathedral,* trans. Eleanor Levieux and Barbara Thompson (Chicago: University of Chicago Press, 1981), p. 3.

II. The Second Coming of Adam Smith

1. Adam Smith, *Lectures on Justice, Police, Revenue, and Arms,* ed. Edwin Cannan (London: Oxford University Press, 1896), p. 179. These lectures are based on notes from students.

2. Adam Smith, *Correspondence of Adam Smith,* ed. Earnest Campbell Mossner and Ian Simpson Ross (Oxford: Clarendon Press, 1987), p. 275.

3. Smith, *Correspondence,* p. 1.

4. Adam Smith, *An Inquiry into the Nature and Causes of the Wealth of Nations,* ed. R. H. Campbell, A. S. Skinner, and W. B. Todd, 2 vols. (Oxford: Clarendon Press, 1976 [1776]), vol. 1, p. 284.

5. Smith, *Lectures,* pp. 172–173.

6. Smith, *Wealth of Nations,* vol. 1, p. 274.

7. Smith, *Correspondence,* p. 102.

8. Peter Gay, *The Enlightenment: An Interpretation,* 2 vols. (London: Weidenfeld and Nicolson, 1967), vol. 2, p. 348.

9. Gay, *Enlightenment,* vol. 2, p. 349.

10. David Hume, *The Letters of David Hume,* ed. J. Y. T. Greig, 2 vols. (Oxford: Oxford University Press, 1932), vol. 2, p. 205.

11. Smith, *Wealth of Nations,* vol. 2, p. 678.

12. Thomas Hobbes, "The Introduction," in *Leviathan* (New York: Collier, 1962), p. 19.

13. Smith, *Wealth of Nations,* vol. 1, p. 341.

14. Smith, *Wealth of Nations,* vol. 1, p. 25.

15. Smith, *Wealth of Nations,* vol. 1, pp. 26–27.

16. Smith, *Wealth of Nations,* vol. 1, p. 456.

17. Recording Industry Association of America, "U.S. Sales Database," https://www.riaa.com/u-s-sales-database/.

18. Smith, *Wealth of Nations,* vol. 1, p. 15.

19. Smith, *Wealth of Nations,* vol. 1, p. 20.

20. Both the preceding Hayek quotation and this Whitehead quotation appear in F. A. Hayek, "The Use of Knowledge in Society," *American Economic Review* 35 (September 1945), pp. 526–528.

21. Smith, *Wealth of Nations,* vol. 1, p. 456.

22. Friedman's argument was based on an essay by Leonard E. Read called "I, Pencil: My Family Tree," Foundation for Economic Education (December 1958).

23. James Ward, *The Perfection of the Paper Clip* (New York: Touchstone, 2015), p. 96.

24. Smith, *Wealth of Nations*, vol. 1, pp. 23–24.

25. See Milton Friedman, *Capitalism and Freedom* (Chicago: University of Chicago Press, 1967), p. 109.

26. Smith, *Wealth of Nations*, vol. 2, pp. 782–785.

27. Paul A. Samuelson, "A Modern Theorist's Vindication of Adam Smith," *American Economic Review: Papers and Proceedings*, vol. 67 (February 1977), pp. 43–44.

28. Smith, *Wealth of Nations*, p. 257.

29. Parmigiano Reggiano Consortium, "Specifications and Legislation," https://www.parmigianoreggiano.com/consortium/rules _regulation_2/default.aspx; Cato Institute, "Reign of *Terroir*: How to Resist Europe's Efforts to Control Common Food Names as Geographical Indications," https://www.cato.org/publications/pol icy-analysis/reign-terroir-how-resist-europes-efforts-control -common-food-names#cite-11.

30. In 2012, these rules protected $72 billion worth of goods. Tanguy Chever et al., *Value of Production of Agricultural Products and Foodstuffs, Wines, Aromatised Wines and Spirits, Protected by a Geographical Indication (GI)*, AGRI–2011–EVAL–042012, October 2012, report for the European Commission prepared by AND International, available at http://ec.europa.eu/agriculture/external-studies/value-gi_en.htm.

31. Smith, *Wealth of Nations*, vol. 1, p. 145.

32. Smith, *Wealth of Nations*, vol. 1, p. 137.

33. For a brief biography, see Todd G. Buchholz, *New Ideas from Dead CEOs* (New York: HarperCollins, 2007), pp. 241–259.

34. Steve Jobs, Stanford University commencement address, *Stanford Report*, June 12, 2005.

35. Sam Peltzman, "Industrial Concentration Under the Rule of Reason," *Journal of Law and Economics* 57, no. 4 (2014), article 7, https://chicagounbound.uchicago.edu/jle/vol57/iss4/7.

36. Even MIT economist Lester Thurow, a fiery adversary of Friedman's, argued against the government breakup of AT&T on these grounds. See "Antitrust Grows Unpopular," *Newsweek*, January 12, 1981.

37. Smith, *Wealth of Nations*, vol. 1, p. 457.

38. Smith, *Wealth of Nations*, vol. 1, p. 471.

39. Bernie Sanders, "So-Called 'Free Trade' Policies Hurt US Workers Every Time We Pass Them," *Guardian*, April 29, 2015, https://www.theguardian.com/commentisfree/2015/apr/29/so -called-free-trade-policies-hurt-us-workers-every-time-we-pass-them;

Tessa Berenson, "Donald Trump Details Plan to Rewrite Global Trade Rules," *Time*, June 28, 2016, http://time.com/4385989/donald-trump-trade-china-speech/.

40. W. Michael Cox and Richard Alm, "How Are We Doing?," *The American*, July 3, 2008, http://www.aei.org/publication/how-are-we-doing/.

41. Mark Perry, "When It Comes to the Affordability of Common Household Goods, the Rich and the Poor Are Both Getting Richer," American Enterprise Institute, October 3, 2013, https://www.aei.org/publication/when-it-comes-to-the-affordability-of-common-household-goods-the-rich-and-the-poor-are-both-getting-richer/.

42. Tom Jackson, *Chilled: How Refrigeration Changed the World and Might Do So Again* (London: Bloomsbury, 2015).

43. Felipe Garcia Ribeiro, Guilherme Stein, and Thomas Kang, "The Cuban Experiment: Measuring the Role of the 1959 Revolution on Economic Performance Using Synthetic Control," working paper (May 21, 2013), https://onlinelibrary.wiley.com/doi/abs/10.1111/twec.12609

44. David Dollar and Aart Kraay, "Trade, Growth and Poverty," World Bank, June 2001, p. 2.

45. Heather Long, "Trump's Steel Tariffs Cost U.S. Consumers $900,000 for Every Job Created, Experts Say," *Washington Post*, May 7, 2019, https://www.washingtonpost.com/business/2019/05/07/trumps-steel-tariffs-cost-us-consumers-every-job-created-experts-say.

46. Gary Clyde Hufbauer and Sean Lowry, *US Tire Tariffs: Saving Few Jobs at High Cost*, Peterson Institute for International Economics, https://piie.com/sites/default/files/publications/pb/pb12-9.pdf.

47. Smith, *Wealth of Nations*, vol. 1, p. 468.

48. Smith, *Correspondence*, pp. 245–246.

III. Malthus: Prophet of Doom and Population Boom

1. William Wordsworth, *The Prelude: 1799* (New York: W. W. Norton, 1979), p. 396.

2. William Godwin, *An Enquiry Concerning the Principles of Political Justice, and Its Influence on General Virtue and Happiness*, 2 vols. (London: 1798), vol. 2, p. 504.

3. Godwin, *Enquiry*, p. 528.

4. Nico Voigtländer and Hans-Joachim Voth, "How the West 'Invented' Fertility Restriction," *American Economic Review* 103 (2013), 2227–2264.

5. The formula for the future value (FV) of a principal amount of money (P) held for (N) years at (R) percent compound interest is $FV = P \times (1 + R)^N$. A helpful rule of thumb is the rule of 72, which states that the number of years it takes for a number to double, when growing at a constant rate, equals 72 divided by that number. For instance, if the economy expands at 4 percent per year, in eighteen years the economy would double.

6. Thomas R. Malthus, *An Essay on the Principle of Population*, 1st ed. (London: Macmillan, reprint, 1909), pp. 139–140.

7. Malthus, *Principle of Population*, pp. 6–7, 92.

8. James Bonar, *Malthus and His Work* (London: Macmillan, 1885), p. 127.

9. Thomas R. Malthus, *An Essay on the Principle of Population*, 2nd ed. (London: Everyman Library, 1914), vol. 2, p. 168.

10. Quoted in Patricia James, *Population Malthus* (London: Routledge and Kegan Paul, 1979), pp. 110–111.

11. Charles Darwin, *The Autobiography of Charles Darwin* (New York: Barnes and Noble, 2005 [1867]), p. 45; Alfred Russel Wallace, *My Life* (London: Chapman and Hall, 1905), vol. 2, p. 232.

12. See Paul Bairoch, "Agriculture and the Industrial Revolution," trans. M. Grindrod, in *The Industrial Revolution*, ed. C. M. Cipolla (Sussex: Harvester Press, 1976), pp. 452–501.

13. André Armengaud, "Population in Europe 1700–1914," in Cipolla, *Industrial Revolution*, p. 48.

14. Thomas R. Malthus, *Principles of Political Economy* (Boston: Wells and Lilly, 1821), pp. 4–5.

15. See Todd G. Buchholz, *The Price of Prosperity* (New York: HarperCollins, 2016), pp. 28–37.

16. Aristotle, *Politics*, bk. 2, http://www.perseus.tufts.edu/hopper/text?doc=Perseus:abo:tlg,0086,035:2.

17. "Family Planning," Walt Disney Productions for the Population Council, 1968, https://www.youtube.com/watch?v=t2DkiceqmzU.

18. See Dennis Meadows et al., *The Limits to Growth* (New York: Universe Books, 1972); Jay Forrester, *World Dynamics* (Cambridge: Wright-Allen Press, 1971); and Robert Heilbroner, *An Inquiry into the Human Prospect* (New York: W. W. Norton, 1974).

19. Gerald O. Barney, ed., *The Global 2000 Report to the President* (Washington, D.C.: U.S. Government Printing Office, 1981).

20. Wassily Leontief, *The Future of the World Economy* (New York: Oxford University Press, 1977), p. 6.

21. Ashok Gulati, "Can India Solve Its Food Paradox?," interview by Knowledge at Wharton, March 28, 2019, https://knowledge.whar ton.upenn.edu/article/can-india-solve-its-food-paradox/.

22. World Bank, *World Development Report* (Washington, D.C.: World Bank, 1984). See Allen C. Kelley, "Economic Consequences of Population Change in the Third World," *Journal of Economic Literature*, vol. 25 (December 1988), pp. 1685–1728.

23. Stephen Buckley, "Africa's Agricultural Rebirth," *Washington Post*, May 25, 1998, p. A18.

24. Charles Kenny, "Is Anywhere Stuck in the Malthusian Trap?," *Kyklos* 63, no. 2, pp. 199–202.

25. Thomas R. Malthus, *An Essay on the Principles of Population*, 2nd ed. (London: J. Johnson, 1803), p. 393.

26. Riham Alkousaa, "Violent Crime Rises in Germany and Is Attributed to Refugees," Reuters, January 3, 2018, https://www.reuters .com/article/us-europe-migrants-germany-crime/violent-crime -rises-in-germany-and-is-attributed-to-refugees-idUSKBN1ES16J.

27. William G. Powderly, "How Infection Shaped History: Lessons from the Irish Famine," *Transactions of the American Clinical and Climatological Association* 130 (2019), https://www.ncbi.nlm.nih.gov /pmc/articles/PMC6735970/.

28. Noel Ignatiev, *How the Irish Became White* (New York: Routledge, 1995).

29. Ignatiev, *How the Irish Became White*, p. 37.

30. See Andres Villareal and Christopher R. Tamborini, "Immigrants' Economic Assimilation: Evidence from Longitudinal Earnings Records," *American Sociological Review*, August 2018; and George J. Borjas, "The Economics of Immigrants," *Journal of Economic Literature*, December 1994. Also see Rachel M. Friedberg and Jennifer Hunt, "The Impact of Immigrants on Host Country Wages, Employment and Growth," *Journal of Economic Perspectives*, Spring 1995, pp. 26–27.

31. See Todd G. Buchholz, *Market Shock* (New York: HarperCollins, 2000), pp. 237–256.

32. See Spencer R. Weart, "The Discovery of the Risk of Global Warming," *Physics Today*, January 1997, p. 34. For the latest IPCC report, see R. T. Watson, M. C. Zinyowera, and R. H. Moss, eds., *Climate Change 1995: The Impacts, Adaptation, and Mitigation of Climate Change* (New York: Cambridge University Press, 1996).

33. Robert Mendelsohn, William D. Nordhaus, and Daigee Shaw, "The Impact of Global Warming on Agriculture: A Ricardian Analy-

sis," *American Economic Review* 83, no. 4 (September 1994), pp. 753–755. For a skeptical (and technical) view of warming, see R. S. Stone, "Variations in Western Arctic Temperatures in Response to Cloud Radiative and Synoptic-Scale Influence," *Journal of Geophysical Research* 102 (1997), pp. 21, 769–770, 776. Easier reading would be Matt O'Keefe, "Solar Waxing," *Harvard Magazine*, May–June 1998.

34. Matthew E. Kahn, *The Review of Economics and Statistics* 87, no. 2 (May 2005), p. 271.

35. Sylvanus Urban, *Gentleman's Magazine and Historical Chronicle*, vol. 94 (London: J. Nichols and Son, 1824), p. 356.

IV. David Ricardo and the Cry for Free Trade

1. David Ricardo, letter to Thomas Malthus, *Letters of David Ricardo*, ed. James Bonar (Oxford: Clarendon Press, 1887), p. 16.

2. David Weatherall, *David Ricardo* (The Hague: Martinus Nijhoff, 1976), p. 2.

3. British History Online, "The Royal Exchange," https://www.british-history.ac.uk/old-new-london/vol1/pp494-513.

4. David Ricardo, *The Works and Correspondence*, ed. Pierro Sraffa (Cambridge: Cambridge University Press, 1951–1955), vol. 6, p. 231.

5. Quoted in Robert Lekachman, *A History of Economic Ideas* (New York: Harper and Row, 1959), p. 143.

6. If the opportunity costs are equal, there are no possible gains from trade. They might as well be self-sufficient. The model works less persuasively if resources cannot be reallocated and prices are extremely "sticky." More complex approaches such as the Heckscher-Ohlin-Samuelson model examine what determines opportunity costs and comparative advantages besides labor hours.

7. David Davies, *The Case of the Labourers in Husbandry Stated and Considered* (London, 1795); Frederick Morton Eden, *The State of the Poor: A History of the Labouring Classes in England, with Parochial Reports*, ed. A. G. L. Rogers (London, 1928); Gregory Clark, *A Farewell to Alms* (Princeton, NJ: Princeton University Press, 2007), table 3.6, p. 30; Joel Mokyr, "Is There Still Life in the Pessimist Case? Consumption During the Industrial Revolution, 1790–1850," *Journal of Economic History* 48, no. 1 (1988), pp. 69–92; Malthus, *An Essay on the Principle of Population* (1798), ch. 1, p. 25.

8. Quoted in Harry Anderson, Rich Thomas, and James C. Jones, "Carving Up the Car Buyer," *Newsweek*, March 5, 1984, p. 72.

9. If Britons dump their dollars, the value of the dollar (the exchange rate) will fall. Thus, trade deficits generally lead to depreciating currencies. But with a cheaper dollar, American exporters find it easier to sell to foreigners, and foreign producers have more trouble selling their goods in the United States. This process eventually reduces the trade deficit. Foreigners may also use their U.S. dollars to buy American assets such as property and factories if they think that the U.S. economy is healthy and will yield returns higher than investments in their own countries.

While an "invasion" of foreign purchasers could give foreigners a larger political voice in the United States, so far the proportion of foreign ownership is still small enough that the political effects remain slight. In the meantime, Americans benefit through more jobs; more tax revenues to towns, states, and Washington; and a transfer of foreign skills and technology to the United States.

10. See Murray Weidenbaum and Michael Munger, "Protectionism at Any Price?," *Regulation*, July–August 1983, pp. 14–22, cited in Benjamin M. Friedman, *Day of Reckoning* (New York: Random House, 1988), pp. 58–60.

11. "Economic Impacts of the Canadian Softwood Lumber Dispute on U.S. Industries," U.S. Senate, Committee on Commerce, Science and Transportation, Hearing Archives (February 14, 2006), pp. 1–53.

12. Frédéric Bastiat, *Economic Sophisms* (Princeton, NJ: D. Van Nostrand, 1964), pp. 56–57. Bastiat also sarcastically suggested that France double its need for jobs by chopping off everyone's right hand.

13. Emily Glassberg Sands and Vinod Bakhavachalam, "Ranking Countries and Industries by Tech, Data, and Business Skills," *Harvard Business Review*, March 27, 2019.

14. World Health Organization, *Global Status Report on Road Safety 2018*, https://www.who.int/violence_injury_prevention/road_safety _status/2018/en/.

15. Todd G. Buchholz, "Burgers, Fries, and Lawyers," *Policy Review*, February–March 2004, no. 123, p. 54.

16. Paul Krugman, "Ricardo's Difficult Idea," MIT, http://web .mit.edu/krugman/www/ricardo.htm.

17. Ricardo, *Works and Correspondence*, vol. 5, p. 55; vol. 1, p. 265. Also see Mark Blaug, *Ricardian Economics* (New Haven, CT: Yale University Press, 1958), p. 33. The German Historical School would later reject Ricardo's approach and apply an organic model to nations. Wilhelm Roscher and Gustav Schmöller argued that nations are

born, raised, and ultimately buried. Policies and principles that work well at one stage in a nation's life may work badly at another.

18. Ricardo, *Works and Correspondence*, vol. 1, p. 97.

19. Ricardo, *Works and Correspondence*, vol. 1, p. 70.

20. Ricardo, *Works and Correspondence*, vol. 1, p. 35.

21. Ricardo, *Works and Correspondence*, vol. 1, p. 120.

22. Ricardo, *Works and Correspondence*, vol. 8, p. 208; also see Ricardo writing in the 1820 *Encyclopedia Britannica*, vol. 8, p. 179.

23. Henry George, *Progress and Poverty* (New York: Schalkenbach Foundation, 1929), p. 545.

24. "Taxing Commercial Properties: Economic Impact Report," Office of the Controller, City and County of San Francisco, Item 19005 (November 11, 2019), p. 4.

25. Eve Baty, "A Castro Restaurant's NIMBY Play to Thwart Competitor Has Failed," *San Francisco Eater*, October 28, 2019, https://sf.eater.com/2019/10/28/20936988/castro-mediterranean-new-falafel-nimby.

26. Malthus, *Principles of Political Economy*, p. 186.

27. Smith, *Wealth of Nations*, pp. 337–338.

28. Malthus, *Principles of Political Economy*, p. 395.

29. John Maynard Keynes, "Thomas R. Malthus," in *Essays in Biography*, in *Collected Writings of John Maynard Keynes*, vol. 10 (London: Macmillan, 1972), p. 100.

30. Ricardo, *Works and Correspondence*, vol. 8, p. 184.

31. Robert Torrens, *Essay on the External Corn Trade* (London: J. Hatchard, 1815), pp. viii–ix.

32. Mark Blaug, *Economic Theory in Retrospect*, 3d ed. (Cambridge: Cambridge University Press, 1978), p. 140.

V. The Stormy Mind of John Stuart Mill

1. John Stuart Mill, *Autobiography* (London: Longmans, Green, Reader, and Dyer, 1873), p. 28. Michael St. John Packe takes a more lenient view of James Mill in *The Life of John Stuart Mill* (New York: Macmillan, 1954).

2. Mill, *Autobiography*, pp. 28, 30.

3. W. L. Courtney, *Life of John Stuart Mill* (London: Walter Scott, 1889), p. 40.

4. Mill, *Autobiography*, pp. 66–67.

5. Mill, *Autobiography*, pp. 98–100.

6. Jeremy Bentham, *Introduction to the Principles of Morals and Legislation* (New York: Haffner, 1948), p. 1.

7. Bentham, *Principles of Morals and Legislation*, pp. 30–31.

8. Quotation from Bentham, "Defence of a Maximum," in *Jeremy Bentham's Economic Writings*, vol. 3, ed. W. Stark (London: George Allen and Unwin, 1954 [1801]), pp. 247–302. See Todd G. Buchholz, "Punishing Humans," *Thought* 59 (September 1984), for a critique of Benthamite justice.

9. Mill, *Autobiography*, pp. 40–41.

10. Beckles Willson, *Ledger and Sword*, vol. 2 (London: Longmans, Green, 1903), p. 429.

11. Willson, *Ledger and Sword*, p. 109.

12. Willson, *Ledger and Sword*, pp. 132–134.

13. Willson, *Ledger and Sword*, p. 49.

14. John Stuart Mill, *The Early Draft of John Stuart Mill's Autobiography*, ed. J. Stillinger (Urbana: University of Illinois Press, 1961), p. 184. See also A. W. Levi, "The Mental Crisis of John Stuart Mill," *Psychoanalytic Review* 32 (January 1945), pp. 86–101.

15. Lionel Robbins, *The Evolution of Modern Economic Theory* (London: Macmillan, 1970), p. 109.

16. John Stuart Mill, "Bentham," in *Essays on Politics and Culture*, ed. G. Himmelfarb (Garden City, NY: Doubleday, 1962 [1838]), pp. 85–131; "Coleridge," in *Essays* (1840), pp. 132–186.

17. Mill, "Bentham," pp. xix–xx.

18. Richard Garnett, *The Life of W. J. Fox* (London: John Lane, 1910), p. 98.

19. Mill, *Autobiography*, pp. 186–187.

20. John Stuart Mill, *On Logic* (1840), p. 617.

21. John Stuart Mill, *Principles of Political Economy*, ed. W. J. Ashley (New York: A. M. Kelly, 1965 [1848]), pp. 199–200.

22. George J. Stigler, "The Nature and Role of Originality in Scientific Progress," *Economica* 22 (November 1955), pp. 293–302.

23. Mill, *Principles of Political Economy*, p. 808.

24. Mill, *Principles of Political Economy*, p. 808.

25. Marcus Eliason and H. Ohlsson, "Timing of Death and the Repeal of the Swedish Inheritance Tax," *Journal of Socio-Economics* 45 (August 2013), pp. 113–123.

26. Joseph Stiglitz, "Notes of Estate Taxes, Redistribution, and the Concept of Balanced Growth Path Dependence," *Journal of Political Economy* 86, no. 2, pt. 2 (1978), pp. S137–S150.

27. Stiglitz, "Notes of Estate Taxes," p. 869.

28. Mary Daly and Joyce Kwok, "Did Welfare Reform Work for Everyone: A Look at Young Single Mothers," *Federal Reserve Bank of San Francisco Economic Letter,* August 3, 2009.

29. Mill, *Principles of Political Economy,* p. 759.

30. Mill, *Principles of Political Economy,* p. 950.

31. Mill, *Principles of Political Economy,* p. 799.

32. Mill, *Principles of Political Economy,* p. 748.

33. Mill, *Principles of Political Economy,* p. 748.

34. Mill, *Principles of Political Economy,* p. 757.

35. Quoted in Gertrude Himmelfarb, "Introduction," in Mill, *On Liberty* (London: Penguin Books, 1986), p. 10.

36. Mill, *Autobiography,* p. 199.

37. Henry Fawcett, "His Influence at Universities," *Popular Science* 3 (July 1873).

38. Edmund Burke, *Reflections on the Revolution in France* (1790), in *The Works of the Right Honorable Edmund Burke* (London: F. C. and J. Rivington, 1808), vol. 5, p. 149.

VI. The Angry Oracle Called Karl Marx

1. David McLellan, *Karl Marx: His Life and Thought* (New York: Harper and Row, 1973), p. 4. See Karl Marx, "On the Jewish Question," in *The Marx-Engels Reader,* ed. Robert C. Tucker (New York: W. W. Norton, 1978), pp. 26–52; Gertrude Himmelfarb, "The Real Marx," *Commentary,* April 1985, pp. 37–43; and "Letters," August 1985.

2. McLellan, *Karl Marx,* pp. 6–7.

3. McLellan, *Karl Marx,* p. 33.

4. Robert Payne, *Karl Marx* (New York: Simon and Schuster, 1968), p. 77.

5. McLellan, *Karl Marx,* p. 53.

6. Saul K. Padover, *Karl Marx: An Intimate Biography* (New York: McGraw-Hill, 1978), p. 179.

7. McLellan, *Karl Marx,* p. 99.

8. Karl Marx and Friedrich Engels, *Collected Works* (New York: International Publishers, 1982), vol. 38, p. 115.

9. Karl Marx, "Introduction to *A Critique of Hegel's Philosophy of Right*," in K. Marx, *The Early Texts,* ed. D. McLellan (Oxford: Oxford University Press, 1971), p. 116.

10. Karl Marx, *The German Ideology,* in Tucker, *Marx-Engels Reader,* pp. 155–156.

11. Karl Marx, *A Contribution to the Critique of Political Economy*, trans. N. I. Stone (Chicago: Charles Kerr, 1904), preface.

12. Karl Marx, *The Eighteenth Brumaire of Louis Bonaparte*, in Tucker, *Marx-Engels Reader*, p. 595.

13. Karl Marx and Friedrich Engels, *The Communist Manifesto*, ed. Samuel Beer (Arlington Heights, IL: Harlan Davidson, 1955), p. 9.

14. Marx, *Critique of Political Economy*, preface.

15. Karl Marx, *Capital*, vol. 1 (Chicago: Charles Kerr, 1906), p. 13.

16. Marx and Engels, *Communist Manifesto*, pp. 13–14.

17. Marx and Engels, *Communist Manifesto*, pp. 13–14.

18. McLellan, *Karl Marx*, p. 98.

19. Padover, *Karl Marx*, pp. 291–293.

20. Payne, *Karl Marx*, p. 295.

21. McLellan, *Karl Marx*, pp. 264, 357.

22. McLellan, *Karl Marx*, p. 284.

23. Marx, *Capital*, vol. 1, pp. 649, 652.

24. Marx, *Capital*, vol. 1, p. 687.

25. Marx, *Capital*, vol. 1, p. 836.

26. Marx, *Capital*, vol. 1, p. 837.

27. Marx and Engels, *Communist Manifesto*, p. 46.

28. Marx, *Capital*, vol. 1, p. 21.

29. Marx and Engels, *Communist Manifesto*, pp. 31–32.

30. Marx, *Capital*, vol. 1, p. 637.

31. Payne, *Karl Marx*, p. 143.

32. Marx and Engels, *Communist Manifesto*, p. 22; Thomas Sowell, *Marxism: Philosophy and Economics* (New York: William Morrow, 1985), p. 138.

33. The question of relative poverty is extremely difficult to assess. First, since there is an income gap between rich and poor, even if the poor gain at a faster rate, the gap in absolute dollars may enlarge. Compare person A, who starts with $10,000 and enjoys a 10 percent raise each year, with person B, who starts at $100,000 and enjoys only a 5 percent raise each year. In about seven years, A is earning about $20,000, while B is earning more than $140,000. Second, in the United States, over the course of a generation there is considerable upward and downward mobility. One major study revealed that about one-third of the children of the most affluent parents in the country received income below the national average. Furthermore, about one-third of the children of the poorest parents climbed up and above the national average. See Christopher Jencks et al., *Inequality: A Reassessment of the Effect of Family and Schooling in America* (New York: Basic Books, 1972), pp. 209–216. For an international

approach to mobility, see W. W. Rostow, *Why the Poor Get Richer and the Rich Slow Down* (Austin: University of Texas Press, 1980). We can confidently say that during most of the twentieth century, all classes in the United States have enjoyed sustained absolute progress. Nonetheless, during the stagflation from 1974 to 1982, all income classes lost ground. The poor especially suffered for economic as well as sociological reasons, as the number of female-headed households jumped by about 40 percent. During the middle and late 1980s the 1973 plateau was reached again and surpassed.

34. John Rawls, *A Theory of Justice* (Cambridge, MA: Harvard University Press, 1971).

35. John Maynard Keynes, *The Collected Writings of John Maynard Keynes*, vol. 28 (London and New York: Macmillan/St. Martin's Press, 1973), pp. 38, 42.

36. See Stephen A. Marglin, "Radical Macroeconomics," Discussion Paper No. 902, Harvard Institute of Economic Research, 1982, pp. 1–26.

37. See Robert Conquest, *The Harvest of Sorrow* (New York: Oxford University Press, 1987).

38. David Masci, "In Russia, Nostalgia for Soviet Union and Positive Feelings About Stalin," *Fact Tank*, Pew Research Center, June 29, 2017, https://www.pewresearch.org/fact-tank/2017/06/29/in-russia-nostalgia-for-soviet-union-and-positive-feelings-about-stalin/.

39. David S. G. Goodman, *Deng Xiaoping and the Chinese Revolution: A Political Biography* (London: Routledge, 1994), p. 3.

40. John Steinbeck, *The Grapes of Wrath* (New York: Penguin Books, 1986 [1939]), p. 537.

VII. Alfred Marshall and the Marginalist Mind

1. We assume that the backpacker cannot return to Italy for more pleasure. Also, the cost of stepping forward includes the opportunity cost—the pleasure derivable from staying home, for instance.

2. Peter Groenewegen, *A Soaring Eagle* (Aldershot, UK: Elgar, 1995), p. 477.

3. Charles Dickens, *Oliver Twist*, ch. 50 (New York: Dover, 2002 [1839]), p. 318.

4. Peter D. Groenewegen, *Alfred Marshall: Critical Responses*, vol. 1 (London: Routledge, 1998), p. 38.

5. John Maynard Keynes, "Alfred Marshall," in *Essays in Biography* (London: Macmillan/St. Martin's Press for the Royal Economic

Society, 1972), p. 164. Though majestic, Keynes's essay contains some factual errors uncovered in Ronald H. Coase, "Alfred Marshall's Mother and Father," *History of Political Economy* 16 (Winter 1984), pp. 519–527.

6. Keynes, "Alfred Marshall," p. 171.

7. *"Economic Journal* 125th Anniversary Special Issue," *Economic Journal* 125 (March 2015), p. 203.

8. A. C. Pigou, "In Memoriam: Alfred Marshall," in *Memorials of Alfred Marshall*, ed. A. C. Pigou (London: Macmillan, 1925), p. 89.

9. Keynes, "Alfred Marshall," p. 175.

10. *Alfred Marshall: The Correspondence of Alfred Marshall, Economist*, vol. 1, ed. John K. Whittaker (Cambridge: Cambridge University Press, 1996), pp. 21, 48.

11. C. R. Fay, "Reminiscences," in Pigou, *Memorials of Alfred Marshall*, pp. 74–75.

12. C. M. Guillebaud, "Some Personal Reminiscences of Alfred Marshall," in *Alfred Marshall: Critical Assessments*, vol. 1, ed. John Cunningham Wood (London: Routledge, 1993), p. 93.

13. J. M. Keynes, "Alfred Marshall, 1842–1924," *Economic Journal* 24, no. 135 (September 1924), p. 346.

14. Alfred Marshall, *Principles of Economics*, 9th ed., ed. C. W. Guillebaud (London: Macmillan, 1961 [1920]), vol. 1, pp. 7–9.

15. Marshall, *Principles of Economics*, p. xv.

16. Marshall, *Principles of Economics*, p. 461.

17. Alfred Marshall, "Letter to Bowley," in Pigou, *Memorials of Alfred Marshall*, p. 427.

18. Keynes, "Alfred Marshall," p. 196.

19. John Neville Keynes, *The Scope and Method of Political Economy* (London: Macmillan, 1891), p. 217n.

20. Marshall, *Principles*, p. xiv.

21. Marshall, *Principles*, p. 366.

22. Marshall, *Principles*, p. 271.

23. Marshall, *Principles*, p. 316. Schumpeter argued that dominant firms and monopolists could help the economy, because their excess profits enabled them to invest heavily in research and development. Schumpeter's position remains controversial.

24. For a profile of the fascinating Sarnoff, see Todd G. Buchholz, *New Ideas from Dead CEOs* (New York: HarperCollins, 2007).

25. John A. Byrne, "Is Your Company Too Big?," *BusinessWeek*, March 27, 1989, pp. 84–94.

26. Marshall, *Principles*, p. 348.

27. Mill, *Principles of Political Economy*, p. 99.

28. Mill, *Principles of Political Economy*, p. 118.

29. Ryan McPhee, "Grosses Analysis: Bruce Springsteen Ends Broadway Residency on High Note," *Playbill*, December 17, 2018, http://www.playbill.com/article/grosses-analysis-bruce-springsteen -ends-broadway-residency-on-high-note.

30. Keynes, "Alfred Marshall," p. 205.

31. Marshall, *Principles*, pp. 587–588.

32. Sharon Terlep, "Clorox Sales Fall as Glad Price Hike Backfires," *Marketwatch*, February 4, 2020, https://www.marketwatch.com /story/clorox-sales-fall-as-glad-price-hike-backfires-2020-02-04.

33. Matthew Boyle, "'Restricted Living' Sparks Online Ramen Frenzy for Walmart," *Bloomberg*, April 3, 2020, https://www.bloom berg.com/news/articles/2020-04-03/-restricted-living-sparks -online-ramen-frenzy-for-walmart.

34. This is a highly complex issue. See Ellen E. Meade, "Exchange Rates, Adjustment, and the J-Curve," in *Federal Reserve Bulletin* 74 (October 1988), pp. 633–644.

35. Alfred Marshall, *Money, Credit and Commerce* (London: Macmillan, 1923), p. 247.

36. F. Y. Edgeworth, "Reminiscences," in Pigou, *Memorials of Alfred Marshall*, p. 70.

37. Alfred Marshall, *Lectures to Women* [1873], ed. Rafaelli Tiziano, Rita MacWilliams Tullberg, and Eugenio Biagini (Aldershot, UK: Elgar 1995), p. 106.

38. Alfred Marshall, Letter to Lord Reay, in Pigou, *Memorials of Alfred Marshall*, p. 462; Marshall, *Principles*, p. 713.

39. Marshall, *Principles*, p. 3.

40. Keynes, p. 173.

VIII. Old and New Institutionalists

1. Auguste Comte gave the same advice to Mill. The neoclassicalists didn't listen. Instead, they derided the even limper "soft" sciences. Ironically, the new institutionalists today meet on the same turf as other social scientists, partly because they bullied themselves into anthropology, criminology, and sociology.

2. Joseph Dorfman, *Thorstein Veblen and His America* (New York: Viking, 1934), p. 79.

3. Thorstein Veblen, "Why Economics Is Not an Evolutionary Science," *Quarterly Journal of Economics* 12 (July 1898), p. 389.

4. Thorstein Veblen, *The Theory of the Leisure Class* (New York: Modern Library, 1934), pp. 42–43.

5. Harvey Leibenstein, "Bandwagon, Snob, and Veblen Effects in the Theory of Consumer Demand," *Quarterly Journal of Economics* 62 (May 1950), pp. 183–207.

6. Jonathan D. Glater and Alan Finder, "U.S. Universities Raise Tuition, and Applicants Follow," *International Herald Tribune*, December 12, 2006.

7. Although he eschewed Marx's approach to exploitation, Veblen accepted Marx's charge that the institution of private property hurts society. Nonetheless, his antipathy toward private property did not stop him from defending his secluded mountain cabin from a trespasser by attacking the intruder with a hatchet.

8. See Todd G. Buchholz, *New Ideas from Dead CEOs* (New York: HarperCollins, 2007).

9. Thorstein Veblen, *The Theory of Business Enterprise* (New York: Scribner's, 1904), p. 309.

10. Veblen, *Theory of Business Enterprise*, p. 286.

11. Thorstein Veblen, *The Engineers and the Price System* (New York: Viking, 1921), pp. 18–19.

12. Thorstein Veblen, *The Vested Interests and the Common Man* (New York: Capricorn Books, 1969), p. 165.

13. Veblen, *Engineers and the Price System*, p. 58.

14. T. Pare and Wilton Woods, "The World's Top 50 Industrial CEO's," in *Fortune* 116 (August 3, 1987), p. 23.

15. Wesley C. Mitchell, *What Veblen Taught* (New York: Viking, 1936), p. xviii; Joseph Dorfman, "Background of Veblen's Thought," in *Thorstein Veblen*, ed. Carlton C. Qualey (New York: Columbia University Press, 1968), p. 129.

16. John Kenneth Galbraith, *The Scotch* (Boston: Houghton Mifflin, 1964), p. 26.

17. John Kenneth Galbraith, *The Affluent Society* (Boston: Houghton Mifflin, 1976), p. 149. Given his forceful critique, it is ironic that Galbraith agreed to write a hardcover book (for Whittle Communications) containing advertisements!

18. Friedrich A. Hayek, "The *Non Sequitur* of the 'Dependence Effect,'" in *Southern Economic Journal* 27 (April 1961), pp. 346–348.

19. Bernie Sanders, "Bernie Sanders on His Plan for Journalism," *Columbia Journalism Review* (August 26, 2019), https://www.cjr.org/opinion/bernie-sanders-media-silicon-valley.php.

20. Lee Benham, "The Effect of Advertising on the Price of Eyeglasses," *Journal of Law and Economics* 15 (October 1972), pp. 337–352.

21. Joseph Pereira, "Pricey Sneakers Worn in Inner City Help Set Nation's Fashion Trend," *Wall Street Journal* (December 1, 1988), pp. A1–A10.

22. Robert Skidelsky, *John Maynard Keynes*, vol. 2 (London: Penguin, 1992), p. 449.

23. Marjorie S. Turner, *Joan Robinson and the Americans* (London: Routledge, 2015), p. 90.

24. Todd G. Buchholz, *Rush* (New York: Penguin, 2011), ch. 7, "How Time and Interest Rates Bring Us Closer"; Barbara A. Hanawalt, *Crime and Conflict in English Communities, 1300–1348* (Cambridge, MA: Harvard University Press, 1979).

25. Richard A. Swedberg, *Joseph A. Schumpeter* (Cambridge: Polity Press, 1991) p. 68.

26. Joseph A. Schumpeter, *History of Economic Analysis* (New York: Oxford University Press, 1954), p. 896.

27. Joseph A. Schumpeter, *The Theory of Economic Development*, trans. R. Opie (New Brunswick, NJ: Transaction, 2008 [1934]), p. 93.

28. Louis Brandeis, "The Living Law," *Illinois Law Review* 10 (1916).

29. United States v. Carroll Towing Co., 159 F.2d 169 (2d Cir. 1947).

30. Ronald Coase, "The Problem of Social Cost," *Journal of Law and Economics* 3 (October 1960), pp. 1–44.

31. George J. Stigler, *Memoirs of an Unregulated Economist* (New York: Basic Books, 1978), p. 76.

32. See Werner Z. Hirsch, *Habitability Laws and the Welfare of Indigent Tenants* (Los Angeles: University of California Press, 1978).

33. Maddy Savage, "The City with 20-Year Waiting Lists for Rental Homes," BBC, May 16, 2017, https://www.bbc.com/worklife/article/20160517-this-is-one-city-where-youll-never-find-a-home.

34. Marc Beauchamp, "Bankrupt Landlords in Wonderland," *Forbes* (March 20, 1989), pp. 105–106. Rent control is another issue that unites economists regardless of liberal or conservative politics. See Alan Blinder's lucid *Hard Heads, Soft Hearts: Tough-Minded Economics for a Just Society* (Reading, MA: Addison-Wesley, 1987), pp. 194–195.

35. See Gary Becker, "Crime and Punishment: An Economic Approach," *Journal of Political Economy* 78 (March–April 1968), pp. 169–217; I. Ehrlich, "Participation in Illegitimate Activities: A Theoretical and Empirical Investigation," *Journal of Political Economy* 81 (May–June 1973), pp. 521–565; D. L. Sjoquist, "Property, Crime and Economic Behavior," *American Economic Review* 63 (June 1973), pp. 439–446.

36. See Todd G. Buchholz, "Revolution, Reputation Effects, and Time Horizons," *Cato Journal* 8 (Spring–Summer 1988), pp. 185–197.

37. Richard A. Posner, *Economic Analysis of Law*, 2nd ed. (Boston: Little, Brown, 1977), p. 22; 3rd ed. (Boston: Little, Brown, 1986), pp. 25–26. See also Todd G. Buchholz, "Punishing Humans," *Thought* 59 (September 1984), p. 290.

38. A. A. Berle and G. C. Means, *The Modern Corporation and Private Property* (New York: Macmillan, 1932).

39. For example, see Lucian Bebchuk and Jesse Fried, "Executive Compensation at Fannie Mae: A Case Study in Perverse Incentives, Nonperformance Pay and Camouflage," *Journal of Corporation Law* 30, no. 4 (2005), pp. 807–822.

40. Adam Grant and Jitendra Singh, "The Problem with Financial Incentives—and What to Do About It," Knowledge at Wharton, March 30, 2011, https://knowledge.wharton.upenn.edu/article/the-problem-with-financial-incentives-and-what-to-do-about-it/.

41. See Dale Arthur Oesterle and John R. Norberg, "Management Buyouts: Creating or Appropriating Shareholder Wealth?," *Vanderbilt Law Review* 41 (March 1988), pp. 207–260; Michael C. Jensen, "Takeovers: Their Causes and Consequences," *Journal of Economic Perspectives* 2 (Spring 1988), p. 21; Benjamin J. Stein, "Loss of Values: Did Amsted LBO Shortchange Shareholders?," *Barron's* (February 16, 1987), p. 8.

42. Bruno S. Frey and Heinz Buhofer, "Prisoners and Property Rights," *Journal of Law and Economics* 31 (April 1988), pp. 19–46.

43. For a theoretical model and an examination of South Vietnam in 1975, see Todd G. Buchholz, "Revolution, Reputation Effects, and Time Horizons," *Cato Journal* 8 (Spring–Summer 1988), pp. 185–197.

IX. Keynes: Bon Vivant as Savior

1. Bertrand Russell, *Autobiography* (London: Unwin Paperbacks, 1975), p. 69.

2. Robert Skidelsky, *John Maynard Keynes*, vol. 1 (London: Macmillan, 1983), p. 180.

3. Milton Friedman, *Dollars and Deficits* (Englewood Cliffs, NJ: Prentice-Hall, 1968), p. 15.

4. Justin Fox, "Bob Lucas on the Comeback on Keynsianism," *Time*, October 28, 2008, https://business.time.com/2008/10/28/bob-lucas-on-the-comeback-of-keynesianism/.

5. Robert Skidelsky, *John Maynard Keynes*, vol. 1 (New York: Penguin, 1983) p. 53.

6. R. F. Harrod, *The Life of John Maynard Keynes* (London: Macmillan, 1951), p. 50.

7. "Professor Keynes Is Optimistic," British Movietone, https://www.youtube.com/watch?v=0PYSFqCSsGU.

8. Skidelsky, *John Maynard Keynes*, vol. 1, p. 118.

9. Dadie Rylands in John Davenport-Hines, *Universal Man: The Lives of John Maynard Keynes* (New York: Basic Books, 2015), p. 293.

10. Harrod, *Life of John Maynard Keynes*, p. 101.

11. Skidelsky, *John Maynard Keynes*, vol. 1, pp. 165–166.

12. Skidelsky, *John Maynard Keynes*, vol. 1, pp. 173, 175.

13. Skidelsky, *John Maynard Keynes*, vol. 1, p. 177.

14. Joseph A. Schumpeter, *Ten Great Economists* (London: George Allen and Unwin, 1952), p. 265.

15. Andrew Sinclair, *The Red and the Blue* (London: Weidenfeld and Nicolson, 1986), p. 17; Michael Holroyd, *Lytton Strachey: A Critical Biography*, vol. 2 (New York: Holt, Rinehart and Winston, 1968), p. 17.

16. John Maynard Keynes, *Economic Consequences of the Peace* (New York: Harcourt Brace, 1919), p. 20.

17. Davenport-Hines, *Universal Man*, p. 91.

18. John Maynard Keynes, *The Collected Writings of John Maynard Keynes* (London: Macmillan/St. Martin's Press for the Royal Economic Society, 1973), vol. 10, pp. 413–415.

19. John Maynard Keynes, *The Economic Consequences of the Peace* (London: MacMillan, 1919), pp. 19, 24–25, 128.

20. Keynes, *Collected Writings*, vol. 17, p. 16.

21. See Milo Keynes, *Lydia Lopokova* (New York: St. Martin's, 1983).

22. Skidelsky, *John Maynard Keynes*, vol. 2, p. 208.

23. David Chambers and Elroy Dimson, "John Maynard Keynes, Investment Innovator," *Journal of Economic Perspectives* 27, no. 3 (2013), pp. 213–228.

24. Davenport-Hines, *Universal Man*, pp. 266–267.

25. For different views on the causes of the Great Depression, see Milton Friedman and Anna J. Schwartz, *A Monetary History of the United States, 1867–1960* (Princeton, NJ: Princeton University Press, 1963); Peter Temin, *Did Monetary Forces Cause the Great Depression?* (New York: Norton, 1976); and Karl Brunner, ed., *The Great Depression Revisited* (Boston: Martinus Nijhoff, 1981).

26. Leo Rosten interviews Friedrich A. Hayek, part 2, November 15, 1978, Hayek Interviews, http://hayek.ufm.edu/index.php?title=Leo_Rosten_Part_II.

27. Gene Epstein, "Mr. Market," *Barron's*, August 24, 1998, https://www.barrons.com/articles/SB903738915698011000.

28. Lawrence H. White, "Did Hayek and Robbins Deepen the Great Depression?," *Journal of Money, Credit and Banking* 40, no. 4 (2008), 763.

29. F. A. Hayek, *The Denationalization of Money* (London: Institute of Economic Affairs, 1976).

30. Paul Samuelson, "Lord Keynes and the General Theory," *Econometrica* 14 (1946), p. 190.

31. Keynes, *General Theory,* in *Collected Writings,* vol. 7, p. 183.

32. Elizabeth S. Johnson and Harry G. Johnson, *The Shadow of Keynes* (London: Basil Blackwell, 1978), p. 102.

33. Keynes, *Collected Writings,* vol. 21, pp. 134, 144.

34. Keynes, *General Theory,* in *Collected Writings,* vol. 7, p. 128. For more elaborate proofs and explanations on why the tax-cut multiplier is smaller than the government and investment multiplier, see any introductory economics textbook.

35. Keynes, *Collected Writings,* vol. 21, p. 296.

36. Keynes, *General Theory,* in *Collected Writings,* vol. 7, pp. 380–381.

37. Keynes, *General Theory,* in *Collected Writings,* vol. 7, p. 129.

38. Samuelson, "Lord Keynes and the General Theory," p. 187.

39. Keynes, *General Theory,* in *Collected Writings,* vol. 7, p. 154.

40. Keynes, *General Theory,* in *Collected Writings,* vol. 7, p. 156.

41. Keynes, *Collected Writings,* vol. 12, p. 57.

42. Keynes, *Collected Writings,* vol. 12, pp. 162–163.

43. Keynes, *Collected Writings,* vol. 12, pp. 383–384.

44. Keynes, *Collected Writings,* vol. 9, pp. 321–332.

X. Milton Friedman and the Monetarist Battle Against Keynes

1. Valentina Sanchez, "Venezuela Hyperinflation Hits 10 Million Percent," CNBC.com, August 3, 2019, https://www.cnbc.com/2019/08/02/venezuela-inflation-at-10-million-percent-its-time-for-shock-therapy.html.

2. A. C. Pigou, ed., *Memorials of Alfred Marshall* (London: Macmillan, 1925), p. 25.

3. John Maynard Keynes, *The Collected Writings of John Maynard Keynes* (London: Macmillan/St. Martin's Press for the Royal Economic Society, 1973), vol. 11, p. 294.

4. Milton Friedman, "Money: Quantity Theory," in *International Encyclopedia of the Social Sciences* (New York: Macmillan and Free Press, 1968), p. 438.

5. Milton Friedman, "Discussion of the Inflationary Gap," *American Economic Review* 32 (June 1942), pp. 314–320, reprinted in *Essays in Positive Economics* (Chicago: University of Chicago Press, 1953), p. 253.

6. John Kenneth Galbraith, *Economics in Perspective* (Boston: Houghton Mifflin, 1987), pp. 270–271. For more on Friedman's life and career, see his memoirs in Milton Friedman and Rose D. Friedman, *Two Lucky People: Memoirs* (Chicago: University of Chicago Press, 1998).

7. In the green room before the NPR radio show, Stiglitz asked what topics we would be discussing. I explained that because he represented President Clinton's push for the North American Free Trade Agreement, listeners would call the program to complain that he was risking American jobs going to Mexico. Stiglitz looked at me and asked, "What do you say?"

8. Milton Friedman and Simon Kuznets, *Income from Independent Professional Practice* (New York: National Bureau of Economic Research, 1945); Todd G. Buchholz, *The Price of Prosperity* (New York: HarperCollins 2016), pp. 119–121.

9. Milton Friedman, *Studies in the Quantity Theory of Money* (Chicago: University of Chicago Press, 1956).

10. Milton Friedman, *A Theory of the Consumption Function* (Princeton, NJ: Princeton University Press, 1957).

11. A. Ando and F. Modigliani, "Tests of the Life Cycle Hypothesis of Savings: Comments and Suggestions," *Bulletin of the Oxford University Institute of Statistics* 19 (1957).

12. Milton Friedman and Anna J. Schwartz, *A Monetary History of the United States, 1867–1960* (Princeton, NJ: Princeton University Press, 1963). For a critical view, see Peter Temin, *Did Monetary Forces Cause the Great Depression?* (New York: Norton, 1976); and Karl Brunner, ed., *The Great Depression Revisited* (Boston: Martinus Nijhoff, 1981).

13. Valerie A. Ramey, "Ten Years After the Financial Crisis: What Have We Learned from the Renaissance in Fiscal Research?," *Journal of Economic Perspectives* 33, no. 2 (2019), pp. 89–114.

14. Gary Fromm and Lawrence R. Klein, "A Comparison of Eleven Econometric Models of the United States," *American Economic Review* 63 (May 1973), pp. 385–393.

15. Milton Friedman, "The Role of Monetary Policy," *American Economic Review* 58, no. 1 (1968), pp. 1–17.

16. Lawrence H. Summers, "The Great Liberator," *New York Times* (November 19, 2006), p. 13.

17. *Economic Report of the President* (Washington, D.C.: U.S. Government Printing Office, 1962), p. 68.

18. Paul A. Samuelson and William D. Nordhaus, *Economics* (New York: McGraw-Hill, 1985), p. 331.

19. *Economic Report of the President*, p. 55.

20. John B. Taylor, "Discretion Versus Policy Rules in Practice," Carnegie-Rochester Conference Series on Public Policy 39 (1993), p. 202; Ben S. Bernanke, "The Taylor Rule: A Benchmark for Monetary Policy?," Brookings, April 28, 2015, https://www.brookings.edu/blog /ben-bernanke/2015/04/28/the-taylor-rule-a-benchmark-for -monetary-policy/.

21. Ben S. Bernanke, "On Milton Friedman's Ninetieth Birthday," Federal Reserve Board, November 8, 2002, https://www.feder alreserve.gov/BOARDDOCS/SPEECHES/2002/20021108/.

22. Marketplace staff, "It's Time to Ask What Pigou Would Do," December 26, 2008, https://www.marketplace.org/2008/12/26/its -time-ask-what-pigou-would-do/.

23. D. G. Champernowne, "Arthur Cecil Pigou (1877–1959)," *Royal Statistical Society* 122, no. 2 (1959), p. 264.

24. Karen Lovejoy Knight, *A. C. Pigou and the Marshallian Thought Style* (London: Palgrave MacMillan, 2018), p. 44.

25. Nahid Aslanbeigui and Guy Oakes, *Arthur Cecil Pigou* (New York: Palgrave/MacMillan, 2015), p. 257.

26. Nahid Aslanbeigui and Guy Oakes, "The Great War and the Genesis of Pigou's *A Study in Public Finance*," *OEconomia* 6, no. 4 (2016), pp. 487–488, https://journals.openedition.org/oeconomia /2471.

27. A. C. Pigou, "Mr. J. M. Keynes' General Theory of Employment, Interest and Money," *Economica* 3, no. 10 (1936), p. 115. When Pigou tried to rebut Keynes in print, Keynes stated that "it is no use whistling a new tune to an organ grinder" (*Collected Writings*, vol. 14, September 1936, p. 87).

28. See A. C. Pigou, *Employment and Equilibrium* (London: Macmillan, 1941), p. 126.

29. "Gazumping Returns to London Property Market," *Telegraph*, February 6, 2009, https://www.telegraph.co.uk/finance/personal finance/borrowing/mortgages/4535006/Gazumping-returns -to-London-property-market.html.

30. A good primer on the matter is Martin S. Feldstein, ed., *Taxes and Capital Formation* (Chicago: University of Chicago Press, 1987). The book contains articles by Summers, President Clinton's deputy treasury secretary, as well as articles by Boskin, Feldstein, and Lawrence Lindsey, key advisers to the Reagan and Bush administrations.

31. Royah Nikkhah, "Sir Michael Caine Warns Further Tax Rises Will Force Him to Move Abroad," *Telegraph*, April 25, 2009, https://www.telegraph.co.uk/finance/budget/5219642/Sir-Michael-Caine-warns-further-tax-rises-will-force-him-to-move-abroad.html.

32. Edward C. Prescott, "The Transformation of Macroeconomic Policy and Research," in *Federal Reserve Bank of Minneapolis 2004 Annual Report*, pp. 19–20.

33. Jason Furman, "Business Tax Reform and Economic Growth," September 22, 2014, p. 8, https://obamawhitehouse.archives.gov/sites/default/files/docs/business_tax_reform_and_economic_growth_jf.pdf.

34. Austan D. Goolsbee and Peter J. Klenow, "Internet Rising, Prices Falling: Measuring Inflation in a World of E-Commerce," National Bureau of Economic Research, Working Paper 24649 (May 2018), https://www.nber.org/papers/w24649.

35. Friedman and Friedman, *Two Lucky People*, p. 380.

XI. The Public Choice School: Politics as a Business

1. James M. Buchanan, *Economics from the Outside In* (College Station: Texas A&M, 2007), pp. 49, 55.

2. David Vesey, "Personality Spotlight: James Buchanan; Nobel Prize Winner for Economics," United Press International, October 16, 1986.

3. Mancur Olson, *The Rise and Decline of Nations* (New Haven, CT: Yale University Press, 1982).

4. Mancur Olson quoted in "The Political Economy of Interest Groups," *Manhattan Report on Economic Policy* 4 (1984), p. 4.

5. Benjamin Franklin, *The Works of Benjamin Franklin*, vol. 10, ed. John Bigelow (New York: G. P. Putnam, 1904 [1783]), p. 72.

6. Todd G. Buchholz, *The Price of Prosperity* (New York: HarperCollins, 2016), pp. 116–117.

7. George J. Stigler, "The Theory of Economic Regulation," *Bell Journal of Economics and Management Science 2* (Spring 1971), pp. 3–21.

8. James M. Buchanan, *The Consequences of Mr. Keynes* (London: Institute of Economic Affairs, 1978), pp. 20–21.

9. Joseph P. Newhouse, *Free for All: Lessons from the RAND Health Insurance Experiment* (Cambridge, MA: Harvard University Press, 1993); Matthew J. Eichner, "The Demand for Medical Care: What People Pay Does Matter," *American Economic Review* 88 (May 1988);

Jonathan Skinner and John E. Weinberg, "How Much Is Enough? Efficiency and Medical Spending in the Last Six Months of Life," National Bureau of Economic Research, Working Paper 6513 (April 1998).

10. Burton A. Abrams, "How Richard Nixon Pressured Arthur Burns: Evidence from the Nixon Tapes," *Journal of Economic Perspectives* 20, no. 4 (June 2006), pp. 181, 187.

11. Mark M. Spiegel, "British Central Bank Independence and Inflation Expectations," *FRBSF Economic Letter*, November 28, 1997, https://www.frbsf.org/economic-research/publications/economic -letter/1997/november/british-central-bank-independence-and -inflation-expectations/.

12. John Maynard Keynes, "The End of Laissez-Faire," in *Essays in Persuasion*, in *The Collected Writings of John Maynard Keynes*, vol. 7 (London: Macmillan/St. Martin's Press for the Royal Economic Society, 1973), p. 379.

13. Paul M. Sweezy, "John Maynard Keynes," *Science and Society* 10 (1946), reprinted in R. Lekachman, ed., *Keynes' General Theory: Report on Three Decades* (London: Macmillan, 1964), p. 303.

14. Keynes, "Am I a Liberal?," in *Essays in Persuasion, Collected Writings,* vol. 9, pp. 301–302.

15. Keynes, *Collected Writings*, vol. 27, p. 387.

16. Keynes, "My Early Beliefs," in *Essays in Biography, Collected Writings,* vol. 10, pp. 436, 437, 446.

17. Robert Skidelsky, *John Maynard Keynes*, vol. 1 (London: Macmillan, 1983), p. xviii.

18. Max Weber, "Politics as a Vocation," in *From Max Weber*, trans. and ed. H. H. Gerth and C. W. Mills (London: Routledge and Kegan Paul, 1948), p. 95.

19. Keynes, *Collected Writings*, vol. 7, p. 384.

20. Keynes, "Can Lloyd George Do It?," in *Collected Writings*, vol. 9, p. 125.

21. Keynes, "Can Lloyd George Do It?," p. 125.

22. Keynes, *Collected Writings,* vol. 10, pp. 440, 448.

23. Keynes, *Collected Writings,* vol. 19, p. 750. See also *Collected Writings*, vol. 2, p. 92; vol. 9, p. 212; vol. 21, p. 201; and Geoff Hodgson, "Persuasion, Exceptions and the Limits to Keynes," *Keynes' Economics*, ed. Tony Lawson and Hashem Pesaran (London: Croom Helm, 1985), p. 23.

24. Quoted in Robert Skidelsky, "The Revolt Against the Victorians," in *The End of the Keynesian Era*, ed. R. Skidelsky (London: Macmillan, 1977), p. 7.

25. Quoted in Charles H. Hession, *John Maynard Keynes* (New York: Macmillan, 1984), p. 258. See also D. E. Moggridge, *Keynes* (London: Fontana, 1976), pp. 38–39.

26. F. A. Hayek, *New Studies in Philosophy, Politics, Economics and the History of Ideas* (London: Routledge and Kegan Paul, 1978), p. 287.

27. Keynes, *Collected Writings*, vol. 10, p. 448.

28. See Leo Strauss, *What Is Political Philosophy?* (Westport, CT: Greenwood Press, 1973), p. 40; Douglas Sturm, "Process Thought and Political Theory," *Review of Politics* 41 (1979), pp. 383–384.

29. Keynes, *Collected Writings*, vol. 2, pp. 22–23. Keynes deleted his more cutting remarks on Lloyd George from *Economic Consequences of the Peace*. They appeared fourteen years later in *Essays in Biography*. See *Collected Writings*, vol. 10, pp. 22–26, and vol. 17, p. 41.

30. See Arrow's "Impossibility Theorem," in Kenneth Arrow, *Social Choice and Individual Values* (New York: Wiley, 1951).

31. Keynes, *Collected Writings*, vol. 9, p. 295.

32. R. F. Harrod, *The Life of John Maynard Keynes* (London: Macmillan, 1951), p. 103.

XII. The Wild World of Rational Expectations and Behavioral Economics

1. Ike Brannon, "Remembering the Man Behind Rational Expectations," *Regulation*, Spring 2006, p. 18.

2. John F. Muth, "Rational Expectations and the Theory of Price Movements," *Econometrica* 29 (1961), pp. 315–335; Dermot J. Hayes and Andrew Schmitz, "Hog Cycles and Countercyclical Production Response," *American Journal of Agricultural Economics* 69, no. 4 (November 1987), pp. 762–770.

3. See P. H. Cootner, ed., *The Random Character of Stock Market Prices* (Cambridge, MA: MIT Press, 1964); Eugene Fama, "Efficient Capital Markets II," *Journal of Finance*, vol. 46, no. 5 (1991), pp. 1575–1617; Paul A. Samuelson, "Challenge to Judgment," *Journal of Portfolio Management* 1 (Fall 1974), p. 17.

4. Chiarella v. United States, 445 U.S. 222 (1980); quoted in *Wall Street Journal*, December 16, 1987, p. 29.

5. Markowitz's seminal paper was "Portfolio Selection," *Journal of Finance* 7, no. 1 (March 1952), pp. 77–91. He expounded on the idea in a book: Harry M. Markowitz, *Portfolio Selection: Efficient Diversification of Investments* (New York: Wiley, 1959). The quotations come

from Peter L. Bernstein's *Capital Ideas* (New York: Free Press, 1992), p. 60. An aside: In 1990 the Free Press asked me whether I would be interested in writing a book on financial economists. Since it would have violated the White House rules, I declined. Instead, Peter Bernstein wrote this excellent book for that publishing house.

6. Franco Modigliani and Merton Miller, "The Cost of Capital, Corporate Finance, and the Theory of Investment," *American Economic Review* 48 (June 1958), pp. 261–297. The "MM" model had to be revised to take account of corporate tax laws, which encourage firms to issue bonds by making interest payments deductible.

7. Quoted in David Warsh, "Nobel-est in Economics: Three Americans Share Prize for Corporate Finance Theories," *Boston Globe*, October 17, 1990.

8. Robert E. Lucas Jr., "Understanding Business Cycles," in *Stabilization of the Domestic and International Economy*, ed. Karl Brunner and Allan Meltzer, Carnegie-Rochester Conference Series, vol. 5.

9. Robert E. Hall, "Stochastic Implications of the Life-Cycle-Permanent Income Hypothesis: Theory and Evidence," *Journal of Political Economy* 86 (December 1978), pp. 971–987.

10. Robert J. Barro, "Are Government Bonds Net Wealth?," *Journal of Political Economy* 82 (December 1974), pp. 1095–1117.

11. Urban Bäckström, "What Lessons Can Be Learned from Recent Financial Crises: The Swedish Experience," Kansas City Federal Reserve Board Symposium, 1997, pp. 1–12.

12. *Financial Times*, July 5, 1994, p. 20.

13. Milton Friedman, *Essays in Positive Economics* (Chicago: University of Chicago Press, 1966).

14. Arjo Klamer, *Conversations with Economists: New Classical Economists and Opponents Speak Out on Current Controversy in Macroeconomics* (Totowa, NJ: Rowman, 1984), pp. 159, 162.

15. David Shariatmadari, "Daniel Kahneman: What Would I Eliminate if I Had a Magic Wand? Overconfidence," *Guardian,* July 18, 2015, https://www.theguardian.com/books/2015/jul/18/daniel-kahneman-books-interview.

16. Daniel Kahneman and Jackson Beatty, "Pupil Diameter and Load on Memory," *Science* 154, no. 3756 (December 23, 1966), pp. 1583–1585.

17. For an example of their work, see Daniel Kahneman and Amos Tversky, "Choices, Values, and Frames," *American Psychologist* 39, no. 6, pp. 341–350. Peter Bernstein's *Against the Gods: The Remarkable Story of Risk* (New York: Wiley, 1996), pp. 270–278, presents their theses clearly.

18. David Genesove and Christopher Mayer, "Loss Aversion and Seller Behavior: Evidence from the Housing Market," National Bureau of Economic Research, Working Paper 8143 (2001).

19. Joshua B. Miller and Adam Sanjuro, "Surprised by the Hot Hand Fallacy? A Truth in the Law of Small Numbers," *Econometrica* 86, no. 6 (2018), pp. 2019–2047.

20. Daniel Kahneman, "Daniel Kahneman: Biographical," Sverges Riksbank Prize in Economic Sciences in Memory of Alfred Nobel, 2002, https://www.nobelprize.org/prizes/economic-sciences /2002/kahneman/biographical/.

21. Quoted in Craig Lambert, "The Marketplace of Perceptions," *Harvard Magazine*, March–April 2006, p. 53.

22. Joseph Schumpeter, *Theory of Economic Development* (New York: Routledge, 2017 [1934]) p. 80.

23. John A. List, "Neoclassical Theory Versus Prospect Theory: Evidence from the Marketplace," *Econometrica* 72 (March 2004), pp. 615–625.

24. Daniel Kahneman open letter, in "Kahneman on the Storm of Doubts Surrounding Social Priming Research," Decision Science News, http://www.decisionsciencenews.com/2012/10/05/kahneman -on-the-storm-of-doubts-surrounding-social-priming-research/.

25. "Open Letter Urges Labs to Replicate Results to Avoid a Looming 'Train Wreck,'" Decision Science News, https://journals .plos.org/plosone/article?id=10.1371/journal.pone.0172636.

26. Chris Mooney, "Why Obamacare Could Produce More Atheists," *Mother Jones*, December 20, 2013, https://www.motherjones .com/politics/2013/12/why-do-atheists-exist/.

27. See John Taylor, "Staggered Wage Setting in a Macro Model," *American Economic Review* 63 (May 1979), pp. 108–113.

28. See Mark H. Willes, "'Rational Expectations' as a Counter-revolution," *Public Interest*, special issue 1980, p. 92.

29. In a 1997 decision, the Supreme Court revisited the insider-trading doctrine and tightened it up, based on change in the Securities and Exchange Commission rules. A financial printer is no longer free to misappropriate inside information. United States v. O'Hagan 97 C.D.O.S. 4931 (1997).

XIII. Dark Clouds, Silver Linings

1. John Maynard Keynes, "Alfred Marshall," in *Essays in Biography*, in *The Collected Writings of John Maynard Keynes* (London: Macmillan/

St. Martin's Press for the Royal Economic Society, 1972), vol. 10, p. 173.

2. See Richard A. Easterlin, "Does Economic Growth Improve the Human Lot? Some Empirical Evidence," in *Nations and Households in Economic Growth: Essays in Honor of Moses Abramovitz*, ed. Paul A. David and Melvin W. Reder (New York: Academic Press, 1974), pp. 89–125.

3. "Math Arrow to Replace Number Line?," Mathematical Association of America, https://www.maa.org/news/math-news/math-arrow-to-replace-number-line/.

4. Joseph A. Schumpeter, *Capitalism, Socialism, and Democracy* (New York: Harper and Row, 1976), p. 61. Paul Romer's "idea gap" discussion appears in his "Idea Gaps and Object Gaps in Economic Development," *Journal of Monetary Economics* 32, no. 3 (1993), pp. 543–573.

5. John Tagliabue, "Yugoslavia's Capitalist Tilt Becomes a Headlong Plunge," *New York Times*, August 14, 1988, p. E2; James Brooke, "Adam Smith Crowds Marx in Angola," *New York Times*, December 29, 1987, p. A6; Larry Rohter, "A Radical Diagnosis of Latin America's Economic Malaise," *New York Times*, September 27, 1987, p. E3.

6. Steven Greenhouse, "The Global March to Free Markets," *New York Times*, July 19, 1987, sec. 3, p. 1.

Acknowledgments

1. Rich Barbieri, "Martin Feldstein, One of the Most Influential Economists of His Generation, Has Died," CNN, June 12, 2019, https://www.cnn.com/2019/06/11/economy/martin-feldstein-obituary/index.html.

Index

About the Author

TODD G. BUCHHOLZ is an internationally acclaimed economist and author. He served as director of economic policy at the White House and managing director of the legendary Tiger investment fund. He taught economics at Harvard University, where he was awarded the Allyn Young Teaching Prize by the Department of Economics, served as a Fellow at Cambridge University, and holds advanced degrees in economics and law from Cambridge and Harvard Universities. He is the inventor of the Math Arrow matrix, and his writing has appeared in the *Wall Street Journal,* the *New York Times,* and *Forbes,* among other publications. He is also the author of *From Here to Economy, Rush: Why You Need and Love the Rat Race,* and *The Price of Prosperity.*